KT-498-519

Qualitative Analysis of Human Movement

Qualitative Analysis of Human Movement

Second Edition
with
CD-ROM

Duane V. Knudson, PhD
California State University at Chico

Craig S. Morrison, EdD
Southern Utah University

Human Kinetics

Library of Congress Cataloging-in-Publication Data

Knudson, Duane V., 1961-
    Qualitative analysis of humam movement / Duane Knudson and Craig Morrison.--2nd ed.
      p. cm.
    Includes bibliographical references and index.
    ISBN 0-7360-3462-5
    1. Kinesiology.   I. Morrison, Craig S., 1946-   II. Title.
    QP303 .K59   2002
    612.7'6--dc21   2001051833

ISBN: 0-7360-3462-5

Copyright © 2002, 1997 by Duane V. Knudson and Craig S. Morrison

All rights reserved. Except for use in a review, the reproduction or utilization of this work in any form or by any electronic, mechanical, or other means, now known or hereafter invented, including xerography, photocopying, and recording, and in any information storage and retrieval system, is forbidden without the written permission of the publisher.

Notice: Permission to reproduce the following material is granted to instructors and agencies who have purchased *Qualitative Analysis of Human Movement* (second edition): pp. 192-197. The reproduction of other parts of this book is expressly forbidden by the above copyright notice. Persons or agencies who have not purchased *Qualitative Analysis of Human Movement* (second edition) may not reproduce any material.

Permission notices for material reprinted in this book from other sources can be found on page xii.

Acquisitions Editor: Judy Patterson Wright, PhD; **Developmental Editor:** Judy Park; **Assistant Editor:** Lee Alexander; **Copyeditor:** D.K. Bihler; **Proofreader:** Sue Fetters; **Indexer:** Bobbi Swanson; **Permission Manager:** Dalene Reeder; **Graphic Designer:** Robert Reuther; **Graphic Artist:** Sandra Meier; **Photo Manager:** Leslie A. Woodrum; **Cover Designer:** Jack W. Davis; **Photographer (cover):** Tony Duffy/The Sporting Image; **Photographer (interior):** Tom Roberts except where otherwise noted; **Art Managers:** Craig Newsom and Carl D. Johnson; **Illustrators:** Tom Roberts, Susan Carson, and Jennifer Delmotte; **Cartoonist:** Dick Flood; **Medical Illustrator:** M.R. Greenberg; **Printer:** Sheridan Books

Printed in the United States of America   10 9 8 7 6 5 4 3 2

Human Kinetics
Web site: www.HumanKinetics.com

United States: Human Kinetics, P.O. Box 5076, Champaign, IL 61825-5076
800-747-4457
e-mail: humank@hkusa.com

Canada: Human Kinetics, 475 Devonshire Road, Unit 100, Windsor, ON N8Y 2L:
800-465-7301 (in Canada only)
e-mail: orders@hkcanada.com

Europe: Human Kinetics, 107 Bradford Road, Stanningley
Leeds LS28 6AT, United Kingdom
+44 (0) 113 255 5665
e-mail: hk@hkeurope.com

Australia: Human Kinetics, 57A Price Avenue, Lower Mitcham, South Australia 5062
08 8277 1555
e-mail: liaw@hkaustralia.com

New Zealand: Human Kinetics, Division of Sports Distributors NZ Ltd.
P.O. Box 300 226 Albany, North Shore City, Auckland
0064 9 448 1207
e-mail: blairc@hknewz.com

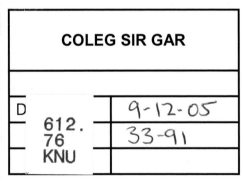

COLEG SIR GAR

D   612.76 KNU   9-12-05   33-91

Contents

PART I An Integrated Approach to Qualitative Analysis 1

PART III Practical Applications of Qualitative Analysis 147

Preface to the Second Edition

Several professionals rely on qualitative analysis for improving the movement of their clients. The athletic coach, physical therapist, dance instructor, and physical education teacher are examples of professionals who use qualitative analysis. How do these professionals make the diagnostic decisions that affect people's lives? This book was written to answer that question by assembling information from the many subdisciplines of kinesiology that contribute to the qualitative analysis of human movement.

The development of qualitative analysis as a subject area and professional skill has been hurt by the lack of a unified approach. The contributions of many subdisciplines of kinesiology to qualitative analysis have not been brought together. Formalizing these largely intuitive processes is very important in improving professional skill development in qualitative analysis. Training future kinesiology professionals in an integrated approach to qualitative analysis is essential to maximizing the movement potential of people of all ages, from athletes to accident rehab patients.

Audience and Scope

Most scholarly work in qualitative analysis has been limited to the perspective of a single subdiscipline of kinesiology (biomechanics, motor development, motor learning, pedagogy, or sport psychology). This text, however, reviews major research and scholarly papers from all of these subdisciplines, integrating the strengths of each separate view. The qualitative analysis of human movement is an interdisciplinary skill relevant to many professions. This book is designed for upper-level undergraduate and graduate courses on the qualitative analysis of human movement. Current and future professionals will find a wealth of information on qualitative analysis and many application examples throughout the book.

Few books guide readers through the process of qualitative analysis of human movement. This book provides sequential illustrations of actual performances as well as written tutorials, guiding readers through the diagnostic process. It shows several fundamental human movements and sport skills, and includes subjects of all ages and ability levels. Case studies and examples realistically illustrate what professionals encounter every day. The addition of a CD-ROM containing video clips of a wide variety of human movements extends the learning experience to qualitative analysis of videotaped replays. Slow-motion replay and computer presentation and illustration on digital video are also illustrated.

Organization and Features

The first edition of *Qualitative Analysis of Human Movement* broke new ground as the first text devoted to the qualitative analysis of human movement. The second edition strives to update and improve the presentation of this important information. The text has been updated with more than 60 qualitative analysis papers from a wide variety of disciplines, and the book has been reorganized to get students into the tasks of qualitative analysis early and progressively practice these important skills.

Part I introduces the interdisciplinary model of qualitative analysis developed in the book and summarizes the development of this approach and the perceptual factors relevant to qualitative analysis. Throughout the text, real-world examples show how the many subdisciplines of kinesiology contribute to each of the four tasks of qualitative analysis. Part II comprises four chapters that fully explore each of the four tasks of qualitative analysis. The book concludes with part III, the application of qualitative analysis in human movement. These chapters guide the reader through real-world examples of qualitative analysis and show how the integration of video and computer technology can be used to improve qualitative analysis.

New to This Edition

In this edition there are even more examples of the application of qualitative analysis throughout the text. Several new features illustrating key points in qualitative analysis are qualitative analysis (QA) Choices, QA Demonstrations, and QA Practice. QA Choices ask open-ended questions on important application issues in qualitative analysis. QA Demonstrations are activities involving two video clips from the accompanying CD-ROM. QA Demonstrations, found in chapters 1 through 7 and 10, illustrate some key point about a task within QA. Suggested answers to QA Demonstrations are provided on the CD-ROM.

QA Practice clips provide opportunities to practice qualitative analysis using four video clips from the CD-ROM. Intended for video-replay practice of the whole QA process, these clips are found in chapter 8. To take advantage of these multimedia experiences, you will need a Pentium PC with at least 32 MB of RAM, 250 MB of hard disk space, a CD-ROM drive, and Windows 95 or later.

This second edition retains the four-task model of qualitative analysis, integrating the many subdisciplines of kinesiology that contribute to the process. The model is comprehensive in scope but simple enough that it can easily be applied to all kinds of human movement. The major purposes of this text are to

- illustrate the interdisciplinary nature of qualitative analysis and detail an integrated model of qualitative analysis of human movement;

- review the research and scholarly writing on the qualitative analysis of human movement from the various subdisciplines of kinesiology;

- provide tutorials and multimedia demonstrations that illustrate the integrated model of qualitative analysis; and

- increase interest in the development of qualitative analysis training in the kinesiology curriculum.

Each chapter begins with a preview box that showcases the topic of the chapter and its importance to qualitative analysis. The major topics of each chapter are highlighted in a list of chapter objectives. Examples are given throughout the text, and a longer discussion of a practical example is presented in the practical applications section of each chapter. Like the previews, practical applications use real-world examples and emphasize how all the subdisciplines of kinesiology contribute to qualitative analysis of human movement.

Other features useful for mastering key concepts in qualitative analysis include key points, chapter summaries, and discussion questions. Key points are small sections that summarize an important concept that has emerged from the qualitative analysis literature. Each chapter concludes with a review that summarizes its major themes and a list of open-ended questions designed to stimulate discussion and interaction among various points of view. A glossary of key terms and an extensive bibliography of qualitative analysis literature are provided at the end of this book.

It is our hope that readers will find themselves thinking critically about their future or present professional practice. We also hope these kinesiology professionals will take steps to improve their skills in qualitative analysis and to help expand the knowledge base on qualitative analysis of human movement.

Acknowledgments

The authors are indebted to many people who helped in the development of this book. The comments of many reviewers are greatly appreciated. We are also indebted to all the professionals at Human Kinetics who improved the quality of this book. Dr. Knudson would like to thank the most important people in his life: his family, scholars whose work this book is built on, and his Lord Jesus Christ. Dr. Morrison is indebted to the scholars who have come before him and especially to those who have been instrumental in his contribution to this book: Joyce Harrison, Jean Reeve, Paul Dunham, and Shirl Hoffman.

Credits

Chapter 1 opener, figures 1.1 - 1.6, 3.2, 3.5, 4.1, 4.2, 4.4, 5.4, 6.1, 6.3, 7.2, 7.3, 8.1 - 8.17, 9.1, 10.1, 10.2 and tables 2.1, 8.2, 8.3, 8.7 Reprinted, by permission, from D. Knudson and C. Morrison, 1997, *Qualitative Analysis of Human Movement,* 1st ed. (Champaign, IL: Human Kinetics).

Figure 2.1 Reprinted, by permission, from J. Hay, 1983, A system for the qualitative analysis of a motor skill. In *Collected papers on sports biomechanics,* edited by G.A. Wood (Perth, Australia: University of Western Australia Press), 97-116.

Figure 2.2 Adapted, with permission, from Jackie Hudson, 1987, "What goes up . . .," Paper presented at the AAHPERD national convention.

Figure 2.3 Reprinted, by permission, from M.N. McPherson, 1990, "A systematic approach to skill analysis," *Sports Science Periodical on Research and Technology in Sport* 11 (1).

Figure 2.5 Reprinted, by permission, from K. Haywood and N. Getchell, 2001, *Learning activities for life span motor development,* 3rd ed. (Champaign, IL: Human Kinetics), 119.

Figures 2.6, 5.2 Reprinted, by permission, from S.K. Gangstead and S. Beveridge, 1984, "The implementation and evaluation of a methodological approach to qualitative sport skill analysis instruction." *Journal of Teaching in Physical Education* 3 (62).

Figure 3.1 Reprinted, by permission, from K.M. Haywood and C.F. Lewis, 1989, *Teaching archery: Steps to success* (Champaign, IL: Human Kinetics).

Figure 3.3 Reprinted, by permission, from R.A. Schmidt and C.A. Wrisberg, 2000, *Motor learning and performance,* 2nd ed. (Champaign, IL: Human Kinetics).

Figure 3.4 Reprinted, by permission, from S. O'Donnell et al., 1994, *Enhancing soldier performance: A non-linear model of performance to improve selection, testing and training* (U.S. Army Research Laboratory, Report ARL-CR-193).

Figure 3.6 Reprinted, by permission, from S.E. Palmer, 1992, "Common region: A new principle of perceptual grouping," *Cognitive Psychology,* 24: 437.

Figure 4.3 Reprinted, by permission, from M.A. Lafortune and P.R. Cavanagh, 1983, Effectiveness and efficiency during bicycle riding. In *Biomechanics VIII-B,* edited by H. Matsui and K. Kobayshi (Champaign, IL: Human Kinetics).

Figures 4.5, 4.6, 4.8 Reprinted, by permission, from C. Morrison and J. Reeve, 1993, "A framework for writing and evaluating critical performance cues and instructional materials for physical education," *The Physical Educator,* 50 (3): 133.

Figure 4.7 Reprinted, by permission, from V. Pinheiro, 2001, "Qualitative analysis for the elementary grades," *JOPERD* 71 (1):22.

Figure 5.1 Reprinted, by permission, from D.R. Bradley and H.M. Petry, 1977, "Organizational determinants of subjective contour: The subjective Necker cube," *American Journal of* Psychology 20(2):254. Copyright 1977 by the Board of Trustees of the University of Illinois. Used with permission of the University of Illinois Press

Figure 6.2 Reprinted, by permission, from D. Knudson, 2000, "What can professionals qualitatively analyze?" *JOPERD* 71(2):19-23.

Figure 7.1 Reprinted, by permission, from H. Hatze, 1976, Biomechanical aspects of a successful motion optimization. In *Biomechanics VB,* edited by P.V. Komi (Baltimore: University Park Press), 10.

Figure 7.4 Reprinted, by permission, from C.M. Balan, and E.W. Davis, 1993, "Ecological task analysis: An approach to teaching," *JOPERD*: December: 54-61.

Table 8.6 Adapted with permission from *Strategies: A Journal for Sport and Physical Educators* Vol. 7 No. 8, pages 19-22. Copyright year 1994 by the American Alliance for Health, Physical Education, Recreation and Dance - 1900 Association Drive - Reston VA 20191.

PART I

An Integrated Approach to Qualitative Analysis

Qualitative analysis is the primary method of improving human movement of clients in many kinesiology professions. Good qualitative analysis requires an interdisciplinary approach that integrates all subdisciplines of kinesiology. The consensus of the kinesiology literature on qualitative analysis can be summarized in a simple, four-task model of qualitative analysis. The tasks of (1) preparation, (2) observation, (3) evaluation and diagnosis, and (4) intervention address the important issues in helping people move better. Chapter 2 reviews how this broader vision of qualitative analysis developed out of fragmented, single-subdisciplinary approaches to qualitative analysis. This section concludes with a summary of how both sensory and cognitive processes are involved in making judgments about human movement.

Interdisciplinary Nature of Qualitative Analysis

Reprinted from Knudson and Morrison 1997: 15.

A golfer is having difficulty with his swing. Essential to his improvement is an instructor's ability to analyze the swing qualitatively. There is a humorous fable about three golf coaches who tried in vain to agree on what would improve the golfer's swing. The conflict arose because each coach had a different perspective on how to help the golfer improve his swing. They were insensitive to the variety of factors from outside their backgrounds that could affect a golf swing. For example, psychological factors, biomechanical factors, or pedagogical factors might limit a golf swing and be misunderstood by the coach.

This story is analogous to the low level of qualitative analysis often used by teachers and coaches who only detect certain errors and provide related corrections. Using an interdisciplinary approach to qualitatively analyzing human movement is better. An interdisciplinary approach to qualitative analysis integrates information from all subdisciplines of kinesiology and enables kinesiology professionals to identify the best way to help movers.

1. Define *qualitative analysis.*
2. Explain the difference between qualitative and quantitative analyses in kinesiology.
3. Explain why qualitative analysis should be an interdisciplinary process.
4. Describe the four tasks of an integrated qualitative analysis model.

Physical education teachers, coaches, and many kinesiology professionals face the challenge of accurate qualitative analysis of human movement every day. Qualitative analysis may be the most important skill that kinesiology professionals can use to improve the performance of their clients. This chapter introduces this important professional skill and explains why qualitative analysis must involve an interdisciplinary approach—integrating the many subdisciplines of kinesiology—to be most effective.

Qualitative Analysis in Kinesiology

Kinesiology is the term used to describe the academic discipline focused on the study of human movement, replacing what was often called *physical education* (Arnold, 1993; Hoffman and Harris, 2000; Newell, 1990). The premier scholarly society in this area (American Academy of Kinesiology and Physical Education) recommends the use of the term *kinesiology* to describe this academic discipline in higher education. Kinesiology professionals work in a wide variety of careers (for example, teaching, coaching, dance, athletic training, sports medicine, physical therapy, fitness, ergonomics) and all use qualitative analysis to improve human movement. Athletic coaches use qualitative analysis to make judgments on technique, strategy, and team selection. Physical education teachers often use qualitative analysis to evaluate student performance and assign grades. Athletic trainers qualitatively analyze gait, exercise, and sport movements to monitor recovery from injury.

Definition of Qualitative Analysis

Qualitative analysis must be defined for the purposes of this text. This is necessary because many terms used in the kinesiology literature to describe qualitative analysis are neither accurate nor all-encompassing. *Movement analysis, clinical diagnosis, skill analysis, error detection, observation, eyeballing, observational assessment, systematic observation,* and other terms have all been used to describe qualitative analysis. We define *qualitative analysis* as the systematic observation and introspective judgment of the quality of human movement for the purpose of providing the most appropriate intervention to improve performance (Knudson and Morrison, 1996: 17). Since *observation, intervention,* and *performance* are used in this definition, it is necessary to define them also.

Observation is defined as the process of gathering, organizing, and giving meaning to sensory information about human motor performances. This definition is very similar to Sage's (1984) definition of *perception,* and the task of observation in qualitative analysis is closely related to perception. *Intervention* in qualitative analysis is defined as the administration of feedback, corrections, or other change in the environment to improve performance. Both observation and intervention are key tasks within the larger process of qualitative analysis of human movement. We will use the term *performance* in a broad sense to mean both the short-term and long-term effectiveness of a person's movement in achieving a goal. This larger view of performance differs from motor learning, which traditionally limits the idea of performance to short-term movement effectiveness, using the term *learning* to refer to long-term ability.

Observation in qualitative analysis is not limited to the use of vision only. All the senses that teachers and coaches can employ to gather information should be used. For example, a gymnastics teacher may rely on kinesthetic information from her arms in spotting early trials of a new skill. Since she is too close to the movement to make reliable visual checks of some phases of the skill, the information from her hand placement and the muscular effort she extends to assist the student in completing the skill is critical to qualitative analysis. Auditory information about the rhythm of students' impacts with the mat can also be important in qualitative analysis for a gymnastics teacher, a dance teacher, or a therapist evaluating gait.

> **KEY POINT 1.1** Many words have been used to describe the process of the qualitative analysis of human movement. We define *qualitative analysis* as the systematic observation and introspective judgment of the quality of human movement for the purpose of providing the most appropriate intervention to improve performance.

> **KEY POINT 1.2** Qualitative analysis is not limited to visual inspection of human movement. Good observation involves the use of all senses to gather information about performance.

Qualitative Versus Quantitative Analysis

Qualitative analysis is by nature a subjective process, a judgment call about the quality of movement. This does not mean that it is unorganized, vague, or arbitrary in nature. In fact, to be most effective, qualitative analysis requires extensive planning, information from many disciplines, and systematic steps.

Figure 1.1 illustrates a continuum of human movement analysis. Any analysis of human movement can be located somewhere along the continuum from qualitative to quantitative. The qualitative end of the continuum involves the nonnumerical analysis of movement information or a judgment on the quality of an aspect of movement. The quantitative end of the continuum involves some measurement of performance. For example, qualitative analysis of baseball pitching could include statements by television commentators or technique reminders given to the pitcher by the pitching coach. Moving along the continuum are more quantitative analyses that use numbers like statistical breakdowns of pitches and their locations, radar measurements of ball speed, or complex biomechanical research.

Information from traditional qualitative analyses in kinesiology falls near the left side of the analysis continuum. Most teachers or coaches use qualitative analysis in everyday practice situations to diagnose and correct errors. Other movement analyses are midway along the continuum. Evaluation of skill or developmental level, such as using a rating scale or timing a 40-yard dash, is at the beginning of quantified performance.

If performance can be expressed in numbers, then the analysis can be based on quantified data. Quantification of data (in seconds, feet, meters, degrees per second) moves the analysis further to the right on the continuum. But even research measurements (quantification of a highly controlled nature) cannot be purely objective. There is some subjectivity in deciding where to place the tape measure or where to take a

FIGURE 1.1 Sample continuum of human movement analysis for analyzing running.
Reprinted from Knudson and Morrison 1997: 5.

FIGURE 1.2 One attempt to catch a fly ball. A qualitative analysis of this situation would help the instructor provide appropriate feedback to this performer. What do you think is the most appropriate feedback?
Reprinted from Knudson and Morrison 1997: 6.

skin-fold measurement. Quantification does not automatically ensure validity and reliability, and the lack of quantification in a qualitative analysis does not automatically mean the assessment is less valid or reliable. Research and writings, discussed later in this book, indicate there is a far richer decision-making base for qualitative analysis than is often thought (Morrison, 2000; Shiffrar, 1994).

The farthest levels of quantitative analyses in sport sciences, such as biomechanics and exercise physiology, are primarily being performed in university research settings or at the Olympic Training Centers for elite athletes. Biomechanists measure instantaneous values of velocity, acceleration, or force for various parts of the body. Physiologists measure the time-varying values of oxygen consumption, body fat, or amounts of lactic acid in the blood. These quantitative analyses of human movement, however, have been and will continue to be too expensive and difficult for widespread use in teaching and coaching settings.

A typical coaching situation where a qualitative analysis would be helpful is illustrated in figure 1.2. An athlete has missed a fly ball during outfield practice. Many teachers might attempt to correct the hand position, as his is clearly not the best hand position for fielding balls above the waist. But a quantitative biomechanical analysis of the hand positions would be overkill and not address the many factors that affect this performance. A good qualitative analysis of this situation would examine all factors affecting performance and then focus on the most important to help the player improve. The real question is whether or not qualitative analysis integrating all sources of information would suggest correcting hand position as the most important feedback.

In the real world, several other factors might contribute to missing a fly ball. The athlete could have poor vision and require glasses. Environmental factors such as the sun or wind may affect his performance. The psychological pressure of a critical time in the game may impair his concentration and perception. Maybe the player has an attention deficit disorder. If he is alert but does not attend to the right information (sound, ball trajectory, and spin), he could misjudge the ball. If he misses several fly balls in a row, the analyst could begin to evaluate the size and direction of errors and decide whether lack of attention was the problem. This example illustrates the many factors that may have to be weighed in qualitative analysis and shows why qualitative analysis involves integration of the many subdisciplines of kinesiology.

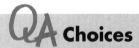 **Choices**

Imagine you are a Little League coach working with the player illustrated in figure 1.2. Which of the following factors do you think is most important in catching and why: readiness, vision, hand/arm position, motivation, or experience? How could you modify practice to confirm your judgment?

Interdisciplinary Nature of Qualitative Analysis

Traditionally, kinesiology scholars have studied qualitative analysis from a single subdisciplinary perspective. For example, scholars interested in motor development have done extensive work in identifying and validating developmental sequences for fundamental movement patterns (Roberton and Halverson, 1984; Wickstrom, 1983). Psychology and motor learning specialists have studied how skills are learned and the conditions of feedback that are related to performance and learning (Ammons, 1956; Magill, 1994; Newell, 1976; Newell, Morris, and Scully, 1985; Schmidt and Wrisberg, 2000).

Experts in the field of biomechanics have formulated general principles of human movement for the purpose of qualitative analysis (Bunn, 1955; Groves and Camaione, 1983; Kreighbaum and Barthels, 1985; Luttgens and Wells, 1982; Norman, 1975; Piscopo and Bailey, 1981). Biomechanists have also proposed specific methods of qualitative analysis, since this subdiscipline was commonly assumed to be a basis for qualitative analysis ability in students (Brown, 1982; Hay and Reid, 1982; Hudson, 1990c; Norman, 1975). Scholars interested in sport pedagogy have also recommended approaches to qualitative analysis (Barrett, 1979a, b; Hoffman, 1974, 1977a; Pinheiro, 1994; Pinheiro and Simon, 1992).

The problem is that qualitative analysis in the real world requires the simultaneous integration of all these and other bodies of knowledge. By *integration*, we mean the simultaneous summing of all subdisciplines of kinesiology into a unified whole that is bigger than the separate constituent parts. We will see in chapter 4 that kinesiology professionals strive to weigh information from experience and the subdisciplines of kinesiology when planning for qualitative analysis. Qualitatively analyzing human movement from a single perspective will result in a fragmented and incomplete understanding of movement. Good qualitative analysis is an interdisciplinary process because all kinesiology subdisciplines contribute to the process. Simultaneously integrating many perspectives is the essence of an interdisciplinary (see figure 1.3) process. In other words, qualitative analysis is not multidisciplinary, where unrelated subdisciplines contribute unique and discrete aspects to the whole (like the golf coaches in the chapter preview). Good qualitative analysis requires that the professional be knowledgeable about and simultaneously integrate information from all the subdisciplines of kinesiology.

An analysis that bases changes in technique solely on principles of biomechanics (the science of technique) is not ideal because it overlooks the relevant information other disciplines contribute to these judgments. In the outfielder example, the athlete's hand position may not be typical of his performance and thus not the most important correction. Knowledge of strength, maturation, and stages of motor development may also apply to the situation being evaluated. Motor development literature would provide information about the typical stages people go through in learning to catch. Motor learning and pedagogy research would also help in shaping the communication of corrections and the appropriate practice schedule. Knowledge of psychology could help in the motivation necessary to sustain the practice and the short-term decrease in performance needed for long-term improvement.

The paradox of qualitative analysis in kinesiology is that it has emerged directly from the major subdisciplines, yet it has not been widely recognized as a distinct area of inquiry in its own right. Some kinesiology

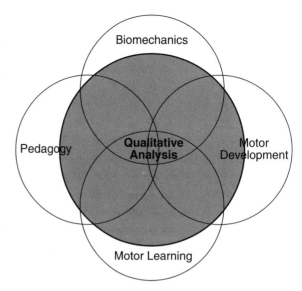

FIGURE 1.3 The interdisciplinary nature of qualitative analysis requires the integration of various subdisciplines within kinesiology. Only four subdisciplines are illustrated to prevent confusion. Reprinted from Knudson and Morrison 1997: 6.

KEY POINT 1.3 Qualitative analysis requires an interdisciplinary approach, the integrated use of information from many subdisciplines of kinesiology. The golf coaches described in the chapter preview must combine information from their subdisciplines to help the golfer improve performance. A coach's knowledge of the performer's strength and flexibility (exercise physiology) must be integrated with knowledge of the various aspects of the technique (biomechanics), the practice required (motor learning), and the anxiety of the performer (sport psychology).

Demonstration 1.1

Observe the golf swing video clips and list the information about the skill and performer that you think is relevant to evaluating their performance. Classify the information by kinesiology subdiscipline or other source.

scholars believe that the whole profession has suffered due to lack of recognition of the importance of qualitative analysis (Huelster, 1939; Hoffman, 1974; Norman, 1975).

It may seem odd that it has taken so long for qualitative analysis to emerge as an entity in kinesiology, but there are several plausible explanations as to why kinesiology has been so slow to address this important ability formally. First, inadequate technology (high-speed film, video equipment, computers) has made it difficult to create knowledge at a deep enough level to affect instructional practice. Because the human body is so complex, it is difficult to create biomechanical models with enough accuracy and all the relevant factors to define optimal movement.

Second, kinesiology faculty have assumed that qualitative analysis ability arises from the undergraduate biomechanics course. While the National Association for Sport and Physical Education (NASPE) guidelines and standards for instruction in introductory biomechanics has an objective to develop qualitative analysis competence (Kinesiology Academy, 1980, 1992), there is considerable criticism and evidence that this objective is not being met (see Knudson, Morrison, and Reeve, 1991). Biomechanics is the science within kinesiology most strongly related to movement technique, but it is not the only relevant subdiscipline. Since qualitative analysis is an interdisciplinary process, qualitative analysis training in kinesiology professional programs should not solely reside in the introductory biomechanics course. Morrison and Harrison (1997) have summarized several strategies for teaching qualitative analysis within the kinesiology curriculum.

Another problem in the last few decades is that most of the research in kinesiology has become highly specialized by subdiscipline. Many kinesiology faculty present and publish their research in specialized academic societies like the American Society of Biomechanics, American College of Sports Medicine, or the North American Society for the Psychology of Sport and Physical Activity. Even faculty interested in the profession of general kinesiology who join the American Alliance for Health, Physical Education, Recreation and Dance (AAHPERD) must select their interests from six national associations and about 90 different interest areas. Since qualitative analysis is based on the integrated use of many of these subdisciplines of kinesiology, it has been difficult to work across these boundaries. An excellent example of how the development of qualitative analysis has been limited by the variety of different approaches, rather than an integrated approach, is the variety of terms used to define the qualitative analysis of human movement (Barrett, 1979a; Hoffman, 1977a; Radford, 1989).

It is likely that scholars from any three subdisciplines of kinesiology would use different terms for the qualitative analysis of human movement. Indeed, scholars have used many terms to describe what we call *qualitative analysis*. Terms like *observation* (Barrett, 1979c), *error identification/detection* (Armstrong and Hoffman, 1979; Cloes, Premuzak, and Pieron, 1995; Vanderbeck, 1979), *qualitative assessment* (James and Dufek, 1993), and *clinical diagnosis* (Hoffman, 1983) have also been used to mean qualitative analysis. The terminology confusion is also apparent in the variety of adjectives other than *qualitative* that are attached to *analysis*: for example, *skill analysis* (Gangstead and Beveridge, 1984; Hoffman, 1974; Wilkinson, 1992b), *movement analysis* (Biscan and Hoffman, 1976), *visual analysis* (Wilkinson, 1992a), and *subjective analysis* (Arend and Higgins, 1976). Another recent terminology problem is the use of the term *systematic observation* in sport pedagogy to mean the observation and classification of teacher and student behaviors for the evaluation of teaching (Behets, 1993; Siedentop, 1991), and not the qualitative analysis of performance.

The consistent use of standardized qualitative analysis terminology across the subdisciplines of kinesiology would be useful in the development of qualitative analysis. The fragmented development of terminology makes the understanding of its origins in kinesiology more important. The next section will briefly preview the integrated and interdisciplinary model of qualitative analysis used in this book. Chapter 2 will provide a closer look at how commonalities in previous models of qualitative analysis lead to the current interdisciplinary model.

Integrated Model of Qualitative Analysis

This text uses a simple four-task model of qualitative analysis. Figure 1.4 illustrates this model and some of the important issues within each task. All four tasks of an integrated qualitative analysis should be viewed as equally important. A weakness in any one task diminishes the effectiveness of qualitative analysis as a whole.

Some important features of the model of qualitative analysis should be apparent in figure 1.4. First, the model is

QA Choices

After the first game of the season, the coach of a junior high school basketball team had a discussion with parents of two of her players. The first parent thought there were a number of technique errors committed by the players on the team. She was concerned that the coach did not give enough corrections about technique. The second parent expressed a concern about the psychological pressure the coach was putting on the players.

How would you respond to the first or second parent? Does one game provide enough information to judge coaching style? Do the parents have an accurate idea of what is important in helping players learn the game? Would most parents understand the technical terminology used in teaching, coaching, and qualitative analysis of movement? Could you explain a balanced approach to helping the player improve their performance and help the team?

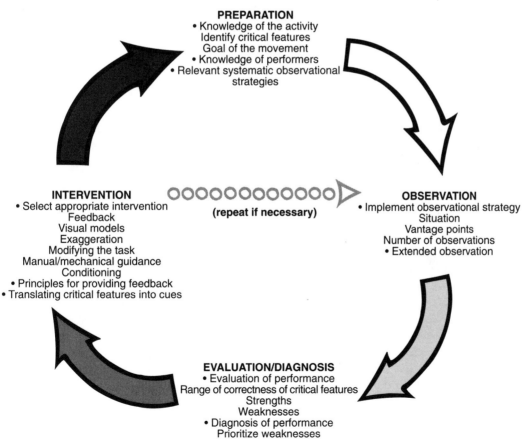

FIGURE 1.4 The comprehensive, integrated model of qualitative analysis. Some of the important issues for each task are listed.
Reprinted from Knudson and Morrison 1997: 27.

Practical Application: A Tale of Three Coaches

Reprinted from Knudson and Morrison 1997: 12.

Three Little League teams started practice for the summer season on the same day. The teams had the same number of players, the same level of skill and talent, the same number of practices and games against the same opponents. The volunteer coaches appeared to be similar, but they had slightly different approaches to qualitative analysis.

Coach A had a treasury of time-honored baseball cues and a keen eye for finding problems in his players' performances. As soon as he observed an error, he provided the related correction. During batting practice, fielding practice, and competition, he bombarded players with a barrage of corrections and helpful pointers. Classic paralysis by analysis was occurring. The children on the team had difficulty improving despite Coach A's advice. Although they didn't win the championship or break any league records, coach and players had an enjoyable season. Parents were not sure why their children were not picking up all the gems of advice from Coach A. Why did it seem as though the children played below their potential while the other teams had most of the good luck?

Coach B had been a good ballplayer in his day. He was a natural athlete and the game came easily to him. Coach B presented the fundamentals of the game as he

remembered them from his playing days, but he didn't have Coach A's keen eye. He couldn't seem to find the problem in a player's throw or swing. Coach B often focused on errors he was familiar with. Unfortunately, he did not notice that these errors were symptomatic of other problems in technique or strength limitations. The parents were impressed with Coach B's demonstrations and believed the children were lucky to have such a skilled coach. Nevertheless, the team didn't make the playoffs, and the players never seemed to look as good as Coach B did when he was demonstrating a technique.

Coach C knew there was a lot the children needed to work on to become skilled players, and he knew they needed to work together to make a good team. He often wanted to help each child with personal coaching, but he knew this wasn't possible. Coach C thought he had better choose his words carefully to communicate effectively and to protect his players' self-esteem and confidence. Almost unconsciously, Coach C praised everyone's effort and often found only one thing each child should work on. The parents were concerned that Coach C didn't look as active, involved, or technical as Coach A. He certainly didn't look as good in action as Coach B. Nevertheless, the children learned quickly and trusted Coach C because he always seemed to find the one thing that helped them hit the ball or get the throw to the right spot. Coach C's players had a great season. They hit, ran, and fielded with confidence. Skill and luck came together, and the team won the postseason tournament. Somehow Coach C must have known that analytical skill was needed to evaluate technique and decide how best to help improve performance.

The astute reader may have noticed that Coach A was a skilled observer and diagnostician of movement errors, but he did not use knowledge from the disciplines of psychology and motor learning to provide the most appropri-

ate feedback. Coach B was knowledgeable about baseball skills but lacked the knowledge and experience to develop his own observational and diagnostic skills. Coach C was a good example of an integrated approach to qualitative analysis. The story suggests that Coach C was skilled in all of the four tasks of an integrated qualitative analysis: preparation, observation, evaluation and diagnosis, and intervention. Neglect of any one of the four tasks limits a teacher's or coach's effectiveness in improving players' performances. The next section of this book details the four tasks of the integrated model of qualitative analysis of human movement.

circular, emphasizing the continuous learning and improvement that are part of professional growth. Second, there is a way to move from intervention directly to observation. For example, an analyst may provide feedback to a performer and immediately begin another observation to continue the qualitative analysis. Third, there can be movement in both directions between observation and evaluation/diagnosis. A skilled analyst may adjust the observational strategy based on an evaluation of information in early observation of a performer.

The following chapters will detail the issues in each of the four tasks in an interdisciplinary qualitative analysis. In the first task of qualitative analysis, preparation, the professional needs to gather knowledge from research and professional opinion, and think critically about the key features of the movement, potential cues, and the common errors clients exhibit. The second task, observation, involves systematically gathering appropriate sensory information about the performance. The third task, evaluation and diagnosis, involves both identifying strengths and weakness as well as prioritizing the possible ways to improve performance. The fourth task, intervention, often involves providing feedback or changes in practice conditions that will lead to improved performance.

Any model of qualitative analysis should be viewed as part of the teaching process in most kinesiology professions. Qualitative analysis is a key teaching skill that should be systematically addressed by the curriculum in teacher preparation and other kinesiology programs. Practicing professionals should continuously read and think critically about how they apply qualitative analysis in the classroom, field, or lab. They should also serve as mentors or teachers of qualitative analysis to students in the field. This cooperative training of future professionals, blending experience and scholarship, has been lacking (Siedentop and Locke, 1997).

Our model is broad enough to include all the major tasks of qualitative analysis yet simple enough not to be overwhelming. Like performers, analysts can also be overcome with *paralysis by analysis,* or information overload (figure 1.5), trying to apply a very complicated qualitative analysis approach or attend to unimportant information. A simple model based on critical movement features reduces the

KEY POINT 1.4 There are four important tasks in a comprehensive view of qualitative analysis: (1) preparation, (2) observation, (3) evaluation and diagnosis, and (4) intervention.

QA Demonstration 1.2

Observe the accompanying video clips and note the most obvious error. Observe the video clips again, this time with a larger vision of qualitative analysis, noting strengths and weaknesses. List these observations and all the kinesiology subdisciplines that provide knowledge relevant to that observation.

FIGURE 1.5 Like a performer, an analyst may be susceptible to paralysis by analysis. Both parties in qualitative analysis must focus their attention and be able to communicate. Reprinted from Knudson and Morrison 1997: 28.

observational and analytic demand on the analyst (although it may increase the demands of preparing for qualitative analysis). In the next chapter we will see that the use of a simple model is supported by the research on the validity and reliability of qualitative analysis.

Summary

Many professions use qualitative analysis to improve human movement. Good qualitative analysis of human movement is interdisciplinary, requiring the integration of information from many subdisciplines of kinesiology. Unfortunately, most research and professional literature on qualitative analysis has not been interdisciplinary; it has been written from the perspective of one subdiscipline (just like the golf coaches in the chapter preview). This text is based on a circular model of qualitative analysis, integrating all the kinesiology subdisciplines into four tasks: preparation, observation, evaluation and diagnosis, and intervention. This larger vision of qualitative analysis uses all the senses to gather information about the strengths and weaknesses of the movement.

Discussion Questions

1. Which kinesiology professions rely most heavily on qualitative analysis to improve human movement?
2. How has terminology been a barrier to the development of qualitative analysis in kinesiology?

3. Why is qualitative analysis an interdisciplinary process? Give examples.

4. Why is *multidisciplinary* a poorer description of qualitative analysis than *interdisciplinary*?

5. In what situations are qualitative analyses more appropriate than quantitative analyses? Why?

6. What does an *integrated* approach to qualitative analysis mean?

7. Which do you think is more important to preparing for qualitative analysis of movement, professional experience or research?

8. Why do you think interdisciplinary approaches to qualitative analysis have been rare in kinesiology?

Role of Models
in Qualitative Analysis

© Carol Simowitz Photography 2000

As explained in chapter 1, good qualitative analysis of human movement should be interdisciplinary. We are treated to this vision through the work of previous scholars and teachers interested in qualitative analysis. Like Isaac Newton said, "If I have seen further, it is because I am standing on the shoulders of giants." This chapter will review the research and writings that contributed to the development of the four-task model of qualitative analysis used in this book. Unlike the cooperative effort in making a pyramid like the one shown here, these contributions have often occurred independently in the many subdisciplines within kinesiology. In fact, even the scholarly and scientific support for the four-task model of qualitative analysis has not resulted in widespread agreement within kinesiology to use this model and terminology.

1. Identify the differences between comprehensive and observational models of qualitative analysis.
2. Identify major contributors and their contributions to the development of qualitative analysis.
3. Explain the contributions of kinesiology subdisciplines to the development of qualitative analysis.
4. Summarize the change in the vision of qualitative analysis over the years.
5. Discuss how the validity and reliability of qualitative analysis of human movement affects the model of qualitative analysis used.

The four-task model of qualitative analysis introduced in chapter 1 did not develop in a vacuum. Many teachers and scholars have contributed to the important professional skill of qualitative analysis of human movement. This chapter will classify the various models of qualitative analysis, show how the vision of qualitative analysis has changed, and trace the contributions of the kinesiology subdisciplines to the development of knowledge about qualitative analysis. This chapter concludes with a summary of the research on the validity and reliability of qualitative analyses of human movement, and how this information impacts a professional's approach to qualitative analysis.

Classifying Models of Qualitative Analysis

There are many approaches or models for the qualitative analysis of human movement in the kinesiology literature. This variety stems from the many subdisciplines of kinesiology that contribute to qualitative analysis. Researchers interested in motor development have documented approaches to qualitative analysis based on phases or levels of motor development. Biomechanics researchers have proposed models to apply the principles of mechanics to the qualitative analysis of human movement. Scholars in sport pedagogy and motor learning have also contributed models for the qualitative analysis of human movement.

If there are many models of qualitative analysis, how do we know which one is best or which features of the models to combine? Before we answer this question, it is important to classify the various models of qualitative analysis. In this book that classification includes two categories: comprehensive and observational.

Comprehensive models deal with the big picture of qualitative analysis, laying the groundwork for the whole process. These models usually provide information on movement goals, preparation for observation, stages of motor development, observation, evaluation, diagnosis of errors, and appropriate feedback. Comprehensive models attempt to summarize all the important tasks relevant to qualitative analysis of human movement.

Observational models of qualitative analysis are focused on the task of observation within qualitative analysis. They therefore fit into comprehensive models. Observational qualitative analysis models tend to fit into what we call the *observation task* of a comprehensive model of qualitative analysis. We will see that some observational models include parts of other tasks (beyond observation) common in comprehensive models.

One could even argue that a continuum probably exists from a strictly observational model to a comprehensive model of qualitative analysis.

Remember that the terminology, scope, and complexity of the qualitative analysis models vary. Scholars from a particular subdiscipline often emphasize the aspects of qualitative analysis to which their subdiscipline is strongly related. Table 2.1 categorizes selected qualitative analysis models in kinesiology as comprehensive or observational. The next section summarizes the development of these models of qualitative analysis.

> **KEY POINT 2.1** Models that have been proposed for qualitative analysis within kinesiology have either focused on the process of observation or had a more comprehensive view of the tasks within qualitative analysis.

TABLE 2.1 Scope of Selected Models for Qualitative Analysis

Comprehensive	Observational
Allison, 1985b	Abendroth-Smith, Kras, and Strand, 1996
Arend and Higgins, 1976	Barrett, 1979c, 1983
Balan and Davis, 1993	Brown, 1982
Hay and Reid, 1982, 1988	Cooper and Glassow, 1963
Hoffman, 1983	Dunham, 1986, 1994
Huelster, 1939	Gangstead and Beveridge, 1984
Knudson and Morrison, 1996	Hudson, 1985, 1995
McPherson, 1990	Pinheiro, 1994
Norman, 1975, 1977	Radford, 1989
Pinheiro and Simon, 1992	Roberton and Halverson, 1984
	Rose, Heath, and Megale, 1990
	Seefeldt and Haubenstricker, 1982

Adapted from Knudson and Morrison 1997: 17.

Overview of History and Models of Qualitative Analysis

Since the kinesiology literature has typically been fragmented into subdisciplines, we have presented the models and historical developments within this subdisciplinary framework. Subdisciplinary contributions are presented in alphabetical order. Although this section is organized in subdisciplinary sections, remember that in an interdisciplinary process of qualitative analysis there should be an integration of all strengths of these models. Readers should take note of the timing of these contributions, think about the development of qualitative analysis, and how the model in chapter 1 includes facets of the models reviewed.

Biomechanical Contributions

In the first half of the 20th century, the term *kinesiology* was used to refer to the course in the physical education curriculum composed of applied anatomy, and possibly some mechanical analyses of human movement. Early leaders in kinesiology/biomechanics were interested in the qualitative analysis of human movement and wrote textbooks for their courses emphasizing qualitative analysis (Broer, 1960; Cooper and Glassow, 1963; Scott, 1942). Early quantitative biomechanical analyses were labor intensive, involving a great deal of hand tracing and calculation from 16-millimeter film tracings.

Thus, qualitative analyses of movement were more common and accepted then than today.

The changing nature of the kinesiology course made for considerable confusion. Before the science of biomechanics developed, students preparing for careers in physical education took a course in kinesiology that was essentially functional anatomy. This course is now the introductory biomechanics course taken by all kinesiology majors. Biomechanists at AAHPERD national conventions in the middle 1970s realized these problems and tried to address them by organizing the first National Conference on Teaching Undergraduate Kinesiology in 1977. The NASPE Kinesiology Academy (now the Biomechanics Academy) appointed a task force to survey kinesiology/biomechanics instructors and to draft guidelines for the teaching of undergraduate kinesiology. After several years of discussion and input, in 1980 the Kinesiology Academy approved the "Guidelines and Standards for Undergraduate Kinesiology."

This proposal of a standard content for undergraduate biomechanics coursework in physical education had two of three main objectives focusing on qualitative analysis. The standards that focus on qualitative analysis recommend that the biomechanics course provide students with:

1. the knowledge necessary to undertake a systematic approach to the analysis of motor skill activities and exercises; and

2. experience in applying that knowledge to the execution and evaluation of both the performer and the performance in the clinical and educational milieu (Kinesiology Academy, 1980: 19).

This essentially qualitative emphasis in undergraduate preparation supports the implementation of qualitative analysis of movement in undergraduate biomechanics courses, and the emphasis is retained in the revised guidelines (Kinesiology Academy, 1992).

As biomechanics began to become the dominant course content (after the 1970s), many instructors did not maintain the focus of the introductory course on qualitative analysis but instead focused on quantitative biomechanical research (Knudson, 2001). Several biomechanists have continued an interest in qualitative analysis in professional preparation, calling for more emphasis on the principles and application of introductory biomechanics course content (Berg, 1975; Brown, 1982, 1984; Davis, 1984; Hay, 1983, 1984; Hudson, 1995; Knudson, 2001; Knudson, Morrison, and Reeve, 1991; Kreighbaum and Barthels, 1985; McGinnis, 1999; Norman, 1975, 1977). These advocates of qualitative analysis in biomechanics conceptualize the process in a variety of ways, so there has been very little systematic development of undergraduate preparation in qualitative analysis in kinesiology. Many kinesiology majors have primarily quantitative analysis experiences in introductory biomechanics.

One of the earliest calls from a biomechanist to focus introductory biomechanics instruction on application to qualitative analysis in the field was Norman (1975, 1977), who proposed that 10 biomechanical principles of motion be used to analyze movement qualitatively (table 2.2). These principles were generated from a decade of experience striving to teach application in the introductory course. His approach has become part of the extensive Canadian coaching-effectiveness programs.

In effect, Norman's model for qualitative analysis is based on these underlying mechanical factors that create human movement. The first step in the analysis is identifying the mechanical purpose or objective in the movement. The mechanical purpose should focus not just on the desired outcome (for example, the distance of a punt) but

TABLE 2.2 Biomechanical Principles for Qualitative Analysis

Summation of joint torques	Summation and continuity of body-segment velocities
Continuity of joint torques	Generation of angular momentum
Impulse	Conservation of angular momentum
Reaction	Manipulation of moment of inertia
Equilibrium	Manipulation of body-segment angular momentum

From "Biomechanics for the community coach," by R.W. Norman. Reprinted with permission from the *Journal of Physical Education, Recreation and Dance* (March 1975): 49-52. *JOPERD* is a publication of the American Alliance for Health, Physical Education, Recreation and Dance, 1900 Association Drive, Reston, VA 22091.

also on the mechanical cause of the outcome. In the javelin throw, the athlete wants to maximize release velocity and optimize release conditions (height and angle). Qualitative analysis is based on identifying errors or violations of the biomechanical principles that limit performance. A diving instructor who observes an overrotated entry position in a dive must decide whether the diver's error was the generation of too much angular momentum or poorly timed manipulation of body segments and their moments of inertia. Many biomechanics textbooks base qualitative analysis on the evaluation of mechanical principles (Groves and Camaione, 1975; Kreighbaum and Bartels, 1985; Luttgens and Wells, 1982). A series of articles by Sanders and Wilson (1989, 1990a, b) proposed 12 biomechanical concepts and their application in teaching and coaching motor skills. All these biomechanical concepts or principles are more specific than Norman's general principles.

Brown (1982) proposed 19 visual evaluation techniques that were developed with the Youth Sports Institute in preparing volunteer youth sport coaches. These techniques are essentially an observational model, organized into five areas: (1) vantage point, (2) movement simplification, (3) balance and stability, (4) movement relationships, and (5) range of movement. The observation and evaluation of movement are based on the application of these 19 techniques, first generally and then specifically. One observes multiple trials by first considering the vantage point, observing slower parts of the movement to simplify observation, and then focusing on faster, more complex parts of the movement. Brown's biomechanics paper concisely summarized the growing body of pedagogy literature of the time, which focused attention on the skill of observation.

Later that decade, at the second national symposium on teaching kinesiology and biomechanics in sports, several key developments occurred. Marett and colleagues (1984) reported on a national survey of kinesiology/biomechanics courses. Undergraduate kinesiology/biomechanics courses were placing a greater emphasis on teaching mechanical principles and applying biomechanics in qualitative analysis, at the expense of functional anatomy. Several other presentations focused on strategies for teaching qualitative analysis in the undergraduate biomechanics courses (Brown, 1984; Daniels, 1984; Hay, 1984; Hoffman, 1984; Hoshizaki, 1984; Kindig and Windell, 1984; Phillips and Clark, 1984; Stoner, 1984). The latest technological advance in interactive instruction, the interactive videodisk, was also demonstrated at this meeting (Zollman and Fuller, 1984). There seemed to be momentum for the goal of teaching the application of biomechanics with qualitative analysis. Unfortunately, this strong start has not grown into a clear consensus to emphasize qualitative analysis over quantitative analysis in the introductory biomechanics course in the United States.

TABLE 2.3 Visual Evaluation Points

Vantage Point

> Select proper viewing distance
> Observe from different angles
> Select with few distractions
> Select setting with vertical and/or horizontal references

Movement Simplification

> Observe slower moving parts
> Observe separate components of complicated skills
> Observe the timing of performance components

Balance and Stability

> Look at supporting parts of the body
> Look at the height of the body and body parts

Movement Relationships

> Look for unnecessary movements
> Look for movement opposition
> Observe motion and direction of swinging body parts
> Look at the motion of the head
> Note the location and direction of applied force

Range of Movement

> Observe the range of motion of body parts
> Look for stretching of the muscles
> Look for a continuous flow of motion

From "Visual evaluation techniques for skill analysis," by E.W. Brown. Adapted with permission from *Journal of Physical Education, Recreation and Dance* (January 1982): 21-25.

About this time, one of the most comprehensive models of qualitative analysis was proposed by Hay (1984). His model, which was the basis for a popular undergraduate biomechanics text (Hay and Reid, 1982, 1988), involves four steps.

1. Development of a deterministic/biomechanical model of the skill
2. Observation of performance and identification of faults
3. Ranking the priority of faults
4. Instructions to the performer

The Hay and Reid approach relies on a strong knowledge of biomechanics to break down motor skills and analyze the movements of performers, and it provides several insightful examples of qualitative analysis of sport skills.

The first step in the Hay and Reid model for qualitative analysis is the development of a biomechanical deterministic model of the skill. First, the mechanical purpose or result is identified—for example, time in a 100-meter dash, horizontal distance for a javelin throw, or height in a vertical jump. Then the biomechanical factors that directly influence or determine the result are identified. Figure 2.1 illustrates a deterministic model of a long jump. Most biomechanics models of qualitative analysis emphasize the importance of understanding the mechanical goal or purpose of movements to be

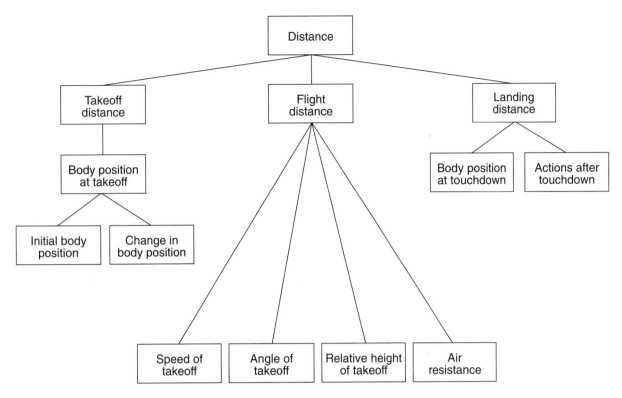

FIGURE 2.1   Deterministic model of a long jump used in preparing for qualitative analysis. Reprinted with permission from Hay, 1983: 106.

analyzed. A recent model of qualitative analysis called *biomechanically based observation and analysis for teachers* (BBOAT) expands the use of these deterministic models by adapting them to traditional organization (phases of the movement and skill level of the learner) of movement information (Abendroth-Smith, Kras, and Strand, 1996; Abendroth-Smith and Kras, 1999).

The second step in the model is the observation of performance and identification of faults. Hay and Reid outline many recommendations for using multiple senses and controlling the setting, vantage points, distances, and numbers of observations. They argue that the focus of observations generally should follow this pattern: observe two or three trials to get a general impression (gestalt) and then focus on parts to be systematically observed in later trials.

Hay and Reid (1988) built on the work of Norman (1975, 1977) and suggested that there are two ways observers identify faults in human movement. The traditional approach is to break the movement down into phases and compare the performer's movement to a mental image of the appropriate movement. They call this the *sequential method*. They suggest that flaws in this method are the assumption of an ideal form, the lack of any valid rationale for determining ideal form, and the typical assumption that champion athletes use ideal form.

Hay and Reid propose that the better approach is to use the *mechanical method* to identify performance faults. The mechanical method is based on using deterministic, biomechanical models to systematically evaluate the model factors to see if performance can be improved. This evaluation begins by identifying the lowest factors on each path. These are the underlying determinants of the effectiveness of the performance. The factors that cannot be changed by the performer are eliminated from consideration, and the observer evaluates what factors can be improved. For example, if the coach feels that initial body position and speed of takeoff are the only critical changes relevant for a long jumper, they can focus subsequent practice on these factors.

Although Hay and Reid claim that the mechanical method does not rely on any visual model of ideal form, they do suggest that their method uses the form of skilled performers as a guide for what is effective and what correction may be appropriate. It appears that the mechanical method proposed is another structure or paradigm on which to base qualitative analysis. In the end it may still rely on the same mental image comparisons as traditional qualitative analyses.

Hay and Reid also expand the vision of qualitative analysis to include the third step, ranking the priority of faults. Hay and Reid advocate that faults be prioritized using two rules: (1) faults are excluded if they are related to or result from other faults, and (2) faults should be corrected in the order that generates the most improvement in the time available. If an observer cannot prioritize some faults based on these rules, they should be ranked in the order in which they occur in the skill.

The final step in the Hay and Reid model for qualitative analysis is providing instruction to the performer. This is a critical step; the results of the analysis can be wasted if feedback is poorly delivered. Hay and Reid note that it is important to check the performer's understanding of the feedback. They also strongly suggest that feedback be limited to one fault at a time. They advocate direct corrections of faults or literal descriptions of what the performer should do. If this is unsuccessful, more figurative feedback that may indirectly lead to the correction should be used.

The Hay and Reid text (1982, 1988) provides a strong comprehensive model of qualitative analysis as commonly used in coaching. Their approach relies on a strong knowledge of biomechanics to break down motor skills. Their book provides several insightful examples of qualitative analysis of several sport skills using their method.

Another biomechanist, Hudson (1985), developed the POSSUM (purpose/observation system of studying and understanding movement) approach to qualitative analysis. A strength of the Hudson model is that the purpose of a movement must be associated with some observable dimensions of the movement. These dimensions are the variables that the observer must evaluate visually. The Hudson model is based on selecting visual variables that are important. They must distinguish between skill levels, be qualitatively observable by the naked eye, and be subject to change by the performer.

Figure 2.2 illustrates how a purpose is linked with visually observable variables. Each visual variable has a continuum that assists in evaluating performance. The visual or spatial analysis of these dimensions is achieved with two kinds of visual foci. The observer may focus at the whole-body, or somatic, level or on the sectional (segmental) level.

Hudson has continued to develop these analyst-friendly descriptions of biomechanical variables. In 1990 she proposed six generic dimensions of value and visual variables. Her research has also focused on examining how experienced and novice observers visualize variables in unfamiliar motor skills and on studying how long and in what phase of the movement visual variables are observed (Hudson, 1990c). Hudson (1995: 55) has expanded this idea and identified 10 core concepts of kinesiology (table 2.4). These concepts are the variables that an analyst can evaluate and give feedback about in order to improve performance. The core concepts

Direction of force

Purpose	Observation
Projection	Initial path
Height	Vertical
	45°
Range	
	Horizontal or below
Speed	

FIGURE 2.2 Examples of the principle of direction of force from the POSSUM model of qualitative analysis. The purposes of motor skills are linked with observable variables for the evaluation of performance.
Courtesy of Jackie Hudson, California State University-Chico.

are, in essence, the technique knobs that an analyst can turn in helping performers improve their movements.

An excellent comprehensive model of qualitative analysis based on previous biomechanical models was proposed by McPherson (1990). Her model of a systematic approach to skill analysis has four steps: preobservation, observation, diagnosis, and remediation, as shown in figure 2.3. Note how the four steps are similar to the four steps of the Hay and Reid (1982, 1988) model. McPherson's article provides excellent discussions of the importance of mechanical principles

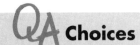

Choices

Biomechanical models of qualitative analysis range from observational models to comprehensive models. When might an observational model approach of qualitative analysis be more appropriate than a more comprehensive model? Is a more comprehensive approach always better?

TABLE 2.4 Core Concepts of Kinesiology	
Range of motion	Coordination
Speed of motion	Compactness
Number of segments	Extension at release
Nature of segments	Path of projection
Balance	Spin

From "Core concepts of kinesiology," by J.L. Hudson. Reprinted with permission from the *Journal of Physical Education, Recreation and Dance* (June 1995): 54-55, 59-60. *JOPERD* is a publication of the American Alliance for Health, Physical Education, Recreation and Dance, 1900 Association Drive, Reston, VA 22091.

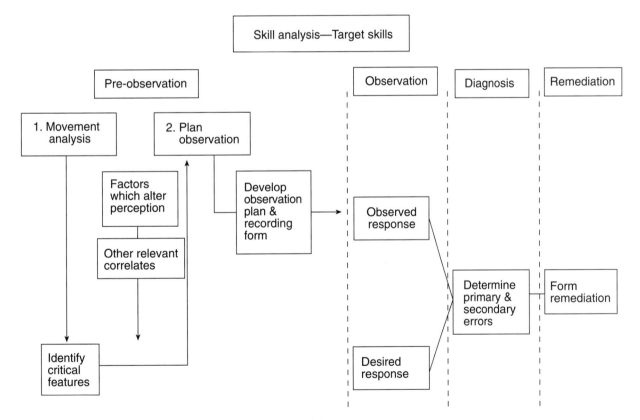

FIGURE 2.3   The McPherson qualitative analysis model.
Reprinted with permission from McPherson, 1990: 2.

and their relationship to critical features. Her discussions on observational plans and diagnosis of errors are also very thorough.

At the third national symposium on teaching kinesiology and biomechanics in sports, fewer papers were presented on qualitative analysis in undergraduate biomechanics compared to the second symposium. Research on the effect of biomechanics instruction and qualitative analysis (Dedeyn, 1991; Knudson, Morrison, and Reeve, 1991), and introductory experiences in qualitative analysis (Bird and Hudson, 1990) were presented. Other presentations described experiences of teaching biomechanical principles in a method aligned with qualitative analysis (Wilkerson, Kreighbaum, and Tant, 1991). After a discussion session at the symposium, a subcommittee was formed to revise the guidelines and standards. In 1992 the revised standards were adopted by the Kinesiology Academy (soon to be renamed the Biomechanics Academy) of NASPE and they retained the qualitative analysis emphasis for undergraduate biomechanics instruction (Kinesiology Academy, 1992). Although the standards retained the emphasis on qualitative analysis, many new biomechanics faculty were more interested in teaching quantitative biomechanical analysis.

At the fourth national conference on teaching biomechanics in sports (Wilkerson, Ludwig, and Butcher, 1997), there was again a noticeable decrease in papers on qualitative analysis of human movement. A survey of instructors at the meeting showed the continued decrease (from 1977 and 1983) in the percentage of class time devoted to the application of biomechanics (Satern, 1999). It is likely that the percentage of courses teaching application to qualitative analysis is even lower. Most students in introductory biomechanics classes do not have experiences in the application of biomechanics in qualitative analysis. The professional skill of qualitative analysis does not appear to be a priority in the majority of biomechanics faculty.

> **KEY POINT 2.2** Early leaders in biomechanics have developed guidelines and standards for the introductory biomechanics course that emphasize qualitative analysis. Not all biomechanics instructors agree with this philosophy of instruction in the introductory course.

Biomechanical contributions to qualitative analysis include scholarly papers (Hay, 1984; Hudson, 1985, 1995; Knudson, 2001; McPherson, 1990; Norman, 1977; Schleihauf, 1983), textbooks designed for implementing the qualitative nature of the guidelines and standards (Adrian and Cooper, 1995; Hall, 1999; Hay and Reid, 1988; Kreighbaum and Barthels, 1985; McGinnis, 1999), and several models of mechanical methods of qualitative analysis. It is clear that biomechanics has contributed to the development of qualitative analysis; however, it is not clear that the majority of biomechanics instructors in the United States follow the recommended emphasis on qualitative analysis in the NASPE guidelines and standards.

Motor Development Contributions

Scholars interested in motor development have documented the typical changes in movement patterns as children mature and become more skilled in many movements. Interest has recently been expanded to life span changes in motor skills. Motor development research on the typical changes of individuals at all ages is invaluable for the kinesiology professional qualitatively analyzing the movement. For example, a youth sport coach would benefit from knowing when growth spurts may influence changes in strength and coordination, or when most children attain mature levels of many fundamental movements.

The nature and description of these developmental changes in movements have been studied in several ways. The developmental changes in movement have been called *developmental sequences* and tend to be described using either a whole-body approach or a movement-components (legs, trunk, arms, and so on) approach. These motor development sequences have naturally been applied as observational models of qualitative analysis.

There are several examples of the whole-body developmental sequence observational models of fundamental movement patterns (Branta, Haubenstricker, and Seefeldt, 1984; Haubenstricker, Branta, and Seefeldt, 1983; Seefeldt and Haubenstricker, 1982; Ulrich, Ulrich, and Branta, 1988; Wickstrom, 1983). A classic example of a whole-body developmental sequence was proposed for overarm throwing by Wild (1938). Wickstrom (1983) has reviewed much of this early work. The development of over-arm throwing in children from two to seven years old generally shows four stages. Stage I involves a flexion and extension of the elbow, essentially in a sagittal plane and without a change in foot position. Stage II generally occurs from age three to five and has several characteristics. There still is no foot movement, but some transverse plane trunk rotation is added to an elbow flexion and extension that may be in a more oblique or horizontal plane. Stage III is usually seen in five- and six-year-olds. The movement begins with a step on the same-side leg (which limits the potential trunk rotation) and arm preparatory movements that are usually straight back. Stage IV is commonly found in boys and girls around six and a half years of age. This mature throwing movement involves a forward step with the opposite side foot, a downward arm backswing, trunk rotation, horizontal adduction of the upper arm, and elbow extension.

Figure 2.4 illustrates stage II and stage IV in the whole-body development of the overarm throw. An analyst can use this approach to know what actions to look for and the typical changes to expect in young throwers.

There are many motor development observational models of qualitative analysis using the movement-component approach (Halverson, 1983; Mosher and Schutz, 1983; Oslin, Stroot, and Siedentop, 1997; Painter, 1994; Roberton, 1983; Williams, 1980). The text by Roberton and Halverson (1984) summarizes many of the component developmental models of fundamental movement patterns studied at the University of Wisconsin. Roberton and Halverson studied the development of overarm throwing longitudinally and cross-sectionally and have validated developmental levels in six components of the overarm throw. A child's developmental level for various body parts of overarm throwing can be observed from the point of view of the trunk, backswing, humerus, forearm, stepping, and stride actions. Roberton and Halverson

FIGURE 2.4 Examples of two whole-body developmental stages of the overarm throw proposed by Wild (1938). Which of the four developmental stages is illustrated and why?
Illustrations courtesy of Steven Barnes, Multimedia Laboratories, Florida State University, Tallahassee.

propose that the trunk action be evaluated first in throwing and striking qualitative analysis. They suggest that the key developmental changes in the other components of throwing and striking are timed to changes in the use of the trunk.

Since the overarm throw is important to many sports, the component model of motor development has also been applied to other sport skills. Rose, Heath, and Megale (1990) developed a component model for observation of the tennis serve, a skill related to the overarm throw. The tennis serve was broken down into developmental levels within six components of the movement. Messick (1991) also reported a prelongitudinal screening study of the motor development of the tennis serve based on six components. Observational models of components of sport skills are quite common. The problem is that these approaches do not point out to the analyst all the factors and subdisciplines to consider in qualitative analysis.

Both whole-body and component observational models are effective in elementary physical education settings. Like youth sport coaches, physical educators need to know developmental milestones of many movements and the typical variability in children reaching these milestones. Maturation rates are typically plus or minus two years of chronological age. Physical educators must individualize teaching and feedback, because children of the same chronological age differ in developmental level and physiological age.

Recent research in motor development has been expanding the scope of the field. Studies are now focusing on the application of developmental sequences to more specific tasks, such as sport skills (Haywood, Williams, and Van Sant, 1991; Messick, 1991; Rose and Heath, 1990; Rose, Heath, and Megale, 1990). Recent motor development theory and research are also focusing on changes in development across the life span by documenting movement changes in older adults (Haywood and Williams, 1995; Williams, Haywood, and Van Sant, 1996). The text by Haywood and Getchell (2001) provides a logical decision tree for rating the developmental level of many movements and provides a CD-ROM with video clips for training in this kind of evaluation (figure 2.5).

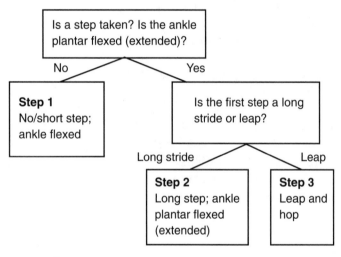

FIGURE 2.5 Logical decision tree.
Reprinted with permission from Haywood and Getchell, 2001.

Motor development research has made significant contributions to qualitative analysis by documenting changes in motor skills and increasing the understanding of ways (whole-body versus components) to observe and rate movement. Motor development has also strongly contributed to our understanding of the validity and reliability of visual observation. Future motor development research could be of even greater value to qualitative analysis if (1) comprehensive models of analysis were used for evaluating developmental level, and (2) it could be learned what corrections and practice are most effective in accelerating motor development. For example, research needs to determine if intervention should be focused on the next developmental level or the mature form to create the fastest skill development.

KEY POINT 2.3 Motor development scholars have contributed to qualitative analysis by carefully documenting the developmental stages of fundamental movement patterns and observational models for identifying these stages or levels.

Motor Learning Contributions

Research in motor learning has focused on issues related to the speed and permanence of learning new motor skills. This research has often used simple motor tasks with performance goals that can be precisely quantified. More and more motor learning research is being conducted in practical and real-world conditions, rather than single joint movements in lab conditions, expanding the opportunity to generalize the research. The major contribution of motor learning research to qualitative analysis in kinesiology is the wealth of information on the effect of many kinds of feedback on learning motor skills.

Feedback is the primary mode of intervention in qualitative analysis. Teachers of discrete movements (for example, a golf swing) may provide immediate feedback as part of qualitative analysis. An understanding of motor learning research on summary feedback might help a track coach provide good feedback in continuous events like sprinting or distance running. There are several good review articles dealing with movement feedback (Annett, 1993; Bilodeau, 1969; Lee, Keh, and Magill, 1993; Magill, 1993, 1994; Newell, 1976; Newell, Morris, and Scully, 1985) as well as explanation in the text on motor learning by Schmidt and Wrisberg (2000). While motor learning scholars have not been leaders in the development of qualitative analysis models, the subdiscipline of motor learning provides critical information in planning intervention (discussed in chapter 7) within qualitative analysis.

Pedagogy Contributions

Pedagogy scholars authored some of the first calls for greater emphasis on qualitative analysis in professional preparation in kinesiology. One of the earliest authors to comment on the need for qualitative analysis of movement was Huelster (1939). She suggested that courses like anatomy, body mechanics, and kinesiology were not enough to give physical education graduates the ability to do real-time qualitative analysis of human movement. Later research proved her right on this point and many of Huelster's suggestions were well ahead of her time. Unfortunately, only a few of her suggestions have been incorporated into the current physical education curriculum.

The next major motivation within pedagogy for the development of qualitative analysis came from research suggesting that good performers do not necessarily make good analyzers of movement (Kretchmar, Sherman, and Mooney, 1949). This view that the kinesthetic sense of skilled athletes may not transfer into qualitative analysis ability has been validated in the research of Girardin and Hanson (1967), Osborne and Gordon (1972), and Armstrong and Hoffman (1979).

A surge in pedagogy research on qualitative analysis in physical education began to appear in the late 1960s and 1970s (Armstrong, 1977a, b; Biscan and Hoffman, 1976; Girardin and Hanson, 1967; Hoffman and Armstrong, 1975; Hoffman and Sembiante, 1975; Landers, 1969; Moody, 1967; Osborne and Gordon, 1972). In 1974 Shirl Hoffman wrote a watershed article about the inability of people who had taken the undergraduate biomechanics class to analyze movement qualitatively. Other scholars have agreed with Hoffman's position that traditional biomechanics courses alone do not adequately prepare students for qualitative analysis and that specific instruction is necessary (Barrett, 1979a, b, c; Locke, 1972). This position has been supported by some research (Knudson, Morrison, and Reeve, 1991; Morrison and Reeve, 1988), although there is evidence that applied and conceptual instruction in biomechanics can affect the physical education teacher's selection of feedback to students (Dedeyn, 1991; Knudson, Morrison, and Reeve, 1991; Nielsen and Beauchamp, 1992). Nielsen and Beauchamp (1992), for example, found that conceptual instruction (generic biomechanical principles like those of Norman or Hudson) improved the amount of corrective, accurate, and specific feedback provided by students who qualitatively analyzed videotaped performances of volleyball and team handball skills.

Other important pedagogy developments in the 1970s were the scholarly reviews of observation literature by Barrett (1977, 1979a, b, c), and a comprehensive model of human movement analysis by Arend and Higgins (1976). The Arend and Higgins model presented a comprehensive picture of movement analysis, both qualitative and quantitative, and may be the first formal call for an interdisciplinary approach to qualitative analysis. Their model was also detailed in a subsequent book (Higgins, 1977).

The Arend and Higgins (1976) paper was important because it provided a comprehensive summary of an interdisciplinary approach to the analysis of human movement. Issues from biomechanics, pedagogy, motor development, and other kinesiology subdisciplines are included in their plan for analysis. Their model also provided for several strategies based on whether the purpose of the analysis was skill or performance. They saw skill analysis as an evaluation of learning, or how human movement changed over time. Performance analysis was the evaluation of the execution of a task or subphase of a task. The Arend and Higgins model is so comprehensive that it was designed to accommodate any kind of analysis of human movement. For example, their model can be used for subjective, anatomical, or quantitative analyses of human movement.

The Arend and Higgins comprehensive model of analysis breaks qualitative analysis down into three phases: preobservation, observation, and postobservation. Preobservation has three levels of decomposition, or levels of the factors important in the movement. Each level provides more specific background information on the movement being analyzed. The third level of decomposition identifies the precise biomechanical, tactical, and morphological factors related to the movement. This model and paper were important because previous articles on qualitative analysis had focused on the observation task, devoting little discussion to the preparatory or analytical activities after observation. Arend and Higgins also were early proponents of the concept of critical features, the key features of a movement that are necessary for optimal performance. We will examine the concept of critical features more closely in chapter 4.

Siedentop (1991) identifies the 1970s as a time when the pedagogy literature changed from research on teaching methods to the beginning of research documenting teaching and learning behaviors. Remember that the term *systematic observation* refers to the observation and classification of teacher and students behaviors in the process of evaluating teaching, not the qualitative analysis of performance. Although the science of sport pedagogy was taking a major turn in focus, many pedagogy scholars continued to contribute to the professional skill of qualitative analysis. By the end of 1979, demand for the implementation of qualitative analysis in the undergraduate physical education curriculum had slowly grown. The initial call to address this need had been made, research had begun, a theoretical basis had been framed, and specific changes in undergraduate preparation had been proposed.

Pedagogical research on qualitative analysis continued to grow in the 1980s. Bayless (1980, 1981) reported two studies indicating that several styles of instruction could improve the error-detection abilities of undergraduate students. It appears that qualitative analysis ability can be developed using a variety of instructional approaches that include guided practice. Hoffman, Imwold, and Kohler (1983) applied the taxonomy developed by Fitts (1965) to analyze children's movements. Also in 1983, two important qualitative analysis scholars summarized their research in key review papers (Barrett, 1983; Hoffman, 1983).

Barrett (1983) summarized her research on observational strategies and brought the professional skill of qualitative analysis to the attention of pedagogy scholars. Hoffman (1983) expanded his observational model of qualitative analysis into a more comprehensive vision called the *diagnostic prescriptive model*. The fundamental requirements were a good mental picture of what a performance should look like and a clear goal/purpose for the movement. The teacher focuses on the difference between the observed response and the mental image of the correct response. If a discrepancy exists between what is seen and what should be, the observer is charged with diagnosing (the extent of discrepancy and possible cause) and prescribing a remedy. His model was further developed into a comprehensive model called the *hypothetical-deductive model*. Differences between observed and desired performance could be related to a lack of a critical ability, a deficiency in skill, or a psychosocial problem. The Hoffman model significantly extended the considerable work on observational models, hypothesizing on the evaluation and diagnosis of movement errors for a more comprehensive vision of qualitative analysis.

Pedagogy scholars with experience in traditional qualitative analysis models in biomechanics courses developed important observational models of qualitative analysis (Cooper and Glassow, 1963). The Gangstead and Beveridge (1984) model was a true observational model, focusing on the observer's attention on the temporal and spatial aspects of the movement. The temporal foci are the preparation, action, and follow-through phases of the movement. The spatial foci are the performer's body weight, path of the hub (slowest moving part), arms, legs, trunk action, head action, and impact/release parameters. Figure 2.6 presents this model as modified from Cooper and Glassow (1963). The Gangstead and Beveridge model is designed to concentrate the analyst's attention on the sequence and the critical features of the movement. This observational framework is useful for observers who have difficulty diverting their attention to different parts of a movement.

Dunham (1986, 1994) proposed the use of task sheets for qualitative analysis and emphasized the importance of getting an overall feeling about the quality of the movement before observing specific components. This gestalt impression in the observational process is different from traditional observational models, which focus on temporal or spatial information first. Dunham instructed the observer to get an overall feel for the way the skill is performed. The basic ideas of a gestalt are that the whole is

Body components	Temporal phasing		
	Preparation	Action	Follow through
Path of hub			
Body weight			
Trunk action			
Head action			
Leg action			
Arm action			
Impact/release			

FIGURE 2.6 The Gangstead and Beveridge (1984) observational model of qualitative analysis. Reprinted with permission from Gangstead and Beveridge, 1984: 62.

greater than the sum of its parts and that the best way to analyze movement is to observe the whole and decide on the quality. If the quality is lacking, then analyze the skill by temporal or spatial means, or use one of the other models proposed in this chapter to find the specific problem. Pinheiro and Cai (1999) found that preservice students were better at diagnosing errors in a badminton short serve when they were able to consult a criteria sheet containing skill information. Pinheiro and Cai go on to indicate that this approach to live movement analysis might be useful at all levels of expertise. Several of these approaches to organizing observation with task sheets (Dunham, 1994; Gangstead and Beveridge, 1984; Pinheiro, 2000) are summarized in chapter 5.

Research on qualitative analysis by pedagogy scholars after 1980 began to expand into visual perception, a natural outgrowth of the early emphasis on observation and improvements in technology. Researchers used eye-tracking recorders to document visual search patterns (Bard et al., 1980; Petrakis, 1986, 1987) and psychological tests to determine the influence of perceptual style on qualitative analysis (Beveridge and Gangstead, 1984; Gangstead, Cashel, and Beveridge, 1987; Knudson and Morrison, 2000; Morrison and Frederick, 1998; Morrison and Reeve, 1989, 1992; Swinnen, 1984a). Recently research has shown that novices can improve visual perception of movement from specific video training programs (Abernethy, Wood, and Parks, 1999).

We will see in the next chapter that visual observation is strongly affected by the analyst's expectations and perception. Petrakis and Romjue (1990) examined the process of mental strategies of experienced observers to see if there were any similarities common to all observers. Procedural knowledge of qualitative analysis appeared to be the same for experienced observers, but their observation strategies appeared to be different. Some observers looked for specific parts of a skill to indicate proficiency; others scrutinized the overall performance. The former approach indicates an analytic perceptual preference, while the latter points to a gestalt approach. Perceptual style, the way a person takes in and organizes sensory information for interpretation, does appear to make a difference in qualitative analysis. The effect of perceptual style has been a focus of recent research on qualitative analysis (Knudson and Morrison, 2000; Morrison and Frederick, 1998; Morrison and Reeve, 1989, 1992). In chapter 5 we will show several ways to organize an observational strategy for qualitative analysis.

Other qualitative analysis issues investigated by pedagogy researchers were the effects of professional experience (Allison, 1987a and b; Barrett, Allison, and Bell, 1987; Imwold and Hoffman, 1983; Pinheiro, 1990), transfer to other skills (Morrison and Reeve, 1986; Nielsen and Beauchamp, 1992; Wilkinson, 1991), teaching qualitative analysis to classroom teachers (Morrison and Harrison, 1985), specific instruction in qualitative analysis (Gangstead, 1987; McPherson, 1988b; Morrison, Gangstead, and Reeve, 1990; Morrison and Reeve, 1988; Morrison, Reeve, and Harrison, 1992; Pinheiro, 1994; Wilkinson, 1990, 1992b), and retention of qualitative analysis ability (Wilkinson, 1992a; Morrison, 1994; Morrison and Harrison, 1985).

In a major theoretical leap, Kniffin (1985) took qualitative analysis to the next logical step. He showed that videotape instruction in the qualitative analysis of movement could produce positive results in live qualitative analysis in the gymnasium. Although these results had been hypothesized by researchers in the field, this was the first real evidence that specific film and videotape training in qualitative analysis would lead to improvement in movement diagnosis in the classroom. Other research has shown insignificant differences in live qualitative analysis proficiency of kinesiology students after videotape training (Eckrich et al., 1994).

Interactive videodisks and CD-ROM technology have been used to store video for instruction in qualitative analysis (Chung, 1993; Harper, 1995; Kelly, Walkley, and Tarrant, 1988; Klesius and Bowers, 1990; Mathias, 1991; Walkley and Kelly, 1989; Williams and Tannehill, 1999). But the small number of studies and inconsistent results in the transfer of video training in qualitative analysis to live settings suggests that more research is needed. The application section of this text and CD-ROM are primarily based on video clips, but we also suggest activities for live qualitative analysis.

Radford (1988, 1989, 1991) added to the review literature on qualitative analysis by pedagogy scholars by defining movement observation and proposing ways of linking observation, feedback, and assessment. More recently, several comprehensive models of qualitative analysis have emerged with a pedagogical heritage (Balan and Davis, 1993; Pinheiro 1990, 1994; Pinheiro and Simon, 1992). Pinheiro has proposed a model that describes the overall processes of qualitative analysis (Pinheiro and Simon, 1992), as well as an observational model (Pinheiro, 1994). The comprehensive model of Pinheiro and Simon (1992) is based on an information processing approach. The three levels in this model are cue acquisition, cue interpretation, and diagnostic decision. Cue acquisition is like the observation task in our integrated, comprehensive model of qualitative analysis. Cue interpretation is analogous to our evaluation step. And the diagnostic decision is analogous to the diagnosis step within the evaluation and diagnosis task of qualitative analysis. All of these processes can also be viewed as part of information processing in qualitative analysis.

Balan and Davis (1993) presented an ecological task analysis approach to teaching physical education derived from the work of Davis and Burton (1991). Their approach includes qualitative analysis as an essential component of the teaching, learning, and evaluation process. Their model also differs from others in emphasizing performer responsibility and control of the observational environment. Responsibility for finding movement solutions is shifted to performers/students, which is appropriate for individualized styles of instruction. The analyst is charged with controlling the physical (practice, equipment, and so on) and social environments to facilitate analysis of the movement. This model is almost like a style of teaching (the pedagogy connection again). This model will be reviewed more extensively in chapter 7.

Pedagogical contributions to the understanding of qualitative analysis are significant. Scholars have focused attention on qualitative analysis instruction in the curriculum, the importance of competence in observation, and enlarging the scope of qualitative analysis inquiry beyond the observation of movement.

> **KEY POINT 2.4** Pedagogy scholars have been early leaders in the call for greater emphasis on the skill of movement observation and teaching qualitative analysis in the kinesiology curriculum. Much of the recent scholarship and research on training qualitative analysis ability has been by pedagogy scholars.

Recent Developments

A growing body of literature and interest in qualitative analysis originated from several subdisciplinary areas within kinesiology. Many subdisciplines of kinesiology have contributed to the development of qualitative analysis, but no consistent terminology or curricular implementation of qualitative analysis training has been agreed on. Unfortunately, much of the recent interest in qualitative analysis has been focused on traditional error detection and correction, purely observational models of the process. At the dawn of the 21st century, three trends in kinesiology show some promise for the further development of qualitative analysis preparation of undergraduates.

First, there appears to be more faculty interest in teaching and research in qualitative analysis. Several recent doctoral dissertations have focused on qualitative analysis

(Chung, 1993; Eckrich, 1991; Harper, 1995; Johnson, 1990; Kwak, 1994; Leis, 1994; Matanin, 1993; Pinheiro, 1990; Raudensky, 1999; Rush, 1991; Taylor, 1995; Williams, 1996). This means that some new faculty may be knowledgeable and interested in promoting a larger, interdisciplinary vision of qualitative analysis. Professional journals like *Strategies* and the *Journal of Physical Education, Recreation, and Dance* (*JOPERD*) have been publishing papers on how to analyze specific sports skills (for example, Jones-Morton, 1990a, b, c, d, 1991a, b; Hudson, 1990b; Knudson, 1991, 1993; Knudson, Luedtke, and Faribault, 1994; Knudson and Morrison, 1996; Tant, 1990). Unfortunately, these papers are few and often not based on a comprehensive and interdisciplinary model of qualitative analysis (Ciapponi, 1999; Coker, 1998; McKethan and Turner, 1999; Wang and Griffin, 1998).

Second, there has been a growing emphasis to focus more attention on how kinesiology curriculum addresses professional preparation. The 1992 National Association for Sport and Physical Education/National Council for the Accreditation of Teacher Education (NASPE/NCATE) guidelines (number 22) required that qualitative analysis be part of the undergraduate curriculum for physical education teacher preparation (NASPE, 1992). Once accreditation agencies require training in qualitative analysis, kinesiology faculty will adjust their programs to meet these requirements. States in Australia (Victoria in 1996) and in the United States (South Carolina in 2000 and Utah in 1999) have picked up on these requirements and developed videotaped instructional units to assist their teachers in analyzing movements qualitatively.

> **KEY POINT 2.5** The time is ripe for the adoption of an interdisciplinary approach to research on and training in qualitative analysis of human movement. Three trends that may support the development of qualitative analysis are (1) more faculty interested in the topic, (2) curricular requirements for training in qualitative analysis, and (3) the gradual acceptance of the value of interdisciplinary research.

Third, there is a greater awareness of a need for interdisciplinary and cooperative approaches to teaching, learning, and research. Funding agencies and journals are encouraging interdisciplinary research. Unfortunately, this trend in greater interdisciplinary efforts has been slow to develop (Harris, 1993). One problem is that true interdisciplinary and applied research is still not the norm and is often unfavorably reviewed by journals. Journals devoted to applied and interdisciplinary papers (namely, *Journal of Interdisciplinary Research in Physical Education* and *Motor Skills: Theory into Practice*) have often folded after a few years in print.

While many faculty may agree with an interdisciplinary vision, they may also lack the skills to conduct this kind of research and continue with the specialized work they have been trained to do. Interdisciplinary cooperation on teaching and researching qualitative analysis, while the ideal approach, will likely take many years to develop acceptance.

Validity and Reliability of Qualitative Analysis

Important questions in any assessment relate to the issues of validity and reliability. In qualitative analysis, *validity* typically refers to the analyst's ability to correctly identify strengths and weaknesses of a performance. *Reliability* refers to the consistency of these subjective ratings. These issues are even more complex when put within the context of a comprehensive model of qualitative analysis. The validity of a qualitative analysis in the real world is affected by the diagnosis of the strengths and weaknesses of performance, and by the intervention the analyst selects. The more judgment and critical thinking used in a qualitative analysis, the greater the difficulty in showing its validity. The research has typically not dealt with this larger view of the validity of qualitative analysis, but rather the ability to visually detect errors or rate movement technique factors. This section will review the research on validity and reliability of qualitative analysis using studies from a variety of human movement disciplines.

Validity

Validity in qualitative analysis has two important levels. The first level is logical validity, which is established by the consensus of the literature and expert opinion on the movement being analyzed. An example of logical validity would be if the qualitative analysis accurately identified the critical features of the movement being analyzed. This first level of validity is very important, although no interdisciplinary conferences have been organized to establish the important aspects of human movements or their analysis. Instead, it is up to each kinesiology professional to remain current so that their qualitative analyses are based on the latest evidence.

The next important level is criterion-referenced validity, or checking the qualitative evaluation and diagnosis of some critical feature of performance with a criterion measurement of that feature. For example, you could check the criterion-referenced validity for visual estimation of knee angle in landing (figure 2.7) by comparing ratings of coaches to high-speed video (see Knudson, 1999) or electrogoniometric measurements of athletes' knee angles. A qualitative analysis of a movement must be valid to be of any value to the performer.

Kinesiology Studies

Qualitative analysis models in kinesiology have typically used panels of experts to provide logical validity for the components used in the analysis, but few studies have documented the criterion-referenced validity of qualitative analysis in kinesiology. Only a few studies (Kilani, Too, and Adrian, 1989; Knudson, 1999; Knudson and Morrison, 2000) have documented the criterion-referenced validity of visual ratings of movement. Both studies showed that very few untrained observers can accurately and consistently rate body angles in a vertical jump. About 50 percent of untrained observers could make holistic ratings of vertical jump range of motion using a visual analog scale (Knudson and Morrison, 2000). Studies are needed on the accuracy of the holistic ratings using visual analog scales, as well as more discrete, ordinal rating approaches to evaluation. Studies are also needed to document whether observers trained in a qualitative analysis system agree with biomechanical quantifications of the same variables.

© Human Kinetics

FIGURE 2.7 Logical validity in the qualitative analysis of knee motion in the landing phase is based upon the hypothesis that knee flexion (critical feature) is an important technique point, while criterion-referenced validity is determined by the actual agreement between the amount of knee flexion rated by the analyst and the actual knee movement measured by biomechanical instruments.

QA Choices

What level of validity of qualitative analysis is most important to you? What level of validity of qualitative analysis should be the primary focus of future research in kinesiology?

Ergonomics/Human Factor Studies

Engineers in the field of ergonomics/human factors routinely develop observational models for evaluation of the physical demands of various work tasks. Ergonomics/human factors studies look at the optimum design of facilities, tools, and tasks for people at work. Ergonomics studies have demonstrated that visual estimation of static body-segment angles in posture assessments are accurate to within 3 to 5 degrees (Douwes and Dul, 1991; Ericson et al., 1991). Note that this is much more accurate than during the movement studied by Knudson (1999) or Knudson and Morrison (2000). In another study untrained observers who visually estimated static shoulder angle from videotapes had slightly greater errors (mean absolute errors of 9 degrees) (Genaidy et al., 1993). The subjects tended to overestimate the true angle in low shoulder angles and underestimate the true angle in medium and high shoulder angles. These overestimations of body angles were consistent with studies of visual ratings of range of motion in the vertical jump (Knudson, 1999; Knudson and Morrison, 2000). These studies confirm the visual perception studies (chapter 3) that show bias in normal perception of still objects or their motions. It is likely that specific training would be required for good criterion-referenced validity of visual ratings of body angles and movement.

A study by DeLooze et al. (1994) examined the agreement between two observers' visual estimations of body actions in a materials-handling task and measurements of the same variables. Coefficients of agreement were not acceptable for torso flexion or for the position of the arms and legs. Only subjective ratings of gross body posture had acceptable agreement ($K = 0.79$) with the criterion measurements. Recently Paquet, Punnett, and Buchholz (2001) found that construction worker postures related to knee flexion and trunk bending and twisting could be accurately classified in three to nine categories. Similar results have been reported in poultry processing tasks (Juul-Kristensen et al., 2001). In summary, the ergonomics literature suggests there is criterion-referenced validity of qualitative analysis of some variables, but not for others. However, few validity studies have included large numbers of subjects who have been systematically trained in qualitative analysis.

Physical Therapy Studies

In the field of physical therapy, several studies have attempted to develop valid qualitative analysis models for evaluating movement quality (Boyce et al., 1995). One study found that observers could estimate step length in walking at slow to normal speeds to within 1.2 to 2.4 inches of accuracy (Stuberg, Straw, and Deuine, 1990). The best accuracy in visual assessment of step length occurred from close observational distances (0 to 3 meters); errors were two to three times larger if faster walking speeds were evaluated. Clearly the validity of qualitative analysis depends, in part, on the speed and complexity of the movement.

One possible reason that visual assessments do not have consistently strong criterion-referenced validity is the perceptual limitations of observers. Saleh and Murdoch (1985) found that biomechanical measurement systems identified more gait abnormalities than skilled visual gait analysts. The perceptual limitations of observing the speed and complexity of human movement are discussed in chapters 3 and 10. Another validity problem documented in the physical therapy literature is the tendency to be influenced by previous assessments (Eastlack et al., 1991; Miyazaki and Kubota, 1984).

More recent physical therapy studies of qualitative analysis validity have found moderate to good validity for several kinds of visual assessments. Bernhardt, Bate, and

Matyas (1998) found that 10 experienced physical therapists had moderate to highly accurate (correlations between 0.68 and 0.87) judgments of hand speed, jerkiness, and hand path using visual analog scales. There was less agreement between therapists because each analyst had a different mapping of actual motion to rating. Consistent with the bias discussed previously, Bruton, Ellis, and Goddard (1999) found consistent 4- to 6-degree visual overestimations of true metacarpophalangeal joint angle in a sample of 40 physical therapists.

KEY POINT 2.6 Although qualitative analysis has been shown to have content validity, the few studies of criterion-referenced validity show only moderate validity of visual assessments of movement in some raters.

Summary

More research is needed, across the subdisciplines of kinesiology, that examines the criterion-referenced validity of visual estimation of important performance variables (joint angles, muscle stretch, step lengths, trunk lean). Studies using a variety of human movements, conditions, and speeds of execution could begin to provide evidence for the criterion-referenced validity of qualitative analysis.

QA Demonstration 2.1

Observe the video clips of the vertical jump and decide if the jumper used enough countermovement. Decide if they bend their knees to at least 90 degrees. What level of *qualitative analysis* validity is being examined in this demonstration?

Reliability

More studies have been done on the reliability of the qualitative analysis of human movement than on validity. Intra-rater reliability is the consistency of the qualitative analyses performed by a single analyst. Inter-rater reliability is the consistency or agreement of the qualitative analyses of several analysts assessing the same performer. There has been a great deal of reliability research on qualitative analysis in the physical therapy and physical education/kinesiology literature. Reliability issues are important to consider when planning qualitative analysis or interpreting the qualitative analyses of others.

Kinesiology Studies

Motor development and adapted physical education studies of the reliability of qualitative analysis are noteworthy because many have used the *generalizability study* (G study) approach. This is important because a G study is designed to examine all variables that affect reliability of any measurement or assessment (observers, occasions, different performers). Roberton (1989) called for future motor development research to emphasize the documentation of the validity and reliability of observational models based on developmental sequences.

Ulrich (1984) reported acceptable reliability (*K*s between 0.62 and 0.84) of a standardized assessment of 12 fundamental motor skills. Ulrich, Ulrich, and Branta (1988) reported a G study of the qualitative analysis using the Michigan State developmental stages of the hop, horizontal jump, and running. Subjects received minimal instruction (one hour) in qualitative analysis of the whole-body developmental level of the three skills. One observer watching three trials could reliably analyze the hop (*G* = 0.88). Reliably assessing the developmental level of the horizontal jump and running required multiple observers and trials. These two skills showed potential observer bias, with 20 to 30 percent of the variance in the ratings being related to interaction between subject and observer. The observers had been warned against this error, but there may have been a tendency to relate the age of the subject to the developmental level assigned. For example, some observers may have been inclined to rate a younger-looking subject lower or an older-looking subject higher.

Observer bias was also observed by Painter (1990, 1994) after training in qualitative analysis. This G study examined the effect of training, academic major, and kind of motor development model (whole-body or component) used to identify 20 female college students' developmental levels of hopping. A key finding was that focusing on hopping components resulted in greater reliability than a whole-body approach that required multiple observers. The component approach (arm or leg action of hopping) to qualitative analysis could reliably rate developmental level with single observers looking at one to five performances.

A recent study of a qualitative rating checklist for folk dance supports the need for training, even using a structured qualitative analysis checklist (Slettum et al., 2001). Good reliability for rating three of six skill components of folk dance was observed after physical educators received four hours of training. It appears that reliable qualitative analyses of complex movements takes considerable planning and practice.

Mosher and Schutz (1983) also found that slow actions of the overarm throw (foot placement and body rotation) could be reliably observed in one trial by one observer. Fast and complex movements are difficult to observe reliably. These studies found that the action of the arms during hopping (Painter, 1990) and throwing (Mosher and Schutz, 1983) was difficult to observe reliably. Painter concluded that one kinesiology student would need at least five trials to observe and rate the arm action in hopping. A single kinesiology student analyst would have to observe 10 trials to reliably rate the whole-body developmental level of hopping.

Physical Therapy Studies

Physical therapy research has supported the moderate reliability of qualitative analysis seen in kinesiology literature. Physical therapy studies have examined the reliability of qualitative analysis of human gait and other clinical measurements. Observational gait assessments have had low to moderate inter-observer reliability, with intra-class correlations between 0.6 and 0.7 (Eastlack et al., 1991; Goodkin and Diller, 1973; Krebs, Edelstein, and Fishman, 1985). The reliability of qualitative assessments of gross motor function in people with cerebral palsy, however, has been good (Gowland et al., 1995). A summary of these studies will shed some light on the issue of the reliability of qualitative analysis of human movement.

Attinger et al. (1987) studied the reliability of visual assessment of gait asymmetry with a jury of eight medical professionals. Reliable identification of the foot on the ground the longest was 80 percent probable and rose to 87 percent probable when the asymmetry was greater than normal. The experts were unable to rate the amount of asymmetry, or reliably identify a limb that was loaded more than the other. Krebs and colleagues (1985) evaluated the inter- and intra-observer reliability of three expert observers with videotapes of 15 disabled children. Intra-rater reliability was moderately reliable. Mean agreement of repeated ratings was 69 percent (31 percent of assessments disagreeing with the same therapist's assessments made a month earlier). For clinicians to be 95 percent sure they had observed a change, there had to be a 10 percent difference in leg kinematics. Mean inter-rater agreement was 67.5 percent, with a mean intra-class correlation of 0.73. A 33 percent difference in walking kinematics would be required to detect differences in walking with different analysts.

In a study of the inter-rater reliability of the qualitative analysis of gait reported by Eastlack et al. (1991), 53 physical therapists rated 10 gait variables (knee kinematics and temporal and spatial variables of the gait cycle) during the four phases of stance from videotapes of patients. Notably, this study was the first to allow the use of slow-motion replay by the observers. The inter-rater reliability of the gait variables was slight to moderate (< 0.69). Joint kinematics had less agreement than temporal or spatial variables. These poor results may be related to the fact that 32 of the 53 physical therapists involved in the study were unfamiliar with any of the four major models for the qualitative analysis of gait in physical therapy.

Other sources of information on the reliability of qualitative analysis in physical therapy include studies of visual estimation of joint range of motion and gross motor performance. Studies of the reliability of visual estimation of joint range of motion have had mixed results. Some studies have documented inter-observer reliability of visual assessment with intra-class correlations above 0.82 (Watkins et al., 1991), whereas others have observed moderate $(0.34 < R < 0.83)$ inter-observer reliability (Youndas et al., 1991, 1993). There is also evidence of poor agreement between visual estimation of ankle range of motion and goniometric measurement (Youndas et al., 1993). Gowland and colleagues (1995) reported good reliability for overall ratings $(R > 0.92)$ and attribute ratings $(R > 0.84)$ of cerebral palsy patients by 19 physical therapists.

Qualitative analyses of physical impairments and disabilities are common in physical therapy. Studies of these clinical assessments have shown results from poor $(K < 0.4)$ to good $(0.7 < K < 0.9)$ reliability depending on the training and nature of the movement being rated (Fife et al., 1991; Hendriks et al., 1997; Keenan and Bach, 1996). The consensus of the physical therapy research on reliability suggests that there is potentially good intra-rater reliability in many situations, while poor inter-rater reliability is likely due to differences in therapists' training or perception of motion.

> **KEY POINT 2.7** Research on qualitative analysis in a variety of disciplines has shown poor to moderate intra-rater reliability and usually poor inter-rater reliability. Careful planning, standardization, and training may improve the reliability of qualitative analysis.

Summary

The physical therapy and kinesiology literature suggests that the reliability of qualitative analysis in actual practice (different analysts, students, number of observations, variable conditions) is likely to be poor to moderate. There are, however, several strategies to increase the potential reliability of qualitative analysis. Specific training and practice using a qualitative analysis model is usually necessary. Increasing the number of observers or the number of trials observed (live trials or videotape replay) tends to increase reliability. Another approach is to increase the specificity of the system/model by analyzing discrete events and providing a simple rating for them (Kerner and Alexander, 1981). Identifying specific critical features and defining rules on how they will be evaluated can help build the potential for agreement in multiple observations of human movement. These strategies are incorporated in the discussion of the four tasks of qualitative analysis in chapters 4 through 7.

Demonstration 2.2

Observe the video clips of the underarm throw and decide if the throwing arm actions are correctly performed. How could you make this evaluation more reliable?

Summary

The research and professional literature on qualitative analysis points to an interdisciplinary and integrated approach to qualitative analysis of human movement. This new vision of qualitative analysis has grown out of contributions from scholars from most kinesiology subdisciplines This larger interdisciplinary vision of qualitative analysis has gained acceptance slowly because institutions change slowly. Several models of qualitative analysis can be used to accurately evaluate human movement, but this ability is not present in all observers and tends to be poorer in fast movements. Qualitative analyses have been shown to have poor to moderate inter-rater reliability with poor inter-rater reliability. Strategies to improve validity and reliability include training, increasing the specificity of the qualitative analysis model, and increasing the number of trials observed.

Discussion Questions

1. What kinesiology subdisciplines have contributed most to the development of qualitative analysis theory? Research? Practice?

2. How might kinesiology foster interdisciplinary cooperation in the development of qualitative analysis research?

3. How should kinesiology programs teach qualitative analysis within the curriculum?

4. What factors are most influential in increasing the potential validity of qualitative analysis?

5. Can *inter-rater reliability* be as good as *intra-rater reliability* in qualitative analysis?

6. What model or approach to qualitative analysis would be most reliable?

7. What model or approach to qualitative analysis would most likely lead to correct decisions about improving movement?

8. What model or approach to qualitative analysis would most likely lead to correct decisions about preventing injury?

Role of Senses and Cognition in Qualitative Analysis

© Charles Westerman/International Stock

A ballet instructor is working hard with her company to finish a piece she has set on them. Movements in this piece must be precise to prevent collisions and to make sure everyone is in time with the music. To make the piece come together, the instructor relies on many of her senses, her perception, and her decision-making ability. She watches to look at dancers' placement as well as their body alignment and limb position. She listens carefully to make sure everyone is in time. Occasionally she participates in the class so that she can gather tactile and kinesthetic information about the progress of the piece. Without information from all of her senses, she would not have a complete picture of what happens in the new dance piece. From her interpretation of what has happened, she then decides how to proceed with the piece.

CHAPTER OBJECTIVES

1. Describe the function of the sense organs associated with qualitative analysis.
2. Discuss some of the limitations of the senses in gathering information for qualitative analysis.
3. Describe the integration process of the senses used in qualitative analysis.
4. Define *perception*.
5. Describe four perceptual tasks as levels of decoding movement information.
6. Explain how qualitative analysis information is processed.
7. List the components of perception and how they relate to qualitative analysis.
8. Summarize the perceptual research on qualitative analysis of movement.
9. How does a gestalt explanation of perception explain the interpretation of visual stimuli?

The ballet instructor presented in this chapter preview is busier than most of us realize. Teaching requires a great deal of activity—and most of it is not visible. This chapter examines only part of this total activity: gathering, integrating, organizing, and giving meaning to sensory information. This teacher must take stimuli from the environment (touch, kinesthetic, auditory, visual) using her sense organs, integrate it, then organize it, and finally assign meaning to the stimuli. Once this information has been processed, it is ready for the evaluation step of qualitative analysis.

This chapter introduces some ideas on how scientists believe the complex processes of perception proceed during the observation of movement. The theories, research, and models presented in this chapter are our best estimate of how information is gathered and processed. Perhaps you can see how the current ideas have evolved and how current ideas will serve to foster future theories, research, and models.

Theoretical Background for Senses and Perception in Qualitative Analysis

To understand how important the senses and perception are in qualitative analysis, let's review what is known about the senses and perception in similar activities, like flying jet fighters. Hartman and Secrist (1991) wrote a seminal article explaining that situational awareness in flying supersonic fighters involves more than exceptional vision and, in fact, requires considerable cognitive activity. Sense of vision is only a starting point for this complex perceptual activity, and many people are unaware of the cognitive element of perception. Pilots must take sensory information, organize it, interpret it, decide on the correct response, and then initiate the response.

Similarly, gathering information by the sense organs is only the beginning of observation within qualitative analysis. We must go through complex cognitive processes in qualitative analysis, just like those fighter pilots do. Fortunately, we have a bit more time to weigh our choices. The complexities of the senses and their contributions to qualitative analysis are staggering, even before we consider the senses' simultaneous interaction. The senses provide the information from which qualitative analysis decisions about human movement are made. The senses and perception are to qualitative analysis of movement what biomechanical instruments are to the quantitative analysis of movement; they gather and organize information about performance.

The cognitive aspects of the senses are also important. Perception of movement is the key to utilizing sensory information. *Perception* is the organization and interpretation of stimuli from our environment, mediated by our senses. Perception involves organizing, or making sense out of, our sensory information (Sage, 1984). This cognitive component of perception is vitally important to what we truly see or hear. For example, if you knew virtually nothing about modern art, would you recognize a masterpiece mistakenly put on sale at a garage sale?

Throughout this chapter this veiled cognitive component of perception will be examined within the context of the qualitative analysis of human movement. Our integrated model has four major tasks that underpin the cognitive processes analysts use in qualitative analysis. A review of what is known about the senses and perception will help us understand the larger challenge of qualitative analysis.

Senses

Although this chapter will examine the four major senses of qualitative analysis—vision, audition, touch (haptic), and kinesthetic proprioception—individually they work in an integrated fashion. This integration of information is part of the first step of perception: organizing sensory information. This organization process takes place in the filters, as explained in the O'Donnell (O'Donnell et al., 1994) model later in this chapter.

This is analogous to the integrated way the senses should work together in the observation task of qualitative analysis (Hay and Reid, 1988; Hoffman, 1983; Radford, 1989). Different senses provide unique information that the observer puts together to improve the observation of performance. The kinesthetic proprioceptive sense an analyst uses while spotting a gymnastics tumbling run may tell more about the forces being exerted by a performer than vision or audition. Audition may be the best sense for gathering temporal information on the timing of the tumbling, while vision is most sensitive to spatial changes in position of the body in flight. All this sensory input must be interpreted and evaluated to gather relevant information for the evaluation and diagnosis task within qualitative analysis. The most dominant sense is typically vision.

Vision

The primary sense used in the qualitative analysis of human movement is vision, so most of the information in this chapter focuses on vision. Until the late 19th century, visual observation was the primary method for studying the biomechanics of movement. This section will review important information about the capabilities and limitations of human visual perception of motion, as well as the three-dimensional expectations we cognitively impose on vision.

There are major limitations to our ability to see fast movements. In fact, the improvements in observational power created by photography and cinematography have dominated the science of biomechanics for the century since their development (Cappozzo, Marchetti, and Tosi, 1992). The initial furor created by the cinematographic photographs of moving animals made by Muybridge and Marey in the late 19th century is a testament to the limited perceptual power of the naked eye. Even today, sports fans feel cheated if they are not shown the slow-motion replay of most of the action.

The sensory receptor concerned with vision is the eye. This receptor takes energy from the visual spectrum of electromagnetic radiation and converts it into nerve transmissions directed to the appropriate parts of the brain.

Functional Components of the Eye

Although the senses are clearly integrated with perception, we can still look at their many functional components separately. The eye has many parts that allow it to gather information from our surroundings. The major functions of the eye are accommodation, static visual acuity, dynamic visual acuity, convergence/divergence, depth perception, eye dominance, tracking, peripheral vision, and fusion. The rest of this section will review how the vision detection system works.

Visibility. The *visibility* of any object or event refers to its detectability by the human eye. This is a complex phenomenon because many levels of detectability are important in qualitative analysis. The lowest level could be just noting or recognizing an event. The latter part of this chapter examines the processes of perception, including detection, in greater depth. At higher levels, the ability to discern information about an event puts greater demands on visual perception. At the lowest level, the two most important factors in visibility are lighting conditions and contrast (McCormick and Sanders, 1982). These two factors will be discussed in the following section on visual accuracy.

Accuracy of Visual Perception. The ability to see details in an object is called *visual acuity*. This ability is strongly related to the adjustment of the eye's lens (accommodation) and the shape of the eye. There are many measures of visual acuity; the most common is minimum separable acuity. A good example of this is the common Snellen eye chart, in which the smallest features discernible (usually letters) are evaluated. This is the most common measure of static visual acuity (SVA). Besides an individual's innate SVA, many factors affect visual discrimination, among them contrast, lighting, motion, time, color, and age. Although most qualitative analysis is concerned with dynamic visual acuity (DVA), SVA is important because many movements have phases with minimal or no movement. Valenti and Costall (1997) indicate there is a great deal of information to be gleaned from situations of limited movement. Their research indicates that the amount of force needed to overcome a resistance can be gleaned from static postures, facial expressions, and/or other body details.

KEY POINT 3.1 Good vision for qualitative analysis is a complex phenomenon. Focal vision and static visual acuity allow the recognition of objects and details. Ambient vision, dynamic visual acuity, perception of color, contrast, accurate eye movements, eye dominance, and peripheral vision all are important in following moving objects.

Contrast is the percentage difference in illumination of the features of an object being viewed. The contrast between the black letters and the white paper of the Snellen eye test (or this book) is very high. The contrast between a dark uniform and a poorly lit athletic field is considerably worse. If the contrast between an object and the background is low, the object must be larger to be as detectable as a smaller object with greater contrast. Professionals selecting colors for uniforms or clothing should think about the potential contrast among the colors selected, the environment, and the equipment.

The amount of light, or illuminance, is an important factor that interacts with contrast to determine the visibility of an object or event. There is extensive research on the effects of lighting on human performance in many tasks. In general, the more illumination, the better the performance (McCormick and Sanders, 1982). There can be too much illumination, however; glare or brightness reflected from the object and background make it difficult to see the object. It is also important to remember that the eye's sensitivity to light changes with illuminance. The transition of sensitivity from darkness to light is relatively quick (less than a minute), while adjustment from light to darkness can take 30 minutes or more (McCormick and Sanders, 1982). Current research in visual discrimination in varying lighting conditions is based on contrast sensitivity function (Kluka, 1991).

Another factor influencing visual discrimination is the perception of color. Recall that the retina has two types of light-sensitive receptors: rods and cones. A human eye has about 130 million rods that are primarily sensitive to light intensity and about 7 million cones that are primarily sensitive to the wavelength of light and are responsible for our perception of color (McCormick and Sanders, 1982). Some people have difficulty discriminating between red and green or between blue and yellow. True color blindness is rare, but color deficiency is usually found in 8 to 10 percent of males and less than 1 percent of females (Gavriysky, 1969). Although these are not large percentages of the population, it would be wise to plan sporting events with contrasting colors that are not combinations of red/green or blue/yellow.

The time available to focus on an object also strongly affects SVA. The greater the viewing time, the better the chance of making visual discriminations. If either the object or the observer is in motion, that reduces the time the eyes will be able to focus on the object. This brings us to DVA, which is the visual discrimination of an object when there is relative movement between the object and the observer. A person's DVA deteriorates rapidly as the eye's angular velocity exceeds 60 or 70 degrees per second (Bahill and LaRitz, 1984; Burg, 1966). Above these speeds the eyes cannot smoothly rotate to keep the object on the fovea. Clearly, then, the faster the movement, the less time the object will be in our visual field, and the less able we will be to see and judge the motion of that object.

Our DVA increases from ages 6 to 20 and then tends to decrease (Burg, 1966; Ishigaki and Miyao, 1994; Morris, 1977). This is why it is developmentally appropriate that baseball/softball leagues for small children use a batting tee rather than machine-pitched balls. As children's visual and hitting skills improve, coaches can incorporate pitched balls and more realistic batting tee drills. For example, older players practicing with a batting tee can focus their eyes forward, quickly saccade their eyes to the ball, and then hit the ball.

Unfortunately, good SVA does not guarantee that a person will have good DVA. Studies have found weak correlations ($R < 0.6$) between SVA and DVA at slow speeds (Burg, 1966; Kluka, 1994) and no correlation at faster speeds (Morris, 1977). The weak association between SVA and DVA is not surprising, since SVA is the ability to observe detail in ideal conditions (static, two dimensions, good lighting, and contrast), while DVA is observational ability in less than ideal conditions (motion, three dimensions, and poor contrast).

Research suggests that DVA can improve with training (Long and Rourke, 1989) and there are large differences between individuals (Morris, 1977). Some people are velocity resistant and are not strongly affected by the relative motion of an object. Others are velocity susceptible: their visual perception is easily disturbed by relative motion of the object (Morris, 1977). Clearly, relative motion and DVA influence the qualitative analysis ability of a teacher or coach. Research on ball catching has also shown that the temporal constraints of the environment affect how the eyes track the object's motion (Montagne, Laurent, and Ripoll, 1993).

QA Demonstration 3.1

Observe the accompanying video clips at normal speed. Can you see where the ball lands in relation to the line? Is this ball in or out if balls striking the boundary line are out? If you use the freeze-frame and slow-motion features, is this discrimination easier?

There are many examples in sport where the relative motion of people or objects past the observer is so great that it cannot be observed reliably. Officiating in sports like basketball and American football has been controversial for many years. The National Football League has experimented with instant replays to make final judgments on difficult calls. In tennis the controversy over calling balls in or out (Vincent, 1984) led to the development of photoelectric sensors to help call the service line in professional matches. Braden (1983) studied the accuracy of judging where tennis balls landed from various court positions. He found that the players were less reliable (11 percent error rate with a mean error of 5 inches) than the linespeople or umpires who usually have a better angle to view shots near boundary lines.

Another problem related to time and DVA is sporting events of very short duration. Examples are collisions or release events in high-speed sports. In most striking sports (for example, baseball and tennis), coaches use cues to have the players watch the ball till it hits the bat or racket. Because ball/bat collisions in baseball and softball last only one or two milliseconds, it is highly unlikely that any athlete can see the ball hit the bat. Seeing the ball hit the bat may be unimportant, in light of our earlier discussion of ambient and focal vision. Focal vision would yield information about the bat/ball contact, whereas ambient vision would guide the bat to the ball. Guiding the bat to the ball for contact is more important than actually seeing the contact, so coaches should cue hitters to focus their attention on the early trajectory of the pitch, not watching the ball hit the bat. Watts and Bahill (1990) reviewed their studies of vision in baseball and concluded that batters cannot track the ball to the point of impact, even in slow-pitch softball! Ball speeds in most sports exceed the eyes' ability to track the trajectory smoothly (Ripoll and Fleurance, 1988). In the following section on eye movements, we will see how the eyes deal with tracking very fast objects.

Events occurring faster than about 1/4 of a second usually cannot be seen (Eastman Kodak Company, 1979). If humans had very fast vision, there would be no illusion of motion when we watch movies, which are really the flashing of 24 distinct pictures per second. There is a clear time limitation in our eyes' ability to perceive information from moving objects in our field of view. Knowledge of this limitation is critical to planning for qualitative analysis and what specific performance information is reliably observable. A complete description of eye motions to track moving objects is presented in the following section on important eye movements. After reading this section, you will know why officials sometimes appear to be looking right at a key play and still miss the call.

Important Eye Movements. The eyes use many kinds of movements to view moving objects. These movements are coordinated to keep both eyes working together. Kluka (1991) classifies eye movement into four types: saccadic, vestibulo-ocular, vergence, and smooth pursuit. Saccadic eye movements are for scanning rapidly and jumping to various points in the visual field. Vestibulo-ocular movements are coordinated with head motion to keep the eyes on some object. Vergence eye movements allow the eyes to focus on objects at different distances, while smooth pursuit eye movements are used to follow slow-moving objects.

The eye movements that make it possible to view objects up close and at a distance are convergence and divergence, respectively. Accommodation and convergence relate to the eyes' ability to focus quickly, smoothly, and accurately as objects approach or recede. This ability is especially important in sports because objects and individuals are always changing their relationships to us. It is equally important in qualitative analysis. These functions are achieved by changes in the tension of the muscles of the lens and the muscles that move the eyes.

To observe this aspect of vision, hold a pencil at arm's length and slowly move it toward your nose. As the pencil gets closer, your eyes move from an almost straight-ahead position in the sockets to a position where they seem to be touching the nose. You are now cross-eyed. Your eyes have converged. At the same time, the lens has changed shape to keep the pencil in focus. The same process takes place as we analyze skills that involve movement that is close to us.

Depth perception is the ability to judge how far away objects are from you or the relative distances objects are away from you and each other. At a distance we generally judge depth by comparing: object size, detail, texture gradient, closer objects, and linear perspective. Look out the window or in the distance and see how many of these factors you can detect. As objects get closer, this perception is mainly a function of eye position as sensed by kinesthetic proprioceptors in the eye muscles as the eyes move closer to the nose or farther outward to the side of the head.

When something has our visual attention, we carefully focus both eyes on the object; this is fixation. We use a very narrow field (about 3 degrees) to fixate our visual focus on the fovea of the retina. To get a feel for how small this area of visual focus is, extend your arm forward. Hold it straight out with your thumb extended vertically. The width of your thumb in this position (the thumb rule) is a good approximation of the focus of your visual field (Groot, Ortega, and Beltran, 1994).

Because information from one eye reaches the brain faster and is processed more quickly, that eye becomes dominant (Kluka, 1991). The dominant eye guides the other eye in the direction of movement and fixations. The use of the dominant eye in sports that require accuracy has been studied for many years. The combination of eye and hand dominance has been a topic of several studies of hockey, batting, and golf putting (Morrison, 1976; Steinberg, Frehlich, and Tennant, 1995; Tieg, 1983). It is easy to establish which eye is the dominant eye. Extend your arms forward, making a small (1 square inch) hole between your hands (figure 3.1). Pick a distant object (such as your partner's right eye) and center it in the hole formed by your hands. Without moving, close one eye at a time. The eye that still has the object lined up in the hole is your dominant eye.

The use of the eyes to track moving objects is a highly complex phenomenon. Eyes move to gather information for processing. This movement takes one of two forms: smooth pursuit or saccade. In the smooth pursuit, the eyes are able to rotate together to keep the eyes on the object they are tracking. In a saccade, the eyes jump from position to position to gather information from the object they are trying to track. The different forms of tracking affect the gathering of perceptual information. These tracking differences can limit potential perceptual information that can be gathered.

• *Smooth pursuit.* When there is slow relative movement between an observer and an object, the eyes can smoothly move together following the object until eye angular velocity reaches between 40 and 70 degrees per

FIGURE 3.1 Simple test to establish eye dominance.
Reprinted from Haywood and Lewis 1989: 38.

second (Bahill and LaRitz, 1984; Ripoll and Fleurance, 1988; Robinson, 1981). People can become skilled at visually tracking objects and predicting their landing or bounce location. With training, angular velocities can reach 100 degrees per second (Buizza and Schmid, 1986; Meyer, Lasker, and Robinson, 1985). A good way to illustrate the accuracy of visual tracking in estimating ball impact or intercept is to toss a tennis ball softly to a person 2 or 3 feet away. Have her catch the ball with one hand. After a couple of trials, ask her to close her eyes when you say "close" early or in the middle of the ball trajectory. Most people will be able to catch the ball with their eyes closed. Unfortunately, many sports or other movements require eye movements beyond our ability for smooth pursuit. In volleyball, for example, eye angular velocities of more than 500 degrees per second are needed to track the trajectory of a spiked ball (Kluka, 1991).

• *Saccade.*   Sports like tennis, badminton, basketball, and baseball generate ball speeds that require another kind of eye movement to track the ball. The quick motion of both eyes from one fixation to another is a saccade. While the eyes are rotating to the next fixation, they are essentially turned off to prevent a blur of light and images as they move. This down time has been called saccadic *suppression* or *omission* (Campbell and Wurtz, 1978). Much of the current research uses the term *change blindness* to describe this phenomenon (Noe, Pesoa, and Thompson, 2000; Simons and Levin, 1997). This term is used because no information is gathered during the saccade.

This research also points out that very little information is stored in short-term memory during saccades (Karn and Hayhoe, 2000; Noe, Pesoa, and Thompson, 2000; Simons and Levin, 1997, 1998). This means that visual information gathered between saccades is the only reference we have for mapping the succeeding saccade. It was formerly believed that a rich short-term memory operated during the saccade, acting as a visual map to the next item of interest in the visual field. In a saccade the eyes can reposition at angular velocities exceeding 700 degrees per second (Carpenter, 1988). Speeds of this magnitude probably negate the need for memory maps of the environment.

Recent research on saccadic eye movements in normal subjects has shown that there is no significant difference between men and women, but saccadic eye movement parameters decrease significantly with age (Wilson, Glue, Ball, and Nutt, 1993). Sports studies have shown anticipatory patterns of saccades relative to the kind of motion of the object that is being tracked (Bahill and LaRitz, 1984; Haywood, 1984; Hubbard and Seng, 1954; Ripoll and Fleurance, 1988). Interestingly, being a skilled athlete in a fast ball game may involve learning to suppress saccades to irrelevant visual stimuli (Lenoir et al., 2000). To observe saccadic eye movement, simply watch someone's eyes in a park or mall. The person's eyes will dart around between the wide variety of visual targets.

• *Limitations of eye movements.*   The limitations of eye motions in the tracking of moving objects, visual suppression during a saccade, and fixations all have implications for sports and qualitative analysis. The analyst must realize that some high-speed events simply cannot be observed. If a key event occurs when the analyst's eyes are in a saccade, it will not be seen. If an observational strategy is not followed, the analyst's eyes may be drawn to and fixated on an extraneous action, causing the analyst to miss an important error in performance. The selection of a viewing distance for observation in qualitative analysis has a major impact on the eye angular velocities required in tracking a performer.

If vision is part of an intervention strategy, it is important not to ask performers to do things their eyes cannot do. The cues "keep your eyes on the ball" and "watch the ball hit your bat/racket" clearly are impossible (Watts and Bahill, 1990) and may be miscues (Kluka, 1991). If a gestalt approach to qualitative analysis is used, it can be a way of limiting this type of visual error. A gestalt observation strategy initially looks at overall performance. A gestalt approach to qualitative analysis and a gestalt observational model will be presented later in the text. *Sports Illustrated* and other sport magazines are filled with photos of baseball hitters or tennis players who usually have their eyes correctly focused forward of ball impact. Coaches making qualitative analyses of officiating should now understand how such terrible (or fortunate, depending on your team) calls are made in sporting events. If it is important to gather visual information about a fast-moving skill or part of a skill, observers should increase their distance so that eye movement velocities are slower.

QA Choices

You are golfing with two friends. After watching your drive, they disagree on the quality of your swing. One of your friends is standing behind you, while the other is facing you square to your shoulders. One friend indicates that you lifted your head during the swing. The other believes you swung inside out. You want to accept feedback from one or both of these individuals. Using the information about vision, can you explain why they might disagree on what they have seen? If you perform the movement again, is there a chance they will see the same thing? Would slowing down your swing on the driving range be effective in reducing disagreement or creating the same technique?

Peripheral Vision.   Peripheral vision is the ability to gather information from the environment other than the point of visual focus. This is a function primarily of the rods in the eyes, as they are situated in areas not central to where light is focused. This ability is particularly sensitive to slight movement and is processed faster than vision requiring color.

Peripheral vision directs our attention to movement in the environment around us so that we can process this information. It also sets the stage and orientation of events so that they can be mapped or matched to general backgrounds (Alfano and Michel, 1990). Restriction of peripheral vision, especially in qualitative analysis, can lead to fewer meaningful reference points and poorer analysis. Peripheral vision only contributes to ambient vision and not to focal vision.

Fusion.   Although the eye has often been compared to a camera, research on visual perception led Johannson (1975) to conclude that the eyes act more like motion-detection systems than still cameras. The eyes do not, in a sense, capture photos; rather, they constantly evaluate a changing flux of light focused on the retina to generate a three-dimensional (3-D) image of the visual field. In normal vision, both eyes send information to the brain, where it is blended and interpreted as a 3-D phenomenon. This blending of each eye's essentially 2-D visual information into a 3-D whole is fusion.

Kluka (1987) presented a simple way to demonstrate this phenomenon. Tape two pieces of paper (8½" x 11"), one white and one red, in a corner at eye level. The white paper is placed in front of you while the red is on the wall next to your left shoulder. Place a pocket mirror in front of your left eye, touching your nose, so that you can see the red piece of paper in the mirror. Look at the white piece of paper with your right eye. If you are the same distance away from both pieces of paper, you should see a single piece of pink paper instead of one white and one red. Another way to illustrate fusion is to hold your thumb vertically at arm's length and aligned with another object in the distance. By focusing your eyes on the thumb (seeing two distant objects) or the distant object (seeing two thumbs) you can see how information from two eyes is blended to create a 3-D representation. Remember that perception requires cognitive processing, so we are not just passive receivers of visual information.

Selective Nature of Visual Attention

Our senses have variable levels of sensitivity, and vision may be the most variable and selective of all the senses. Without a conscious effort to attend to one object, the eyes will dart about the visual field, moving to unusual or quickly moving objects. In short, normal vision will pay attention to any number of things in a person's view. The perception discussion in this chapter gives some examples of how the eyes search the visual field in order to make sense of visual stimuli.

The implications of this fact for qualitative analysis are interesting and varied. One perspective is to consider this selectivity a barrier to systematic observation and therefore plan a specific observational strategy to compensate. The other perspective is to use this sensitivity to locate and focus on unusual features of a movement. A problem with the second approach is that we are not always conscious of what our eyes are focused on. We may not be sure if we waste observational time looking at unimportant aspects of performance or focus on important aspects by ignoring the unimportant ones.

Demonstration 3.2

Observe the basketball shooting video clip. Watch the flight of the ball and indicate what happened. While watching the ball, can you also gather information about the foot or hand position? How much information can you gather if you are tracking the flight of a projectile? Can you judge the qualities of the shooter's movement if you are focusing on object motion?

Focal and Ambient Visual Perception

To illustrate how closely tied the senses and perception are, we can use the example of two encompassing visual systems: ambient and focal. By examining these two systems, we can see that the senses are inseparable from perception. Although senses and perception will be discussed as separate entities in this chapter, they are, in fact, intrinsically linked in their function.

There appear to be two visual perceptual systems working to provide information for decisions in movement and movement analysis: focal and ambient (Schmidt and Wrisberg, 2000). Their function seems to explain many of the reasons why SVA and DVA are not strongly related, why batters cannot keep their eyes on the ball, and especially why biological motion is seen differently than object motion (Shiffrar, 1994). Further work on these two systems may change the way we talk about vision, especially as it relates to biological motion.

KEY POINT 3.2 Ambient and focal vision are important to us in everyday life, but they are extremely important in the analysis of movement. Realizing how ambient and focal vision work and what information they give us can enhance our visual data-gathering processes.

Focal vision tells us *what* an object is and uses a small portion of the retina, whereas ambient vision tell us *where* an object is and about its motion, or about its motion relative to the observer. Ambient vision uses information from the whole retina (focal and peripheral). Focal vision just uses information from the most accurate point on the retina, the fovea. The fovea is a small point that is limited to about 3 degrees of the visual field (Kluka, 1991). As you read this book you move the fovea across the words. Focus your eyes on a word in the text and notice you cannot see words to either edge of the paper. Focal vision may have its greatest value when a particular detail of a movement must be seen, as opposed to determining relationships of body parts in a movement sequence.

Schmidt and Wrisberg (2000) have summarized the types of information provided by the optical flow (movement of objects across the retina) in ambient vision. The types of information provided by ambient vision useful for qualitative analysis are as follows:

- Velocities of the movement through the environment
- Direction of the movement relative to the position of fixed objects in the environment
- Movement of environmental objects relative to the observer
- Time until contact between the observer and an object in the environment (Schmidt and Wrisberg, 2000: 112)

Biases in Visual Perception

There are several biases in visual perception that may be hardwired into the 3-D perceptual set of vision. Many of these phenomena are related to the geometry of the situation. The farther an object is from the viewer, the smaller it appears and the smaller the displacement past the observer, compared to a similar object moving at the same speed close to the observer. For example, on a late-night walk, nearby objects move past at the speed of your gait while distant objects appear to move past slowly. This is why people tend to overestimate the speed of objects close to them and underestimate the speed of objects at greater distances (Johansson, 1975).

The large horizontal perspective of our visual field also leads to a tendency to overestimate the lengths of vertical lines compared to horizontal lines (Prinzmetal and Gettleman, 1993). A novice coach, for example, might more readily perceive that the up-and-down motion of a runner is exaggerated before perceiving overstriding. Other biases are a tendency to underestimate object size with an inward shift of accommodation (Meehan and Day, 1995) and a tendency for dimmer objects to appear farther away (Kluka, 1991).

Many readers are familiar with some of the many images that can be interpreted as two different things (for example, two faces or a vase). You can see only one interpretation of the image at a time. An example of the 3-D bias of vision is illustrated in figure 3.2. What two things does it show? The image is literally two lines that touch at a point. The objects are typically interpreted as parallel lines (a road stretching to the horizon). Figure 5.1 (page 97) illustrates our 3-D bias.

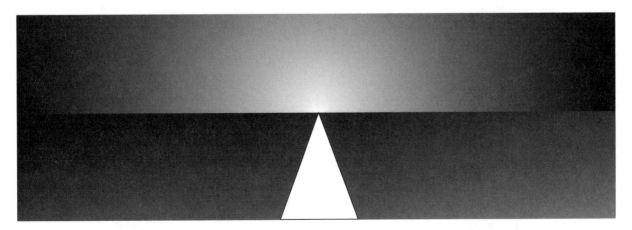

FIGURE 3.2   What objects do you see in this image? Do the lines intersect or are they parallel? Even simple drawings tend to be interpreted as 3-D objects.
Reprinted from Knudson and Morrison 1997: 40.

QA Choices

You are a cross-country skate-skiing instructor qualitatively analyzing skate skiing in an activity class. Your students want to have fun, but you also have them focused on improving. What sensory information should you attend to the most? Are there specific senses that are most appropriate for the critical features of skiing?

Assume you are skiing behind a skier who needs a push-off correction. As you begin observing again, what senses are most relevant? A good approach would be to give feedback on the important sounds from the skis and then give verbal cues/prompts on when to signal the next weight shift or pole plant. Your auditory senses monitor the force and duration of the push-off, while your sense of vision provides information on balance during the next glide. You need to pay attention to these senses and integrate the sensory information to provide good qualitative analysis in this situation.

Sports Vision

As the interest in vision in sports has grown, several articles have been written on visual skills in sports (Abernethy and Neal, 1999; Blundell, 1985; Fisk, 1993; Knudson and Kluka, 1997; McNaughton, 1986; Regan, 1997; Sherman, 1980). Research has also been conducted on commercial programs for training DVA, such as "eyerobics" (Cohn and Chaplik, 1991; Long, 1994; MacLeod, 1991) and "dynavison" (Klavora, Gaskovski, and Forsyth, 1994, 1995). The International Academy of Sports Vision, established in 1984, is an organization that encompasses many professions interested in vision in sport. It sponsors professional meetings, *Sportsvision* magazine, and the *International Journal of Sports Vision*. Another organization interested in vision in sport is the Sports Vision Section of the American Optometric Association. Kluka (1991) summarized the research, noting that there are 14 important visual skills relevant to learning motor skills and other factors affecting visual perception.

Coaches need to observe how performers use their eyes in many sport skills. Knowledge of how the eyes work and their limitations is important for analysts so that they know what is observable and what feedback on the use of the eyes is helpful. For example, the miscue of "keep your eye on the ball" may not interfere with performance in some sports, but the cue "watch the ball hit your bat" could adversely affect performance by encouraging head motion and less visual attention earlier in the trajectory of the ball. The trajectory of the ball is ascertained by ambient vision. Accurate placement of the bat is concerned with where the ball will be, not the state of contact between the bat and ball. Where the bat moves is a function of ambient vision, while the state of contact of the bat and ball will rarely be identifiable with focal vision. Cues on ball tracking should emphasize focused attention, minimal or smooth head motion, and characteristics of the ball (seams, spin, and so on). The adage to coach "from the eyes down" may be very important in some skills. It is also important that any intervention regarding vision be accurate and effective, not just a cliché.

Audition

KEY POINT 3.3 The information gathered by our ears (frequency and amplitude of sound) is vitally important to the qualitative analysis of rhythmic movements (dance, hurdles, and so on). Auditory information from discrete events is also important. The sound of impact in baseball and the sound of a gymnast landing are important sources of information about performance.

The interaction of the ears and the brain allow us to perceive sound. From what we hear, we can make sense of the frequency of sound waves (interpreted as pitch) and the amplitude of sound waves (interpreted as loudness). The small muscles in the ear attached to the eardrum and ossicles can contract or relax to modify the sound. This is analogous to the way the muscles of the eye work with the lens to focus light in vision. This ability is demonstrated in the case of loud noises such as a jet aircraft departing. The eardrum muscles tighten to reduce vibration and sound transmission.

We can also best determine the tempo of activity from the input gathered by our ears. This information comes from alterations in frequency and pitch. Dance provides many examples of combining these elements of sound as factors for qualitative analysis. The desirable timing of actions in a dance can be counted aloud (1, 2, 3, . . .). The loudness of each number can vary to show the emphasis placed on the action occurring at that time. This emphasis in sound connects to the cognitive aspect of the activity facilitating the whole movement.

Touch

The haptic senses of touch (Meisner's and Ruffini's corpuscles, Merkel's disks) and pressure receptors (Pacinian corpuscles) send information to the brain when they are stimulated. These receptors are found in the skin and attached to hair follicles. Either the gentle pressure (touch) on the skin or the movement of the hair in the follicles triggers these receptors. When these stimuli breach the threshold of the nerve, signals are transmitted to the brain indicating direct contact with or close proximity to an object.

> **KEY POINT 3.4** The tactile system (sense of touch) can provide a great deal of information about performance to the analyst and the athlete. This information is gathered primarily by pressure and touch receptors.

The pressure receptors (Pacinian corpuscles) have a higher threshold than touch receptors. They react when touch becomes pressure. Then information about the stimulus is sent directly to the brain. This pressure can help us determine whether or not a person can perform the movement independently or still needs spotting.

Kinesthetic Proprioception

The kinesthetic proprioceptors work to tell us about movement in our limbs and body. They do this by sending information to the brain from the stretch receptors in the muscles, the Golgi tendon organs (GTO) in the tendons, and the senses in the joints. The stretch receptors tell the brain about speed of contraction and muscle length. The muscle spindle works by stimulating the nerve wrapped around it. It is highly sensitive to the slightest change in length. Information is sent to the brain by type Ia afferent nerve endings. The flower spray endings associated with the spindle are less sensitive and harder to trigger. This information is sent to the brain by type II afferent fibers. The contrast between the signals of these two sensory receptors gives us information about the speed of movement.

> **KEY POINT 3.5** Kinesthetic feedback is another source of information about performance. It is gathered by GTO, muscle spindles, and other joint receptors. An analyst might ask an athlete to tell her how much knee flexion he used in the last trial and to focus on that sense in practice.

The GTO tells us primarily about the load on a muscle. It does this via the tendon's stimulation of the nerve endings. Joint receptors give general information to the brain that movement has taken place. The combination of this information allows us to understand the relationships between body parts and muscle tension.

Using Senses to Understand Movement

We all know that eyes allow us to see and ears permit us to hear, and that we can sense movement and recognize touch. However, our senses provide more than general information via vision, audition, kinesthesia, and touch. Each sense can elicit qualities from the energy forms it interprets to provide highly specific information about what is occurring in our environment. The integration and interpretation of this information allow us to make decisions about how to proceed in qualitative analysis.

As you may recall, we defined *perception* as the organization and interpretation of stimuli from the environment, mediated by our senses. Each of our senses provides us with a great deal of specific information from our environment, and this information becomes the basis for decisions. The following section gives examples of how the parts of the sensory system work together. By this we mean how vision interacts with touch and sound, and maybe even with kinesthesia.

Perception of Sensory Information

Part of the work of these four major sensory receptor groups is done by either electrical, chemical, or mechanical energy. The other part of their work involves perception. For example, think of tracking the flight of a kicked ball. Electrical energy is used in nerve transmission, chemical energy for color vision, and mechanical energy for transmitting sound waves through the eardrum to the bones in the middle ear. The perceptual component is easily demonstrated by the adjustments of the eye and head movement to the direction of the energy received by the senses.

For an example of how all the senses might be used to understand movement and provide feedback to an athlete, consider a coach spotting an athlete vaulting in gymnastics. The athlete runs the approach, hurdles onto a board, places her hands on the horse, and flies to a landing. In this skill the coach can use all of his senses to gain information about the performance to provide feedback.

Sound contributes to feedback decisions. The tempo, loudness, and pitch of the run-up approach, hurdle, hand placement on the horse, and foot landing on the mat all provide useful data. The tempo of the run-up, the different pitch from hitting the vaulting board, horse, or mat correctly or incorrectly, and the loudness of any of these parts tell the coach something about the quality of the skill.

While the athlete is moving, the coach's visual system can track her and provide information about body position, body placement in relation to the apparatus, and the relationship of body parts to one another. Interestingly, the linear and angular velocities may be so great when the athlete is on the board and horse that the coach cannot get any usable visual information. The situation forces him to make decisions about performance based on data from the other sensory systems.

The coach will then have to rely on the systems of sound, touch, and kinesthesia to judge performance quality. During flight or landing, he will likely touch the athlete and may even push to help her in rotation or flight. At this point, touch and pressure information will be added to the input being processed by the coach. Proprioceptive kinesthetic information will flow to the central nervous system as the coach moves his body parts to support the gymnast. Clearly there is an incredible flow of data bombarding the brain. All of this information must be organized, given meaning, and then combined into a total picture to describe what has occurred.

To say the least, the perceptual process is an incredibly large and efficient system. It is even more amazing to think that we use all of these systems to gain information about a particular movement. Even if we use only two or three of these systems, we can imagine what the other systems would feel, look, or sound like. If the coach in our gymnastics example moved away from the horse, he could still imagine what a good vault would feel like, kinesthetically and haptically, as opposed to a bad vault.

Integration of Senses

As you can see, the perceptual system is continually bombarded by sensory input. How do we pay attention to what is important? How do we use all the information available from the senses to make decisions? The complex process of intersensory integration is the perception of an event, as measured in terms of one sensory modality, being changed in some way by the concurrent stimulation of one or more other sensory modalities (Welch and Warren, 1980). In other words, our perception of an event through one sense is affected by our perception of the same event through other senses.

Martino and Marks (1999) point out that senses are better categorized as interrelated than separate. They indicate that senses seldom work alone and perception is suited to working with combined input. They hypothesize that there are two levels of processing when integrating information from the senses: linguistic or prelinguistic. At the prelinguistic level, perceptual information commingles before it is coded semantically. This occurs for visual and auditory stimuli. In the other level of processing, linguistically instead of semantically, input is combined from different senses semantically before it is processed for information. As you might guess, prelinguistic processing is faster than semantic processing (Martino and Marks, 1999).

It is even likely, as when spotting in gymnastics, that we use our haptic and kinesthetic proprioceptive senses as well as vision and audition. The sound of the block on the horse could be compared to the visual or proprioceptive information the coach has just observed. The approach and block sounded vigorous, but there still was not enough rotation. What sense might a gymnastics coach put the most confidence in when sensory information conflicts?

How does the brain deal with the input from competing senses, and how does this flow of information from the different senses interact? The types of information the brain deals with fall into three general categories: detection of an event, spatial stimuli, and temporal stimuli. The cognitive handling of inputs from these three sources can be explained by the information processing issues that will be discussed in the next few sections. In a trained observer, there appears to be an ability to prepare for and attend to potentially important stimuli. This is the theoretical approach used in expert-novice research.

> **KEY POINT 3.6** With a great deal of practice, the brain can automatically integrate sensory information and prioritize it based on its importance to the qualitative analysis being performed. A skilled coach might hear an unusual rhythm in an athlete's performance and then visually observe the movement in qualitative analysis. A diving coach concentrating on observing the dive might use the sound of the diver hitting the water to aid her visual interpretation of the athlete's entry.

Sensory Detection of an Event

Relatively strong auditory and tactile stimuli take about 110 to 120 milliseconds to detect. Visual stimuli take slightly longer, about 150 milliseconds (Riggs, 1971). It appears that with intense training, however, people (like fighter pilots) can speed up their visual detection and integration of stimuli to 33 milliseconds (Secrist and Hartman, 1993). Note that reaction time is inversely related to stimulus intensity. That is, the more prominent the stimulus, the faster the response. It might take concentrated effort for a coach to use auditory observation in a competitive environment with crowd noise.

Stimuli in the analyst's environment rarely act in isolation. The effect of other accessory stimuli (stimuli that we are not attending to selectively) on a primary stimulus (the sense we are using selectively) is one of either inhibition or facilitation. If the accessory stimulus is low to moderate in intensity, it generally facilitates perception of the primary stimulus. If the accessory stimulus has a high intensity, it may have an inhibiting effect (Shigehisa, Shigehisa, and Symons, 1973; Shigehisa and Symons, 1973). For this effect to be optimized, these stimuli must occur close together.

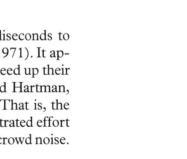

Demonstration 3.3

Observe the dancer and the runner in the video clips. What did you notice? Why? How did your mind try to reconcile (logically fix or explain) the situation?

These effects may be due to physiological reasons or selective attention (Welch and Warren, 1980). The physiological effects that seem to enhance detection relate to muscle tonus of sensory organs (the muscles of the ossicles in the ear or muscles of the pupil in the eye). Selective attention may cause someone to pay more attention to a particular movement because of a secondary stimulus. Studies that have examined the effects of touch and hearing on vision support the idea of synesthesia for these senses (Marks, 1987; Martino and Marks, 1999). This synesthesia appears to broaden and enhance selective attention. Rather than just attend to one stimulus, the observer is able to attend to and use information from both senses.

Spatial Stimuli

For spatial stimuli the order of dominance changes. The visual sense predominates, followed by audition, proprioception, and then touch (Welch and Warren, 1980). Another major difference between vision and audition is that audition is accurate only in the horizontal plane, while vision is accurate in all planes. Sound received from the horizontal (left, right) is perceived more accurately than sound from above or below. It is interesting to note how closely auditory and visual perception interact in processing spatial information. Visual perception appears to provide a framework for auditory information (Platt and Warren, 1972; Warren, 1970). It seems that our visual memory provides a basic map to which auditory information can be applied.

Kinesthetic proprioception of hand movements can detect spatial differences of about plus or minus 1.25 centimeters (Magill and Parks, 1983), which suggests that we can gain accurate information concerning movement from our kinesthetic receptors. We can sense the slightest movement of a body part of someone we are spotting. That is, we can sense an arm or leg movement of less than 1 inch.

QA Choices

You have to prepare to analyze a beginning swimmer doing the breaststroke. Supporting this learner in the water will provide you tactile, kinesthetic, and visual stimuli about the quality of the movement. Which stimuli will be available for processing first? Can you enhance your sensory detection of events in this analysis? Can accessory stimuli degrade sensory information and how can you allow it to enhance analysis? Which sense would you rely on most for analysis in the time after the event has occurred?

Temporal Information

When short-duration stimuli are processed, it seems that audition is most accurate, followed by touch and then vision (Welch and Warren, 1980). Auditory stimuli also appear to last longer than other stimuli (Behar and Bevan, 1961), so we can analyze auditory information for a longer time than other information. The temporal accuracy of kinesthetic proprioception relative to other senses is not clear. Thus, a qualitative analyst might want to have a visual focus for the take-off of the long jump, using the sound of the approach and take-off as supplementary information.

Knowledge and Perception

Along with the senses and skill knowledge, perception forms the basis of qualitative analysis. Knowledge of the components of a movement and their sequence is useless unless the analyst can resolve meaning from the performance being analyzed. Essentially, information processing organizes and gives meaning to information from the sensory receptors. Remember that this is essentially the definition of perception (Sage, 1984).

The process of perception appears to have two major parts. The first is the organization of sensory information, which involves sending information from the sensory receptors to the appropriate areas of the brain. The second deals with interpreting this information and assigning meaning to it. Once this meaning has been established, the qualitative analysis tasks of evaluation and diagnosis can follow.

> **KEY POINT 3.7** Perception has two major components: organizing sensory information and assigning meaning to that information.

Perceptual Tasks

"The simple perception of natural forms is a delight." Emerson

This quote by Emerson is true, in that perceiving natural phenomena (for example, animals, plants, rivers, and human motion) can be delightful. It may be wrong, however, to assume perception is simple. In fact, perception is a highly complex process we are only beginning to understand. Perception has been studied primarily from the point of view of the types of tasks used in perception. These tasks or experimental conditions allow us to understand what is required of the cognitive processes that attempt to decode environmental stimuli. According to Proctor and Dutta (1995), these tasks (in order of increasing cognitive requirements) are detection, discrimination, recognition, and identification. People involved with movement analysis will readily associate with the different tasks described here. Although the term *detection* was discussed in relation to vision, it is now used to illustrate a level of information processing based on the amount of information available for a decision.

In detection tasks a person need only indicate when a stimulus has occurred. A typical subject might be asked to indicate if a light flashed or if there was a sound. Usually studies dealing with detection attempt to ascertain the lowest threshold at which a stimulus can be detected. These studies are often conducted to see if the person's detection ability can be adapted to stimuli that are below the initial thresholds. With training, this effect is often achieved.

In sport an example of this type of task might be this question: Did the offensive lineman move his hand? To a game official, detection of this event would lead to a penalty if it occurred before the snap of the ball. Similarly, a teacher's or coach's perception might work at the level of detection in skill analysis. For example, a teacher might decide whether or not a child's elbow preceded the forearm in an overhand throw. Either it did or it did not. Could the elbow/forearm relationship be detected?

> **KEY POINT 3.8** Perceptual tasks have four levels: detection, discrimination, recognition, and identification. All four levels of perception are used in qualitative analysis.

Discrimination tasks generally require a subject to attend to various stimuli and to distinguish among them. Are the stimuli the same or different? Or do they have more or less of some quality? A batter in baseball has to attend to the flight of the pitch and the spin on the ball, as well as discriminate among possible types of pitches in order to adjust his swing. Generally speaking, good batters have this perceptual ability developed to a higher level than poor batters. They can discriminate among pitches and adapt. This ability is important for teachers analyzing movement. For example, did the hands land on the front, middle, or back part of the horse in a vault? The analyst knows that the hands made contact with the horse but, in order to provide good feedback, must discriminate where contact occurred.

Recognition tasks require more perceptual processing than either detection or discrimination tasks. This type of task usually involves stimuli that have been presented previously, as opposed to those that have not. People can distinguish stimuli learned previously from stimuli that they are not conversant with. In a gymnastics floor routine, spectators would be able to recognize and name all of the tumbling moves they were familiar with. They would not be able to recognize moves they had not seen before.

Recognition implies that a good deal of knowledge is needed to help with the analysis. A spectator or coach who did not know the whole routine of a gymnast would not know if a part was missing or changed. In qualitative analysis, recognition is important because it is the level of perception that allows us to start perfecting skill performance. It is the level where we look for complete matching of a performance and its critical features with a prototypic skill.

Identification tasks stress the perceptual processes even more than recognition. These types of tasks require that a person respond to a stimulus in a specific way, that they make a judgment in response to a stimulus. These responses can be the same for different or similar stimuli. A guard in basketball might encounter the stimulus of a certain defense set up by an opponent. She might respond by running this play or that play in order to beat that defense. Once the player has identified the stimulus (defense), she can decide on the appropriate answer(s).

QA Choices

You are preparing to observe a person throwing a ball overhand. You have never observed this person doing this movement before. Knowing you have four levels of information processing, which one do you think would be the best for your initial observations? Should this level of observation change as you continue your observations? How would you prepare yourself to work at each of the four levels? Do you think different observers would work better at different levels? Is there a common, or agreed on, level comfortable to most observers?

Similarly, a teacher or coach might identify a certain error in movement, such as stepping on the wrong foot during a throw. His correction might differ based on the knowledge he has about the skill or performer. Skill-related feedback might be appropriate in one situation, while motivational feedback might be more effective in another. The process of identification is similar to the third task in qualitative analysis, that of evaluation and diagnosis.

As you can see, information processing and perceptual processes are complex and require a great deal of cognitive processing when applied in qualitative analysis. The complexities of qualitative analysis are far more intricate than most of us imagine. In truth, we have just begun to describe the cognitive-perceptual picture. This process is elaborated throughout this chapter.

Models of Information Processing

Several models have been postulated to describe the way information is processed from the initiation of a stimulus to the completion of a response. These models are useful for both the description of motor responses and the principally cognitive solutions required by qualitative analysis. All these models attempt to explain how information is processed, regardless of the level: detection, discrimination, recognition, or identification. Historically, two major categories of processing have been postulated: single channel and multiple resources (O'Donnell, Moise, Warner, and Secrist, 1994). Although these models only postulate how we deal with environmental stimuli, they can be useful in helping us understand how we could come to conclusions about movement that are different from the conclusions of others watching the same movement.

Single-Channel Models

Single-channel models have generally fallen out of favor because they do not explain the huge amount of sensory input people are capable of handling. In 1958 Broadbent proposed the limited-capacity model of information processing, which described the processing activity of the stimulus as only one channel, similar to a one-lane, one-way street. Only so much information could pass through the brain in one direction at a time. The capacity model described by Kahneman (1973) supported this point of view.

In 1960 Treisman (in Anderson, 1990) said that a certain amount of processing must take place before information is filtered into a single channel. A screening process allows pertinent information to be attended to and passed on to higher levels of processing. Building on this line of thought, Deutsch and Deutsch (1963) proposed the pertinence model, which attempted to explain the filtering (screening) process as a matching of all stimuli with long-term memory.

> **KEY POINT 3.9** Information processing models have evolved over the years from single-channel, limited-capacity models to multiple-channel, parallel-processing models. Practice and education allow us to develop information processing to its optimum. This development needs to be purposeful and focused.

Multiple-Resource Models

Because the human brain can handle so much information, the limited-capacity models fell out of favor. But they did lead to two ideas carried forward to later models: filters and channels of information. Filters are the processes used by the brain to help organize information. They are believed to deal with information such as color, lines, language, spatial information, intensity of stimuli, and duration of stimuli, to name a few. Channels are pathways for information and communication in the brain. These channels can be parallel or serial and can move information forward, sideways, and backward.

Multiple-resource models succeeded the limited-capacity models. Wickens's model (1984a, b) proposed that sensory input is processed by multiple parts of the brain. He also suggested that processing resources are separate from response processes. Pribram and McGuinness (1975) postulated the cognitive-energetic stage model, which depicts information processing as dependent on internal and external sources of energy.

Following this came the model of automaticity formulated by Schneider and Shiffrin (1977) and Anderson (1990). This model explains information processing as automatic for well-learned and highly practiced sensory input. Little or no attention is required for familiar information.

Pattern recognition models were espoused as extensions of the multiple-resource explanation of information processing. The two types of pattern recognition models are template matching and feature integration. Template matching models (Anderson, 1990) indicate a continual matching process of stimuli to stored templates. The themes of template matching and feature integration will be further discussed later in this chapter. The feature-integration theory (Treisman and Gelade, 1980) postulated preattentive and focused attention parts to information screening. The first level does not demand much attention, but the second is far more intensive if features are deemed important at lower energy levels. Further research by McLeod, Driver, Dienes, and Crisp (1991) has supported this idea and indicates that visual search is active and based on cognitive mapping. This map may be interpreted as knowledge about the features of interest.

In 1992 Pinheiro and Simon presented a general information processing approach of how qualitative analysis proceeds. This theoretical explanation was the first attempt to apply an information processing model to qualitative analysis of movement. They based much of their model on schemas (ways of encoding and storing information in memory). They explain skill analysis as information processing at two levels: short-term memory and long-term memory. They add that information is stored as either semantic (information about things) or recognition (dealing principally with visual stimuli). They explain qualitative analysis as chunks of information being recognized as relevant in short-term memory and therefore being passed on to long-term memory for further processing. This involves a matching process with previously stored relevant data about the incoming information. They suggest various levels of processing in qualitative analysis, such as information acquisition (the senses), processing (short- and long-term memory), and decision making.

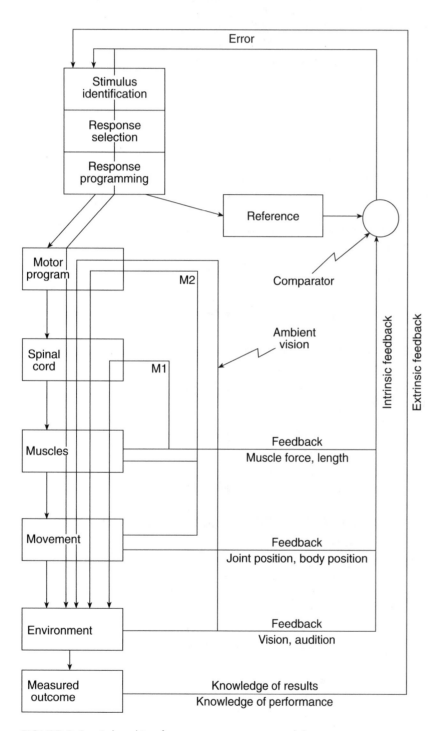

FIGURE 3.3 Schmidt's information-processing model.
Reprinted with permission from Schmidt and Wrisberg, 2000:

Schmidt's Information Processing Model

Perhaps the most familiar information processing model is the one proposed by Schmidt (Schmidt, 1991; Schmidt and Wrisberg, 2000) and shown in figure 3.3. This model explains motor control information processes concerned with human movement problems. It is presented here because it can illustrate points important to terms and ideas already expressed in this chapter.

The lines from one section to another represent channels. (There are also channels within each box representing major functions or brain activities.) For example, the filter system (or screening process) can be seen in the stimulus-detection box of Schmidt's model. The input box in the Schmidt model parallels the energetics section of the O'Donnell et al. model. The "comparator" in the Schmidt model is the place where an observed performance would be compared to what is considered a good performance of the skill. Finally, the response system in the O'Donnell model matches the response-selection box in the Schmidt model.

O'Donnell, Moise, Warner, and Secrist Information Processing Model

O'Donnell et al. (1994) proposed an information processing model that draws on much of the work already cited and provides an excellent structure on which to base a description of the complex activity of sensory organization and interpretation. This advanced theoretical approach posits a framework that the many components of qualitative analysis can be hung on. There are three major steps in the progression of this model: (1) the energetics system, (2) the attention allocation system, and (3) the response system. Figure 3.4 shows this model.

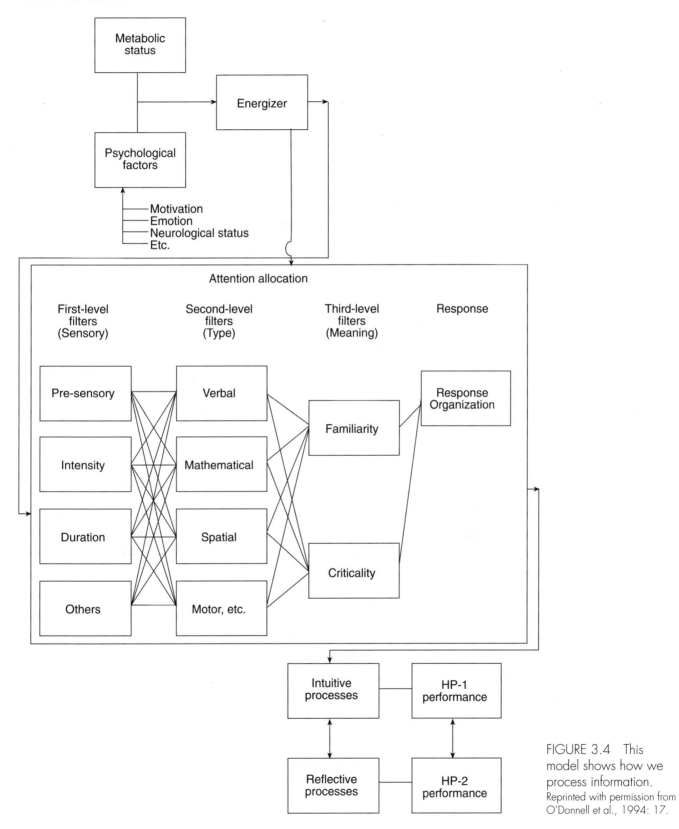

FIGURE 3.4 This model shows how we process information.
Reprinted with permission from O'Donnell et al., 1994: 17.

Energetics System

The energetics system drives the potential of information processing by the metabolic and psychological state of the individual. Metabolically, the body must provide energy to allow for the physiological processes to occur. Psychologically, emotions, neurological status, and motivation increase or limit the release of energy from the metabolic pathways, which allow sensory information to flow. The qualitative analyst must use energy to pay attention and focus that attention in observing human movement.

Attention Allocation System

The filters in the model's attention allocation system are of great interest to qualitative analysis. This is where sensory information is organized so that it can be matched with the knowledge base. This organization process is extremely complex and not fully understood. It is hypothesized that this is where activity relating to spatial (verbal and nonverbal) perceptions, imagery, motion, topology, mental rotation, critical features, and more takes place to sort through sensory information. This is analogous to template matching (Anderson, 1990) and feature integration (Treisman and Gelade, 1980). The filters are also called *constraints* by some psychologists (Shiffrar, 1994). Constraints are assumptions or prior knowledge about the physical world. These will be discussed later in this chapter with biological motion perception. It is in the filters that information is organized and channeled for further processing so that the final filters can deal with stimuli recognition. Filters might be explained by Pinheiro and Simon (1992) as part of short-term memory.

Again, it is difficult to say how much information is attended to and how much is stored. This model proposes multiple channels and parallel processing, so a great deal of information can be handled. At some point, however, a single channel is used and the relevant information in this channel is what is attended to. Although we may retain information in our central nervous system for a short time, it appears we can attend to only one thing at a time in a controlled fashion. This is especially true when information is new and continually changing. When we deal with familiar, predictable information, we can attend to several stimuli simultaneously. This is controlled or automatic processing of information and will be discussed later in this chapter.

Response System

In the third stage of this model, the response domain, responses are either intuitive or reflective. Because the O'Donnell et al. (1994) system is designed to explain both slow and fast information processing, both the intuitive and the reflective modes are presented. Most qualitative analysis responses pass through the reflective (slower) processing track. This would be true even if we quickly intuited the correct response from the analysis of a movement. Although we might want to respond to a movement quickly, it is important not to jump to conclusions and consider knowledge from different disciplines to optimize the intervention.

To illustrate how the O'Donnell et al. (1994) theoretical model might apply to qualitative analysis, figure 3.5 presents a skill to be analyzed. The observer looks at and also listens to the movement because the hurdle is rich in both auditory and visual information. If the sounds and what is seen match what is expected, the quality of the hurdle is probably acceptable. Matching sound and vision, however, may be difficult.

The analyst should observe the performance using as many senses as possible. The sensory input is then organized in the filters and passed along to the decision centers in the brain. A response is formulated and the specific type of intervention is given. Then the analyst begins the process again, perhaps by watching another performance

A teacher analyzing a skill using a gestalt (holistic) approach to qualitative analysis exemplifies the parallel processing of a great deal of information that experienced minds can handle. The whole performance is examined and a feel for the quality of the performance is developed. The teacher picks up many visual, auditory, kinesthetic, and tactile stimuli. These stimuli then pass through the filters in an attempt to organize and integrate them. At the next level, these stimuli are matched with previous information from the teacher's knowledge base. In hurdling, for example, the sound information would be matched with expected visual information. If the match is not good, analysts need to gather more information or delay intervention until the differences can be resolved. This process moves forward, backward, and sideways in the filters until the stimuli have been organized to present a coherent, understandable picture.

If the stimuli cannot be resolved into a coherent picture, then the process is started again. In this case, the analyst may try to resolve the problem by focusing on a particular part of the skill (the arms or the legs). Recall that the observational model proposed by Gangstead and Beveridge (1984) was designed to help analysts use a more organized approach to observation. This back-and-forth sensory integration and interpretation is never ending and is fundamental to qualitative analysis.

If one attentional focus is not useful, then we can switch to another and access the acquired information about that focus remaining in our memory. When processing stimuli, we must try to get the best information. This information is then sent on to the response area so that the stimulus can be interpreted appropriately.

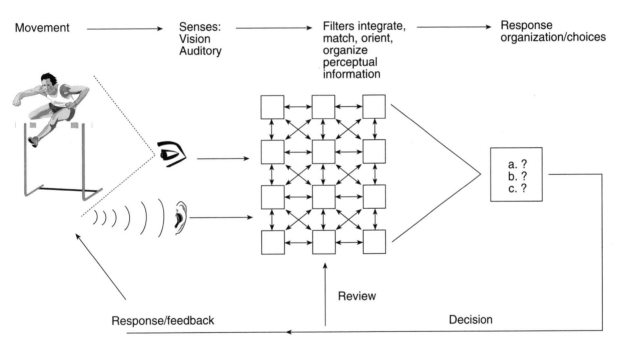

FIGURE 3.5 Perception model with skill illustration.
Reprinted from Knudson and Morrison 1997: 56.

or by pulling information from short-term memory to develop appropriate feedback. This is why it is important to be aware that many senses gather information for qualitative analysis and that memory can hold traces of sensory performance information for short periods of time.

Comparisons Between Schmidt and O'Donnell Models

In comparison, the closed loop in Schmidt's (Schmidt and Wrisberg, 2000) model is similar to the reflective (type II) processing path of the O'Donnell et al. (1994) model.

In the type II O'Donnell et al. model, feedback would be given only after the observer had time to reflect on the movement and all possible types of intervention. The open loop in Schmidt's model (Schmidt and Wrisberg, 2000) would be like the fast processing in the O'Donnell et al. intuitive response (type I), in which feedback is often given before the skill performance has been completed. This type of feedback from the analyst may be correct, but it has limited value, since the response has not been completely considered.

This type of situation is seen in the case of a basketball player throwing a desperation shot and having the coach respond by yelling out, "Oh, no! Don't shoot!" after the ball leaves the player's hands. As often as not, the ball goes in the basket. When it does, the coach usually yells out, albeit with egg on his face, "Great shot!" The fast response, given before completion, does not consider all of the relevant information. The slow reflective response considers all relevant information and is more likely to result in correct intervention.

We suggest a reflective approach in qualitative analysis. That is, reflect on the skill performance once it has concluded. It often appears that analysts rerun the images of the movements in their minds before responding. This is can be explained by short-term memory (Anderson, 1990; Pinheiro and Simon, 1992). Therefore, it is wise to be more reflective when dealing with qualitative analysis information. Most experts recommend watching several skill performances before making feedback decisions.

KEY POINT 3.10 Research linking perception to qualitative analysis has been limited but should be an area of focus in the future. Factors examined by qualitative analysis research so far include perceptual styles, eye tracking, and imagery. Much needs to be learned about the visual perception of movement and the critical features of movement, since these two components are the foci of qualitative analysis.

Research on Perception in Qualitative Analysis

Evidence for the importance of perception in the qualitative analysis of movement has slowly accumulated over the years. The two major sources are investigations that (1) use perception or facets of perception directly in various qualitative analyses of movement and (2) examine perception in general. The information from these latter investigations can be applied indirectly to qualitative analysis. They are undoubtedly the basis for investigations of perception in qualitative analysis.

Again, we can hypothesize that considerable and complex cognitive activity takes place in the filter system. The research in qualitative analysis that examines filter function has dealt primarily with spatial ability, imagery, types of examples (good only versus good and bad), and observational models.

Imagery and Qualitative Analysis

As part of the information processing model reviewed in this book, imagery is part of the filters (O'Donnell et al., 1994). It appears that vivid mental images of performances can be used to match information in the filters. This process is like template matching (Anderson, 1990), feature integration (Triesman and Gelade, 1980), and recognition (Pinheiro and Simon, 1992). This matching process is part of the analysis that decides the merits of a performance. Because verbal and visual information is stored differently, it is communication between the verbal and the visual abstract representations in the mind that allows for performance evaluation. This information is then fed to the response system, and feedback or other interventions are formulated depending on the purpose of analysis.

We are not completely sure how images are stored. Farah, Hammond, Levine, and Calvanio (1988) believe there are two kinds of imagery: spatial and visual. These concepts are extremely complex and beyond the scope of this text. They are mentioned here to alert the reader that mental images are complex and can be different for different analysts.

The results of the studies of imagery and qualitative analysis are less than conclusive, but they do illustrate the importance of vivid mental imagery in the analysis of movement. In 1975 Hoffman and Sembiante studied whether a person analyzing human movement holds a mental image of the movement in memory. They concluded that the ability to formulate and hold a vivid mental image was related to qualitative analysis ability. In the second Hoffman study (Hoffman and Armstrong, 1975), visual imagery did not appear to be a discriminating factor in qualitative analysis ability. The factors under examination here relate directly to the question of how a person analyzes a skill. Although the jury is still out, imagery would intuitively seem to be an important factor in matching a systematized skill performance with a prototypic skill performance. This topic deserves further research.

Spatial Ability and Qualitative Analysis

People's ability to deal with spatial information in qualitative analysis has been only superficially investigated. It seems obvious that the more easily we can process visual-spatial information, the more easily we can analyze movement, since movement is essentially change of position in space.

Researchers have assessed spatial ability by examining perceptual style (field dependence/independence), whether or not subjects can use background cues to extract information from the environment. A tennis player who tends to be field independent does not rely heavily on reference points such as court lines, the net, and other environmental information to play. This type of player can gather sufficient information from the opponent to decide on appropriate responses. An analyst who can separate performers from background factors will be less susceptible to a disorganized sensory background and may not need to spend much time manipulating the observational situation. By contrast, an analyst who has difficulty observing movement without reference to floor lines or background markers tends to have a field-dependent perceptual style. This person must make sure the qualitative analysis environment is well organized.

Five studies (Gangstead, Cashel, and Beveridge, 1987; Knudson and Morrison, 2000; Morrison and Frederick, 1998; Morrison and Reeve, 1989, 1992) have looked at spatial ability from a verbal and nonverbal (nonanalog and analog) point of view and its effects on qualitative analysis. A test of spatial ability can sometimes be solved using verbal clues, while other spatial tests resist verbal help. The Group Embedded Figures Test (Whitkin, Oltman, Raskin, and Karp, 1971) is one in which verbal self-talk appears to aid in the solution of the visual problems. The mental-rotations test (Vandenberg, 1971) and the portable rod and frame test (Whitkin, 1954) seem to resist verbal clues. Gangstead, Cashel, and Beveridge (1987) found a weak ($R = 0.27$) relationship between qualitative analysis and field independence. They used the rod and frame test (Whitkin, 1954) to determine analog spatial ability. Morrison and Reeve (1989, 1992) and Morrison and Frederick (1998) used the verbal-spatial Group Embedded Figures Test (Whitkin, Oltman, Raskin, and Karp, 1971) to see if spatial ability was important to qualitative analysis. Morrison and Reeve (1989, 1992) found that those tending toward a field-independent style of analysis were better than those who were more field dependent. Morrison and Frederick (1998) uncovered a weak relationship ($R = -0.33$) between disembedding and absolute error in qualitative analysis.

A recent study (Knudson and Morrison, 2000) added the Vandenberg mental rotation test (1971) to the Group Embedded Figures Test (Whitkin, Oltman, Raskin, and Karp, 1971) to assess mental rotation ability and disembedding in the assessment of angles and range of motion in the vertical jump. They reported no significant associations between disembedding and mental rotations on either linear or angular measures of movement in a sample of 43 untrained undergraduates.

The studies of the effects of spatial ability on qualitative analysis are not conclusive but tend to indicate that spatial ability may have little effect on qualitative analysis compared to other factors (knowledge, experience, and so on). Some people appear to use a combination of analog spatial ability and verbal spatial ability to help organize movement information as part of the filter system. Although more research is needed, present data suggests a need for explicit verbal skill descriptions (see pages 81, 88, and 136) as well as practice with movement examples to develop qualitative analysis.

Good and Bad Examples As Types of Information

A number of authors have used good and bad examples of skill performances to teach qualitative analysis (Beveridge and Gangstead, 1984; Gangstead, 1984; Kelly, Walkley, and Tarrant, 1988; Morrison, 1994; Morrison and Reeve, 1989). Only Gangstead (1984), Morrison and Reeve (1989), and Morrison (1994) attempted to differentiate between the two types of information and qualitative analysis ability. Gangstead found that for qualitative analysis instruction, examples of good and bad performances were superior to good examples only. Morrison and Reeve and Morrison found no significant difference for type of training information on qualitative analysis ability.

These research projects were initiated to establish the value of more and contrasting instructional information to the development of qualitative analysis ability. The authors felt this information would be valuable in the filter stage of the O'Donnell et al. (1994) model or the comparator stage of the Schmidt model. Despite the conflicting results for types of examples, this book and CD-ROM present both good and poor technique for examples and tutorials in qualitative analysis.

Observational Models

As part of the idea of the attention allocation system (O'Donnell et al., 1994) or the stimulus recognition stage (Schmidt and Wrisberg, 2000), Gangstead and Beveridge (1984) developed an observational model for qualitative analysis. This model was designed to help focus an analyst's attention on specific parts of a performance and to reduce extraneous information. Those who recommend a gestalt approach to the initial analysis, such as Dunham (1986, 1994), tell analysts to first allocate their attention to the whole performance and then look for general stimuli on which to judge the performance. A systematic observational strategy using either a structured approach such as a gestalt or an observational model is crucial to the perceptual process in observation of movement (Gangstead and Beveridge, 1984).

Development of Spatial Perceptual Ability

Studies of spatial perceptual ability could lead to enhancement of qualitative analysis ability. It has been demonstrated that visual spatial ability can be enhanced by training.

Since spatial ability appears to correlate to analysis ability, development of spatial ability could underlie enhancement of qualitative analysis ability. Pinheiro and Cai (1999) found that undergraduate students who used an observational model similar to Dunham's (1986, 1994) were superior in their qualitative analysis than those who did not use an observational model.

So far, there appears to be only one perceptual training system shown to improve perceptual spatial abilities (Secrist and Hartman, 1993). This system is available only to F-15 and F-16 fighter pilots. Essentially, it is a rapid-fire presentation of visual situations normally encountered by pilots on combat missions. Short bursts of combat sequences (lasting 5 to 6 seconds) are presented, and subjects are required to make nearly instantaneous decisions (in 0.33 to 0.67 seconds). All challenges are adapted to a subject's current level of performance. A similar system could be used with skill analysis instruction to sharpen information processing abilities. To some degree, systems like this already exist in videotape and videodisk presentations, but they are much slower and are not purposefully matched to the live environment and current ability level of the analyst.

Perception of Biological Motion Research

Recent psychological research has tied the idea of the *what* of focal vision and the *where* of ambient vision to the analysis of biological motion (Heptulla-Chaterjee, Freyd, and Shiffrar, 1996; Shiffrar, 1994; Shiffrar and Freyd, 1993; Thornton, Pinto, and Shiffrar, 1998).

Shiffrar (1994) indicated that these two visual systems converge in the higher centers of the brain and are used in the cognitive interpretation of biological motion. The two systems she mentions are the ventral (the *what*) and the dorsal (the *where*). She does not call these two systems the *focal* and the *ambient,* although she does appear to be referring to these two systems. In her experiment she demonstrated that even when no movement path was given for apparent biological motion, the visual system constructs paths for the apparent motion consistent with biomechanical limitations. It appears in this case that the mind is working at the identification level of processing. That is, presented with enough time, the mind fills in the path of biological motion even though no real motion occurred. We cannot dismiss how active our perception is in the analysis of human movement.

In 1990 Shiffrar and Freyd reported that when looking at apparent body motions (motions that were inferred from two still pictures but never actually occurred), an observer will interpret motion as occurring in the shortest path for fast motions regardless of how impossible that motion is. They also found that the slower the stimulus motion, the more anatomically possible the motion path observed by the subject. In faster motions hands and arms appeared to move through the body, whereas at slower speeds the mind perceived the body parts as taking the anatomically correct way around the body. Without sufficient time, the mind notes the different positions of the body parts and seems to be operating at the detection level of movement. That is, the brain simply notes a change has occurred without adding extra information such as the biomechanically possible path of the body part.

The visual perceptual system may also be seen to function as a hierarchy (Thornton, Pinto, and Shiffrar, 1998): a lower level system with brief temporal and spatial limits and a higher level system with longer temporal and larger spatial information. Although these levels are difficult to define, local information seems to be derived from the level of the joint and adjacent limbs; the global level acquires information from about half of the human body. Temporally, the local works within about 50 milliseconds or less, while the global works over longer periods of time.

Perceptual research has implications for the two main approaches to organizing observational strategies: the gestalt approach and a more structured or localized approach (for example, Gangstead and Beveridge, 1984). Both strategies correspond to styles of information processing and have a common connection. The commonality between these two approaches (what and where, local and global information) appears to be temporal demands for processing sensory information.

The practical implications for these observations are that both approaches to observing human movement take time. This is because they use either local or global information as well as ambient and focal vision. Whatever observational strategy is used for qualitative analysis, the analyst should allow time for information processing and not rush to judgment. This admonition speaks strongly to the ideas suggested throughout this text, namely, that good qualitative analysis relies on careful attention to all four tasks of the QA process.

Knowledge about how perceptual information is processed is becoming more and more specific. At times we appear to integrate previous knowledge. At other times we appear to provide information that supersedes previous knowledge. As with any area of study, it will take time to sort out relevant ideas from irrelevant ones. Only further research from psychologists and analysts interested in qualitative analysis of human movement will clear up areas of confusion. From an information processing perspective, it does appear that the recent research findings presented here support our suggestions on how to best qualitatively analyze movement.

Another interesting concept emerging from psychological research on biological motion is the idea that the recognition of biological motion may be tied to the motor aspect of that movement (Thornton, Pinto, and Shiffrar, 1998). Psychologists have linked the visual and motor systems in the perception of human motion by noting significant effects for the recognition of human motion in conditions of relative masking. They believe that the ability to recognize a type of motion is related to a person's ability to use the motion they are asked to recognize.

Recalling the discussion earlier in this chapter on movement ability and analysis ability, it may appear that the psychological research on biological motion contradicts the findings from kinesiology (Armstrong and Hoffman, 1979; Girardin and Hanson, 1967; Osborne and Gordon, 1972). This is not the case, however. These kinesiology studies found that higher skill levels did not indicate higher qualitative analysis of movement abilities. The psychological research on biological motion simply indicates that the ability to move in a certain way is tied to perception of that movement (Thornton, Pinto, and Shiffrar, 1998).

QA Choices

You have to observe an unfamiliar movement and analyze it qualitatively. You are not sure about where to look for information during the movement. You decided beforehand that the most important information will come from the relationship of the limbs to each other and to the body. Will you take time to focus on each body part separately? Will you focus on the left or right side, or the top or bottom? How will you eliminate distracting movements? Is it better to use ambient or focal vision? Can a model help?

Related Information Processing Research

Research that deals not directly with qualitative analysis of skill but with related areas of information processing has allowed conjecture on factors that could be important to movement analysis. These studies deal with information processing concepts such as expert/novice differences, topological features, encoding of spatial information, attention and selective attention, and completion.

Expert Versus Novice Studies

The research that may have relevant information for qualitative analysis of movement is the research on expert versus novice differences in anticipation of movements (Abernethy, 1989, 1993; Abernethy and Russell, 1987; Abernethy and Zawi, submitted; Buckolz, Prapavesis, and Fairs, 1988; Davids, DePalmer, and Savelsbergh, 1989; Goulet et al., 1988). The essence of this research is the question, how much information does it take for an expert as opposed to a novice to anticipate an opponent's shot in racket sports? These studies have used direction of shot and different amounts of movement information to examine these questions. Generally speaking, experts are better than novices at anticipating the end results of opponents' shots. They appear to acquire this information earlier in the stroke and need information from fewer body parts to make these decisions. This type of research appears to hold promise for the qualitative analysis of movement. Examination of the difference between expert analysts and novice analysts could produce information that indicates which body parts are most important for good qualitative analysis and when this information is acquired.

Topological Features

Topological features are prominent structural components of objects that attract attention. They may affect information processing at the level of filters. Chen (1982) concluded that topological information is a basic factor in perceptual organization. This organization process may direct the flow of information to the correct succeeding filters for further organization and processing. For example, if critical features of a movement can serve as topological features, then focusing attention on those critical features can improve cognitive processing in qualitative analysis. Sparrow and Sherman (2001) postulate that for movement analysis, especially using point of light displays, topological features are an important component in the analysis process.

Encoding of Spatial Information

Information storage is the next major consideration in the last part of the perception sequence. The storage of information, both verbal and visual, is the part of memory where stimuli from the environment are matched. An important factor in qualitative analysis is that we appear to encode movement information differently from verbal information (Minas, 1977; Simon, 1979; Theios and Amarhein, 1989). Minas reported a study where subjects were asked to describe a movement in words or copy the movement physically. They did much better at reproducing the movement physically than describing it verbally.

The coding of information in the mind is abstract, neither strictly linguistic or imagistic. Nevertheless, information encoded from a visual-spatial source must be reconciled with verbal information. This process tends to take time, and poor correlations between words and movement information can lead to errors (Theios and Amarhein, 1989). Words and pictures are stored separately, as are the other senses relevant to qualitative analysis. This means that when movement (spatial) information is processed, it must be matched for spatial and movement information stored in memory. Then words must be attached to describe the movement if feedback is desired. Cue words serve a purpose as information storage for the analyst, not just the performer.

Having a good vocabulary or well-defined skill description based on correct language can help not only with feedback but also with information storage. Chunking of information may explain this storage process. Experts appear to be more efficient at information storage than novices.

Attention and Selective Attention

Attention and selective attention are appropriately placed with perception. To some degree, selective attention is demonstrated by the eye-tracking studies previously mentioned (Petrakis, 1986, 1987; Petrakis and Romjue, 1990). These types of studies show where a person is looking for critical information as a result of her knowledge of movement or information gaps in past observations. The analyst's attention should be directed by the information stored as images and verbal information encoded, in the brain, for the matching process.

A good deal of research activity has dealt with attention (Abernathy and Russell, 1987). It has essentially examined factors that make experts more efficient at handling the large amounts of information in skill performances. Differences appear to include the facts that experts chunk information, encode more efficiently, and retrieve information more quickly. Regardless of what we are doing, our attention is always attracted to certain features in our field of vision. In qualitative analysis, we must use our knowledge base to attend selectively to skill components that will yield valuable information. An inability to direct our attention reduces our qualitative analysis potential.

Some skills have so many components, especially skills like those in gymnastics, that it is easy to become distracted and lose track of particular parts of the skill we need to see. Certainly observation models like the one proposed by Gangstead and Beveridge (1984) can help us direct our attention to the important factors in a skill.

Completion

Williams (1989a, b) demonstrated how partial movement clues could be used to build a complete picture of an activity. His studies demonstrated the pattern-seeking nature of human perception. With only limited movement information, subjects could fill in the missing parts of a skill and name the movements presented. These subjects were able to take pieces of information, orient them, match them to information stores in memory, and then successfully describe the movement as it would appear whole. These studies again demonstrate the importance and the potential of the perceptual system. They also explain how some coaches may think they see things that are faster than human vision. Information processing allows their minds to infer what they think happened even though their senses did not gather direct visual information of the event.

Most times the skill is interpreted correctly. But we can always be fooled. We need to be careful when we are not absolutely sure of the basic sensory information. This is yet another argument for viewing skills several times, especially in fast movements.

Automatic and Controlled Processing

No discussion of information processing would be complete without an examination of the ideas of controlled and automatic processing of information (Naatanen, 1990; Schneider and Shiffrin, 1977). As Schneider and Shiffrin explain it, automatic processing involves a sequence of neurons that become active in response to certain stimuli.

This activation needs no dynamic control on the part of the subject and is a well-learned sequence. Stimuli are mapped or sent directly to the correct response areas in the brain with limited processing.

Controlled processing is a temporary sequence (not well learned) directly under the control of the subject's active attention. This process has limited information handling capacity and can be quite slow. Automatic processing has a much greater capacity and is much faster at mapping stimuli to correct responses. Familiarity with the stimuli is a hallmark of automatic processing.

Automatic and controlled processing can be seen in sport situations. A point guard, dribbling the ball down the floor to set up a play, processes information automatically until unfamiliar stimuli force him into a more controlled mode. The dribbling, the running, and the way the team sets up are all expected stimuli, so processing them is automatic. But if the opposition sets up an unfamiliar defense, then the point guard will have to process the new information in a controlled fashion. Often the team with the ball takes a time-out to solve the unanticipated defense. Many experienced coaches and teachers plan their observation to reduce the potential for unexpected occurrences that would interfere with the smooth operation of the class. This allows them to direct the controlled processing to the analysis of the skill being observed. If anything unexpected occurs in the movement, they can devote their efforts to dealing with it.

In qualitative analysis most of the visual, auditory, and tactile stimuli are processed automatically until something unexpected or strange occurs. The more familiar the analyst is with the skill, the student, and the environment, the more automatically the information about the performance will be processed. Since automaticity is an indication of learning and requires less effort on the part of the analyst than controlled processing, those interested in improving their qualitative analysis ability should learn all they can about qualitative analysis, the skill to be analyzed, the subjects to be analyzed, the analysis environment, and the possible feedback for a skill performance. This learning will facilitate a greater analysis capacity and greater ease of analysis, and should lead to better teaching, as will be shown in chapter 5. Automatic processing is so quick and effortless that it does not appear to be conscious. But we usually have to learn the process, and we all have different capacities for it.

> **KEY POINT 3.11** Controlled and automatic processing are important components of qualitative analysis. The more automatic we can make our information processing, the faster and more efficient we will be as analysts.

Two studies that examined biases in gymnastics judging (Ste-Marie and Lee, 1991; Ste-Marie and Valiquette, 1996) point to the need for observers to be aware of prior knowledge of a performer in movement analysis. They found significant effects for judges who had watched warm-ups of gymnasts. Final or competition scores were related to how well a gymnast warmed up. Those who had poor warm-ups were more likely to receive lower scores in competition than their performance deserved. Those who had good warm-ups were more likely to receive better scores in their competitive performance. Based on this research, then, a concerted effort must be maintained in order to see each performance with a fresh eye.

A Gestalt

Perhaps the best place to end our brief discussion of information processing is at a place where perception starts, with suggestions to novice teachers and coaches on how to analyze qualitatively. Different people have varying approaches on how to look for meaning in movement—for example, "just watch the arms in this skill" or "watch

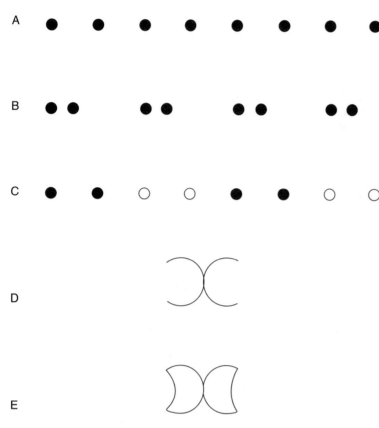

FIGURE 3.6 Illustrations of the gestalt concepts of proximity, lightness, continuity, and closure.
Reprinted with permission from Palmer, 1992: 437.

for the follow-through in this movement." In a conversation with one of the authors, a volleyball coach said she could tell how well a spike was performed by watching the follow-through. While this suggestion may be helpful to some, it may be confusing or ineffective to most.

A good way for most people to begin observing movement for analysis is to build a gestalt representation of the movement to be analyzed (Chen, 1982; Treisman, 1986). A gestalt representation is a picture whose totality is greater than the sum of its parts. Four basic principles (Anderson, 1990; Yantis, 1992) are proximity, similarity, good continuation, and closure. Figure 3.6 from Palmer (1992) demonstrates these organizing principles.

The mind tries to extract information from the stimuli presented by organizing them into patterns that have meaning. Recent research and theoretical interpretation of a gestalt have formulated the idea of uniform connectedness as the foundation of information processing. That is, uniform connectedness (regions of homogeneous properties, such as lightness, color, or texture) is the first perceptual factor in a gestalt (Palmer and Rock, 1994). After uniform connectedness come proximity, similarity, continuation, and closure.

Although no qualitative analysis studies have directly addressed grouping, Petrakis (1986, 1987; Petrakis and Romjue, 1990) may have indirectly demonstrated grouping of stimuli by uniform connectedness as a factor in qualitative analysis. Her research examined eye-tracking patterns to see if experienced observers looked at skills differently than inexperienced observers; she found that this was the case. The research further showed that the experts' visual search patterns were more systematic than the novices' and may have been based on the uniform connectedness of sections of the body. The experts tended to look for information concerning the movement being examined from the same regions of the body, while the novices searched wildly over the body for meaningful information. The experts seemed to group information by areas that appeared to be connected in a uniform fashion; novices did not. These results may further support the ideas of focal/ambient vision or what/where perception (Schmidt and Wrisberg, 2000; Shiffrar, 1994). The eyes appeared to be focused on a central point but were actually gathering information from ambient vision as to where the limbs were in relation to the body and each other. Focal vision could not have gathered information about these relationships.

Rather than watch for one specific aspect of a skill, qualitative analysts should base their initial response on an overall impression or feeling about the quality of the performance. This may be especially true in continuous activities such as swimming, running, and rowing. Since we often get to see several repetitions of a skill performance when we are teaching or coaching, we can go back and look for specific skill components after

KEY POINT 3.12 The idea of a gestalt is important to anyone interested in qualitative analysis. It provides a less structured approach to gathering information in observation.

making an overall decision about the quality of the performance. Then we can focus on the critical features that are organized (grouped) by knowledge and experience, or on the previous observations. Even if we do not get to see several performances of the skill, our short-term memory (Simon, 1979) may allow us to reformulate the performance in our minds so that we remember the individual parts of the skill.

Perception is a highly complex area of study. It can, at best, be hypothesized by indirect measures of brain function and observed behaviors. Although we do not have extensive hard evidence on how perceptual processes occur, perception is crucial to the qualitative analysis of movement and needs to be examined and understood if progress is going to continue in this area of our discipline.

Summary

All of the senses are extremely important in the qualitative analysis of movement. Too often, analysts disregard the importance of the various senses and how these senses work together to provide information. Vision is generally the sense that predominates in the qualitative analysis process, but the best observation incorporates auditory, haptic, and kinesthetic information as well. Processing of information from the senses is primarily driven by the function of attention. Different senses process information at different speeds, and different senses may have primacy when dealing with certain types of information. The processing of input would be confused if we did not know what stimuli to focus on in different situations.

We process cognitive information on four levels (detection, discrimination, recognition, identification) based on how information is available and what kind of responses we need to provide. Regardless of the level of processing, information for responses seems to pass through the same series of perceptual steps. Sensory information is first organized then meaning is assigned to it. Research indicates that perception measured by disembedding and mental rotations may affect qualitative analysis. Related research indicates that we need to be aware of the differences between biological and object motion, topological features, attention and selective attention, completion, automatic and controlled processing, and a gestalt. General and specific qualitative research has attempted to explain these steps. Having a representative figure of these steps can help us better understand the process. It can also help us prepare for better qualitative analysis.

Discussion Questions

1. What visual limitations are most strongly related to a blown call by a sports official? For a given sporting event, who is more likely to make a visual mistake: an athlete, an official, or a spectator? Why?

2. For the movements you analyze qualitatively, which sense provides the most relevant information? What are the limitations of this sense?

3. Go to a driving range and compare the distance the golf ball travels to kinesthetic (feel of swing and impact), auditory (impact sound), and visual (initial flight) information. What sense seems most accurate?

4. Experiment with a metronome or weights to determine the accuracy of your sense of audition or kinesthesis. Which sense is more sensitive?

5. How are the senses related to information processing? Is it possible to see something and not understand it? Think of some optical illusions you have encountered.

6. Where in the information processing model is sensory information organized?

7. What is the difference between controlled and automatic processing? In a trip to the beach, what parts of processing would be controlled and what parts would be automatic? Can these processes change? (That is, can automatic processing be changed from controlled to automatic and back again?)

8. What types of research have been done that relate to information processing for qualitative analysis?

9. What does the term *gestalt* mean? How is this approach useful for people involved in qualitative analysis? Will the ideas of proximity, grouping, and continuation work in movement situations?

PART II

Four Tasks of an Integrated Qualitative Analysis

We have seen that the many subdisciplinary views of qualitative analysis can be summarized in an interdisciplinary model with four important tasks. Preparation, observation, evaluation and diagnosis, and intervention are the tasks of qualitative analysis where the knowledge of all kinesiology subdisciplines must be integrated. Chapter 4 outlines the knowledge that must be gathered in the preparation task. Several approaches to the second task of qualitative analysis, observation, are illustrated in chapter 5. The third task of qualitative analysis, perhaps the most difficult of the four, has two parts: evaluation and diagnosis. These two parts are reviewed in chapter 6. Part II concludes with a review of the many kinds of intervention that can be used to improve human movement in chapter 7.

4

Preparation: Gathering Relevant Knowledge

© Tony Demin/International Stock

The booster club just asked you to judge the slam-dunk contest at the local junior college's basketball tournament. Since you are the local movement expert, the boosters want you to develop a rating scale and train the other judges before the contest. What are the key elements of a dunk in basketball? What aspects of a dunk should the judges look for and rate? Should the judges consider the height of the hand above the rim or the height of the jump? What is the range of correctness for a successful dunk? Could the judges make a fair and consistent rating without knowing the physical requirements and key elements of difficult dunks? How would you qualitatively analyze the dunk? Think about how different a qualitative analysis would be when teaching safe dunking versus judging a dunking contest with skilled players.

1. Identify areas of prerequisite knowledge that are important in the preparation task of qualitative analysis.

2. Define the critical features and explain how they are identified in the preparation task of qualitative analysis.

3. Explain how preparation in qualitative analysis is related to effective teaching and systematic observation.

4. Explain how preparing for qualitative analysis can be integrated with planning for teaching.

The first task in the qualitative analysis of human movement is the continuous process of building a prerequisite knowledge base. In our integrated model of qualitative analysis, this task is preparation. Other scholars have called this the *preplanning step* (Philipp and Wilkerson, 1990) or the *preobservation phase* (Arend and Higgins, 1976; McPherson, 1990), or have simply noted that prerequisite information is needed before observation and analysis can begin (Hay and Reid, 1988). We believe that professionals must continually read and research to build a knowledge base and must think critically about the practice of their profession. For example, physical educators should keep up with current research in the sport sciences and pedagogy, while physical therapists should keep up with research on the qualitative analysis of gait and other everyday movements.

This chapter will review important areas of prerequisite knowledge that professionals interested in human movement should be aware of in preparing for effective qualitative analysis. Good preparation involves weighing evidence from many subdisciplines of kinesiology. The three major areas of this prerequisite information are

1. knowledge about the activity or movement,
2. knowledge about the performer(s), and
3. knowledge about effective instruction.

KEY POINT 4.1 The first task of qualitative analysis is preparation: gathering knowledge about the activity and performers. Professionals should continuously gather detailed prerequisite knowledge in order to be good qualitative analyzers of movement and they should strive to integrate their analyses with instruction to maximize their effectiveness.

The chapter concludes with a brief acknowledgement that another area of critical knowledge relates to the next task of qualitative analysis, observation. Professionals need to have the knowledge to develop and practice a systematic observational strategy for the movements they analyze.

The philosophy of this approach to qualitative analysis is that knowledge is transient. Our state of knowledge and the standards of professional practice are dynamic. Professionals must realize that career is a never-ending search for the latest knowledge, our best approximation of the truth that can be applied to practice. For a qualitative analysis of human movement to be most effective, the analyst needs to maintain an up-to-date knowledge base. Otherwise, analyses may be based on erroneous or invalid information. A coach who is unaware of the rapid changes in sports equipment, for example, may be teaching inappropriate technique for the equipment his athletes are using.

Knowledge of Activity

An extensive knowledge base about an activity is essential to a good qualitative analysis of that activity. The knowledge base for any activity comes from all the subdisciplines of kinesiology (Vickers, 1989). An elementary physical education teacher needs current information about motor skill development and the fundamental movement patterns related to those skills. This includes validated developmental sequences, ages of typical stages, rate of advancement, and outcome measures. The subdiscipline of motor learning contains important knowledge on practice schedules and stages of motor learning that affect all kinesiology professions attempting to teach someone a new movement. Professionals must seek out the information they need from a variety of sources.

In secondary physical education, teachers and coaches need to know about the skills, strategy, and physical requirements of sports. They should update detailed knowledge of the individual skills and techniques. The goal or purpose of each sport skill needs to be determined (Gentile, 1972; James and Dufek, 1993). If the goal of a skill can be precisely defined, then the technique factors that lead to success in that skill can be more clearly identified for qualitative analysis. Recall that many models of qualitative analysis systems begin by defining the purpose of the movement (Arend and Higgins, 1976; Broer, 1960; Hay and Reid, 1982; Hoffman, 1983; McPherson, 1990).

A good example of a situational or strategic change in the goal of a movement is in the tennis serve. The first serve generally emphasizes placement, speed, or spin in order to put the opponent at a disadvantage, while the second serve's goal shifts toward greater accuracy to prevent a double fault. The importance of technique versus tactical errors changes depending on which serve is being attempted. In planning to qualitatively analyze the serve, the analyst will plan to observe both kinds of serves in practice and match play.

Sources of Information

Three main sources of information contribute to the prerequisite knowledge of an activity: experience, expert opinion, and scientific research. All three are important sources to consider in developing a prerequisite knowledge base for qualitative analysis. Two difficulties confront kinesiology professionals in this area: gathering the information from sometimes fragmented sources and weighing the evidence from each source.

Experience

Experience in any profession is invaluable, as evidenced by improvements in employability and salary with increasing years of experience. Most professionals develop positions on issues based on experiences with several patients or clients. This professional experience has the advantage of being population specific and environmentally relevant. Thoughtful coaches are likely to make valid generalizations from experience if their players are relatively homogeneous.

The weaknesses of experience as a source of valid information are that it is anecdotal and can be influenced by personal bias. Also, experience cannot control all the factors that may affect a particular issue, so professionals should search other sources to verify or refute their own conclusions.

Expert Opinion

The opinions of experts carry a lot of weight in many professions. People with a wealth of experience deserve the attention of their peers. The places to seek out this expert opinion are professional periodicals and professional meetings. In physical education, journals like *Strategies* and *JOPERD* feature articles written for professional practice. There are also professional magazines and newsletters that publish teaching tips and expert opinions, such as *Physical Education Digest* and *Peak Performance* (NASPE, AAHPERD). Professional organizations also usually produce professional magazines (for example, *TennisPro, Addvantage*). Sport-specific popular publications (for example, *Tennis* or *Golf Digest*) are also useful, often featuring interviews with successful coaches or analysts. Professionals can also seek out these expert opinions personally at professional meetings or over the Internet, or by consistently attending professional meetings and conferences where experts are often invited to speak.

The weaknesses of expert opinions are that they may conflict (figure 4.1) and that opinions often change. Teaching motor skills is often affected by the technique of a current champion or the agenda of the most prominent expert at that particular point in time (Hay and Reid, 1982). The latest rehabilitation protocol or technique in vogue may or may not be an improvement, and may still be far from the ideal.

FIGURE 4.1 Expert advice is often conflicting. This makes the task of building correct prerequisite information for qualitative analysis difficult.
Reprinted from Knudson and Morrison 1997: 69.

Both expert coaches and athletes have held opinions about performance in a particular skill that research has shown to be false. The history of sports is full of examples of incorrect notions about key points in many skills. Interested readers can find examples from track and field (Hay, 1993; Hay and Reid, 1982) and golf (Torrey, 1985). Skilled performers commonly have mistaken ideas about what is going on when they are performing. It is important to remember that championship athletic performance does not require expert knowledge about the kinesiology or qualitative analysis of the athlete's sport. The hallmark of a champion is to perform consistently and effectively, with little conscious thought about the process.

Scientific Research

Another source of prerequisite information for qualitative analysis is scientific research. Research in all the subdisciplines of kinesiology provides the most valid and accurate information available for basing decisions in qualitative analysis. Research can be either descriptive or experimental. For example, descriptive studies of injury rates of various populations of athletes or for modes of training would be relevant to the critical features selected for qualitative analysis. Experimental research on how different styles of teaching or teacher feedback affect learning also provides knowledge relevant to professionals planning qualitative analysis. Unfortunately, the controls needed in experimental research often limit its real-world application. It is also difficult for practitioners to gather relevant information from research, for many reasons. Often research is published in technical journals with difficult vernacular. Reading and interpreting research may be difficult because of the abstract nature of the topics, the technical demands of some measurements, and the complex experimental or statistical designs. Advanced degrees and constant updating may be needed to fully interpret research.

Some periodicals have the mission of bridging the gap between research and practice (Boyer, 1990). One of the first publications to attempt this was *Motor Skills: Theory into Practice*, but it ceased publication in 1985. Examples of good periodicals with scholarly research-based articles for practitioners are *Sports Coach, Track and Field Coaches Review, JOPERD, ACSM's Health and Fitness Journal,* and *Strength and Conditioning Journal.* In physical therapy, *Journal of Orthopedic and Sports Physical Therapy* has a reputation for readable and practitioner-friendly research. There are also many newsletters associated with professional organizations or interest groups that provide current information. Examples are *Physical Activity Today* (Research Consortium, AAHPERD), *Physical Activity and Fitness Research Digest* (President's Council on Physical Fitness and Sports), *Sports Science Periodical on Research and Technology in Sport* (Coaching Association of Canada), *Sports Sciences* (National Collegiate Athletic Association), *Fitness FACTS* (American Association for Active Lifestyles and Fitness), and *Olympic Coach* (United States Olympic Committee Division of Coaching Development).

Research also has the problem of accessibility for many professionals, although the advent of powerful computers, data storage, and communication technology has begun to make it easier to acquire sport science information. This access increases the impact of good information, but unfortunately, it also increases the impact of poor research and incorrect expert advice. Computer-compiled databases of articles and abstracts are available in print, can be searched on-line, and are stored on CD-ROM. Some of the best databases are the Sport and Leisure Index, SPORT (Sport Information Resource Center [SIRC], Ottawa, Canada), MedLine (National Library of Medicine), and ERIC (from the U.S. Department of Education). The CD-ROM version of SPORT, SPORT Discus (Institute for Scientific Information, Philadelphia), is now available in many university libraries. Excellent published versions of computer-compiled sources are available in the PE Index (Ben Oak Publishing Co., Cape Girardeau, Mo.), Sport Bibliography (SIRC), and Physical Fitness/Sports Medicine (President's Council on Physical Fitness and Sports).

The explosion of journals, articles, and discussions on the World Wide Web (WWW) has made access to information on human movement faster and easier. Unfortunately, much of this information is available only with paid subscriptions. The important thing to remember about the WWW is that it usually provides fast access to information but not necessarily accurate information (knowledge or the truth). People have a variety of motivations for posting information on the WWW, so professionals need to weigh the quality of evidence presented and the motivation or purpose of the Web page. WWW readers must beware and look at the language and tone (citations and statistics) of the page for cues as to its potential accuracy. A good place to start a search might be the Human Kinetics home page (www.humankinetics.com). This site has more than 200 links to specific professional organizations, sports, and exercise sites.

QA Choices

Suppose you are a volunteer coach for your daughter's softball team. As you discuss the upcoming tryouts and draft with the other coaches, you wonder which aspects of hitting, catching, and throwing to look for in drafting the best team. What sources of information are most valid: your experience, other veteran coaches, or coaching literature?

Professionals in human movement must weigh the evidence based on their own experience, expert opinion, and research to establish the most valid background information for qualitative analysis. Scientific research should be given the greatest weight because of the control, greater objectivity, and validity of the observations. The most important issue is to think critically about professional practice and the various sources of information.

Terminology

One approach to studying and organizing knowledge of an activity is to compare the movements to those of similar activities. Although the terminology varies among authors and disciplines, many experts suggest that the study of human movement be based on classifications usually called *fundamental movement patterns* (Broer, 1960; Cooper and Glassow, 1963; Daniels, 1984; Philipp and Wilkerson, 1990; Wickstrom, 1983). We will use the terminology in figure 4.2 for this book.

Fundamental movement patterns are broad categories of movements for a general purpose. Examples are walking, running, throwing, kicking, jumping, catching, striking, or carrying. Fundamental movement patterns can be adapted for specific purposes or combined with other fundamental movement patterns to complete a specific task. Some experts break movements into even smaller categories. A motor skill is an adapted fundamental movement pattern for a specific activity or goal. Typically these are related to specific sports. Some skills related to throwing and kicking are football passing, baseball pitching, punting, and place kicking.

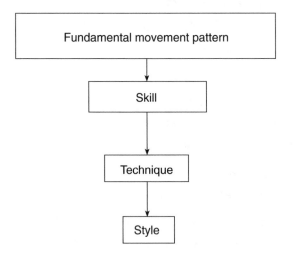

FIGURE 4.2 Hierarchy of terminology for describing human movement.
Reprinted from Knudson and Morrison 1997: 71.

Techniques are skills with even more specific purposes. The selection of appropriate technique varies with each situation. A banana shot (a kind of placekick), for example, is appropriate in soccer, while the hang- and hitch-kick techniques are appropriate in the skill of long jumping for maximum flight into the pit. Techniques are further divided into variations in style. Style aspects of movement are personal differences, idiosyncrasies, or actions related to a specific performer. At this level, qualitative analysis is extremely difficult because the analyst must decide whether minor variations in the movement detract from performance.

Whatever the level of analysis, critical features of the movement can be specified. An integrated qualitative analysis uses critical features as the standards for observing, analyzing, and improving movement. The term this book uses for short-term or long-term improvement in a motor skill is *performance*. In the subdiscipline of motor learning, performance often refers to short-term changes in motor skills; *learning* refers to long-term or permanent improvements (Shea, Shebilske, and Worchel, 1993). This distinction between short- and long-term changes in a motor skill is important. Motor learning research has shown that long-term improvement often results from practice conditions that challenge the performer, making practice execution (short-term results) look worse (Schmidt, 1991; Shea, Shebilske, and Worchel, 1993).

Critical Features

One of the most important areas of knowledge about an activity is establishment of its critical features. *Critical features* have been defined many ways. Arend and Higgins (1976) define the term as parts of a movement that can be least modified to be successful. They have also been defined as important aspects of performance that are related to the efficiency and effectiveness of the movement (Jones-Morton, 1990a). McPherson (1990) defined the term as statements describing specific body movements that are observable and that are then used to evaluate whether the key mechanical factors of the movement have been performed ideally. Critical features are sometimes called *critical elements* or *critical performance elements.*

We believe that critical features should be viewed as key features of a movement that are necessary for optimal performance. They are aspects of movement that are the most invariant across performers and are the least adaptable if the goal of the movement is to be achieved safely and efficiently. Critical features are the points defining good form that are used in teaching and should also be used to help determine the teacher's focus in the qualitative analysis of the skill. For example, the knee angle at deepest knee flexion (an indicator of the countermovement) in a standing vertical jump may be anywhere from 90 to 115 degrees because of range of motion, leverage, and muscle mechanical properties. Critical features for a conditioning exercise like the squat are knee angle, trunk lean, and neutral lumbar lordosis, and are strongly related to training effects on muscle and risk of injury.

In other words, critical features are the most important aspects of a movement; they need to be performed in a certain way in order to be successful. We will see that it is useful for the analyst to establish a range of correctness for the critical features and decide which are most important to performance. Integral to critical features is the idea of correct sequence. It does little good to have the correct critical features but the wrong sequence. (Imagine a softball batter starting the forward swing of the bat before the stride.) Chapter 5 will show how to organize an observational strategy to take advantage of the sequence or temporal organization of the critical features of the movement being analyzed. Understanding of critical features and their order is important, as one suggested format for intervention is based on where in the movement sequence the error occurs.

Although it is helpful to express critical features in behavioral terms that can easily be evaluated visually, this may not always be possible. Some critical features of human movement are constructs or other abstract ideas rather than clearly defined biomechanical parameters. A teacher/coach may believe strongly in these ideas and may be struggling to find cues or ways to affect this aspect of performance. A good example related to several sports, among them baseball batting and pole vaulting, is fear. There are many ways coaches try to evaluate the attitude and confidence of athletes where fear of injury has a dramatic impact (no pun intended) on performance.

Three issues can be used to justify the identification of critical features or desirable technique: safety or risk of injury to the performer, effectiveness in accomplishing the goal of the movement, and efficiency of goal attainment. Biomechanics is the primary sport science involved in identifying the quantitative underpinnings for the critical features of a movement. Biomechanical research provides kinematic (range of motion, body angles, length) information on elite and other performers. This kind of research can be of practical use because teachers/coaches may be able to observe some of these variables (Hudson, 1990 a and c).

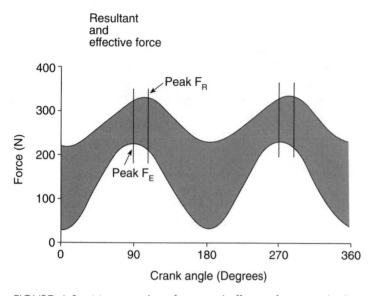

Resultant and effective force

FIGURE 4.3   Mean resultant force and effective force applied to the pedals of a bicycle. The shaded region shows the amount of force not effective in rotating the pedals.
Reprinted with permission from Lafortune and Cavanagh, 1983: 933.

Another branch of biomechanical research is kinetics, the study of how forces create the movement. Kinetic data determine which technique effectively applies force or provides smaller loads to tissues and may have a lower risk of injury. For example, biomechanical research on the effectiveness of force application in cycling has found that only about 76 percent of pedal forces are used in driving the bike (Lafortune and Cavanagh, 1983). Figure 4.3 illustrates the total force on the pedal and the effective (rotary) force on the pedal. The shaded region shows the forces that are not effective in creating rotation. The complex interaction of muscle mechanical properties and musculoskeletal geometry may preclude the body from applying forces in a mechanically optimal direction in many movements.

Safety Rationale

A professional must decide if a particular action or technique is safe. Does it have a low probability of acute or chronic injury? These safety decisions depend on many factors, such as the age of the performer, level of conditioning, injury status, previous activity, and rest. For example, how much follow-through in pitching is desirable to help prevent shoulder injury? How much knee flexion in landing from the vertical jump? Greater knee flexion clearly decreases the peak force from the ground on the body in landing, but as knee flexion increases, the shearing forces on the knee increase. So the amount of knee flexion needed to cushion landings could vary among individuals with knee injuries.

Effectiveness Rationale

Each human movement has an associated goal or outcome. The appropriateness of a person's form can be judged based on its effectiveness in achieving the movement goal. Principles of biomechanics can be used to evaluate whether a particular movement pattern or form is optimally effective in achieving a particular outcome. Does a particular body posture in a motor skill allow for desirable stability or the application of force in the direction of the target?

Many striking or throwing techniques employ weight shifts and linear motion that flatten the arc of the hand/implement toward the target, making the athlete more accurate. The linear momentum of the weight shift is transferred to the rotary motions (angular momentum) of the upper body. This weight shift is crucial for the effectiveness of these skills.

Efficiency Rationale

The appropriateness of a movement technique can also be evaluated on its efficiency, or the economical use of energy in achieving the goal. Some inefficiencies may be easy to spot. A large pause or hitch in a movement or the excessive up-and-down movement of a distance runner may be easily identified as wasted energy. Some small variations in technique may be exceedingly difficult to evaluate, however, particularly in terms of

KEY POINT 4.2 All human movements have critical features, the key factors that are necessary for optimal performance. Critical features are based on the safety, effectiveness, and efficiency of the movement. Their exact sequence or coordination is also very important.

which is more efficient. Biomechanists have had difficulty establishing how to document the mechanical energy used to create a movement (Cavanagh, 1990; Cavanagh and Kram, 1985).

Rationales in Action

Human movement is highly dependent on the environment or context, so the importance of safety, effectiveness, and efficiency can vary within and between techniques. For example, during preseason workouts, a cross-country coach noticed that an athlete appeared to have excessive rear foot pronation as he ran. Inspection of the athlete's shoes tended to confirm this diagnosis. The coach encouraged the athlete to change to shoes with more medial support and frequently change training routes to minimize the influence of a consistent slope of the terrain and streets he trained on.

The safety rationale, or reducing the risk of injury, was deemed most important in this case. The athlete may have felt that he was a better runner (more effective) with his old shoes, but the coach's knowledge of the rear foot motion and the deterioration of running shoes provided a powerful rationale for changing the athlete's equipment. Another safety example is changing one's walking gait in icy conditions. Even nonathletes shorten their stride lengths considerably to make up for the loss of horizontal friction forces.

Range of Correctness for Critical Features

Critical features in a skill should be defined as precisely as possible, bearing in mind that a range of correctness is needed to accommodate the variations inherent in people. Schleihauf (1983) suggested that the range of effective movement solutions varies with the nature of the movement. For example, the weight shifts are very different for a golf swing and a fencing lunge. Knowing the range of correctness of critical features makes evaluation and diagnostic decisions easier in qualitative analysis. Good examples are differences in stance and weight shift in throwing and striking. Weight shift is a critical feature in many skills because a weight shift followed by hip and trunk rotation is an efficient and effective way to generate speed in the upper extremity.

In baseball hitting, the emphasis is on bat accuracy because of the difficulty in hitting an unpredictable pitch. Baseball coaches should be aware that open, square, and closed stances may all be appropriate, but the step of the front foot should be a short distance (3 to 8 inches) toward the pitch. A forceful overarm throw, however, should have a square stance with a longer leg drive. The range of correctness that can be observed for qualitative analysis of high-speed throwing may be a forward step from half of standing height (Roberton and Halverson, 1984) to 90 percent of standing height, typical in baseball pitchers (Atwater, 1979; Hay, 1993). If research can establish desirable ranges of correctness that are observable, the reliability of qualitative analysis of the movement will improve.

There are two problems in defining the range of correctness: conflict between expert opinions and conflict between biomechanical theory and research. We have already mentioned how experts in a particular area (sport, conditioning, therapy) often have conflicting opinions on the best practice. The field of biomechanics has only recently begun to attempt to define optimal performance in a particular task for a given environment, so the field is ripe for different theories and interpretations of research data.

QA Demonstration 4.1

Observe the vertical jumps in the accompanying video clips. List the critical features for the whole jump from the initial movement to the end of the landing. Try to keep your list to less than seven features that you believe are supported by research and have pedagogical value in teaching jumping.

KEY POINT 4.3 Qualitative analysis will be easier and more reliable if the analyst can establish a range of correctness for the critical features and technique points of a movement. This is often not easy because desirable and optimal movement patterns have not been established.

There have been major limitations to the development of theories of optimal human movement. The complexity of the neuromuscular and musculoskeletal system, experimental technique, computing power, optimization theory, psychological factors, and theoretical research have all limited the answers to the question of what is good or optimal form. Biomechanists may disagree on what determines optimal form and how the musculoskeletal system is creating the movement.

Biomechanical research has shown that many optimization criteria (minimizing energy expenditure, muscle stress, or acceleration) can predict the overall patterns of EMG and movement kinematics exhibited by subjects. Indeed, some would argue that the inherent variability of the body's physical abilities and of the learning process makes it impossible to establish one ideal form for a particular movement (Brisson and Alain, 1996; Duck, 1986; Gentile, 1972; Hay and Reid, 1982; Norman, 1975; Spaeth, 1972). What might be possible with biomechanical research is the documentation of a range of desirable form suited to human and environmental constraints (Schleihauf, 1983). Skills with a closed environment will have a narrow range of correctness, while skills with an open environment will have a wider range of correctness (Higgins and Spaeth, 1972).

Most of the examples of critical features used so far have related to the movement of the body itself. We will see in chapter 7 that motor learning research calls this *knowledge of performance* (KP). It is important to understand, however, that critical features can also be related to the outcome of the movement, called *knowledge of results* (KR). For example, the initial trajectory of a typical basketball shot is between 49 and 55 degrees above the horizontal (Knudson, 1993). This angle of release is KR and may be a critical feature of shooting that coaches and teachers should plan to observe. These angles of release provide a range of correctness for the shot because they offer a good compromise between the angle of entry and the speed needed to reach the basket (Knudson, 1993). Many activities have distinct outcomes that may give an athlete an advantage and consequently should be evaluated in a qualitative analysis of the activity.

Critical features and their sequence can be complex ideas, subtle points, common knowledge, professional jargon, or precise values based on modeling or research. Whatever the source or type of critical feature, the analyst needs to gather teaching cues that correspond to it. Teaching cues translate critical features (usually expressed technically) into easily understood or highly descriptive language. For the analyst to communicate effectively with the performer, critical features should be expressed in behavioral terms. This process involves the collection and organization of a wide variety of cue words and phrases. The analyst now has a repertoire of cues to help communicate a point. This flexibility is important because people often interpret cues in different ways. Chapter 7 will review the important points in providing appropriate intervention to improve performance.

Information about motor development is an important prerequisite to qualitative analysis of skill. Teachers should know the relevant developmental sequence people usually progress through and the typical ages for key milestones. Motor development information is useful in knowing what to look for in early stages of motor learning (although many adults do not reach the mature level of many fundamental movement patterns). It also provides developmental information useful in teaching adults new skills. Motor develop-

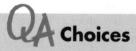 **Choices**

The psychological aspects of many sports are crucial, but these factors are often difficult for analysts to judge. If you were coaching beginning pole-vaulters, is it more important to attend to apparent confidence and other psychological cues or should you emphasize technique-oriented critical features? Revisit this question after reading the next section on knowledge of performers.

ment knowledge, along with information on common errors, tells the analyst some of what to look for in qualitative analysis.

Taxonomies and Common Errors

The physical education literature contains many books that provide basic skill information for teaching sport skills. Some books provide an overview of key skills for many sports; others provide detailed analysis of the skills of a particular sport (for example, Human Kinetics's *Steps to Success* activity series). In AAHPERD and the related district and state organizations, there are groups interested in basic instruction in physical activities.

Despite all this literature and interest, however, there is still a need for taxonomies of critical features of fundamental movement patterns and sport skills (Hoffman, 1974). We will see later that some books provide general technique points and cues for teaching motor skills, but often these are just recent versions of old instructional books. It would be most desirable to get experts together with scholars from many subdisciplines of physical education to create universal or official taxonomies of critical features for the skills and fundamental movement patterns of specific sports. These taxonomies should also include common errors and an exhaustive list of cue words or phrases.

Qualitative analysis of novices is bound to be more effective if analysts are knowledgeable about the most common errors of the skills they teach. Analysts can also provide a variety of feedback if they are familiar with several of the most effective cue words or phrases for each critical feature and the associated common errors. In analyzing softball batting, for example, it would be desirable for experts from teaching, coaching, and softball research to get together and identify the critical features of batting, the common errors, and the best teaching cues.

Knowledge of Performers

Extensive background knowledge about students, athletes, dancers, or clients is also needed to prepare for qualitative analysis. Performers come to an activity with a wide variety of abilities based on genetics, anthropometrics, age, gender, experience, training, and skill-related fitness components. The more knowledge the coach can gather about their mental and physical abilities, the better the coach can analyze and evaluate performance.

For example, knowledge about the upper-extremity strength limitations of young basketball players could be used to prescribe additional strength training, establish strength guidelines for initiating certain shooting techniques, or justify the purchase of different equipment. Research on the forces and risks of heading in soccer (figure 4.4) resulted in changes to the size and mass of the ball. The areas of motor development, anthropometrics, and kineanthropometrics all contribute valuable information on typical changes in the characteristics of humans in motion.

Knowledge about performers can serve as the basis for equipment and facility modifications that speed up the development of correct technique. Physical educators can select age-appropriate balls, while physical therapists with precise information on typical strength or flexibility of patients with

QA Demonstration 4.2

Watch the accompanying video clips and try to determine performer characteristics (strength, flexibility, motivation, development, and so on) that most strongly affect performance.

FIGURE 4.4 Physical limitations of performers and appropriate equipment are important sources of information in qualitative analysis. Reprinted from Knudson and Morrison 1997: 75.

a specific injury can select appropriate rehabilitative aids. Better knowledge of these functional capacities at various stages of rehabilitation can be used to improve diagnostic decisions in treatment. Potential sources of this information about clients include professional literature, clinic records, and communication with professional organizations or peers.

There are many good examples of dramatic changes in people as a result of normal development. The cognitive development of children in early primary grades does not typically allow them to grasp and use abstract strategic information. So in the first few years of school, a teacher should probably not try to provide feedback related to a complex team tactic that fulfills a strategic game plan. One of the most dramatic changes in a short period of time is puberty. Over the course of a few months, adolescents may find it harder to coordinate their new, longer and larger body segments. One adolescent may experience a minor improvement in strength, while another may have substantial increases in strength and stamina.

The science of motor development has begun to study components of movement (rate controllers) that influence the development and coordination of movements. Rate controllers may be the slowest-changing components in children, while aging adults may lose them more rapidly than other components of movement (Haywood and Getchell, 2001). Analysts must also adjust the kind of feedback they give and the practice they prescribe to each client's stage of motor development. Clearly analysts of movement must be knowledgeable about the physical characteristics of the people they work with, because physical status can dramatically affect the level of performance that can be achieved.

KEY POINT 4.4 Knowledge of the physical, cognitive, and emotional characteristics of performers is important in preparing for qualitative analysis.

Knowledge of Effective Instruction

All kinesiology professions involve some teaching of human movement. Teachers of motor skills need to be aware of pedagogical and motor learning research on appropriate and effective presentation of information. There is a natural connection between presenting movement information and giving similar information as feedback that will be effective intervention. To communicate effectively, the analyst and the performer must share a common vocabulary. To build this vocabulary and teach the

© Human Kinetics

In the preparation task of qualitative analysis, coaches must maintain up-to-date knowledge of the performers they coach. In youth sports, this means a good working knowledge of motor development and exercise physiology. Imagine you are the coach watching a child swinging a bat that is obviously too large and heavy for him. Is the child's swinging with a bent arm a problem of technique, immature level of performance, or strength?

The science of motor development describes the typical stages and changes in the development of motor skills. Arm-striking patterns tend to develop from an overarm to a sidearm pattern. Are you familiar with the three major stages of sidearm striking proposed by Wickstrom (1983)? Does the child's performance look like it was created by an arm-dominated action, a simultaneous body action, or a sequential strike? Motor development literature is extremely important to the understanding of the status of a person's movement, common actions, and typical changes with development.

When this knowledge of motor development is combined with an understanding of movement energy systems and training (exercise physiology), youth coaches have powerful tools to understand the physical limitations of children and how to overcome them. The cramped swing illustrated could occur because of poor technique in the readiness and preparatory phases of the movement. Is this performer old enough to have developed the visual perceptual skills (Nelson, 1991) needed to track a moving ball?

If the problem is strength, there are several intervention strategies that could be effective. The child could choke up on the bat, use a lighter bat, and work on increasing upper-body strength. Do you know about developmental changes in strength (Malina and Bouchard, 1991; Nelson, 1991; Roemmich and Rogol, 1995)? Did you know that prepubescent strength training results in strength gains related to neural factors rather than muscle hypertrophy (see Wilmore and Costill, 1999)? If you know the child is strong enough, how should you try to change the technique? Should intervention focus on achieving the next developmental level or should the child try to emulate adult form? The practical application of qualitative analysis is clearly an interdisciplinary process that must integrate many perspectives affecting a particular performer and performance. Consistent review of professional literature is essential to the preparation task of an integrated qualitative analysis.

movement skills, analysts must follow good instructional procedures. The two major factors in this teaching process are presenting appropriate information and presenting it effectively.

Presenting Appropriate Information

An essential task in presenting motor skill information for initial instruction and as feedback is translating the critical features into teaching cues. The teacher/coach must look for the most appropriate language to communicate the critical features. The performer's age, experience, and interest level may affect the choice of cue words or cue phrases to communicate skill information. Good qualitative analysts collect and update a variety of teaching cue words and phrases to get through to the performers they are helping. Because people make different inferences about words, it is helpful to be able to provide the same correction several different ways. A good cue phrase for the preparatory weight shift in golf is "shift your weight to your rear foot." "Straight" is a cue word a golfer could use to remember to keep his upper arm comfortably straight during the swing.

KEY POINT 4.5 There is an important connection between teaching motor skills and later analyzing qualitatively to improve performance. A common language base and understanding of the critical features of a movement make qualitative analysis easier and more effective.

Authoritative taxonomies of cue words for sport skills would be invaluable in physical education and coaching. Unfortunately, kinesiology scholars and experts have not come to an agreement on the important critical features and cures for these skills. Good sources for teaching cues include Dunham, Reeve, and Morrison (1989), Fronske (2001), Fronske and Dunn (1992), Kovar et al. (1992), Landin (1994), and Masser (1985, 1993).

Teaching cues are among the best forms of communication and feedback for performers. One key word, usually a verb (for example, "coil," "step," or "oppose"), can communicate the essence of a critical feature. These words can be derived from the execution phase of Dunham's model (1994), presented later in this chapter, if these phrases are written behaviorally. A cue phrase describes the critical feature in behavioral terms. A figurative or descriptive phrase ("arch your back as you block on the horse") is often better than a literal description of the action. Most diving coaches know that "wrap your arms" is a better cue phrase for a twisting dive than "decrease your transverse plane moment of inertia," even though the latter is more accurate. Another example is the figurative cue to "scratch your back" with the tennis racket when you serve. Skilled tennis players do not literally scratch their backs with the racket, but they do drop the racket head behind their backs to make it easier to rotate the racket. Remember that cues need to be relevant to the performer. Small children relate better to "reach into the cookie jar" than "follow through high" as a cue for the follow-through in a basketball shot.

Good cue phrases communicate the essence of a critical feature or technique point concisely so that the performer can remember them during practice. Try to keep these behavioral descriptions to less than six words, the limit of most people's short-term memory. Remember that you can attach more information to the cue later and add finer points or details to build on the essentials. It is ironic that children can often teach each other a game or movement and get into action much more quickly than many physical education teachers or coaches. Really good teaching/coaching introduces the critical features of a skill quickly and in terms the performers can understand and relate to.

Housner and Griffey (1994) suggest that learning cues can be categorized based on verbal, visual, and kinesthetic/tactile information. These categories can help instructors select the most appropriate information for the needs of a specific learner. Verbal information presented too metaphorically may confuse a young person but can be quite helpful to adults. Tactile information and visual demonstrations may help young children more than verbal skill instruction. Auditory information is important in qualitative analysis because, we believe, it can help the performer. Information on the rhythm of a movement may be an important addition to more traditional verbal or visual cues in helping students understand movement.

Using cues or simple word labels as substitutes for a more complex description of a movement is verbal pretraining (Christina and Corcos, 1988). The phrases "hit and step" in baseball and "right left" for a basketball lay-up carry a great deal of information. Verbal pretraining is important for conveying complex information about human movement. The use of cue words or phrases in instruction can be helpful in the qualitative analysis process.

Some authors have begun to address miscues, common teaching cues that are incorrect or can be easily misinterpreted (Adrian and House, 1987a, b). This is a tricky subject because sometimes cues that are incorrect still result in improvements or the correct movement. For example, one method of intervention is to exaggerate or overcorrect a problem area of performance, which often brings about the smaller, desirable change in the person's technique. It is clear that some cues, although less than the truth, have a history of success with performers. Two classic examples are "run on your toes" for sprinting and "throw by your ear" in throwing a baseball. More research is needed to determine how age, skill level, and aspects of cues interact to foster communication of movement information and aid learning of motor skills.

A variety of cues are also needed because of cognitive and perceptual style differences among performers of different ages. If a qualitative analysis of a novice in elementary school and an adult revealed the same problem, the cues that would best communicate to each learner would most likely be different. The small child with a short attention span would probably respond well to a figurative cue such as "open a window when you toss the ball." The adult might respond equally well to a literal cue if she could attach the desired meaning to it. Until more research is done to identify the most effective cues, professionals should strive to develop and refine cues and to share them with others.

One the best methods of writing cue phrases may be the method proposed by Morrison and Reeve (1993), based on Vickers's (1989) method of writing technical or qualitative objectives. The Morrison and Reeve approach uses the four parts of Vickers's behavior objectives: action, content, qualifications, and special conditions. The action is a verb that describes the desirable motion. The content is a short description of what is doing the action. Qualifications are a short description of how success can be gauged. And special conditions can be added to the teaching cues if more information is needed to evaluate the performance. This structure is illustrated in line 4 of figure 4.5: "Swing" indicates the action, "arm" indicates the content, "forward" qualifies the action, and "level to ground" is a special condition defining the movement.

Relevant cues for movements can be created for each phase of a movement (preparation, execution, and follow-through), with variations for performers of different ages and levels of expertise (Vickers, 1989). This identification of special cues for various ability levels has also been emphasized by Strand (1988) and Abendroth-Smith, Kras, and Strand (1996). Future research should help professionals develop a variety of effective and developmentally appropriate cues.

Turn side to target
Step on opposite foot/transfer weight
Rotate hips and trunk
Swing arm forward level to ground
Snap wrist
Follow through to target

FIGURE 4.5 Six behavioral teaching cues for overarm throwing based on the Morrison and Reeve (1993) method.
Reprinted with permission from Morrison and Reeve, 1993: 133.

KEY POINT 4.6 Cue words and phrases are effective ways to present information to performers. Cues need to be concise, accurate, and appropriate to the age and ability level of the performer.

If cues are highly effective as teaching and intervention tools, how can cues be integrated into effective instruction? Qualitative analysis would improve if the analyst can plan instruction to support later qualitative analysis of clients. One relevant approach is the format for preparing teaching information in motor skills proposed by Dunham (1986, 1994). This format breaks movements into two phases, anatomical and motor, rather than the traditional three phases of preparation, execution, and follow-through. The anatomical phase occurs just as the skill performance starts. The motor phase describes the major actions and the follow-through.

Teaching cues used in the motor phase can be phrased behaviorally, as suggested by Morrison and Reeve (1993), to create a task sheet. Figure 4.6 shows such a task sheet for the overhand throw. Using task sheets for teaching physical education with examples from many activities has been published (Dunham, Reeve, and Morrison, 1989). The first word in the execution or motor phase can be used as the key cue word for feedback. These action words may also serve as cues or verbal pretraining for the performer (Christina and Corcos, 1988).

Task sheets tell performers exactly what to do for the execution of a movement. Additional details can be added to the teaching cues as they become necessary. As a part of their research, Pinheiro and Cai (1999) used a similar format that differs only slightly from the Dunham (1994) approach (figure 4.7). Task sheets like those in figure 4.7 can be posted on the gym wall to augment instruction and provide a structure for observation (chapter 5). Which kind of task sheet depends on the skill being analyzed and the observational strategy preference of the analyst.

The preparation of task sheets can be evaluated using a process proposed by Morrison and Reeve (1993). Figure 4.8 illustrates the components of effective movement instruction materials. The two most important content factors (behavioral cues and their sequence) are weighted the most. The score sheet has been separated from the explanation of each section because the score sheet needs to be short and concise. Once instructors have used the score sheet a few times, they will not need the explanation of scoring. In fact, instructors may modify the score sheet to suit their teaching situations. A task sheet effectively provides the basis for a teaching loop. It is first used to present information to students, then it is used as the basis for movement evaluation, finally it provides for feedback directly related to what was taught and evaluated. Thus, consistency between teaching, qualitative analysis, and the evaluation or grading of movement can be established in physical education (Pinheiro and Cai, 1999).

It is important to have clear teaching cues for instruction. Not only do they aid the learner in acquiring the skill, but they also serve as the criteria against which the teacher judges the skill and the performer interprets feedback. Any discrepancy between what the analyst teaches and the feedback can confuse the student. An example is the tennis instructor who taught his class the forehand but forgot to tell students to keep their

---

Overhand throw

Anatomical phase

Body orientation: Non-throwing side to target
Feet: Shoulder width apart
Knees: Slightly bent
Hips: Slightly bent
Trunk: Back straight
Shoulders: Non-throwing shoulder to target
Arms: Throwing arm extended back at shoulder height
Hands/fingers: Three middle fingers on top of ball
Head: Eyes on target

Motor phase

1. *Step and point* with foot closest to target
2. *Rotate* hips then trunk
3. *Elbow comes through first*, staying high
4. *Follow through*—bring throwing hand close to floor

FIGURE 4.6 Sample overarm throw task sheet for teaching the overarm throw.
Reprinted with permission from Morrison and Reeve, 1993: 133.

SOCCER

Observer's name: _____

Date: _____

Skills to be diagnosed: _____ **Throw in** _____ [specific skill]

Performer: _____

Illustration	Critical elements	Yes	No	Comment / Dx
Preparatory phase	1. Face the target. 2. Feet shoulder width apart or stride. 3. Feet **behind** the side-line. 4. Secure the ball **overhead** with both hands. 5. Fingers spread to form "**W**" on the ball.	_____ _____ _____ _____ _____	_____ _____ _____ _____ _____	
Execution phase	1. Bring ball behind the head. 2. Body **arched** backwards. 3. Body uncoils to release ball. 4. Ball released forward by both hands. 5. Release ball "**up in the sky.**" 6. Feet **in contact** with the ground.	_____ _____ _____ _____ _____ _____	_____ _____ _____ _____ _____ _____	
Follow through	1. Feet **still in contact** with the ground. 2. Arms extended forward. 3. Body **follows direction** of throw.	_____ _____ _____	_____ _____ _____	

FIGURE 4.7   Observational model proposed by Pinheiro.
Reprinted with permission of Victor Pinheiro, University of Akron.

FIGURE 4.8 Analytic scale developed by Morrison and Reeve to help instructors evaluate their skill instruction. Reprinted with permission from Morrison and Reeve, 1993: 133.

Analytic scale

Reader _____ Author _____

	Low		Middle		High
1. Content and sequence					
a. Keys/cues/critical features	2	4	6	8	10
b. Sequence	2	4	6	8	10

Total _____

	Low		Middle		High
2. Appropriately presented					
a. Concise description phrases	1	2	3	4	5
b. Accurate language	1	2	3	4	5
c. Consistency of terms	1	2	3	4	5
d. Extraneous information	1	2	3	4	5
e. Repetition	1	2	3	4	5

Total _____

Grand total _____

Scoring: Higher score means better content.

1. a. Keys/cues/critical features—Are the major parts of the skill all included? Are only the most important selected (5 to 6)?
   b. Sequence—Are the keys/cues/critical features presented in the correct order, beginning to end?
2. a. Concise—Is the information presented as briefly as possible?
   b. Accurate language—Does the word selection describe what happens?
   c. Consistency of terms—If technical/description terms are used (flexed/extended, abducted/adducted) are they used throughout the presentation?
   d. Extraneous information—Are thoughts and ideas included that do not really apply to skill?
   e. Repetition—Is information presented in ways that are unnecessary and redundant?

wrists stiff on contact. His first correction was to keep the wrist stiff. How was the class to know this critical feature was important if they were not taught it?

This poor preparation for instruction illustrates the connection between instruction and qualitative analysis. An explicit method of information preparation and presentation would have avoided or minimized the forehand problem and allowed for greater learning. Also, a method of checking information presentation could have caught the omission. If the skill or task sheet for the forehand had been prepared properly, the process of instruction and qualitative analysis would have proceeded more smoothly. How does an analyst take appropriate skill information and plan effective instruction? Although this text is not meant to explain teaching methods, since the actual presentation of skill information to performers relates to qualitative analysis, we will summarize it here.

Effective Presentation of Information

Once appropriate instructional information is identified, the analyst needs to present that information effectively. Pedagogical research has shown that highly effective teachers present information to students more efficiently than less-effective teachers (Siedentop, 1991; Werner and Rink, 1987). The starting point for effective presentations is the preparation of teaching materials. If the skills to be taught can be organized in a systematic way and presented consistently, students can learn under any of a variety of teaching styles (Mosston and Ashworth, 1986; Siedentop, 1991).

This organization of information about motor skills for instruction is important because poorly taught skills will not be learned and will require greater qualitative analysis. Intervention will also become more difficult. Research on information presentation shows that certain components of instruction are essential for effective teaching. Most good teachers provide good demonstrations, explicit verbal explanation, summary cues, direct student attention to important factors, and have a way to check for student understanding (Brown, 1995; Graham, 1988; Graham, Hussey, Taylor, and Werner, 1993; Harrison, 1999; Kwak, 1994; Masser, 1985, 1993).

Many pedagogy experts see the effective presentation of motor skill information and qualitative analysis as part of effective teaching or coaching. Graham (1988) tied the idea of good teaching presentation to the use of appropriate feedback and organization of the teaching environment. Kwak (1994) emphasized the importance of cognition in learning. Cognition is a cornerstone of understanding and using qualitative feedback. Masser (1985, 1993) provided evidence for the use of refining tasks in skill acquisition. This refining process relates instruction directly to suitable feedback. Reynolds (1992) describes monitoring, the process of following students carefully during class time so that feedback on performance can be tied directly to instruction. Finally, Harrison (1999), in a 10-year review of her research findings on teaching, supported these assertions on teaching for learning. She found that the more successful trials students had, the better they acquired a skill. She suggested that learning activities must be chosen carefully and that the learner must participate fully in the learning situation.

These results may seem obvious, but they explain why some teachers are more successful than others. Teachers and coaches can likely improve the effectiveness of qualitative analysis by planning for effective presentation of skill information and practice that set up effective qualitative analysis. All kinesiology professionals can improve their qualitative analysis of motor skills by studying pedagogical research on the effective presentation of motor skill information.

Preparing for Next Task

In preparing for qualitative analysis, the analyst should be aware that the next task is the observation of human movement. A key component of observation in qualitative analysis is the use of a systematic observational strategy (SOS), a plan to gather relevant information about a movement. Information from many subdisciplines of kinesiology affects the selection of the best SOS for a particular movement. In preparing for qualitative analysis, the analyst may begin to plan a systematic observational strategy. If the movement is fast and complicated, an analyst may practice the anticipated SOS to improve qualitative analysis on the job. This practice may help to create positive visual habits in the actual observation of live movement. Unfortunately, the question presented by Kretchmar, Sherman, and Mooney (1949)—namely, what are the best visual habits for observing human movement?—is still not answered. The next chapter provides a detailed review of important factors in the second task of qualitative analysis: observation.

Summary

The first of the four tasks of qualitative analysis is preparation. Kinesiology professionals preparing for qualitative analysis must weigh evidence from the many subdisciplines on the activity or movement, the performers, and effective instruction. Professionals must continuously update their knowledge in all of these areas. Analysts weigh interdisciplinary evidence from three major sources: experience, research, and expert opinion. Since qualitative analysis is often part of the larger process of teaching motor skills, analysts must keep their knowledge about appropriate and effective presentation of information up to date. They often prepare for the observation of human movement, the next task of qualitative analysis.

Discussion Questions

1. In preparing for qualitative analysis, what factors should you weigh in evaluating the importance of various sources of information on human movement?

2. What sources of knowledge should be emphasized by professional teachers/coaches in preparing for qualitative analysis?

3. What factors are most important in selecting the *critical features* of a movement?

4. What subdisciplines of kinesiology are most important in selecting *critical features* of movements?

5. What factors are most important in establishing the range of correctness for the *critical features* of a movement?

6. In a world of rapidly changing knowledge and technology, how important are specialized publications that bridge the gap or summarize the application potential of scholarly research?

7. How can professional organizations help their members integrate the many subdisciplines in preparing for qualitative analysis?

8. How can the integration of preparation with *effective pedagogy* (instructional strategies) make subsequent qualitative analysis more effective?

Observation:
Developing a Systematic
Observational Strategy

© Terry Wild Studio

A friend has asked you to videotape her tennis match in the finals of a regional tournament. What key strokes, player movements, and ball motions would be useful to a tennis player? Should both players be in the field of view? What vantage points would provide the best view of the action and what actions would be missed from those vantage points? These are some important questions to think about in planning to observe human movement. The videotape images, like the visual information that coaches collect in qualitative analysis, must be carefully selected to get as much important information as possible.

1. Explain how to compensate for perceptual limitations by planning a systematic observational strategy.
2. Identify the key elements of a systematic observational strategy.
3. Identify several effective systematic observational strategies.
4. Explain how all the senses can be integrated to improve observation.

"You can observe a lot just by watchin'." Yogi Berra

The observation of human movement is the second task of an integrated qualitative analysis. The quote from Yogi Berra implies that movement observation is an easy, natural task. We disagree. Not only is it untrue about visual observation but it also leaves out the other senses that can contribute to the task of qualitative analysis. Once analysts have organized prerequisite information in the preparation task of qualitative analysis, they use this information to create a systematic observational strategy (SOS), a plan to gather all the relevant information about a human movement. This chapter will review several proposals for observational strategies, identify key elements of an SOS, and discuss the integration of all the senses that contribute to the task of observation in qualitative analysis.

An SOS is necessary in qualitative analysis for many reasons. First, large amounts of information about the movement from many subdisciplines must be condensed into critical features that will be observed. Second, sensory and information processing limitations (discussed in chapter 3) must be considered. Third, the knowledge and expectations of the observer strongly influence what is observed. Edgar Dale (1984: 58) pointed out the importance of prerequisite knowledge in observation: "We can only see in a picture what our experience permits us to see." In other words, analysts must have a background that allows them to know what to look for. A good SOS will enable analysts to gather appropriate and unbiased multisensory information on a person's performance of a motor skill.

Demonstration 5.1

Select one of the movements in the video clips that is new to you. Observe the movement twice and make a list of the performer's good and bad techniques. Was it easy or difficult to determine the performer's skill with unguided visual observation? Why?

The goal of an SOS is to provide a platform to gather relevant information on the status of a person's movement performance. All kinds of information must be attended to and apprehended. Remember that observation includes all sensory information a teacher/coach can garner about human movement. In the past the predominant thinking has limited observation to identifying errors in performance based on some "good form" model envisioned by the teacher/coach. We believe that the task of observation should be broad enough to encompass many modes of sensory perception but limited to the collection of this multifaceted information. The observation task of qualitative analysis includes only collecting and interpreting information, not evaluating or diagnosing its quality.

We have chosen to separate the information gathering or perceptual task (observation) from the diagnostic task (evaluation and diagnosis in our model) to emphasize the two different processes. Radford (1989) reviewed the research on observation in kinesiology and concluded that observation and subsequent decision making must be conceptualized as separate. (This is the view expressed by the information-processing model used in this text.) Some scholars argue that these two tasks are related and can occur at the same time (Pinheiro and Simon, 1992). But we define *observation* as the process of gathering, organizing, and giving meaning to sensory information about human motor performances. Most information processing models consider this process separate even if they use direct mapping from the perceptual components to the decision areas.

A simple view of observation of human movement essentially involves two main decisions: *what* (focus) to observe and *how* (a plan to observe). The preparation task of qualitative analysis identified the critical features of the movement. It also provided format for observation. Later in this chapter the Gangstead and Beveridge (1984) and Dunham (1994) observational models will be used. These models are the same models presented in chapters 2 and 4. Use of models such as these may improve observation of human movement (Pinheiro and Cai, 1999). Critical features are the focus of the SOS, so observing them is crucial to gathering useful information. The next section summarizes key proposals from the kinesiology literature on how to observe human movement. The *how* of an SOS is more complicated than the *what* and may be different for different analysts.

We started this chapter with a quote from Yogi Berra. The following quote better illustrates that perception is a large part of the observation process and that it is subject to change depending on many factors. A change in our perception of an event can enhance or diminish our powers of observation.

> "Whilst part of what we perceive comes through our senses from the object before us, another part (and it may be the larger part) always comes out of our own mind."

> William James

Before we continue with our discussion of observation, it is important to reinforce the idea that observation relies strongly on the perceptual abilities of the observer. Perception is an active process and we bring a great deal of our own informational and organizational structure to the process. This is one reason why, in many cases, we see things differently than others. In figure 5.1 the Necker cube (Bradley and Petry, 1977) illustrates how we can perceive things differently.

In their research on this version of the Necker cube, Bradley and Petry (1977) reported several interesting findings on observation. Even though there are eight separate disks containing three intersecting lines, most people's minds form these lines into a cube. Further, most people report that the white lines can be seen between the dark disks. This holds true until the disks are understood as holes in a surface and the cube is behind the surface containing the holes. Another phenomenon of a person's perceptual set can also be demonstrated. To some observers, the cube projects down and to the left; while others see it projecting up and to the right. Some observers are able to reverse their initial perception, initially seeing the cube project down and to the left and then changing this perception to up and

KEY POINT 5.1 The second task of qualitative analysis is observation. In this task, analysts gather information from all the senses about a movement with a systematic observational strategy (SOS). There are several ways to organize an SOS for the qualitative analysis of human movement.

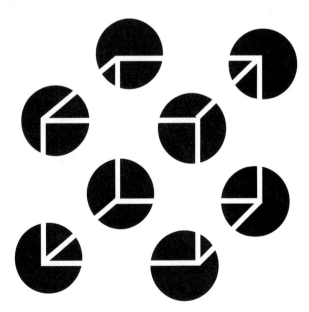

FIGURE 5.1 Necker cube illustrates individual perceptual sets related to subjective contours.
Reprinted with permission from D. R. Bradley and H. M. Petry, 1977: 254.

to the right. This demonstration alerts us to the fact that perception is an active process and can lead to a different interpretation of reality based on what the observer brings to the event.

Proposals for Observational Strategies

Several scholars have proposed guidelines for developing skill in observing human movement. They offer different approaches for an SOS. Observation is only one task within qualitative analysis, and several observational strategies are effective. Different plans of observation may even be needed to accommodate the perceptual differences among observers.

Barrett's System

Barrett (1977) identified three key tasks in the development of observational skill in physical education: analysis, planning, and positioning. She suggested that the lack of professional preparation for observational skill may be due to trends in education that emphasized the importance of reliability and outcome scores rather than process variables. Barrett (1979b) later published a review paper on the growing body of literature that addresses the task of observation within the qualitative analysis process.

Her ideas on how to apply this research in planning observations were nicely summarized by Barrett (1979a, c). According to Barrett, three components are needed in planning a observational strategy: deciding what to observe, planning how to observe it, and knowing what factors influence the ability to observe. In 1983 Barrett presented a model of observation and indicated that observation was a key skill in teaching motor skills. A subsequent paper based on her work suggested that the first task, deciding what performance variables to observe, is the most important in planning movement observation (Allison, 1985b).

Radford's System

A paper by Radford (1989) reviewed the literature on observation in kinesiology and proposed a theoretical framework for movement observation. Observation was seen as three independent subprocesses: attention, template formation, and motivation. Attention is the process of limiting sensory information and can be controlled from the top down or the bottom up. For example, viewing the overall action draws attention to extraneous movements (bottom-up processing), while top-down processing is a conscious decision to direct observation. Viewing the overall performance would develop a gestalt of the skill, while an observational model such as the one presented by Gangstead and Beveridge (1984) could be used for bottom-up processing. A gestalt is an overall feeling of the quality of a movement. The Dunham model (1994) employs a gestalt process. The Gangstead and Beveridge model (1984) is a temporal and spatial model designed to draw your attention to specific parts of a movement. These models are presented in this text to allow for exploration of two different approaches to movement observation: a specific part of a movement approach and a general feeling approach.

Template formation (analogous to deciding on critical features and their acceptable ranges) is the cognitive, abstract, symbolic representation of a model of human movement. Templates of human movement are multilayered, plastic (shapeable), and generalizable to many performers. A template is not an image of an ideal movement but a generalized paradigm that accommodates differences within a definable range. This idea is similar to range of correctness presented in the previous chapter. The last subprocess, motivation, is involved throughout the whole process because good observation requires persistence, effort, practice, and the subsequent elaboration of movement templates (Radford, 1989: 23).

James and Dufek System

James and Dufek (1993) proposed seven steps for the observation of movement. The focus of their paper is similar to qualitative analysis in this book. The steps in their observational strategy are to classify the skills to be analyzed, divide the movement into phases, observe several times in order to evaluate each phase critically, and focus attention on four major areas.

They deem the first step, classifying the fundamental movement pattern or the mechanical objective that is the focus of the skill, important to planning observation. Knowing the number and location of movement phases may assist in planning observations to see the important events in each phase. The last two steps are the guidelines for planning observation: focusing attention either on phases or on four different areas. The authors suggest that the plan for observation first focus on the total body (the rhythm or continuity of the whole body). Next, focus on the pelvis and trunk (the center of gravity) and the large muscles, which initiate most movements. The third focus is the base of support and how it changes, because it is often the source of balance and reaction forces that drive the movement. Fourth, focus on specific actions of the extremities. These movements are often fast and difficult to see, so the authors advocate focusing on joint actions rather than specific segments. This model starts with a gestalt and concludes with a system of observation (temporal and spatial) advocated by other authors (Beveridge and Gangstead, 1984, 1988; Gangstead, 1984; Gangstead and Beveridge, 1984).

Practical Applications: What's the Call?

The stolen-base leader in the conference is taking a big lead off first base. You are the field umpire of a two-person umpire crew. You crouch into position, anticipating the pitch and the runner's break to second base. Out of the stretch, the pitcher rockets a throw to the first baseman, who applies the tag as the runner dives back to the base. What's the call?

Your qualitative analysis of this situation strongly depends on your attention and your ability to get into the correct position and systematically observe the movement of the ball and the runner. Were you attending to the pitcher at the time of release? Were your body, head, and eyes positioned at a 90-degree angle to the path of the runner? How close were you to the action? Where did you focus your eyes during the flight of the ball and when the tag was applied? Did your observation focus on the determining factor in the judgment of whether the runner was out or safe? Did the defense have to qualitatively prove the runner out, or did the runner have to prove he was safe?

A baseball umpire's systematic observation is similar to observation within other qualitative analyses of human movement. Choosing what to focus attention on prepares the analyst for observation, but it may bias the observer to see some events and be less sensitive to others. How can analysts prepare to observe systematically to increase their accuracy, yet limit the effect of observer expectations in biasing information gathering for qualitative analysis?

KEY POINT 5.2 A good systematic observational strategy should include what critical features to focus attention on, how to control the situation, the vantage points of observation, the number of observations needed, and a decision on whether extended observation will be needed.

Key Elements in a Systematic Observational Strategy

Our review of the observation literature in kinesiology leads us to propose that there are five major areas that professionals should consider in developing an SOS. They should (1) plan to focus attention on critical features to aid in the analysis; (2) exercise as much control over the observational situation (teaching, coaching, therapy environments) as possible; (3) plan the angle of view, or vantage points, from which to view the performance; and (4) plan the number of observations they expect to need. Finally, (5) they may need to include plans for extended observation. The primary sense involved is often vision, although the other senses will also be used to gather information about the movement.

Focus of Observation

The first task of qualitative analysis outlined the critical features of the movement to be analyzed. These critical features and any other variables that may be related to the performer and the situation become focal points for the systematic observational strategy to follow. Barrett (1979c) calls this idea of planning the focuses of attention in observation a *scanning strategy*. A scanning strategy is a plan to define what to look for, when, and how long to look. Planning for a gestalt or observing with an observational model can achieve the goal of a scanning strategy.

Besides critical features, there are many variables an analyst may need to observe in qualitative analysis. Aspects of the movement that relate to the rules of the sport need to be observed. For example, a badminton coach will need to focus on the racket head in some serves because the shuttle must be contacted below the waist. Other observational variables to plan might be environmental factors that constrain the appropriate technique in open motor skills, deviations in movement rhythm, extraneous motions, and cues that fatigue or psychological stress is affecting the performer. For example, a beginning swimmer's fear may prevent proper execution of swimming skills.

With all these aspects of performance to observe, how does one organize the scanning strategy? The qualitative analysis literature has proposed four approaches. Observation can be organized to follow (1) the phases of the movement, (2) balance, (3) the most important features, and (4) the path from general impressions to specific actions.

QA Choices

You have two new students in class. You have never seen these students perform any of the skills you are teaching. You need to make a quick assessment of their abilities so that you can decide how to work with them. Which scanning strategy do you think would give you the most information in a quick observation?

Observation by Phases of Movement

The most common scanning strategy in qualitative analysis may be to observe critical features within the normal order or phases of the movement (Gangstead and Beveridge, 1984; James and Dufek, 1993; Philipp and Wilkerson, 1990; Pinheiro, 1994). This observational strategy decreases the perceptual overload by focusing attention on the three primary phases of most movements: preparation, execution, and follow-through. It is often not clear what phase should be observed first, however, although it is assumed that observation follows the sequence of the movement. This observational strategy may be most appropriate in open motor skills. Since open skills are highly dependent on the environment, a strategy to observe the environment and how preparatory actions match the environment is very important.

This observational strategy is exemplified in the work of Gangstead and Beveridge (Beveridge and Gangstead, 1984, 1988; Gangstead, 1984; Gangstead and Beveridge, 1984). The focus is primarily on knowledge of performance for various parts of the body during three phases of the movement (figure 5.2). The movement itself is of primary concern, although it is important to remember that knowledge of results can be relevant to improving performance too.

Body components	Temporal phasing		
	Preparation	Action	Follow through
Path of hub	Over base of support	Shift forward to target	Continue movement to target
Body weight	Over base of support	Shift forward to target	On front foot closest to target
Trunk action	Non-throwing side to target	Rotate open to target	Follow arm to target
Head action	Face target	Eyes on target	Eyes on target
Leg action	Apart, weight on back leg	Step to target with closest leg	Bring back leg up to front leg
Arm action	Throwing arm extended back	Bring throwing arm forward	Throwing arm across body
Impact/release		Snap wrist	

FIGURE 5.2 Observational model proposed by Gangstead and Beveridge with overarm throwing cues. An example of observation by phases of the movement.
Adapted with permission from Gangstead and Beveridge, 1984: 62.

If this observational strategy is used without a gestalt, then a body component of interest is observed through the temporal phases of the movement. For example, the path of the hub (belt buckle or slowest moving part of the body) is observed in the preparation, action, and follow-through phases. Any other body components are observed in a serial fashion. Descriptive phrases, like those about throwing illustrated in figure 5.2, can be inserted in the observational model to help guide the analyst.

If an analyst prefers a gestalt observational strategy, either of the Gangstead and Beveridge (1984) or the Dunham (1994) models can be easily adapted to focus on specific aspects of performance. Recall that in a gestalt the analyst observes for an overall impression of the movement. If the analyst suspects a problem in a particular part of the movement, the observational model will help the analyst focus on specific weakness in performance based on the technique factors on the task sheets. Use the technique points from the temporal and spatial model (Gangstead

QA Demonstration 5.2

Use the Gangstead and Beveridge (1984) overarm throwing observational model (figure 5.2) to observe the video clip. Observe the throws three times and focus on one temporal phase of the movement each time. Does the timing of the phases seem correct? Does the initiation of arm movement follow the beginning of the rotation of the hips and trunk? Does the throwing elbow get in front of the hand before it moves forward?

Demonstration 5.3

Use the Gangstead and Beveridge (1984) overarm throwing observational model (figure 5.2) to observe the video clip. Observe the throw several times and focus on specific body components (spatial). Which approach to organizing observation (temporal or spatial) was easier? What parts of the movement were difficult to see?

Dunham Model

Body Orientation:

Preparation:

Feet:

Knees:

Hips:

Trunk:

Shoulders:

Arms:

Hands:

Head:

Execution:

   1.

   2.

   3.

   4.

   5.

   6.

FIGURE 5.3 Task sheet for the qualitative analysis of the overarm throw using the Dunham (1994) model.

and Beveridge, 1984) of the overarm throw in a Dunham model (1994) to analyze the movements in the qualitative analysis demonstrations. Figure 5.3 is the gestalt (Dunham, 1994) model to be used in this analysis.

Observation of Balance

There is a saying in construction that you can't build a cathedral on the foundation of a house. The second way to organize an observational strategy is rooted in this philosophy. A scanning strategy can be based on the concept of balance and the origins of the movement. Many coaches like to focus on the base of support and the initial movements of the lower extremities for some skills because they believe that balance and the actions of the legs (or arms) strongly affect the actions of subsequent segments. Observing movement from the base of support and initial movements is especially appropriate for gymnastics and any other activity where balance and base of support can dramatically affect subsequent actions. Movement in many sports requiring great accuracy, like baseball pitching, is strongly affected by variations in balance. DeRenne and House (1987) deem balance one of the four most important aspects of baseball pitching.

Observation Based on Importance

The third type of observational strategy organization is based on a ranking of the importance of the critical features identified earlier. This approach is favored in research by Morrison (1994; Morrison and Harrison, 1985; Morrison and Reeve, 1986, 1988a, 1989, 1992). This approach evolved from an earlier study by Harrison (1973). Obviously, if an analyst believes that a particular critical feature is most important for safe movement, that feature should be observed first. The logic behind this observational strategy is similar to the origins of movement approach, because some critical features may influence other aspects of the movement. Examples of this approach can be seen in typical feedback from cross-country skiing coaches and ice hockey coaches. It is not uncommon for a skate-skiing coach to say to a performer, "You can only be on one ski at a time," meaning the weight must be squarely over the gliding ski and may be considered the most important factor to successful skate-skiing technique by many coaches. The hockey coach may say to a performer; "Sit down while skating," meaning the player must balance over the skate blades. Again, many coaches may consider this factor the most important for success in hockey skating.

Generally, the sequence aspect of this approach drives this system of observation. Professionals who have thoroughly researched a movement and reflected on their practice to identify critical features may have definite opinions on what aspects of the movement deserve the most attention. Biomechanical models of qualitative analysis tend to emphasize this approach by selecting variables for analysis that are related to the goal or primary mechanical purpose of the movement.

Observation From General to Specific

The fourth approach is to move from the general to the specific. It has been proposed by several authors (Brown, 1982; Hay and Reid, 1982; James and Dufek, 1993; McPherson, 1990). It is what Radford (1989) called *bottom-up attentional processing,* and chapter 3 referred to as a *gestalt observational model* (Dunham, 1986, 1994). This approach is also similar to the gestalt talked about in chapter 3, in which the analyst considers all the parts of a movement and develops an overall impression of the quality of the movement. The whole, complete skill is greater than the sum of its parts. If the analyst feels there is something wrong in the skill, he can pinpoint the deficiencies by looking at the phases of the movement or individual body parts, or a combination of phases and body parts.

Whatever the approach used to organize the observational strategy, some experts advocate written plans for observation. Examples may take the form of checklists (Adrian and Cooper, 1989; Bayless, 1981; Davis, 1980; Frederick, 1977; Hoffman, 1977b; McPherson, 1990; Pinheiro, 1994), diagrams (McPherson, 1990), task sheets (Dunham 1986, 1994; Klesius and Bowers, 1990; Morrison and Reeve, 1993; Reeve and Morrison, 1986), or rating scales (Hensley, 1983; Hensley, Morrow, and East, 1990; Rose, Heath, and Megale, 1990).

Demonstration 5.4

Use the Dunham (1994) task sheet (figure 5.3) to rank the most important technique points within all the phases of the overarm throw. Observe the throw focusing on the most important critical features in each phase. Does your judgment of the most important critical features predispose you to analyzing some technique points and missing others? Do you end up using similar results to the Gangstead and Beveridge (1984) observational strategy?

Choices

You are a physical education teacher who has to teach several different skills in several different units. One of your units involves fundamental gymnastics skills. Another contains fundamental volleyball skills. As part of your SOS, would you observe skills in each unit differently? If so, why?

Situation for Observation

The exact nature of the movement task and the environment in which the task is performed should be controlled as much as possible by the analyst. Yet the task performance must be as realistic as possible for the qualitative analysis to be most effective. The Balan and Davis (1993) model (chapters 2 and 7) could provide an answer to the problem of how to teach in a way that improves qualitative analysis while successfully structuring an environment that is friendly to both analysis and practice. Unfortunately, qualitative analyses are most often performed in situations where the lack of environmental control either minimizes or exaggerates relevant technique problems. The environment should be carefully planned so that modifying for speed, competition, distractions, or psychological pressure will elicit realistic performances.

For example, most qualitative analyses of tennis ground strokes should be conducted during normal play and practice rallies or with a ball machine that can project balls in an inconsistent fashion. A player's forehand or backhand strokes are often dramatically affected by the environment. At the advanced level of open motor skills, the athlete's movement and tactics may be of primary interest. Coaches need to plan situations for their observations of open skills that mimic the competitive environment—for example, a point guard dribbling the ball up the floor who must adjust his dribbling to the defense.

Since closed skills are performed in a relatively stable environment, they do not need adjustment as they proceed. But even they can be made more realistic with psychological pressure. An excellent situation for the qualitative analysis of free-throw shooting in basketball is a free-throw competition at the end of practice. The combination of fatigue and psychological pressure to perform (to win or avoid penalty) creates a situation in which the coach can evaluate good and bad habits that may affect the outcome of a game. Remember, the very fact that the instructor or coach is watching has an effect on performers. Some thrive on the attention and pressure; others perform worse. Analysts must take this factor into account when setting up observations and later when evaluating and diagnosing performance.

The speed and timing of movements for observation should be matched as closely as possible to the situation in which the movement occurs in competition or public performance. For example, a novice tennis player usually encounters slower ground strokes from opponents and should not consistently be observed in a time-stressed position of returning shots with great speed or spin. Early skill practice and systematic observation by instructors should take place in closed environments. Unfortunately, practice routines in sports are often organized for convenience rather than for effective qualitative analysis. For example, coaching or teaching a movement with players in a shuttle position (fielding a ground ball, throwing to first, and returning to the back of the line) does not allow the analyst to observe several trials. And multiple observations are essential to evaluation and diagnosis.

Once the play/movement situation is as realistic as possible, the analyst may have control over the background only from her vantage points (Brown, 1982). An effort should be made to set up the subject's movement to allow for a stable background.

Vantage Points for Observation

The analyst should specify the optimal positions for observation for a particular movement. A specific vantage point may be crucial to seeing the critical features identified for the qualitative analysis. In most cases, the best vantage point for observing a particular movement or critical feature is at right angles to the plane of motion. This often

FIGURE 5.4 Split-screen video images of the address position of a beginning golfer from two vantage points. Which aspects of performance are visible from only one vantage point?
Reprinted from Knudson and Morrison 1997: 90.

means that a movement needs several vantage points. Figure 5.4 illustrates split-screen video images of the address position of a beginning golfer. What different aspects of his technique are observable from the different vantage points?

Because most human movement involves important motions in all three cardinal planes, observation often requires several vantage points to obtain undistorted views of key actions. An example is the apparent excessive elbow flexion in preparing to throw a ball illustrated in figure 8.11 (frame d, p. 171). The knowledgeable analyst knows that this rear view can exaggerate the appearance of elbow flexion due to the extreme external rotation of the shoulder in this phase of the throw.

Brown (1982) suggested that vantage points should have stable backgrounds, without distractions or moving objects. A uniform background with a contrasting color relative to the subject would be ideal. Horizontal or vertical references in the background make the visual estimation of motion and angles easier. The practical matter of getting to and from desirable vantage points may also affect the fine tuning of what to observe in the SOS.

Demonstration 5.5

Observe the video clips and try to rate the vertical motion of the shoulders. Which background and vantage point facilitated the rating of this aspect of motion? Why?

The observer's distance from the movement is also an important factor in selecting vantage points for observation. It is clear from the research on vision (chapter 3) that this distance affects the angular motion of the analyst's eyes as they track the movement. Therefore, the distance from the movement should be as large as possible while still allowing for observation of important details. Sufficient distance provides a background on which to have the movement superimposed and reduces the tracking demand on the eyes.

How much distance should there be between the observer and the movement? There is no universal answer because the speed and complexity of human movement varies, the critical features of interest vary, and the environment may limit the selection of a viewing distance. The faster the movement, the greater the viewing distance should be to limit the demands on the observer's eyes. Hay and Reid (1982) advocated viewing distances of 10 to 15 meters for movements that have limited ground speed or take place in small areas and 20 to 40 meters for movements that are fast or cover a large distance.

But viewing distances beyond 10 meters are much larger than many physical therapists or physical educators can use. The lab or gym space may not allow these large distances. They would also require the observer to travel to the performer to provide feedback or intervention. We suggest that 5 to 10 meters is a good rule of thumb for the minimum distance for observation of most human movements. If the movement or event is very small and slow, the analyst may want to observe from closer vantage points in order to consistently see the action of interest. For example, a golf coach may not be getting enough information on ball spin from the flight of the ball and may choose to stand close to the golfer to examine the location of divots. This provides a clue about the path of the club and, consequently, the spin on the ball.

The evidence suggests that the best rule when using visual observation is to observe from as far away as pragmatically possible. If the distance is too great, however, it may limit the gathering of auditory, tactile, and kinesthetic information. Particularly when using the latter senses, the observer must be able to touch the performer.

Demonstration 5.6

How much elbow flexion do these runners have? Which distance and vantage point is most likely to result in a good estimate?

Peripheral vision should also be taken into account as part of the vantage point. If clothing (hats, visors, and so on), people, or objects limit peripheral vision, understanding of skill performance may be inhibited. Peripheral vision is important in the development of cognitive maps. This concept is explained in chapter 3. Peripheral vision may be seen as ambient vision (Schmidt and Wrisberg, 2000) and provides us with the *where* of movement (Shiffrar, 1994). The *where* of movement allows us to understand the relationship of different body parts to each other.

Number of Observations

The analyst needs to plan the number of observations that should be necessary to gather enough information for diagnosis and intervention. Clients need to repeat the movement because of the analyst's perceptual limitations and because the consistency of good or bad technique points is an important issue in diagnosis and intervention. Clark, Stamm, and Urquia (1979) found that the observation of six trials of a balancing task for children was sufficient to provide a reliable relative estimate of performance.

The problem is that many teaching, coaching, or clinical situations do not allow for large blocks of time for individual attention and observation of many trials. Unlike the elite level, where most coaching is one on one, typically most coaches must divide their attention among several athletes. Therefore, they must compromise between gathering enough information for a good evaluation and diagnosis of the performance and bowing to the time constraints of the situation.

There are few guidelines for planning the number of observations needed for a qualitative analysis. The exact number is probably best determined by the individual doing the analysis for a particular situation. It can also vary between observers, depending on the complexity of the skill and the ease of observation. Logan and McKinney (1970) recommended observing a minimum of eight trials, while Hay and Reid (1982) suggest 15 trials as a guideline. Based on qualitative analysis instruction studies by Morrison (Morrison and Harrison, 1985; Morrison and Reeve, 1989, 1992), some sport skills require only five repetitions for consistent qualitative analysis.

In Morrison's original videotape skill analysis test, the children performed each skill five times in sequence and then that sequence was repeated. The latter two studies cited did not use the second set of performances because those viewing the test analysis tapes (in intervening projects) felt they had decided the merits of the performances during the first sequence. Initial scores on the latter studies with similar subjects were in the same range as scores for the original study. Reliability studies (Mosher and Schutz, 1983; Painter, 1989; Ulrich, Ulrich, and Branta, 1988) also suggest that five observations are usually enough.

Clearly it is best if multiple trials are observed systematically before any intervention is decided. Based on this discussion and the reliability studies reviewed in chapter 9, a reasonable rule of thumb for the number of trials observed systematically in most qualitative analysis situations is between five and eight observations. Although some simple and slow body actions can be reliably observed in one trial, it is important to observe more because of the variability of performance. More observations also let the observer focus on information from all the senses. Unfortunately, sports officials and gymnastics judges must base their judgments on the observation of a single event.

Perceptual limitations and the variability of human performance suggest that multiple trials are needed in qualitative analysis. It is not appropriate to correct a performer after observing only one attempt (unless it is a situation or competition with only one observable performance). The consistency of a performer's strengths and weaknesses are key issues in the evaluation and diagnosis task of qualitative analysis (chapter 6). The number of trials observed may also vary according to the skill of the performer, the skill of the analyst, and other aspects of the situation. For example, novices to a motor skill often exhibit inconsistent performance and errors, so they should be observed more times than skilled performers.

Extended Observation

Extended observation is a plan for gathering more information on a movement than is usually observable. Good examples of extended observation are recording a performance on videotape, using multiple senses, and using multiple observers. Of course, observational power is greatly increased by using freeze-frame, frame-advance, and slow-motion replay features. A detailed discussion of using videotape to assist in qualitative analysis is presented in chapter 10. The use of other senses besides vision is also an example of extended observation. A coach or therapist may use the sounds created by a performer to gather information on the rhythm or identify a weak phase of a movement.

Demonstration 5.7

Observe one replay of the vertical jump and rate the amount of knee flexion at the bottom of the countermovement. Observe the video clip several more times and estimate deepest knee flexion again. Discuss how many observations you think were needed for you to get an accurate estimate or feel for the amount of knee flexion this subject uses. Compare your impressions to other students' as well as freeze-frame and slow-motion replay of the clip.

If a critical feature of interest in a qualitative analysis is difficult to see, extended observation is called for. For example, a gymnastics coach who thinks the athlete has adequate height on a stunt but still fails to rotate enough for consistently good landings may choose to spot several attempts. The sense of touch during spotting gives the coach a feel for the level of performance and what intervention should work best.

If videotape is not available and the senses are not enough, Hay and Reid (1982) suggest a visual trick that may help analysts get a look at fast movements. They suggest the eye-close technique, in which analysts close their eyes at the instant of an important event of the movement to fix a temporary image of it. This trick relies on the short-term sensory memory and/or short-term memory described by Pinheiro and Simon (1992). Short-term sensory memory allows you to hold a sound, vision, or haptic sensation in memory for a few seconds after the senses have been stimulated. Short-term memory allows you to remember a limited amount of information about an event for a slightly longer time. The idea can be transferred to other senses as long as no competing stimuli are allowed to compromise the most recently gathered information.

Integrated Use of All Senses

How can analysts extend their observational power by using all the relevant senses? Several authors have suggested that all the senses work together in the observation task of qualitative analysis (Hay and Reid, 1982; Hoffman, 1983; Radford, 1989). Hay and Reid stated that aural, tactile, and kinesthetic observation can supplement visual information. Chapter 3 summarized the research that supports this holistic view of observation.

Many sports generate distinct sounds that can be used to provide information on an outcome or the movement itself. The sounds of preparatory footwork in the tennis forehand or the rhythm of the final steps in the long jump, for example, supply valuable information about how the athlete performed the skill. The sound produced by the slice technique in tennis is quite different from that of the flat serve. These sounds of impact provide important cues on the amounts of spin and speed applied to the ball.

The sense of touch can also be used to increase observational power in qualitative analysis. Teachers who spot gymnastics, diving, or other skills can sense the athlete's ability to generate the forces and torques required. Teachers or coaches with good physical skills may compete with performers to simulate various styles of play. This provides a great deal of information on the strengths and weaknesses of an athlete. Smart coaches who use the sense of touch can quickly check the appropriateness of equipment or the strength of a performer.

Hay and Reid (1982) use *kinesthetic observation* to describe the assessment of a performer's sensation of movement. They suggest that good qualitative analysis is a cooperative effort between performer and analyst. As performers increase their skill level, they usually develop a greater kinesthetic sense and feel for their performance. Skilled athletes can often tell the coach exactly what position their body was in or what mistake they made in a particular trial. Wise coaches and teachers of skilled performers use the performers' observations to supplement their qualitative analysis. Baseball batters or tennis players may be asked whether they hit the "sweet spot" on particular trials. Players can assist the coach and learn to evaluate shots by the sound of the impact and vibration they feel. Good communication with performers is essential and may help motivate them to implement the corrections prescribed.

Summary

The second task of qualitative analysis is observation. Good observation of human movement is based on a systematic observational strategy (SOS) to gather information about the critical features of a movement. An SOS can be organized based on the phases or sequence of the movement, by balance or base of support, by the importance of critical features, or from a general impression to specific aspects of performance. The key elements of an SOS are to focus attention, control the situation, plan vantage points, plan the number of observations, and extend observational power if needed. Analysts can extend observational power by getting information from all their senses, using more observers, or recording the performances on videotape. The information gleaned from observation will be used in the next task of qualitative analysis, the evaluation and diagnosis of performance.

A review of important points in an SOS follows:

- Observation is based on knowledge of the activity, the performer, effective instruction, and a systematic observational strategy.

- Observation is based on a variety of sensory information and the interaction of all the senses, not just vision.

- Because attention is an important component of observation, attentional focus is necessary in an SOS.

- An SOS can be organized by the phases of the movement, by balance, by ranking of critical features, or from the general to the specific.

- Analysts should control the situation to optimize observation and the subject's performance.

- It is important to select appropriate vantage points, viewing distances, and numbers of observations.
- Coaches and teachers of skilled performers should integrate their observations with the performer's perceptions to supplement their qualitative analysis.
- Tools such as slow-motion video replay can extend observational power considerably.

Discussion Questions

1. What factors make the use of a *systematic observational strategy* necessary in qualitative analysis?

2. How do differences in analysts' psychological and cognitive styles affect the choice of observational strategy?

3. What kinds of motor skills are best suited for visual observation? Auditory observation? Tactile observation?

4. Does specific knowledge about the critical features of a movement and about a performer's physical limitations improve or bias the observation?

5. Do specific observational strategies bias an analyst toward certain critical features?

6. How much practice in using a specific observational strategy is needed to become proficient and consistent in identifying characteristics of movement?

7. Do different critical features require different observation strategies?

Evaluation and Diagnosis: Critical Thinking Within Qualitative Analysis

© Mary Langenfeld

This young person who has several obvious faults in their bowling technique asks for your help. After viewing a few performances, you tell them the four major flaws you detected. They have a bounding and inconsistent approach, an exaggerated backswing, and an inside-out downswing. They respond, "Yes, but what can I do to knock down more pins?" This young person has put your qualitative analysis of the situation to an important test. How do you know which fault is most strongly related to pin count? How will you select the intervention that will help this bowler the most? What is more important, short-term or long-term score improvement?

1. Explain why evaluation of performance errors is necessary for qualitative analysis.
2. Discuss the four major difficulties in evaluating strengths and weaknesses of performance.
3. Discuss six strategies for prioritizing weaknesses that serve as performance diagnosis.

After observing a performance, the analyst must identify desirable and undesirable aspects of that performance. A critical evaluation of these aspects and a diagnosis of the performance lead to a ranking of priority for the intervention the analyst will provide the performer. Evaluation and diagnosis are the two parts of the third task of an integrated qualitative analysis. This chapter will review the various rationales for prioritizing possible intervention in improving performance. Because of the many interrelated factors involved in human movement, the evaluation and diagnosis of performance may be the most difficult task in qualitative analysis.

The systematic observation of human movement results in a large amount of information about a person's performance. This information must be processed in the analyst's mind. Essential skills in this third task of qualitative analysis are the ability to evaluate the strengths and weaknesses of performance and to diagnose the implications for those strengths and weaknesses. Diagnosis identifies the weaknesses that directly limit performance so that they can be corrected in the intervention task of qualitative analysis. Not all "errors" or differences in movement technique are related to performance, and providing too much or incorrect intervention will have a negative effect on performance.

In evaluating and diagnosing performance, the analyst essentially becomes a human-movement detective or physician. The analytical tasks of deciding "whatdunit," what caused the problem, are difficult and may have far-reaching consequences because the intervention selected could do harm rather than good. An analyst who focuses the performer's attention on minor or symptomatic errors at the expense of more important problems may indirectly contribute to an injury. A coach who focuses practice on errors symptomatic of another problem is wasting valuable practice time. Evaluation of performance is the important first step in making sense out of the information gathered in the systematic observation of human movement.

Evaluation

The terms *evaluation* and *diagnosis* are used to emphasize the essential processes in the third task of qualitative analysis. *Evaluation* typically refers to a judgment of quality, to ascertaining the value or amount of something. This is important because the analyst often must establish the good points of the performance as well as the errors or weaknesses.

Much of the early literature on qualitative analysis has focused only on errors or faults in performance. Early in its development, qualitative analysis was often referred to as *error detection*. This is understandable, because the primary method of qualitative analysis involves comparing a model of good form to the observed performance, with the goal of identifying differences or errors. Some motor-development scholars argue that it makes little sense to judge performance as right or wrong; movement should be interpreted in reference to a continuum of development (Painter, 1989).

An integrated qualitative analysis is interested in more than identifying errors. The evaluation of a performance's strengths will affect the diagnosis of the weaknesses and how the analyst chooses intervention. A good evaluation should take into account the critical features of the movement that are within a desirable range, noting these as strengths of the performance. Those critical features not within that range are the weaknesses or errors. The Arend and Higgins (1976) model of qualitative analysis used the term *evaluation of performance*, noting that evaluation should focus on the efficiency of the movement and its appropriateness to the environment.

KEY POINT 6.1 The third task of an integrated qualitative analysis has two distinct processes: (1) evaluation of the strengths and weaknesses of performance and (2) diagnosis to select the most appropriate intervention to improve performance.

Process of Evaluation

It has often been assumed that professional experience and knowledge allow analysts to observe and evaluate human movement. There has been little research on the process of evaluation in qualitative analysis, and only a few authors have hypothesized as to what occurs in this process. It is likely that several cognitive methods are used to identify strengths and weaknesses of critical features. What is known about the accuracy of these methods was reviewed in the validity section of chapter 2.

The kinesiology literature about qualitative analysis suggests there are two distinct ways the evaluation of performance can occur. Hay and Reid (1988) call them the *sequential method* and the *mechanical method*. The sequential method involves comparing mental images of body positions throughout each phase of the movement. Most coaches use this mind's-eye image of the desirable actions and phases of a movement to compare with the actual performance. Figure 6.1 illustrates how this visual comparison might look in the evaluation of a volleyball bump or pass. This focusing on the difference between a model of good form and the actual movement has been hypothesized to be the primary method of evaluation in qualitative analysis (Arend and Higgins,

FIGURE 6.1 The evaluation of performance in qualitative analysis typically compares the observed performance with a mental image of desired performance. Evaluation is more than just identifying errors.
Reprinted from Knudson and Morrison 1997: 97.

113

ℚA Choices

Experts in a particular sport may find the sequential method of evaluation appealing for qualitative analysis of that sport. Should they try to improve their qualitative analysis of their sport by blending biomechanical principles into their evaluation (mechanical method) strategy? If new techniques develop in their sport, should they rely more on sequential or mechanical evaluation in the new variations in their sport?

1976; Hoffman, 1983; Pinheiro and Simon, 1992). This likely contributed to the overemphasis on error detection.

The mechanical method, illustrated in chapter 2 (figure 2.1), uses a model of the mechanical factors that affect performance. The evaluation task of qualitative analysis then becomes a process of deciding to what extent each mechanical variable was achieved. Qualitative analysis models based on this approach suggest that knowledge of a few biomechanical principles can be used to evaluate a variety of motor skills and that these principles are directly related to corrections that can improve performance (Hay and Reid, 1988; Hudson, 1995; Knudson, 2001; Norman, 1975). Examples of critical features using mechanical principles are the concepts of sequential coordination, inertia, optimal projection, and range of motion. Like different observational strategies, different approaches to evaluation can be effective in the qualitative analysis of human movement.

We propose that the process of evaluation within an integrated qualitative analysis can benefit from using either the sequential or the mechanical methods. The majority of observers are probably most comfortable using mental images of desirable form for critical features of the movements they analyze qualitatively. To keep the task manageable, evaluation of performance should be based on a few (about four to eight) critical features. So the quality of the critical features of the movement becomes the focus of the evaluation task. This evaluation is not viewed as dualistic; the performer's technique is not judged either correct or incorrect (error).

If a performer consistently exhibits technique outside the range of correctness for a critical feature, this must be evaluated as a weakness or performance error. These errors should eventually be corrected because of their negative effect on performance or risk of injury. This is why it is important to specify as completely as possible in the preparation task the range of correctness of all critical features of a movement to be evaluated. The range of correctness can be defined or quantified in the analyst's mind (for example, step with the left foot 3 to 7 inches), but correctness is usually expressed behaviorally to performers. A baseball coach may teach hitters to "step over a bat" to achieve the small, controlled weight shift that fosters the quick and accurate swing required in baseball.

The evaluation of critical features in an integrated qualitative analysis should result in an unbiased, accurate assessment of the critical features relevant to performance. There are two approaches to evaluation using the sequential or the mechanical method that have the potential to be accurate and reliable, rating performance on a three-point ordinal scale or a visual analog scale (figure 6.2). The ordinal scale uses three categories, rating critical features into one of three levels: inadequate, within the desirable range, or excessive. The major advantage of this approach is that the categories lead directly to diagnostic decision making and intervention. This approach increases reliability by decreasing the chance of disagreement due to artificial precision.

The second approach evaluates the quality of the movement with a more holistic impression using essentially a visual analog scale. Analysts attach some personal meaning to the ends of a continuum and use their intuitive feel for the quality of performance of a critical feature to place a mark/rating on the scale. If the ends of the scale represent too much or too little of the critical feature (the middle of the scale usually meaning

KEY POINT 6.2 Evaluation in qualitative analysis is concerned with identifying the strengths and weaknesses of performance. Effective approaches include rating critical features into one of three categories (inadequate, within the desirable range, or excessive) or the use of a visual analog scale.

Ordinal Scale:

Inadequate	Within the desirable range	Excessive

Visual-Analog Scale:

Too little ROM ———————————————— Too much ROM

FIGURE 6.2   Two approaches to evaluate the range of motion information gathered in an observation of a vertical jump. The vertical jump illustrated can be rated on the visual analog scale or an ordinal scale. A balance must be struck between accuracy and potential inconsistency.
Reprinted with permission from Knudson, 2000: 22.

good performance), the visual analog scale is much like the ordinal approach to evaluation.

Difficulties in Evaluation

There may also be deviations from prototypic form that are difficult to judge as in or out of the range of correctness of critical features or desirable form. The variety of environmental constraints and differences in performer anatomy and physiology may lead to differences in technique that cannot easily be identified as errors or bad technique. Some important difficulties in evaluating performance are variability, kinds of errors, differences between critical features and ideal form, and analyst bias.

Performance Variability

A major problem in establishing whether a critical feature is within the desirable range of correctness or is a weakness is the issue of performance consistency or variability.

This is why the systematic observational strategy should include at least five to eight observations. The analyst should evaluate an inadequate level of a critical feature differently if it occurs once or across several trials. Early in motor development, performers exhibit a wide variety of errors, and an error in one trial may not be significant. The more advanced the performer, the more consistent performance becomes. In advanced performers the strengths and weakness are often more subtle, but tend to be more consistent over repeated trials. Whatever the performer's level, use repeated observations to help you evaluate the critical features of a movement.

Unfortunately, movement consistency is not the only problem in the evaluation of performance. Other problems are finding agreement on the critical features, their range of correctness, and their order of importance to performance. Chapter 5 discussed some of the areas of disagreement on what is important to performance. This is a problem since there is no universal agreement about which features are critical for a movement, much less which critical features are more important than others. Analyst must use their own knowledge and experience to establish critical features and their range of correctness, and how to deal with movement consistency.

Kinds of Movement Errors

Even if evaluation were limited to error detection from an agreed set of critical features, it would still not be a simple task. Several authors have discussed how problems or errors in performance can have several sources. Hoffman (1983) proposed that errors could be related to critical abilities, skill, or psychosocial factors. A schematic of these classifications of errors is presented in figure 6.3. Note that even when errors are isolated as skill related, they may still have three different causes: technique, perception, or decision.

A similar approach was proposed by Philipp and Wilkerson (1990), who classified errors as biomechanical, physiological, perceptual, or psychological. Biomechanical errors relate to technique problems in body position or timing. Physiological errors are deficiencies in physical capacities such as strength, endurance, or flexibility. Perceptual errors are misunderstandings of technique or mistakes in evaluating environ-

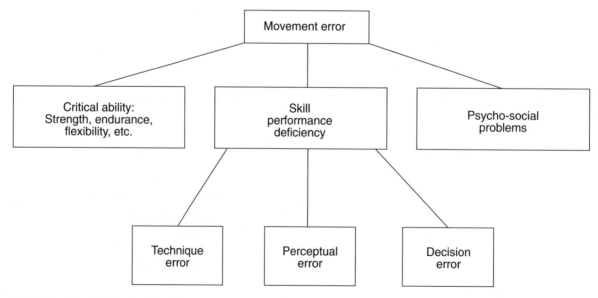

FIGURE 6.3 The kinds of performance errors that form the basis of Hoffman's diagnostic problem-solving approach to qualitative analysis (1983).
Reprinted from Knudson and Morrison 1997: 99.

mental cues. Psychological errors are motivational and attitude problems that interfere with performance. These error classifications are built into the Philipp and Wilkerson model of qualitative analysis and are linked to specific interventions to improve performance. The problem with this approach is that a performance problem may be caused by the interaction of several of these errors, and there is no diagnosis process to select the best intervention to improve performance.

These factors may arise from a particular deviation in prototypical performance, making evaluation and diagnosis of performance difficult. For example, an analyst would want to determine whether a volleyball player is missing passes to the setter because of bumping technique, fatigue, or perceptual problems in tracking the serve.

Critical Features Versus Ideal Form

The underlying assumption in the teaching of most motor skills is that the teacher knows what is the best or most appropriate movement response. The belief that a certain technique or form is best has been at the core of motor skills instruction for years. Brown (1982: 21) illustrates this belief: "While some performers may compensate for the lack of 'good form' through excessive practice, strength and speed of movement, improper form usually limits the ultimate level of performance." Most motor skill instructors would agree with this premise, but most have also had experiences similar to the disagreement illustrated in figure 4.1. There is a large difference between maintaining current knowledge to refine critical features and knowing what optimal form is for a specific person and situation.

If optimal form and the critical features for a movement are easy to establish, why have some skills undergone radical changes in technique independent of changes in equipment or rules? Why do many sports go through cyclic changes in predominant technique based on the best-known athlete or teacher at a given time? Why do experts in biomechanics disagree on the causes of particular movements? Why do some scholars argue (Gentile, 1972) that it is inappropriate to assume that the teacher can specify one ideal form that would help all learners succeed?

Clearly the evaluation of human movement is a difficult task complicated by a lack of consensus and knowledge about how humans move. For example, there are two highly effective techniques for the basketball free throw, the underhanded technique of Rick Barry (a professional basketball player who lead the league in free-throw percentage) and the traditional set shot technique used by Michael Jordan. Is there an ideal form for a free throw? Even if there was, the free throw is a closed motor skill, while shooting in game conditions is an open motor skill. Skills in closed environments are more likely to have a tighter range of correctness approaching the idea of ideal form. Skills in an open environment require greater flexibility to accomplish the goal and will have fewer restrictions on effective technique.

The critical features of any skill are dynamic and interact with a multitude of other factors that affect performance. This interaction of critical features, performer traits, movement environment, and other factors makes it difficult to establish one ideal form for a particular movement. Kinesiology professionals should make a concerted effort to summarize the body of literature by inviting scholars from many subdisciplines and practitioners to begin to develop

Demonstration 6.1

An important critical feature of overarm throwing is the amount of abduction of the shoulder. The upper arm should be held about 90 degrees to the spine (like an extension from the line of the shoulders) to maximize the effect of trunk rotation and protect some interior shoulder structures. Evaluate the video clips and determine if this critical feature is a strength or weakness. Use a visual analog scale or an ordinal scale to evaluate the performances. Is one method of evaluation better than another? Do you think one method would be better for different types of skills (open versus closed, discrete versus continuous)?

taxonomies and position papers on motor skills. Defining the critical features of motor skills and their range of correctness would make the evaluation of performance in qualitative analysis easier.

Analyst Bias

Whatever the approach to evaluation, an unconscious tendency or bias may creep into evaluation in qualitative analysis. The reliability study by Ulrich et al. (1988) discussed in chapter 2 found statistically significant interactions between observers and performers. The age of the performer tended to color the analysts' evaluations. Young performers' skill levels tended to be underrated, while older performers' levels tended to be overrated. Two studies on bias in gymnastics judging (Ste-Marie and Lee, 1991; Ste-Marie and Valiquette, 1996) found that prior knowledge of a performer could also influence current judgments of performance.

Other Considerations

Morrison (2000) suggested that there are some other factors we should take into consideration when trying to reduce the difficulties in evaluating movement. Along with some of the ideas earlier, he indicated that a systematic way of defining movement (possibly an observational model) was essential to aid in evaluation. He also indicated that we should be aware that we all see things differently due to different perceptual abilities, experiences, and perceptual illusions.

Remember that observational assessments of human movement have not been as reliable as quantitative analyses. Some scholars believe that the strong measurement and reliability emphasis of the physical education profession has hurt the development of qualitative analysis (Barrett, 1979b). The difficulty of achieving consistent, unbiased evaluation of human movement is not an argument against using qualitative analysis. Qualitative analysis can be reliable and unbiased when analysts plan and conduct their analyses carefully.

The more specific the range of correctness of a critical feature can be made, the less sensitive the observer will be to any unconscious tendency to rate a performer differently from the standards. Too much specificity, however, reduces reliability by decreasing the potential agreement among different analysts. A 10-point rating scale or visual analog scale may go beyond the analyst's ability to discriminate true levels of performance of some critical features.

Evaluating human movement within qualitative analysis involves judging the strengths and weaknesses of a person's performance. Critical features in a movement should be evaluated only after an adequate systematic observation has been performed to gather relevant information. A few (four to eight) critical features should be evaluated using a three-category ordinal scale (inadequate, within the desirable range, excessive) or a visual analog scale. These evaluation approaches are not complicated and, if there is a problem, point logically to the intervention appropriate for that critical feature. In the following section we will see that diagnosing the strengths and weaknesses is also a difficult process.

Diagnosis

Once the characteristics of performance have been evaluated, the analyst must diagnose the situation to establish what specific intervention is best for the performer. *Diagnosis* usually refers to critical scrutiny and judgment in differentiating a problem from its symptoms. The many subdisciplines of kinesiology have often used other terminology for these steps or included them within the process of observation. It is not surprising that several subdisciplines have slightly different names or definitions for this process.

What is surprising is that with well over 100 years of history in kinesiology in the United States, there is no consistent rationale for the diagnosis of movement errors. This is analogous to medical schools teaching anatomy, physiology, and the variability of these parameters but forgoing courses in the diagnosis of symptoms and the clinical rotations used to teach this skill. What would a patient think of a doctor who had no basis for diagnosing disease and prescribing a remedy? Doctor to nurse: "I'm not sure what's wrong with Mrs. Smith. She's the fifth patient today with a sore throat. Have her take a sample of medication X home. I'm not sure why or if it will work, but it's what my old doctor always used." (Insert "coach" to make this story more familiar.)

One problem that may account for the lack of a theoretical basis for diagnosing movement is the difficulty of establishing critical features discussed in chapter 4 and the previous section of this chapter. Another potential barrier to the development of a theoretical basis of diagnosis is the erroneous belief that qualitative analysis is easy and teachers/coaches will develop a talent for it with experience alone. Remember that in the early stages of motor learning/development, errors are often obvious deviations from good form. The difficulty is in the frequency and variability of these errors. Despite these controversies, one aspect of diagnosis appears to be agreed on. It should narrow the strengths and weaknesses in performance to focus the performer and analyst on the single most important intervention (Arend and Higgins, 1976; Hay and Reid, 1982; Hoffman, 1983; McPherson, 1990).

Prioritizing Intervention

Focusing on one intervention in qualitative analysis is important because the research in psychology and motor learning suggests that most learners can focus on only one correction at a time during practice (Christina and Corcos, 1988; Schmidt and Wrisberg, 2000). To prevent paralysis by analysis, the teacher/coach must prioritize intervention and select one solution as the best (Arend and Higgins, 1976; Hay and Reid, 1982; Hoffman, 1983; McPherson, 1990). Due to the lack of guidelines for the diagnosis of performance to select the best intervention, we believe, this is not an easy task. Diagnosis is also difficult because the cause of a particular problem may be far removed from its observable effect(s) (Hay, 1993; Luttgens and Wells, 1982).

The subdiscipline of kinesiology traditionally associated with diagnosis of motor skills is biomechanics. Hoffman (1974: 6) stated the following: "Diagnosis appears to rely on the observer's ability to use biomechanical concepts to accurately interpret the visual data at hand. The nature of the task suggests that a thorough understanding of principles in biomechanics, including the structural and functional relationships of joints and skeletal segments, is a prerequisite for diagnosis." Biomechanics is the science of how forces and torques move the human body.

The best diagnosis of performance should use knowledge integrated from many subdisciplines of human movement (Hoffman, 1983). Even if an optimal form could be established for a task, the analyst would still have to decide whether the performer was flexible and strong enough to use that form. If a performer is several developmental stages from desirable or mature form, is it wise to try to emulate this form if it is beyond his or her physical abilities? Biomechanics, motor development, exercise physiology, motor learning, pedagogy, and psychology all affect the answer to this question.

Does kinesiology research support any theories or guidelines for prioritizing movement errors into appropriate intervention? Do we know what is the best feedback or intervention to help a person move from, say, an immature level of throwing to a mature overarm throwing pattern? Unfortunately, the answer to both questions is no. There has been limited research to test which kinds of diagnostic decisions result in faster short-term and long-term improvement.

The kinesiology literature has only begun to stress that diagnosis is a critical task in qualitative analysis (Hoffman, 1974, 1983; Hay and Reid, 1982; Knudson, 2000; McPherson, 1990; Pinheiro and Simon, 1992). Pinheiro and Simon (1992) proposed a three-stage model of motor skill diagnosis based on their research on novice and expert analysts of the shot put and medical diagnosis literature. They found that expert analysts were better at the observation task of qualitative analysis, called *cue acquisition* in their diagnosis model. The second stage was the interpretation of cues, or making connections between the cues and the cognitive representation (schema) of the skill. This finding of meaning in the information observed is what we call the process of evaluation. The last stage of the model was considering the causes of the errors observed and making a decision. Pinheiro and Simon suggested that experts in qualitative analysis simultaneously use these three stages in their thinking when they analyze movement.

> **KEY POINT 6.3** Diagnosis within qualitative analysis involves a judgment that identifies the underlying causes of poor performance from the observed strengths and weaknesses. Diagnosis is used to set priorities for possible intervention.

Few qualitative analysis scholars have tried to hypothesize about how the diagnosis process occurs. The papers by Hoffman (1983) and Pinheiro and Simon (1992) are among the few that have addressed this problem. Most qualitative analysis models do not elaborate on how the diagnosis of performance occurs. Since there has been little systematic research to examine which approaches to prioritizing corrections results in faster and longer-term improvement, we can only review some logical approaches and discuss their merits based on research that has been focused on other kinesiology issues.

Rationales for Prioritizing Intervention

In prioritizing possible intervention, it is very important to keep in mind the goal or purpose of the movement being analyzed. Just as a physician's diagnosis is based on knowledge of many possible outcomes of a disease, diagnosis within qualitative analysis must be based on knowledge of the possible outcomes of intervention. The diagnosis of a person's overarm throw would differ depending on its purpose. The purposes of a throw from the outfield, from the catcher to second base, and from the pitcher to home plate are different. Clearly the analyst must understand the goal or purpose of the movement and the goals of the performer. This knowledge of goals and outcomes will shape the priorities of corrections.

A review of the kinesiology literature on diagnosis within qualitative analysis supports the view that prioritizing possible intervention or corrections is important. Christina and Corcos (1988) warn analysts against rushing to provide feedback if they are uncertain about the diagnosis, because inappropriate feedback may frustrate the performer and damage the analyst's credibility.

In reviewing the variety of qualitative analysis literature, we found six logical rationales that scholars have proposed for prioritizing intervention in the diagnosis of performance. These rationales may be summed up by the following phrases: relationship to previous actions, maximizing improvement, in order of difficulty, correct sequence, base of support, and critical features first.

Teachers or coaches may unconsciously be using one or more of these criteria when they select specific feedback or corrections over other possible interventions. Other coaches may just have strong opinions on what types of movement errors must be corrected first. No one rationale for prioritizing intervention should be considered the best, because research has not directly compared the various rationales and the best rationale may be specific to the person or the motor skill. For gymnastics skills that are strongly determined by balance, corrections should likely be prioritized from the base of support up. A coach's experience and reading may lead her to emphasize execution actions over preparatory or follow-through actions in a particular sport skill. The variety of successful approaches is like the different strategies for the systematic observation of movement, which can all be used to gather information about performance.

Relationship to Previous Actions

The first rationale for prioritizing intervention is to relate actions to previous actions in a movement (Hay and Reid, 1982, 1988). It may be possible to identify errors or weaknesses that are only symptoms because they are caused by another problem. This rationale is similar to Hoffman's (1983) idea of primary and secondary errors. Some deviations from the desirable form, or other style differences, may be less important or mere symptoms of more important problems. If a missed ball (secondary error) can be related to a previous action (primary error) like improper preparation, vision, or directed attention, it would be foolish to correct the swing mechanics that are merely symptomatic of the real problem.

Knowledge needed to relate an action to a previous action comes from biomechanical principles, research, and practical experience in qualitative analysis. For example, if the goal of an overarm throw is distance, it is important to know the critical features of throwing that relate to the ball's height, angle, and speed of release. These three factors (along with release considerations for a football) determine the distance of the throw. The throwing actions that relate to these parameters will help the analyst diagnose throwing performance. This is one of the strengths of qualitative analysis models based on the principles of biomechanics. The evaluation and diagnosis of performance are focused on key movement issues that lead directly to potential intervention (Norman, 1975).

Teachers, coaches, and athletes often have good hunches or opinions on what action relates to another. If the majority of coaches and professional athletes in a sport have the same opinion, it is most likely correct. It should not be assumed, however, that the opinions of athletes and coaches are always correct; there have been many instances where they have been wrong. Researchers have a difficult time relating actions to previous actions even in controlled biomechanical research and computer modeling. The two biggest problems in relating biomechanical actions to other biomechanical actions are the interaction of the segments and the effects of muscle actions at joints they do not even cross (Zajac and Gordon, 1989). These and other biomechanical research issues make it difficult to establish exactly what actions are related to what other actions.

Good examples of relating an action to an earlier action can be found in both open and closed motor skills. Suppose a gymnast overrotates in a vault and stumbles in landing. Biomechanics tells the coach that two things can result in too much rotation: conditions at take-off that determine angular momentum or the timing and changes of body position that manipulate the resistance to rotation (moment of inertia). If the analyst's evaluation of the take-off was good (trying to relate to a previous action), he may focus corrective efforts to the flight phase of the vault.

An open motor skill like baseball batting might have several factors related to an awkward action in the follow-through of the swing. The pitch may have been in a bad position, the batter may have been fooled by the pitch, or a loss of balance could have accounted for the poor follow-through.

Another example relevant to many overarm patterns involves sequential coordination. The powerful trunk rotation in an overarm pattern (throw, spike, tennis serve) results in the arm lagging behind because of its inertia. This humeral horizontal abduction and external rotation create an eccentric stretch of important muscles (pectoralis major, subscapularis) that contribute to the last 50 milliseconds of the movement. For performers to have advanced arm actions in overarm patterns, they must have good leg drive and trunk rotation. Cues to keep the arm back will not lead directly to the coordination and timing needed in elite-level overarm skills. Students interested in coordination in overarm patterns can examine the video clips from QA Practices 8.4 (page 175) and 8.5 (page 183) for overarm throwing and the tennis serve.

Attentional, psychological, or motivational factors may create performance errors. The awkward baseball swing could be related to nervousness or just a lack of attention and concentrated effort. An analyst may notice that one performer is rarely enthusiastic and is very attentive to other students' reactions to his performance. If this performer has confidence and self-esteem problems, the best diagnosis may be to emphasize success and praise. Future work with this performer could get him to focus more on the movement and less on the result. Relating actions to previous actions in the diagnosis of motor skills must be based on principles from all the subdisciplines of kinesiology.

The science of biomechanics studies how muscles and external forces create motion of the human body. Biomechanical research on throwing technique and exercise will provide information on which to base a diagnosis of the throwing problem of this baseball player. What muscle groups would you emphasize in weight training or conditioning exercises to help improve her throwing? Most professionals would likely emphasize the triceps. It might surprise you to learn that biomechanical research suggests that one of the most important joint actions is humerus internal rotation (Adrian and Cooper, 1995; Hong et al., 2001). The high angular velocities of elbow extension appear to be related to the coordination and interaction of the arm segments (Atwater, 1979). Roberts (1971) reported on a study by Dobbins that paralyzed the triceps with a radial nerve block. The subject could create about 82 percent of initial throwing velocity after several practice trials. Triceps do appear to contribute to throwing speed, but probably not to the extent that many coaches expect. Coaches should review recent research on testing and conditioning for overarm throwing (DeRenne et al., 1990,

Practical Applications: Deciding on Focus

One of your best infielders is having trouble creating speed on her overarm throw. Fast batters and long throws to first base will be problems unless you can improve the speed of release. This player has good technique on the major critical features of the overarm throw. This leads you to believe that improvement will be difficult and will require improved coordination or conditioning. (See chapter 8 for the critical features of the overarm throw.) How do you decide if conditioning or throwing technique should be the focus of intervention?

2001; Janda and Loubert, 1991; Jones, 1987; Lachowetz et al., 1998) to optimize performance and, more importantly, to minimize the risk of overuse injuries.

If you already have a good conditioning program, this athlete may improve if you prescribe appropriate practice to improve the sequential coordination of her throw. Unfortunately, biomechanical research is not conclusive on why sequential coordination is best in all kinds of throwing of light objects. Biomechanists have not even agreed on a way to define *coordination* using biomechanical variables. There are various approaches to documenting the kinetics or mechanical causes of movement. The biomechanical research on the kinetic chain/link principle, commonly seen in a proximal to distal sequential coordination of high-speed movements like throwing and striking, is not conclusive. It is not clear whether the slowing proximal segment speeds up the distal segment or the acceleration of the distal segment slows the proximal segment (Feltner, 1989; Hong et al., 2001; Phillips, Roberts, and Huang, 1983; Putnam, 1991). Currently biomechanics research is not in a position to provide a great deal of guidance for coaches trying to improve coordination in throwing and other sequentially coordinated skills.

QA Demonstration 6.2

Observe the video clips and use a gestalt observational strategy to get an overall feel for the movement and identify the most obvious movement weaknesses and strengths. Students not familiar with tennis may need to review the critical features of groundstrokes. Observe the performances again and check to see if any preceding actions contributed to the weakness you observed. Compare your results to another student's diagnosis.

Maximizing Improvement

Another rationale for prioritizing intervention is to select intervention that can be expected to maximize improvement (Hay and Reid, 1982, 1988). In 1988 Hay and Reid proposed that diagnosing performance is a two-step process of excluding faults that appear to be effects of other faults and prioritizing the faults that are left based on the improvement that can be expected in the time available. On the surface this seems like a logical approach to selecting corrections. The problem, however, is that it is not clear how to judge which correction leads to the most improvement and what time frame should be used.

Prioritizing to maximize improvement is probably a good approach, but it needs research to determine what factors are most significant in both short-term and long-term improvement. One technique change could create a lot of initial improvement but in the long run make it difficult to achieve advanced levels of performance. On the other hand, motor-learning research has shown that more randomly assigned practice conditions (high contextual interference) create lower initial performance but better long-term performance (Schmidt and Wrisberg, 2000).

In Order of Difficulty

Research in psychology, pedagogy, and motor learning has shown the importance of positive reinforcement and success in motivating practice and the learning of motor skills. These disciplines tend to recommend that the easiest corrections be made first if movement errors seem unrelated and cannot be ranked in importance (Christina and Corcos, 1988). The explanation is logical, since easy technique changes lead to the performer's perceived success, improvement, and greater motivation to continue practice. Selecting intervention in order of difficulty may produce small but consistent increases in skill. The question is, however, what

QA Demonstration 6.3

Observe the video clips and diagnose performance based on intervention to a weakness you believe would result in the most long-term improvement. Why would this intervention create the most improvement? Can you suggest another intervention that might work as well? Does the type of intervention depend more on the performer, the activity, or the skill level of the performer?

Demonstration 6.4

Observe the video clips and diagnose performance based on the intervention that would be the easiest for the performer to implement. Why do you think this is easiest for the performer? Does skill level affect the ease with which a performer can implement an intervention strategy?

is the best way to prioritize intervention to get the most improvement? A correction that is easy to communicate to a performer may not lead to improvement, especially if the action in question is related to another action. Like the rationale for prioritizing intervention, selecting intervention in order of difficulty for the performer is logical, but there is no clear research showing that it is most effective in improving performance.

Correct Sequence

Another rationale for prioritizing intervention is to correct in sequence, or provide intervention in the sequence of the actions in the motor skill. First correcting actions in the preparation phase of a movement may have effects on the execution and follow-through phases. This approach has been used by Morrison and Harrison (1985) in teaching qualitative analysis to classroom teachers with no background in kinesiology. This order of priority may also be implied by the many qualitative analysis models that break the movement into preparatory, execution, and follow-through phases.

There is little scientific evidence to support this domino theory of technique. It is logical that some skills could be highly sequential; actions in preparation might strongly influence later actions. The correct-in-sequence rationale may be a good approach for making tough decisions between two very similar corrections, or for analysts without a strong background in biomechanics and other subdisciplines. A volunteer youth sport coach or early childhood specialist at a day-care center might be able to help children improve a variety of motor skills by providing corrections in sequence. Fast sport skills in open environments are highly dependent on preparatory movements and might benefit from prioritizing intervention in sequence.

Base of Support

In many activities, coaches choose to provide intervention to improve performance from the base of support up. For activities requiring balance or the control of large forces generated by the strong muscles of the lower extremities, this approach may be logical. Often gymnasts must support their body weight with their upper extremities and very small bases of support. One of us knows a golf pro who bases teaching and qualitative analysis of the golf swing (a closed motor skill) from the stance/base of support up. This PGA professional, who has a master's degree in kinesiology, has come to the conclusion that most errors later in the golf swing are a result of actions in the setup and backswing. The golf swing requires great precision to strike the ball with the correct speed and path for a specific shot.

Demonstration 6.5

Observe the video clips and diagnose performance based on the intervention related to the base of support and performer balance. Do you think this is the best intervention in these performers? Why?

A target-shooting analogy illustrates the importance of stance and balance in accuracy sports. Tell performers to compare the accuracy and stability of an Olympic marksman to the accuracy they can expect with their current lower-extremity technique in an accuracy skill. As with the other approaches to diagnosis, research is needed to see whether balance or precision motor skills improve the most with intervention directed to the base of support and balance compared to other kinds of intervention.

Critical Features First

The last rationale for prioritizing intervention is to improve critical features first, before minor variations in performance. The kinesiology literature is full of professional articles offering opinions on the most important aspects of motor skills. This is not what we mean. By definition, critical features are the most important factors in determining the success of a movement. They are established by rigorous review of professional experience and research. If the right critical features have been established, correcting them before addressing other general points of good form or style should help the performer achieve the movement goal faster.

> **KEY POINT 6.4** There are six logical rationales for prioritizing corrections to select the best intervention: relating actions to previous actions, maximizing improvement, making the easiest corrections first (working in order of difficulty), correcting in sequence, moving upward from the base of support, and fixing critical features first.

The problem with this approach to diagnosis is that most movements have several critical features, and we have seen that it is difficult to establish which are the most important. An analyst may have strong convictions about several critical features but may have only educated guesses or beliefs regarding their relative importance.

Sport-specific research and experience can make a professional believe that the sequence of a skill is very important. That professional may then diagnose performance based on the sequence of the critical features of a movement. A therapist may prioritize intervention in gait analysis by relating actions to previous actions and maximizing improvement. The definition of maximum improvement may change as the goals of therapy change from safe or pain-free gait to a more cosmetically normal gait. The best diagnosis of performance may use information from all relevant subdisciplines of kinesiology to try to relate actions to previous actions in combination with another prioritization rationale relevant to that motor skill.

Further Practice

You can continue to practice evaluation and diagnosis of performance in any situation where you can observe movement. If you videotape a televised sporting event, the comments of color commentators can be good practice examples. Replay the movements they are referring to and evaluate the performance to see if your diagnosis results in similar judgments. Remember that television experts are usually former sport/activity stars who may or may not have extensive coaching experience and training in kinesiology.

Another way to use videotape replay to practice evaluation and diagnosis is to tape practice sessions or competitions of local sports. Does your evaluation and diagnosis of the performances point to the same interventions selected by the coach? This idea could also be extended to exercise movements in conditioning or rehabilitation settings.

Summary

The third task of qualitative analysis of human movement requires skill in two processes, the evaluation and the diagnosis of performance. This may be the most difficult task of an integrated qualitative analysis. The analyst must evaluate the strengths and weaknesses of the movement's critical features, which were identified in the observation task. The process of diagnosis involves prioritizing these strengths and weaknesses so that one intervention can be selected to improve performance. There are six rationales that may be used to prioritize intervention: relating actions to previous actions, maximizing improvement, making the easiest corrections first (working in order of difficulty), correcting in sequence, moving upward from the base of support, and fixing critical features first.

In the absence of kinesiology research to show what kind of intervention creates the most improvement in performance, it's up to the professional to decide what rationale or combination of rationales to use. One good way to diagnose performance is to combine the rationale of relating actions to previous actions and another rationale relevant to the movement being analyzed. Once a critical feature has been selected as most likely to improve performance, the analyst is ready for the fourth task of qualitative analysis, intervention.

Discussion Questions

1. How do the processes of *evaluation* and *diagnosis* differ?

2. What factors in the evaluation of performance affect *accuracy*, *reliability*, and potential *bias* of the qualitative analysis?

3. What subdisciplines of kinesiology contribute knowledge necessary for prioritizing strengths and weaknesses identified by the evaluation of performance?

4. What important research questions need to be answered to improve the diagnoses of performance in qualitative analysis?

5. Does accurate performance evaluation make diagnosis easier?

6. What rationale for prioritizing intervention do you think is the best approach to diagnosis in most qualitative analysis situations? Why?

7. If you were to combine several diagnostic rationales, which would you combine and why?

8. Should kinesiology establish standard critical features and their range of correctness for human movements?

Intervention: Strategies for Improving Performance

© Tom Putt/Sport The Library

This badminton player is having difficulty getting the desirable speed and downward trajectory of the smash. Your observation of several trials suggests that the player positions himself poorly, letting the shuttle get over or behind his head. Your feedback to the player is to stay back a little before hitting the shot. Because the player has been learning the smash with his body turned at a right angle to the net, your cue is misunderstood to mean that he should move back toward the sideline. Clearly feedback must be phrased carefully to be effective. What other intervention would help this player? Would general feedback to "hustle" be effective, or should a more specific cue relevant to this performer be used?

1. Identify the variety of intervention strategies used in qualitative analysis to improve performance.
2. Identify research-supported guidelines for the provision of augmented verbal feedback.
3. List the functions of feedback as intervention in qualitative analysis.
4. Describe how to develop appropriate cue words and phrases.
5. Identify situations where the intervention of exaggeration, modification of practice, manual or mechanical guidance, conditioning, or ecological intervention would be appropriate to improve performance.

Once a systematic observation has been conducted and the strengths and weaknesses of the movement have been evaluated and diagnosed, the last task of qualitative analysis is intervention. Intervention is the analyst's administration of feedback, corrections, or other changes in the environment to improve performance. This is a critical step in the qualitative analysis process where the instructor communicates with the learner about the desired change that will lead to improvement. Intervention requires the integrated use of knowledge from all kinesiology subdisciplines. Improper intervention can result in decreased performance.

In other models of qualitative analysis, the task of intervention has been given a variety of names. Some scholars call it *feedback* (Arend and Higgins, 1976), whereas biomechanists call it *remediation* (Knudson and Morrison, 1996; McPherson, 1990) or *instructions to performers* (Hay and Reid, 1988; McGinnis, 1999). The integrated model of qualitative analysis uses the more general term of *intervention* because it encompasses all possible actions a kinesiology professional can take. Intervention is not limited to the various forms of feedback, instruction, or remediation of previous qualitative analysis models. Instructors can choose to give verbal feedback—or they can choose not to intervene, positively reinforce good aspects of performance (technique or effort), use modeling, provide physical guidance, modify practice, prescribe training, and adjust competition or equipment. This chapter will discuss how to optimize the intervention to improve performance.

> **KEY POINT 7.1** The fourth task of qualitative analysis is intervention, which may involve providing feedback to performers, making technique corrections, or prescribing practice in order to improve performance.

Feedback

The predominant mode of intervention in teaching motor skills is verbal feedback from the teacher. Whenever a person executes a movement, information about the outcome is available immediately. This information is intrinsic feedback. The physical sensations of walking in deep sand, the kinesthetics of carrying a heavy object, and visual information on the path of a thrown ball are examples of intrinsic feedback.

The other major kind of feedback is extrinsic or augmented feedback. It comes from an external source after the movement has been completed. Augmented feedback is the primary mode of intervention in most qualitative analyses in kinesiology. Examples of augmented feedback are praise, corrective instructions, and specific information about the completed movement. This section will focus on how analysts can use feedback as intervention to improve performance. A great deal of research has been conducted on feedback in learning motor skills. Before we summarize the research, providing principles for using feedback as intervention, the next two sections will review the various classifications of feedback and the functions it serves in learning movements.

Functions of Feedback

Movement feedback has three major functions in helping people improve their performance: information, reinforcement, and motivation (Schmidt and Wrisberg, 2000). Each function of feedback can be used as a target of intervention in the qualitative analysis process. Arguably the most important function of augmented feedback is guidance, or information about how to perform the next practice trial.

Information

The information function of feedback is essentially instructing performers how to correct movement errors. Performers use the information function to plan the next movement response in the process of practicing and learning the movement. A therapist who wants to improve the safety of a patient's gait with a cane can use feedback to teach the patient how to position the cane relative to the injured leg.

The primary power of good augmented feedback is the guidance it gives in shaping future responses. Motor learning scholar Charles Shea illustrates this idea by describing feedback as cognitive training wheels for performers. Skill feedback provides the most appropriate mental images that help the person shape the next response, similar to bicycle training wheels set to an appropriate height. For example, a dance instructor might ask a dancer to keep his trunk more upright or vertical during a particular move.

> **KEY POINT 7.2** Feedback used as intervention in qualitative analysis has three major functions: information, reinforcement, or motivation. These functions of feedback help the performer improve.

A classic example of failure to use the information function of feedback occurs when a coach provides poor feedback, often in frustration as a performer repeats the same error over and over. Teachers or coaches may get caught in a correction complex that is sometimes manifested by a stream of don'ts: "Johnny, don't step in the bucket, son." "You did it again; don't lift your head!" Feedback with a don't message does not directly inform performers what they *should* do. It also communicates a negative and discouraging message. More effective intervention would be to provide feedback that helped the performer get an idea of what to do. For example, the teacher could say, "Johnny, remember to take a small step toward first base for outside pitches." Or, "Remember to step about the width of a bat, Johnny."

A common error of novice golfers is to lift their head during the swing, which often affects the trunk and the plane of the swing. It would be poor feedback to say to such a student, "Don't lift your head." A more creative coach might use the information function of feedback: "I would like you to really focus on the ball. Pick your head up and away from the ball only when I say 'lift!'" The student takes his practice swing, concentrating on "head down, eyes on the ball," and executes a nice shot. "Hey! You didn't say 'lift,'" he would say. His nice shot and the coach's silence would have made the point.

Reinforcement

The second function of feedback is reinforcement, which can be either positive to help encourage correct technique or negative to diminish the frequency of undesirable actions. Readers may remember Thorndike's law of effect (1927). When applied to

Choices

You are coaching a junior high school wrestling team and several boys have been causing trouble: wrestling dangerously in drills with boys in smaller weight classes. Safety is important, but so is an aggressive attitude in wrestling. Initially you use negative feedback and punishment, but how can you use positive feedback to reinforce safe but competitive wrestling?

learning motor skills, Thorndike's law would say that people tend to repeat responses that are rewarded and avoid responses that are punished. Feedback to a performer should begin with reinforcement of the strengths of performance identified during evaluation. This is why it is important for evaluation to identify both strengths and weaknesses. If good movement components cannot be found, reinforcement feedback cannot be given. A therapist might tell a patient, "Great job! I know that was hard, but those were your smoothest, most even steps so far." A strength coach might tell an athlete, "Nice job, Sheila! You kept your back straight through some very heavy squats."

It is sometimes appropriate to provide negative feedback. Behavior that is inappropriate or dangerous may warrant a swift, negative response from the instructor. But this type of feedback should be used sparingly and only in the right circumstances. Relying on negative feedback can result in an adversarial relationship with clients, which is neither productive nor pleasant. Psychologists also say that several positive reinforcements are needed to compensate for one negative reinforcement or criticism. Emphasizing positive reinforcement of appropriate behavior tends to decrease inappropriate behavior.

Motivation

The third function of feedback is similar to reinforcement, but it focuses on providing motivation to practice. Indeed, many psychologists argue that this type of feedback is of primary importance. Teachers and coaches should provide positive feedback that rewards consistent effort and tends to create a positive attitude and climate. For example, elementary physical educators should carefully provide positive feedback that reinforces an "I can do it" attitude in each child. Pedagogy research has shown that good teachers provide a great deal of praise and positive feedback (Siedentop, 1991).

One study showed that specific, corrective feedback in a volleyball unit increased the number of successful practice trials in a junior high school physical education unit (Pellett et al., 1994). Clearly a good intervention approach is to provide feedback that lets the performer know what to do next. This feedback should be expressed in a positive, encouraging manner. In coaching athletics or other high levels of performance, the coach is responsible for motivating the intense practice and training needed to prepare for competition.

The higher the skill level of the performer, the more important the motivation function of feedback becomes as intervention. The muscle memory that is the hallmark of skilled performance becomes a problem when an analyst tries to correct a weakness in performance. Intermediate and advanced performers often resist the intervention (Langley, 1993). They are often not motivated to make these difficult technique adjustments unless performance improves immediately, but performance usually suffers until the new motor pattern is learned.

Langley (1993) makes some useful suggestions for overcoming learners' resistance to intervention. Performance is improved in these performers by individual attention that focuses on the performance limitations of a technique problem and personal motivation to make changes. The next section summarizes the research on how to select feedback that is effective in improving performance.

Classifications of Feedback

The two major classifications of feedback used in motor learning research are important to understand so that the analyst may select appropriate feedback as intervention. Feedback can be classified as either knowledge of results (KR) or knowledge of performance (KP). KR is information about the outcome of the movement or the extent to which the goal of the movement was achieved. KR is easily observable in some activities, such as when a ball misses the basket or an arrow hits the bull's-eye. Other times KR may be unknown or less obvious to the performer. A sprinter may believe she won the race, but the photo and times generated will provide more precise KR.

KP is information about the movement process, the actual execution or movements of the body. For example, a basketball student shooting a free throw receives KP from a physical education teacher who comments on her good wrist action at release. KP feedback in softball hitting might be to "keep more weight on your back foot at the beginning of the swing."

In some human movements the outcome or goal is to move the body in a perfect or stylistic way. Judges at dance, diving, or gymnastics competitions have the difficult task of analyzing movement qualitatively. Coaches and teachers must realize that KP and KR are one and the same in these situations. The outcome of interest is the actual movement of the body. But usually these two classifications of feedback are different and provide unique information to performers when used as feedback during qualitative analysis. When providing augmented feedback as intervention in qualitative analysis, analysts should remember that KP is often more powerful in most situations.

Since the main function of feedback is to guide the learner in the next practice response, information on the actual movement and how it should be changed is often more valuable than the outcome or result of the movement. Several studies have examined motor learning when giving KP as feedback. A classic study that provided both KR and KP showed the power of KP feedback (Hatze, 1976). A 10-kilogram mass was attached to the foot of a subject, who attempted to minimize movement time in a leg-raising task. For the first 120 practice trials the subject received KR as movement time, producing the classic negatively accelerating learning curve (figure 7.1). With the effects of KR at a plateau, KP was provided as velocity curves of the optimal and subject's movement. A second learning curve occurred that approached optimal movement.

Studies have shown the superiority of KP over KR if KP is provided as a continuous graph of the performance (Howell, 1956; Newell, Sparrow, and Quinn, 1985; Newell et al., 1983). Biomechanical studies have shown how graphic presentation of KP can improve performance in cycling (Broker, Gregor, and Schmidt, 1989; Sanderson and Cavanagh, 1990). Research has shown that allowing the learner to control when the instructor provides KP results in greater learning than other fixed schedules of KP feedback (Janelle et al., 1995,

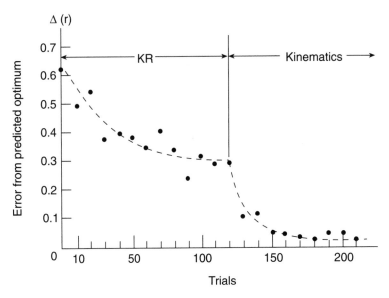

FIGURE 7.1 The guidance power of KP over KR in a kicking task. Reprinted with permission from Hatze, 1976: 10.

1997). But don't let all this evidence give you the impression that KP is always the most effective form of feedback; in many of these studies the goal of the movement can be easily defined in biomechanical terms.

In the real world of a clinic or gymnasium, much of this carefully controlled research is hard to apply. Gentile (1972) argues that too much emphasis can be placed on KP feedback in teaching motor skills. She proposes that KP is most appropriate when the movement itself is the goal of interest, as in a dive or a gymnastics routine. She also hypothesizes that undue emphasis on KP, when the goal of the movement is some other outcome, could interfere with motor learning.

Gentile emphasizes that kinesiology professionals may direct the learner's focus to form and teacher feedback, limiting attention on the outcome (KR) of the movement. In these more open environment movements, skill is essentially the ability to achieve the goal by reacting to changes in the environment. KR, therefore, is also an important and powerful feedback. Remember that critical features can be related to the movement itself (KP) or a different outcome (KR). The trajectory of a basketball shot and the break of a baseball pitch are crucial aspects of performance and provide important information to the performer.

Another promising line of research involves the combined use of KP and KR feedback (McCullagh and Caird, 1990; McCullagh and Little, 1990). Kinesiology professionals performing an integrated qualitative analysis should select the mode of feedback that matches the movement and environment. When the analyst is confident that a critical feature related to body motion needs improvement, the research suggests that KP feedback is more effective.

Principles for Providing Augmented Feedback

To summarize the kinesiology research on augmented feedback, we propose seven guidelines that will help the analyst shape the intervention chosen after the diagnosis phase. These feedback guidelines are based on the general consensus of the literature and are not meant to be a scholarly review of the subject. There are several good review articles dealing with movement feedback (Annett, 1993; Bilodeau, 1969; Lee, Keh, and Magill, 1993; Magill, 1993, 1994; Newell, 1976; Newell, Morris, and Skully, 1985). There are also good professional articles on providing feedback (Chen, 2001; Sharpe, 1993; Tobey, 1992). Tobey suggested that the three main issues are that feedback be specific, immediate, and positive.

These guidelines are not intended to define an optimal approach to feedback. They are presented here to allow you to consider factors you might include in your feedback. Kinesiology research has just begun to study what kinds of observational models (correct form, incorrect form, developing/learning form) given as feedback create the most learning (Martens, Burwitz, and Zuckerman, 1976; McCullagh and Caird, 1990; McCullagh, Stiehl, and Weiss, 1990). Other studies have tried to identify modeling and critical cues that improve performance best in children (Fronske, Abendroth-Smith, and Blakmore, 1995; Masser, 1993; Weiss, 1982). More such studies are needed. The best intervention for short-term versus long-term performance, for open or closed skills, and for the different stages of motor learning (Gentile, 1972) or motor development must also be determined. The best we can offer at this time are some guidelines that have consistent support within the kinesiology literature.

1. Don't give too much feedback.
2. Be specific.

3. Don't delay feedback.

4. Keep it positive.

5. Provide frequent feedback, especially for novices.

6. Use cue words or phrases.

7. Use a variety of approaches.

Limit Feedback

A common mistake made by many professionals, especially novices, is to provide too much feedback to performers. Even if they understand the feedback, performers are often overloaded with several corrections, making it impossible for them to plan future executions to practice the movement. Coaches with a correction complex often rifle off a stream of corrections and feedback. This creates information overload (figure 7.2) for the performer and leads to paralysis by analysis. Remember that this problem is the reason there is an evaluation and diagnosis step in qualitative analysis. Diagnosis of performance results in the selection of one intervention to help the performer improve (Arend and Higgins, 1976; Hay and Reid, 1982; Hoffman, 1983; McPherson, 1990). Any feedback selected should also be directed at only one aspect of performance.

Practice and game performance can suffer from the psychological pressure of keeping too many things in mind. Too much information can be worse than no information. This overanalysis and extra feedback can create greater problems during competition. Psychological research has shown that in sports competition the brain of a skilled right-handed performer has a highly active right hemisphere (visual, spatial functions) and the left hemisphere (analytical functions) is essentially turned off (Torrey, 1985). The phenomenon is similar for left-handed players. When an athlete is so confident, focused, and relaxed that peak performance is achieved, this is called playing *in the zone*. This experience may be accompanied by altered perception of effort, time, and pain. A coach who provides too much information, forcing the athlete to overanalyze what she is doing, may hinder performance.

Be Specific

For feedback to guide the performer's next practice trial, it should be as specific as possible. Specific feedback focuses on the exact element and how it needs to be changed

FIGURE 7.2 Too much augmented feedback as intervention can cause paralysis by analysis in performers. The subtle irony is that the important message of relaxation (essential in high-speed movements) is negated by the excessive corrections.
Reprinted from Knudson and Morrison 1997: 112.

(Christina and Corcos, 1988). The feedback should also be specific to the motor skill and at the student's level of understanding (Lee et al., 1993).

A good example of specific feedback is a coach helping a Little League hitter. Saying "step" to remind players to stride in the direction of the throw could be too vague. It would be more helpful for the athlete if the coach said, "Sally, remember to step toward the target at least 2 feet." Using the cue "step" could then be a reinforcement for continued batting practice. In teaching and analyzing weight training, "take a wider grip on the bar" is less useful than "line up your hands on the hash marks right here." Remember, if you prepare well for qualitative analysis and have developed task sheets and teaching cues, you already have a set of relevant cues for the movement. These cues are the action words in the execution phase of the movement description. One of the most important functions of cue words is building a common movement vocabulary between teacher and learner.

An excellent way to make feedback specific and motivational is to tailor the feedback to each individual. Many factors interact to determine what will be effective feedback for a particular person and situation. The performer's stress level, age, and personality are all factors in the choice of feedback. A good coach or therapist tailors (make it specific) the exact mode of feedback, cue used, and tone of voice to the individual. To do this, the professional needs a feel for the person's attitude, body language, and interaction with others.

Research in pedagogy has demonstrated that the pattern of instruction in physical education usually results in initial general feedback regarding a common error of many students (Siedentop, 1991). Later the teacher begins to provide more specific feedback focused on the individual. Unfortunately, the majority of feedback in physical education is general rather than specific (Siedentop, 1991). How can analysts create specific, individualized feedback as intervention?

Considerable research from psychology on personality and learning styles is helpful in individualizing feedback. In general, learners tend to be visual, auditory, or kinesthetic. Visual learners respond well to pictures or diagrams; thus, demonstrations or videotape replays are effective for them. Auditory learners tend to relate to and remember the words used by an instructor; cues are very helpful for them. Kinesthetic learners tend to use their bodies to help them learn. They could benefit from manual guidance or limited verbal feedback intended to focus their attention on a specific aspect of their movement during practice trials.

Perceptive analysts use their insights about their clients' learning styles to devise specific feedback for each individual. An analyst might choose to use a cue emphasizing proper technique with verbally oriented novices to help them get the basic coordination or motor program. For visual or kinesthetic learners, the analyst would supplement traditional verbal feedback with other kinds of intervention like manual guidance.

Give Immediate Feedback

Coaches' corrections or augmented feedback should be provided as soon as possible after the performance or trial because the feedback will be used to plan the next practice trial (Lee et al., 1993). Immediate feedback helps learners make connections between that feedback and their kinesthetic sense and proprioceptive information (intrinsic KP) from the trial. Remember that the analyst will be observing several trials, evaluating and diagnosing the movement before feedback is used as intervention. The kinesthetic sense, proprioceptive information, and muscle memory of the movement must be processed by the learner before an analyst provides augmented feedback (Chen,

2001). Part of the art of intervention is finding the minimal delay where the intrinsic feedback can be combined with intervention and not lost.

The performer must focus on how the movement felt and relate this feeling to a judgment of its correctness. This takes time to think about the feedback and its association with the person's intrinsic KP. If feedback is nearly immediate (within a few seconds), the performer has time to compare it with the experience. At least five seconds should also be allowed for the performer to process and integrate these two sources of information before further practice (Schmidt and Wrisberg, 2000).

Research suggests that feedback need not be instantaneous and that summary feedback or bandwidth feedback is effective in learning motor skills (Chen, 2001; Schmidt and Wrisberg, 2000). Analysts can provide effective feedback that summarizes the performance of a block of several trials, although the potential link of the feedback with the performer's perceptions will be weaker. In bandwidth feedback the instructor only provides KP when performance is outside the range of correctness. The mover gets implied reinforcement if the analyst provides no feedback after a performance. Many real-world settings are not like research settings, where one-to-one feedback can be given. Creating ideal feedback conditions may not be possible in most clinical and field situations.

Keeping feedback close to the actual performance is another reason the evaluation and diagnosis step of qualitative analysis is difficult. The analyst must not only evaluate and diagnose the performance effectively but also attempt to do it almost immediately. Certainly the validity of the judgment is most important, but it is also desirable to maximize the guidance function of the feedback by responding as quickly as possible.

Keep It Positive

To be most effective, augmented feedback should be worded to instruct the performer with a positive connotation (Christina and Corcos, 1988; Lee et al., 1993). Unfortunately, some teachers of motor skills have not followed this advice. Because motor skill teachers typically use visual models to identify errors in performance, their feedback may lapse into a series of don'ts. Selecting cues that are positive still tells the performer what to do, but without sending a negative message. Remember, a good qualitative analysis focuses on the qualities of a skill and not just on errors.

Research in typical physical education settings has shown that the majority of feedback is negative (Siedentop, 1991). Negative feedback is sometimes appropriate, but it should not be the primary mode of feedback. There is a big psychological difference between "let's work on this" and "you still haven't done this right!"

In short, feedback should convey the message that the analyst believes in the performer so that the performer is more likely to think, *I can do it*. When performers have problems with self-confidence and self-concept, positive feedback is very important. Feedback should encourage students and paint a positive picture of their potential (Ziegler, 1987).

James and Dufek (1993) suggest that intervention in qualitative analysis should refine strengths before correcting weaknesses in performance. Reinforcing or rewarding good performance characteristics helps athletes learn that part of the performance. It may also help motivate continued practice. This is a good intervention strategy to make sure the feedback has a positive tone. A coach should suggest, "Step with your left foot over the blue line" rather than "You stepped with the wrong foot, Chet!"

So far we have focused on the tone of verbal feedback, but nonverbal communication should also be positive. Gestures, facial expressions, and other body language can strongly communicate positive or negative messages to performers. Analysts need to choose their intervention carefully and make sure their nonverbal communication is consistent with their positive verbal feedback. Patients and athletes will begin to doubt your credibility when they read differences between what you say and what your body language says.

Provide Frequent Feedback, Especially for Novices

Early in motor learning it is important for the teacher to provide frequent feedback to guide the learner's subsequent practice trials. To help prevent confusion, provide some time for young learners to mentally process the feedback. In large classes teachers do not usually have a chance to provide too much feedback to any one student. Thus, pedagogy research suggests that feedback rates should be high enough that every individual receives some feedback. In situations where there is more one-on-one qualitative analysis, intervention should follow the motor learning principle of faded reinforcement. It is best to provide relevant feedback with every few trials initially, with decreasing feedback as practice proceeds or skill improves (Schmidt and Wrisberg, 2000).

As learners become more skilled, they need to rely more on their kinesthetic and proprioceptive intrinsic feedback than on the augmented feedback from the teacher. This is why analysts need to decrease the frequency of their feedback as performers become more skilled. In the advanced stages of motor skill, the kinesiology professional may question performers on what they feel were the good and bad points of their performances. Enlisting the athlete's help in the diagnosis can focus attention on the occasional correction.

Use Cue Words or Phrases

Kinesiology professionals have known for years that performers can remember and use information in practice better if it presented in concise cue words or phrases (Masser, 1993). Many books are available that provide cues for teaching the skills of specific sports. There are also articles that suggest cues for teaching motor skills (for example, Fronske, Wilson, and Dunn, 1992; Kovar et al., 1992; Parson, 1998). Fronske (2001) has compiled an excellent book of cues for teaching many sports. A particularly effective approach is to use metaphors to communicate the desirable technique (Gassner, 1999).

Good dance instructors are highly effective in their use of cues. Dance instructors must carefully time their cues to the music, use as few words as possible, and combine nonverbal cues to lead the group effectively (Shields, 1995). Simple cue words like *grapevine, box, cross*, and *plyo* can carry a great deal of information to a performer who has been taught these movements. A way to translate critical features into cue words or phrases was discussed in chapter 4.

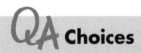

QA Choices

You are teaching beginning, intermediate, and advanced tennis classes at the local junior college. Would the cues, for the serve, be different in these classes? If so, which classes and how many of the cues? In which classes might students need more positive feedback with corrective cues to keep their confidence up?

KEY POINT 7.3 In general, verbal augmented feedback should be specific and expressed positively with cue word or phrases appropriate to the performer.

Use a Variety of Approaches

A dictionary may lead a foreign tourist to believe that words in the English language have multiple but stable meanings. Teachers who have written test questions or experimented with various cue words, however, know that words have a variety of meanings and that changes in those meanings may be quite dynamic. This is why kinesiology professionals should

Imagine you are a physical education teacher in a typical gym with 50 fifth-graders. Your basketball unit is under way and you have the class at eight stations practicing shooting and ball-handling skills. Research in sport pedagogy suggests that to be effective, the teacher should move randomly throughout the gym, actively supervising practice, providing positive feedback to motivate students, and qualitatively analyzing their performances. Motor learning research has shown that the many novice subjects in this class require frequent augmented feedback to improve. How are you going to work it all in?

Your attention is drawn to Hugo, who is having difficulty hitting the spot on the wall for the chest pass. Observation and evaluation and diagnosis suggest that his step is correct, but his arms do not appear to propel the ball with enough speed. How do you select appropriate intervention when you focus on one performer to qualitatively analyze shooting? Your mind flies. *Quick! Hugo's throw, shooting, and push-up score are above average. Hugo is a great little person who always tries his best. I bet he needs a little more pronation and coordination with the extending arm.* Your voice and smile turn on. "Nice pass,

Hugo! I bet you could pass like Jason Kidd if you used your hands more. Give me that upside-down five (hand slap) on this next pass. Great!"

Moving on to the next performer, in your gym voice you give another general prompt to hustle to the whole class: "Squad four looks great! Kim and Hugo almost knocked the targets off the wall!" Looking over to squad five, you think, *Bobby looks like he needs some praise. Let's see what looks good in his shot.* In 15 seconds you have weighed information from many subdisciplines of kinesiology. Pedagogy and psychology considerations made it important for you to praise the effort and good aspects of the children's performances. Knowledge of the children made diagnosis and intervention of their basketball skills more accurate. You were also sensitive to the body language of a child who might need a little attention and praise to feel good about his shooting ability. The intervention you used for Hugo included augmented verbal feedback about the forearm action of the pass. You linked the feedback to a previous cue (upside-down five) and used some manual guidance by putting your hand in the follow-through position for Hugo's next pass.

collect cue words or phrases for each critical feature of the motor skills they teach. They will then be able to provide several cues to communicate the essential idea of each critical feature they evaluate.

Professionals should also try to have a variety of modes to communicate these cues as feedback. Some performers respond best to a verbal cue, others to a visual one, and still others to a kinesthetic one. Cues for the last step in a basketball lay-up might be verbal ("long step and jump"), visual (footprints on the floor), or kinesthetic ("Make it feel like stepping over a beach ball.").

Analysts need to use age-appropriate cues when teaching small children and cues using current slang when teaching in elementary and secondary schools. Most veteran physical educators or coaches will have had an experience similar to that of Jeanne Jones, who was teaching a basketball unit to junior high students. A particular student was having trouble shooting along the appropriate trajectory. Jones had worked with this student over several class periods, providing cues such as "shoot with a high arch" and "shoot upward" to help correct the angle of release. Finally she found a cue that clicked with the student: "Shoot up through the top of a phone booth." When the student began shooting better, he said, "Why didn't you tell me this before?!" Jones smiled, even though she wanted to say, "I've been telling you for the past week!" Jones knew that she needed a variety of cues to communicate with the culturally diverse students she taught.

To determine if different feedback is needed, question students or clients on what feedback was given. A dance teacher could ask, "John, what were we working on with your waltz last time?" If the student is not making the changes you want, repeat or rephrase your feedback. Questioning is a good technique when you can't tell whether the performer understands what you want her to work on specifically (Christina and Corcos, 1988).

Kinesiology research has shown that feedback is an effective intervention in the qualitative analysis of human movement. Feedback should be as specific as possible, given as a cue about a single aspect of performance, and phrased in positive terms. Feedback is most effective when it is provided as KP with minimal delay. Analysts must be careful to focus feedback on the movement itself (KP) or the outcome of the movement (KR). They should also decrease the frequency of feedback with increasing skill level and be prepared to provide feedback in a variety of ways.

There are some tricks of the trade beyond traditional augmented verbal feedback for providing intervention to improve motor skills. They include teaching suggestions already used by many good teachers.

- Using visual models
- Exaggeration or overcompensation
- Task modification
- Manual or mechanical guidance
- Conditioning
- Attentional cueing
- Ecological intervention

While some of these could be viewed as some kind of feedback (i.e., manual or mechanical guidance, attention cueing), others are clearly not classic verbal feedback. Unfortunately, a narrow view of intervention (traditional feedback) can limit the effectiveness of some professionals' qualitative analyses. These forms of intervention, which typically do not qualify as traditional feedback, have not been studied from an interdisciplinary perspective to determine which are the most effective. The following sections describe some of these methods; analysts must make their own decisions about which methods are most appropriate.

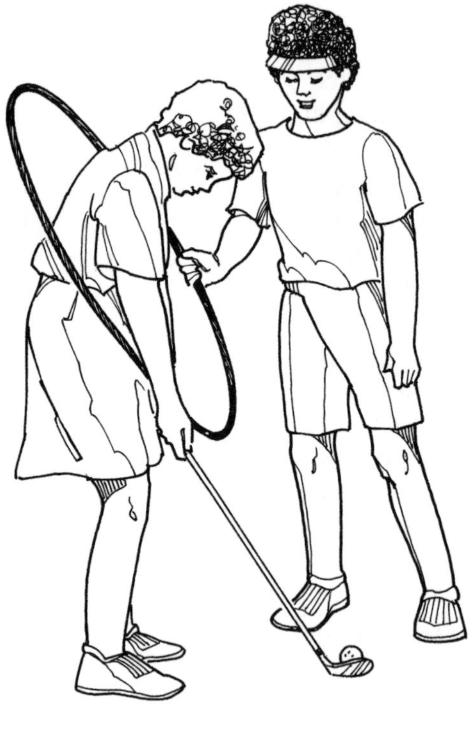

Visual Models

There are several ways to provide visual feedback on the status of performance or a desirable correction to a performer. Demonstrations by the instructor may be effective because most people have a visual learning style. Years of motor learning research have shown that modeling observational learning is the most effective way to convey information to people who are learning a new pattern of coordination or are establishing coordination in the early stages of learning a skill (McCullagh and Caird, 1990; Messier and Cirillo, 1989; Wood et al., 1992). In observational learning the analyst provides visual information like a picture or demonstration to a learner.

Posters of key body positions in exercise are highly effective in the weight room. The walls of elementary school gyms could have key cues and corresponding pictures for teachers to use as intervention. Such visual aids are excellent for improving the atmosphere of the

FIGURE 7.3 An instructor can use the visual image of a hoop to illustrate the desirable swing plane of the golf swing. Reprinted from Knudson and Morrison 1997: 116.

gym and decreasing the stress on a teacher's body caused by demonstrations in many classes every day of the week. Figure 7.3 illustrates how a golf instructor can use a hoop to create a visual image of the swing plane of the golf swing.

Several scholarly reviews of modeling or observational learning research can assist the qualitative analyst in using this form of intervention (Gould and Roberts, 1982; McCullagh, Weiss, and Ross, 1989). Wiese-Bjornstal (1993) summarized the research, in observational learning for practitioners, in order to propose guidelines for providing good demonstrations. Multiple trials should be presented by a skilled model similar to the performers (McCullagh, 1986, 1987; Wiese-Bjornstal, 1993) with verbal guidance by the instructor (Williams, 1989a,b,c). The demonstration should also be presented from the performer's perspective (Ishikura and Inomata, 1995).

It is important, however, for analysts to understand that there are two situations where observational learning has not been shown to be superior to other feedback as intervention. Observational learning is not very effective (1) in creating improvement in motor control and (2) for refining and customizing a movement to situational constraints. For example, watching a pitching coach demonstrate a pitching technique is not likely to help a high school pitcher improve control or pitch location.

Another common form of visual intervention is the videotape replay. There has been a great deal of research on the effectiveness of motion pictures, loop films, and video replays in teaching motor skills. A classic review of video replay as intervention in learning motor skills was reported by Rothstein and Arnold (1976). The review examined 52 studies; the majority found no significant difference between video replay and normal teacher feedback. More recent research on video intervention has supported these results (Emmen et al., 1985; Miller and Gabbard, 1988; van Wieringen et al., 1989). Although there is little scientific evidence that video replay as intervention is superior to traditional teacher feedback, its use for qualitative analysis may be justified. Chapter 8 discusses how to maximize the effectiveness of videotape for all the tasks of qualitative analysis, not just intervention.

Exaggeration or Overcompensation

The muscle memory that is necessary for skilled movement is also our biggest obstacle in creating changes in a movement. Because even small changes in technique can be very difficult for players to create, many experienced teachers and coaches exaggerate the desired correction in feedback. Good examples of this are the serve in tennis and shooting in basketball.

The initial trajectory of the ball in the tennis serve of recreational players needs to hit nearly horizontal or slightly upward. A common error is to hit downward on the serve and net a lot of serves. Players who have trouble getting the feeling of the upward action of the serve can be encouraged to try to hit the back fence with the serve. Often this results in the desired upward service action and a serve that lands deep in the service box.

Exaggeration or overcompensation can also be used to correct a common error in basketball shooting. Players often shoot on a low trajectory at the rim when they should have a higher angle of release. Telling players with this problem to shoot with a high arc is effective in improving shooting, although skilled basketball players do not really shoot with a high trajectory (Hay, 1993). This cue and the qualitative analysis of the jump shot are reviewed in chapter 8.

KEY POINT 7.4 Some techniques of intervention beyond traditional verbal feedback in qualitative analysis are the use of visual models, exaggeration of corrections, task modification, manual and mechanical guidance, conditioning, attentional cueing, and ecological intervention.

An analyst using overcompensation as intervention should do so with care. Whether the exaggeration is effective or not, the performer should be informed later that the cue words were not literally the truth. The analyst can explain that the exaggeration was necessary to create the desired change, or just that it is a good description of what the desirable technique may feel like. Do not let misconceptions about performance persist in athletes. Eventually the exaggerated technique may develop, or the cue may be passed on to other performers when it is inappropriate. Remember that the performers of today are often the instructors of tomorrow, and they are likely to teach as they have been taught.

Modifying the Practice

An option often overlooked by professionals is to change practice as intervention to improve performance. The kind of practice used varies with the kind of motor skill being learned and the performer's skill level. Analysts must often make the practice easier for novice performers to accommodate deficits in strength and skill. Coaches working with advanced athletes should change practice tasks frequently to challenge the athletes and maintain their motivation to practice. Remember that advanced performers require a great deal of practice to improve a small amount.

Fortunately, there is a large body of motor learning research on the effectiveness of various forms of practice and practice schedules. For example, the first (cognitive) stage of motor learning is focused on learning the basic motor program for a particular task. Good intervention for a person having trouble in this stage might be a combination of feedback and modified practice. Breaking the task into parts, making it easier, or eliminating attention to outcome could all be effective ways to help learning. Schleihauf (1983) demonstrated that a successful way to modify breaststroke swimming practice was exaggerating the glide phase to give the athletes more time to cognitively process the coach's feedback.

The Practice Environment

The large cognitive demands of learning a new motor skill usually require that any change in practice as intervention should be performed in a closed environment, in which the conditions of the immediate environment do not change a great deal. The external factors of performance are reasonably consistent. Conversely, in an open environment, the conditions (opponents, obstacles, and so on) are changing.

Modifying practice in progression for a beginner learning to dribble a basketball would typically mean moving from a closed to a more open practice environment. The performer would dribble in a small area, dribble moving slowly in one direction, dribble around objects, dribble with others moving randomly, and finally dribble to avoid defensive pressure. In the early stages of learning, cognitive attention is focused on the movement. As the performer learns, attention can progressively be moved from the skill to the environment.

Practice Equipment

Another possible intervention in qualitative analysis is to change the equipment used by performers. Practice with different equipment can improve performance in several ways. Improvement in performance can be dramatic when appropriate equipment for a performer is identified, like the correct club length for a golfer's height or a child's tennis racket for a young learner. Equipment that is lighter or heavier than normal may be used in practice to provide an overload or training effect. Training with under- and overweight baseballs has been shown to improve throwing velocity more than normal throwing (DeRenne, Ho, and Blitzblau, 1990).

Another way to improve performance with the modification of practice equipment is the use of teaching aids. This approach is common in golf and simple homemade aids have recently been proposed for beginning golf instruction (Pinheiro and Marson, 1998). An analyst can modify equipment for practice or long-term use as an intervention strategy to improve movement.

Practice Scheduling

The prescription of practice and practice schedules has been a major area of motor learning research. The classic practice scheme in athletics of repeated practice trials without rest may not be the best way to learn motor skills. The practice of a movement may be organized (practice to rest schedule) along a continuum from massed practice to distributed practice. In massed practice there is little or no rest between trials, while in distributed practice longer rest intervals are scheduled between trials.

For discrete motor skills (tennis serve, basketball shot), massed practice does not result in degradation of learning. For continuous motor skills where fatigue can be a factor, however, massed practice tends to decrease practice trial performance but has a small effect on learning (Schmidt and Wrisberg, 2000). When prescribing practice as intervention, carefully evaluate the performer's situation and goals. Modification of practice interacts with many other aspects of physical training and learning other motor skills.

Planning practice with multiple skills or tasks then becomes a factor in modifying practice as intervention. Practice of several movements can be either blocked or random. Blocked practice involves many repetitions or trials of a task in a block before another practice task is introduced. Motor learning research suggests that this kind of practice leads to good performance in practice and an exaggerated sense of skill, followed by poorer long-term learning. Early in learning a new movement, blocked practice is effective in helping performers develop a basic motor program. In random practice, trials alternate rapidly among different movements. This results in poorer practice performance but better long-term motor learning (Schmidt and Wrisberg, 2000).

If a complex movement can easily be broken into phases, it might be a good idea to provide intervention by progression. Part-whole learning is generally not as meaningful or as easy to put together as whole-part learning, but it's a good remedial approach for someone who is having a problem. An example is a student having trouble with footwork in the basketball lay-up. It might be good intervention to modify the task by allowing the student to carry the ball and work on the approach footwork in isolation.

The consensus of research suggests that if practice is to be modified to help improve motor learning, the approach should depend on the level of the performer, the kind of movement, and the other movements being learned. The quality of practice is highly important; the time spent on a task is less important than was once thought. It is clear that frequent changes in practice conditions, tasks, and repetitions assist in motor learning. A challenging practice session may look worse in execution, but the retention and transfer of skill is better in the long run (Schmidt and Wrisberg, 2000).

Frequent changes in task and feedback are important if a performer is working on a difficult correction or change in a movement pattern. A good intervention strategy in situations like this is to change the practice task and then return to the observation task of qualitative analysis. Remember that in the real world the analyst can move from intervention back to observation. This immediate gathering of new information on performance and on the effectiveness of the intervention should speed up the improvement in the client's performance.

The last thing to remember about modifying practice is that competition may be a big help in qualitative analysis. Most coaches know that you cannot use practice to predict performance in actual competition. Some people thrive on pressure, while others fold in competitive situations.

Motor learning research shows that there is no simple association between practice performance and performance in retention trials (learning). Drills and practice should be changed frequently, with many activities involving competition and gamelike situations. Making practice drills competitive can help nervous performers get used to playing under pressure. In an intermittent activity like tennis, practice can mimic match conditions with short, intense drills followed by a short rest. Coaches can use this intervention and teach relaxation techniques for players to use during these rest breaks.

Manual and Mechanical Guidance

Sometimes a teacher physically moves or holds a performer's body in specific positions to give the athlete a feel for the position or action. This is manual guidance. Spotting in gymnastics and having athletes freeze on command so that the coach can manually change the athlete's body positions are examples of manual guidance. Giving performers this kinesthetic sense of the position or action can be highly effective, but the analyst must be careful not to violate people's cultural or personal taboos against being touched. Kinesiology professionals need to be sensitive to these concerns of their clients.

Mechanical guidance involves using some aid or mechanical device to help the performer make the appropriate movements (Lockhart, 1966). For example, in golf mechanical guidance may be provided by a swing aid, brace, or strap. The sports of golf and basketball seem to have a continuous stream of mechanical devices being introduced that are supposed to help players groove the right swing or shot.

One of the problems with both manual and mechanical guidance is transferring the new feeling into practice movements and unlearning the older muscle memory or faulty motor program. It is difficult for players to unlearn motor programs, especially if they have been using the movement for some time. Manual guidance should be used carefully; the analyst needs to make sure the performer understands that it will take concentrated effort and a lot of perfect practice to make movement changes. Manual and mechanical guidance may be most effective when the performer is at a low skill level and is comfortable with instructor contact (Lockhart, 1966).

Another problem is that guidance can increase the risk of injury. An example of this risk is given by tennis pro Vic Braden (1983). A tennis pro wanted a player to get the feel of keeping his feet on the court during the serve to correct an early jump in his serve. The pro asked the player to serve with his foot in a shoe that had been fixed to a board, which had been nailed to the clay tennis court. The player served and got the feeling of an injured ankle! Helping the performer feel the correct movement can be effective, but it must be done with care. A tennis player dragging her toe and a golfer with a weight-shift problem can better feel their performances if they remove their shoes to focus their attention on the foot in question.

Conditioning

If the analyst believes that a critical ability is lacking, appropriate intervention may be physical training or conditioning. A student who lacks strength to perform a skill might be helped by several intervention strategies: changing equipment, modifying practice, or prescribing physical training to increase strength. If a performer lacks dynamic flexibility to perform a skill optimally, an integrated qualitative analysis might prescribe a static stretching program in conjunction with modified skill practice to gradually increase range of motion. If a lack of critical ability poses a risk of injury, intervention should focus exclusively on this issue until safe practice is possible.

Qualitative analysts often try to verify their judgments of physical limitations with physical tests (40-yard dash, vertical jump, three-hop test). Advancements in motor development, exercise physiology, kineanthropometrics, and sports medicine research may help identify key quantitative measurements and fitness variables related to performance and potential injury.

Attentional Cueing

Attentional cueing refers to learners' ability to take themselves through a movement with specific cue words (Janelle et al., 1997; Minas, 1977; Morrison and Reeve, 1993). This process can involve the instructor providing intervention as cue words to guide subsequent performance, or the cue words can be developed cooperatively with the performer. Cue words should focus on the actions of the movement and the most meaningful parts of the movement, like the Vickers teaching cues illustrated in chapter 4. The action words or the first words in the execution phase of the movement description become the cues to movement. The overarm throw examples (figure 4.5, page 89) include "turn," "step," "rotate," "swing," "snap," and "follow through." This intervention strategy can teach performers to become more aware of the movement as they are learning it and can be a useful skill for self-instruction in the future.

Ecological Intervention

The ecological approach to skill acquisition is primarily founded on the notion of direct realism (Handford et al., 1997). This approach says that biological systems do not need a highly developed mental representation to use sensory information. Skilled movements are based principally on the relationship between the performer and the environment (Handford et al., 1997). There is a continual revolving relationship between perception and movement that shapes the movement form. The movement product is not based on a schema of the movement but is continually adaptable to the changing environment. This is seen in a hockey player adapting the backswing on a slap shot based on defensive conditions.

To enhance this interaction between perception and movement, the environment needs to be manipulated in relation to the responses the performer will make in varying game situations. This is vital if the performer is to enhance her particular movement responses within the constraints of a particular environment. Because the number of environments is nearly infinite, infinite responses are available. An analyst sensitive to an ecological approach would provide interventions with as much variety in the environment as possible for the level of the performer. Recall that the environmental adjustments need to take into account the level of the learner. Appropriate environmental changes that add contextual interference can enhance learning.

The goal of an ecological approach is the performance of a particular movement. An objective for a movement is established and attainment of that objective is sought. Take, for example, the objective of throwing a ball for distance as opposed to throwing a ball for accuracy. The objective of the movement is distance, while attaining the form to throw the ball that distance is the goal of the ecological instruction. The importance of how the movement proceeds is paramount. The quality of the movement is the desired outcome of the ecological approach.

Balan and Davis (1993) have shown that an ecological approach to intervention in qualitative analysis has four main components: task goals, choices, manipulation, and instruction. Figure 7.4 expands on this description.

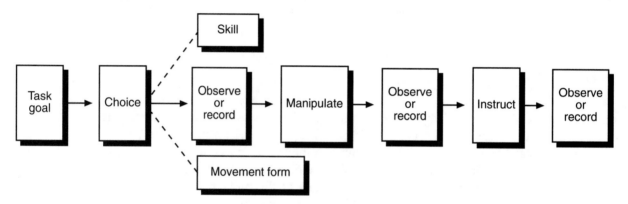

FIGURE 7.4   Balan and Davis (1993) model for assessment and instruction in an ecological approach to teaching.
Reprinted with permission from Balan and Davis, 1993: 56.

Each of the four levels has components designed to improve the quality of the movement. When considering the goal (the way a movement is performed) of a new movement, the practice environment should be designed to elicit the desired movement for analysis. The second stage of the model suggests allowing the performer to move in a way that will achieve the goal of the task in a particular environment. Again, the observer records the quality of the movement within the context of environment. Intervention may again focus on changing the environment to change the action of the performer. Finally, the observer may actually instruct the performer in order to enhance the movement. Implicit in this overall approach is that performers develop a movement pattern optimal for them and more closely matched to the environment.

In an ecological approach to intervention, it is crucial that the analyst understand the *range of correctness* concept advocated by this text. Other principles that seem to underlie this intervention strategy of movement enhancement include the following (Handford et al., 1997):

• Practice should be variable.

• The majority of skills are seen as open skills.

- High cognitive and contextual interference enhances acquisition.
- Practice conditions should match competition conditions.

Biomechanical analysis may define an apparent optimal movement pattern for cross-country skiing, but an interdisciplinary and ecological approach to qualitative analysis remains open to a range of correct techniques. Physiological, psychological, anatomical, along with other environmental conditions might suggest that different movement patterns are optimal rather than the idealized form. The focus of the ecological approach is to get the performer to be as biomechanically efficient as possible within the environmental constraints. If analysts do not take these constraints into account, they will not be able to manipulate the environment in a way to optimize the learner's performance. The ecological approach to intervention in cross-country skiing may be practicing on different types of snow: granular or powder. Skiers should also practice on well-groomed and ungroomed tracks as well as up and down slopes and on cambers where one ski is higher than the other. All these variations should be mixed and combined to provide environments with different perceptual challenges, which should stimulate a variety of responses to enhance performance.

Demonstration 7.1

Ever wish you could turn back time and take something you said back? Here is your chance. Observe the video clips and decide if the analyst provided appropriate intervention for each performance. For each clip ask yourself the following questions: Was the intervention appropriate? Why? Is there a better intervention? Why?

Further Practice

For ethical reasons, we do not recommend that you try out various kinds of feedback and intervention on people. A thoughtful professional always strives to give the most effective intervention and, following many interactions with clients, critically examines the effectiveness of past intervention. New kinds of practice or cues always need to be tried out, but professionals should not experiment with clients unless there are good logical and empirical reasons to try the new intervention. Further practice for intervention will have to happen over the long term, within a career-long vision of professional development.

Summary

The fourth task of qualitative analysis is the provision of some intervention to help the performer improve. Intervention is not limited to traditional augmented verbal feedback. It includes other methods to teach and train a person to move better. A rich history of research on feedback suggests that augmented verbal feedback, used as intervention, should be limited to a cue word or phrase that is as specific as possible and is given with minimum delay. Augmented feedback can be highly effective if it is given in positive terms, as knowledge of performance (KP), and in language that is age-appropriate or specific to the individual. Another consideration for those who wish to improve performance is the use of beyond verbal feedback intervention techniques. Simple changes in the environment can add to the effectiveness of the intervention.

Discussion Questions

1. What kinds of *augmented feedback* are best for a novice, an intermediate, and an expert performer? Do these kinds of feedback vary with different sports or activities?

2. What motor skills would benefit from a performer's focusing attention on *intrinsic feedback* as intervention?

3. How does the age of the performer affect selection of the mode of intervention in qualitative analysis?

4. You are a high school soccer coach. What hand signals can you use to provide intervention to players who cannot hear you in competition?

5. Are there ideal cue words for particular movements, or must skill level and ecological factors be considered in selecting cues?

6. What rationale for intervention is best?

7. Should intervention focus on short-term or long-term performance?

8. Which kind of intervention is most important, reinforcement or corrections?

Practical Applications of Qualitative Analysis

Part III is dedicated to the practical application of our integrated model of qualitative analysis. The best way to illustrate such a model is to describe the process in several examples. Chapter 8 presents selected examples from a variety of human movements that are designed to highlight the interdisciplinary nature and tasks of qualitative analysis. Video from real movement situations was isolated and illustrated or stored on the CD-ROM for these tutorials. Chapter 9 poses hypothetical situations where qualitative analysis could help solve a problem in human movement. These "theory into practice" situations are effective in beginning discussions on qualitative analysis with other professionals. Chapter 10 provides important technical and practical information on using video technology to enhance qualitative analysis.

Tutorials in Qualitative Analysis of Human Movement

© Caroline Wood/International Stock

Like the children in this picture, you may be asking yourself, "When do I get a turn?" This chapter will lead you through selected tutorials and practical examples of the qualitative analysis of six human movements. The skills are illustrated from video images of actual performances and links to video clips stored on the CD-ROM that accompanies this book. Several approaches to integrated qualitative analysis are illustrated. Explanations of the critical features, systematic observational strategies, evaluation and diagnosis, and intervention are presented for each movement. It is important to think about the differences in the depth of analysis required for different movements and performers.

1. Illustrate an integrated approach to qualitative analysis of selected motor skills.
2. Discuss how the approaches to qualitative analysis of the presented skills differ.
3. Discuss how similar movement patterns may have different qualitative analysis strategies.
4. Develop skill in the qualitative analysis of videotaped movements.
5. Generalize qualitative analysis skills to live movement conditions.

Research has conclusively shown that instruction in qualitative analysis improves ability at qualitative analysis, but this ability tends to be sport or movement specific. Research has also shown that practice with many examples of good and bad performances are necessary for the development of skill in qualitative analysis. This chapter cannot provide enough experience to make a reader a skilled analyst of human movement, but it does provide a progressive set of examples of interdisciplinary qualitative analysis from a variety of human movement activities. Fundamental movement patterns (catching, overarm throwing, walking) and sport skills (placekick, jump shot, tennis serve) are presented to illustrate the process of an integrated qualitative analysis. The tasks of qualitative analysis are presented using drawings and video clips stored on the CD-ROM.

The critical features and sample teaching cues are identified for each of the movement examples. These critical features and cues are based on research and the opinions of the authors. We present them not as the only right or perfect choices but simply as examples of an integrated qualitative analysis of human movement. As the performances get more complex, the amount of discussion of the critical features and the diagnosis of the performances will naturally increase.

The figures in this chapter are drawn from selected frames of normal video to illustrate critical features of real-world examples as closely as possible to the actual performance. The size of subjects is maximized to make them easier to see and because there is essentially unlimited viewing time. In real-world qualitative analysis, the analyst must be far enough away from the performer to use background objects to judge the motion of the body. The time between images is noted in the figure captions.

For each movement sequence, systematically observe the changes in body position based on the critical features and observational strategies presented. Use as much information from the text, illustrations, background, and figure captions as possible to inform your qualitative analysis. It is important for professionals interested in developing skill in qualitative analysis to practice various observational strategies and approaches to qualitative analysis using videotaped and live movements. Good analysts also need to remain open to cues that help identify contextual and nonbiomechanical factors that might affect performance (table 8.1).

The drawings are not meant to replace your observation of live human movement. To help you develop skill in the observation of the movements presented in this chapter, video clips of other performers are included in the CD-ROM. QA Demonstrations include the references to these clips. This chapter is designed in a qualitative analysis progression, from line drawings, to video replay, and finally to live human movement. It is up to each kinesiology professional to practice the important skill of qualitative analysis.

TABLE 8.1 Nonbiomechanical Factors Which Can Affect Performance	
Psychological	**Emotional**
Fear	Excitement
Aggression	Boredom
Showing off	Happiness
Seeking attention	Sadness
Easy distraction	Depression
Processing deficit	
Physiological	**Physical**
Strength	Vision
Flexibility	Maturity
Fatigue	Kinesthetic
Body composition	Haptic

Analyzing Catching

The fundamental pattern of catching is a good movement to use for illustrating several important points about an integrated qualitative analysis. Qualitative analysis of this movement can be fine-tuned to apply to other specific catching skills. Qualitative analysis of catching is somewhat simplified because the goal or mechanical purpose of catching is clear and easy to evaluate. This, combined with an understanding of the sequential nature of the movement, makes the diagnosis of performance within qualitative analysis easier.

Critical Features

Several authors have reported models for the qualitative analysis of catching (Jones-Morton, 1991b; Kelly, Reuschlein, and Haubenstricker, 1998; Morrison and Harrison, 1985). The majority of the technique points mentioned by these authors can be summarized in four critical features of catching in table 8.2, listed roughly in order of their occurrence in catching.

TABLE 8.2 Critical Features and Cues for Catching	
Critical Feature	**Cues**
Readiness	Watch the ball.
Intercept	Move to meet the ball; reach for the ball.
Hand position	Thumbs in or out, fingers up or down.
Ball momentum absorption	Give with the ball; retract hands and arms.

Reprinted from Knudson and Morrison 1997: 125.

FIGURE 8.1 Sequence images of a child catching a bouncing tennis ball. What would be the best intervention to help this child improve her catching ability? Time between pictures is 0.07 seconds.
Reprinted from Knudson and Morrison 1997: 126.

FIGURE 8.2 Sequence images of the same child catching in the trial immediately after the one illustrated in figure 8.1. What is the appropriate intervention in this case? What does this second observation tell you about the previous feedback? Time between pictures is 0.07 seconds.
Reprinted from Knudson and Morrison 1997: 126.

Systematic Observational Strategy (SOS)

An SOS for analyzing live or videotaped catching performances is based on the sequence or phases of the catching movement. Teachers should first observe the performer's state of readiness and attention to the object being caught. Next, observation is focused on the motion of the body and arms to intercept the object. The final two critical features to observe are the position of the hands and how the body, arms, and hands give to dissipate the motion energy of the object. Figure 8.1 illustrates the performance of a child catching a bouncing tennis ball. Use the critical features in table 8.2 to perform an integrated qualitative analysis of the movement.

Subject 1

The subject uses a typical immature approach to catching, trapping the ball against her body. It looks as if the performer has her attention focused on the ball, is lined up with the ball, and is bending down with her feet apart. Her readiness and preparation are a baseball coach's dream come true. Her hands are in correct position, but her arms have limited forward reach to intercept the ball. Intervention could focus on motivational efforts to closely attend to the flight of the ball and anticipate where it will go. Providing feedback about giving with the arms is inappropriate if the subject can-

d   e   f

d   e   f

not first move the arms forward to intercept the ball in a position to "give with the ball." Good intervention might be the following: "Good job! On the next try, watch the ball closely and move your hands to the ball." Or "Guess where the ball will be and move your hands there first." Is there any additional information that would improve the diagnosis and intervention? Would it be useful to observe additional trials?

Figure 8.2 shows the same subject catching another bouncing ball in the very next trial. What intervention would be appropriate if you had just observed these two trials? Is this intervention different from what was suggested by figure 8.1? Why or why not?

The diagnosis of performance after the observation of two trials is easier and may result in different intervention compared to the diagnosis of only one trial. The child can catch correctly in an almost identical trial. Figures 8.1 and 8.2 are typical in teaching young children to catch. Teachers need to expect movement variability and plan to observe several performances. The best intervention may be to reinforce good attention and effort and to focus feedback on the critical feature of ball intercept. Good feedback could be "Great job! Remember to reach forward to catch the ball away from your body." The importance of reaching for the ball in catching has been supported by recent research showing that visual information on hand position is used in catching (Donkelaar and Lee, 1994). Notice that some of the intervention is biomechanical (hand and body position) while the other psychological (motivation).

Although not evident from figures 8.1 and 8.2, this girl frequently attempts to catch with her arms/hands to one side, with trunk and head motion away from the ball. Fear of the ball is an important issue for young children and may continue into adulthood. A good analyst should be aware of these fears and might change the observational situation to supplement observation. Throws could be faster or more difficult, or a soft foam ball could be introduced to see if the subject changes her approach to catching in different situations. Clearly, observing more catching trials would help improve performance diagnosis and intervention. An analyst who takes an integrated approach tries to observe multiple trials and evaluate all relevant factors about the performer and the situation.

Subject 2

Figure 8.3 illustrates an attempt to catch a playground ball by a young child playing catch with another child. Perform an integrated qualitative analysis of this performance. (Assume that several trials showed similar strengths and weaknesses.) This child and her partner are being cooperative by tossing the ball directly to each other from a short distance. How could an analyst modify the task to gather additional information on this child's catching ability?

This girl exhibits several common errors that are typical at immature levels of catching motor development. She catches by attempting to trap the ball between her forearms and her chest. Her body reacts after the ball has struck her body, turning her head to avoid contact with the ball. A good intervention strategy should modify the task to see if she would use more mature catching form if the task were made even easier. The analyst could provide a smaller and softer foam ball, or the analyst could toss the ball to the child.

Good feedback for this performer would be to praise her attention and success at catching the ball. The analyst could use an indirect style of teaching and ask, "Does

FIGURE 8.3   Sequence images of a child catching a large playground ball. What is the appropriate intervention in this case? Time between pictures is 0.07 seconds.
Reprinted from Knudson and Morrison 1997: 126.

the ball sometimes bounce out of your grasp? What catching cues that the class learned would help you?"

Analyzing Soccer Instep Kick

Placekicking is an adapted striking pattern of the lower extremity where the foot impacts the ball as it lies on the ground. A variety of sports require skill in this movement, which we are calling the *soccer instep kick*. How should an American football or soccer coach qualitatively analyze placekicking? The examples in this section and the CD-ROM include children and adults kicking in soccer and kickball.

Critical Features

High-speed kicking in a variety of sports has been extensively researched. The integrated qualitative analysis we suggest is based on this body of research and several models proposed by previous authors (Barfield, 1998; Jones-Morton, 1990a; Kelly, Reuschlein, and Haubenstricker, 1990; Levanon and Dapena, 1998; Morrison and Reeve, 1986; Tant, 1990). There are six critical features to be evaluated in a qualitative analysis of the soccer instep kick (table 8.3). These critical features are also presented roughly in the order of occurrence in the movement. Does the movement sequence in kicking correspond to the potential influence of the critical features? If the objective of a placekick changes, do the critical features change in importance?

Practice 8.1

Qualitatively analyze the catching skills in the following video clips. Justify your evaluation, diagnosis, and choice of intervention. See if you can translate the qualitative analysis of catching examples in the text to an integrated qualitative analysis of videotape replay. In all QA Practice examples, we challenge you to focus on the observation, evaluation and diagnosis, and intervention tasks of qualitative analysis. In the preparation task for qualitative analysis, review our critical features in the text and decide if they are the ones you want to use. Note how many times you watched the clips before you felt sure you could judge the quality of the movement. Professionals can certainly disagree on the qualitative analysis of movement, so the most important point is to justify your answers to the tasks of qualitative analysis.

TABLE 8.3 Critical Features and Cues for the Soccer Instep Kick

Critical Feature	Cues
Eye focus	Head down and watch the ball
Opposition	Turn your side to the target
Plant	Plant your foot next to the ball
Sequential coordination	Rotate your hip and leg
Solid impact	Kick through the center of the ball
Follow-through	Follow through toward the target

Reprinted from Knudson and Morrison 1997: 128.

Systematic Observational Strategy (SOS)

It is likely that several SOSs are effective for the qualitative analysis of human movement. It is, however, difficult to actually practice different SOSs with the figures in this chapter. Readers should try three SOSs when analyzing live or videotaped kicking performances. The most common strategy is to observe according to the sequence or phases of the movement. A similar strategy is to observe from the origins of movement (from slower-moving to faster-moving segments). The third observational strategy is the gestalt approach, moving from general impressions to specific. Which observational strategy is easiest or most comfortable? Why do you prefer one over another? In the absence of evidence that a particular rationale for diagnosis is best, should novice soccer coaches observe in sequence and provide intervention according to the sequence of the movement?

The soccer kick is an excellent example of a motor skill involving sequential coordination for generating high speeds of a distal segment. Some soccer kick techniques have minor variations in these critical features to meet situational requirements. The kick will be dramatically different if the purpose is to travel accurately 10 feet to a

FIGURE 8.4   Sequence images of a child kicking a stationary soccer ball. What correction would help this player improve the most? Time between pictures is 0.07 seconds.
Reprinted from Knudson and Morrison 1997: 130.

teammate, versus getting as far from your own goal as possible. For example, the critical feature of solid impact would be less important in the short pass than in the long pass. Slow-speed kicks do not require sequential coordination and may use the side of the foot to push the ball to a target. This leads to a common misconception that the side of the foot is the desirable striking point for high-speed kicks. In reality, the neutral position of the hip and foot and the flat surface of the instep when the foot is pointed make the instep kick a proper technique for high-speed placekicking. For the long pass, the analyst would pay closer attention to the foot position at impact, the sound of the kick, and the trajectory of the ball to evaluate the quality of the impact.

Another common error is to minimize opposition by not approaching the ball at an angle. Efficient use of hip rotation and the levers of the lower extremity can be made by an approach angle to the ball between 30 and 60 degrees (Tant, 1990). The other common errors are not focusing attention on the ball, planting the foot behind or in front of the ball at impact, and an exaggerated concern for accuracy that typically results in slow foot speed and a limited follow-through.

Subject 1

Perform an integrated qualitative analysis of the kick illustrated in figure 8.4. The subject is kicking a stationary soccer ball toward a target to maximize speed and accuracy. What would be the best intervention in this situation? For figure 8.4 and the rest of the movements illustrated in this chapter, assume that the performance strengths and weaknesses apparent in the figures were consistent across several trials.

The young person in figure 8.4 essentially achieves the goal of kicking the ball toward the target and keeps good eye focus on the soccer ball. There are weaknesses in the critical features of opposition, foot plant, sequential coordination, and solid impact. Note that the foot position at impact with the ball is not totally clear; this judgment is even more difficult in real-time qualitative analysis of kicking. Is there anything else that can be modified in this situation? It would be quite obvious if the student

were trapping, receiving passes, or blocking a shot on goal. If possible, it would be appropriate for the analyst to provide a smaller soccer ball instead of the full-size soccer ball.

Intervention beyond a change in equipment must be focused on one critical feature, even though the player has quite a bit of kicking development ahead. Remember that in kicking development young children have difficulty impacting the ball, so they typically approach the ball from behind and may even stop before kicking the ball. This player has enough experience to aggressively approach the ball, keep his eyes focused, and impact the ball. Intervention should focus on the foot plant or the opposition (an angled approach) because coordination is related to opposition and correct foot position is difficult in a straight approach to the ball. A soccer coach could say, "That's a powerful kick, Billy. I bet you can get even more power if you remember to plant your foot next to the ball." Or, "That's a great kick, Billy. I would like you to try an angled approach to the ball. You can get more power if you approach from the side and turn your side to the ball." Once these basic techniques have been established, the analyst should focus on the correct foot position (toe down and kick with the shoe laces) at impact, which will maximize energy transmitted to the ball for a given foot speed. For a young person like this subject, a powerful sequential coordination of the hip and leg is likely the last critical feature to develop.

Subject 2

Try another integrated qualitative analysis, this time of the instep kick illustrated in figure 8.5. This subject is also kicking for speed and accuracy in a game of mat ball (kickball with large mats for bases). Select appropriate cues for intervention. Remember that the strengths and weaknesses illustrated have been consistent across several kicking trials. Do you think the subject in figure 8.5 is more or less skilled than the one in figure 8.4? Think about what critical features are most related to this decision.

a   b   c

FIGURE 8.5 Sequence images of a child kicking a playground ball in a game of mat ball. What correction would help this player improve the most? Time between pictures is 0.1 seconds.
Reprinted from Knudson and Morrison 1997: 130.

The performer in figure 8.5 is kicking in a more open environment than placekicking a stationary ball. The smooth motion of the ball prior to the kick suggests that this trial may not be a difficult kick for this subject. The critical features this player needs to improve are foot plant, opposition, coordination, and solid impact. Movements that may have caught an observer's eye are an upright trunk early in the approach, the knee bent at impact, and the very high and straight follow-through of the leg.

The subject approaches the ball straight on and places the plant foot too far forward for the speed of the ball. The optimal point of impact is passed because the plant foot is ahead of the ball by the time impact occurred. A good evaluation and diagnosis of this situation would likely lead to intervention on the foot plant or the approach angle/opposition. Providing cues on foot plant will be helpful only if the subject is consistently placing the foot too far forward. In an open environment like mat ball or soccer, the analyst needs many observations to make this evaluation. The ability to coordinate hip rotation and leg actions to create a solid impact (get the leg, ankle, and foot almost completely extended at impact) is related to the approach and foot plant.

Providing a cue to work on an effective approach angle would be the best intervention. Examples might be "turn your side to the target" or "approach the ball from the side." The teacher might say, "That was a great kick, Cory! I bet you could get more power. Try to approach the ball from the side." The analyst could then repeat the qualitative analysis to monitor how that intervention affected critical features and overall performance.

Subject 3

The person illustrated in figure 8.6 is kicking a stationary soccer ball for speed and accuracy. Perform an integrated qualitative analysis of this kicking performance in order to provide appropriate intervention for this performer.

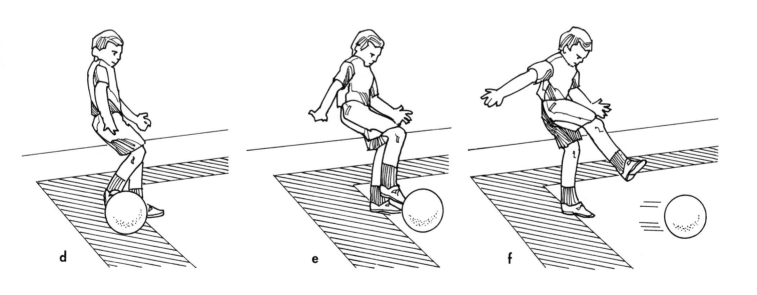

FIGURE 8.6   Sequence images of an adult kicking a stationary soccer ball. Are there any weaknesses in kicking technique? Time between pictures is 0.1 seconds.
Reprinted from Knudson and Morrison 1997: 132.

Practical Applications: Observational Models for Kicking

Before we look at video clips of kicking, let's review some of the ways to organize critical features into an observational model. Look at the following examples and see if you prefer the gestalt approach (Dunham, 1994) or the spatial/temporal approach (Gangstead and Beveridge 1984).Fill out the temporal/spatial model, based on the gestalt model, whether or not you plan to use the temporal/spatial model in the analysis.

Gestalt Model (Dunham, 1994)

Body Orientation: Facing ball at 45-degree angle to line of kick

Preparation:

    Feet: Weight on non-kicking foot, one foot from ball
           Kicking foot back away from ball

    Knees: Slight bend of non-kicking, deep bend of kicking

    Hips: Slight bend of non-kicking, slight extension of kicking, rotated back from ball

    Trunk: Straight and slight extension, rotated back from ball

    Shoulders: Non-kicking slightly forward, kicking back

    Arms: Non-kicking forward, kicking back for balance

    Hands: Relaxed

    Head: Down, eyes on ball

Execution:

  1. Rotate hips and trunk to ball.

  2. Bend kicking hip and straighten leg forcefully.

  3. Point toes; contact ball with laces.

  4. Bring kicking leg through to target.

  5. Balance with arms.

  6. Follow thorough to target.

continued ➡

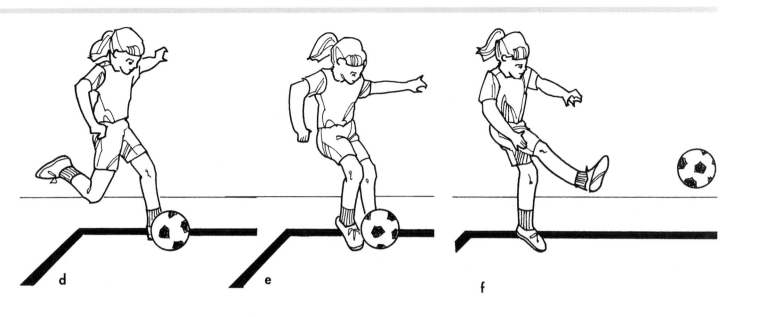

d   e   f

Temporal and Spatial Model (Gangstead and Beveridge, 1984)

Instep Kick:

Body components	Temporal phasing		
	Preparation	*Action*	*Follow-through*
Path of hub			
Body weight			
Trunk action			
Head action			
Leg action			
Arm action			
Impact/release			

There are no major weaknesses in the critical features in this performance. Note the subject's strong hurdle, foot plant, kicking foot position before impact, and forward body motion creating a low ball trajectory. Analysts must use care in prescribing technique changes in skilled performers and avoid the tendency to overcorrect. Because skilled performers have developed great consistency and control, changes in technique will take tremendous effort. Changes in technique should only be prescribed if they improve performance or prevent injury, and when other interventions (conditioning, competition, practice, rest) will not produce similar results. Good intervention for this performer should be infrequent reinforcement and praise, followed by frequent modifications of the task. The main challenges for the analyst are maintaining the variety and intensity of practice.

QA **Practice 8.2**

Qualitatively analyze the kicking skills in the following video clips. Justify your evaluation, diagnosis, and choice of intervention. Assume the performance of these young people are consistent across trials.

Analyzing Basketball Jump Shot

Shooting in the game of basketball takes a variety of forms. The most common shot, however, is the jump shot. Jump shots in competition are difficult because of the small margin for error and the uncertainty of defensive pressure. This section will illustrate the qualitative analysis of jump shooting, paying special attention to physical differences in performers.

Critical Features

The discussion of critical features for the qualitative analysis of the basketball jump shot is based on the review of the jump shot by Knudson (1993). Teachers and coaches of basketball need to be keenly aware of the open nature of basketball. The uncertainty imposed by the defense, teammates, and the clock can dramatically affect how a player shoots the ball. Factors like shot distance and release height also affect the optimal release conditions for a shot. Some recent studies of basketball shooting with relevant technique information are Hamilton and Reinschmidt (1997), Miller and Bartlett (1993, 1996), Liu and Burton (1999), and several papers in the proceedings of the 11th International Society of Biomechanics in Sports (ISBS) symposium.

Knudson reviewed the biomechanical research and identified six critical features for typical midrange jump shots (table 8.4). The critical features of the jump shot focus on both the motion of the athlete's body (KP) and the outcome variables of the ball motion (KR). This is an example of selecting critical features based on a consensus of biomechanical research. Performer characteristics like age and strength, or environmental factors (defense, basket height, ball size), can all influence the critical features of shooting in a specific situation.

Systematic Observational Strategy (SOS)

The SOSs to use with this model include moving from movement origins, moving from general to specific technique points, and rating the importance of the critical features. Carefully review the critical features of the jump shot and determine which are most important to improving shooting success. Are any other key points of shooting a basketball left out? Prioritize the critical features and use them to guide your observation of the jump shot illustrated in figure 8.7. The performer is shooting a junior basketball in a game situation toward a lowered (7-foot) hoop. What is the most appropriate intervention for the subject in figure 8.7?

TABLE 8.4 Critical Features of the Basketball Jump Shot

Critical Feature	Cues
Staggered stance and vertical jump	Boxer's stance
Shooting plane	Shooting plane; powerline
Optimized height of release	Release at the top
Angle of release	Golden arch; best path
Cooperation of upper and lower extremities	Smooth; jump and shoot
Ball rotation	Flip the wrist for ball

From "Biomechanics of the basketball jump shot: Six key teaching points," by D. Knudson. Reprinted with permission from the *Journal of Physical Education, Recreation and Dance* (February, 1993) 67-73. *JOPERD* is a publication of the American Alliance for Health, Physical Education, Recreation and Dance, 1900 Association Drive, Reston, VA 22091.

FIGURE 8.7 Sequence images of a child shooting a junior-size basketball at a 7-foot basket during a game. What intervention would be appropriate based on the qualitative analysis model presented? Time between pictures is 0.1 seconds.
Reprinted from Knudson and Morrison 1997: 134.

Subject 1

The performance in figure 8.7 illustrates a typical transition period from a set shot to a jump shot. The person is also exhibiting a common error of many basketball players. The key outcome variables of the shot—the speed and angle of release—are not optimal for the ball to pass cleanly through the hoop. This weakness of shooting out instead of up is related to the low height of release. Many performers tend to shoot the ball directly toward the rim (low arch and higher-speed shot) rather than up over the rim. These flat shots require greater ball speeds to reach the rim, since gravity makes the ball drop throughout the trajectory of the shot. This is a very important error because the hoop was low enough for the person to use the desirable trajectory.

The other common errors in this performance are jumping toward the basket and shooting during the jump. These errors could be related to a lack of strength or could be technique errors that developed through practice with regulation basketball equipment. The strengths of the performer are good alignment with the basket, cooperation of the arms and legs, and good backspin on the ball.

How does the analyst weigh these many factors in evaluating and diagnosing this performance? How does information from the disciplines of motor development, psychology, and motor learning contribute to the diagnosis? See if you agree with the following diagnosis and intervention.

The best intervention for this situation would be cues to correct the shot's angle of release. The performer has good cooperation of the upper and lower body and has good wrist action in shooting the ball. A higher angle of release might indirectly improve the height of release; more importantly, it would increase the probability of making a basket. One good approach to intervention would be to use the following augmented feedback: "Excellent release and ball rotation!" Follow up with cues such as "remember to shoot upward" or "remember to shoot with a high or golden arc." Another cue using a visual image would be "shoot up through the top of a phone booth," as if the shooter were standing in a phone booth.

Observation of subsequent shots could focus on the angle of the shot, the height of release, and the direction of the jump. All three of these factors can strongly affect the path of the ball. Cues such as "release at the top" to increase the height of release might be helpful. With improvement in release parameters, intervention can focus on a more balanced position and vertical jump. For young basketball players like this, the least important factors to correct are the fine points of arm preparation not related to the shooting plane. As strength develops, the preparatory arm position can be moved up to the forehead from the set shot position in front of the shooting shoulder. The most important critical feature for shot accuracy is the shooting plane. It is easier to build from the strengths of the performer who shoots from a lower position with good technique than it is to put a young player in the position of imitating a mature performer (ball above the eyes, jump, and shoot) when they do not have the strength to do so.

What aspects of performance were difficult to observe in these drawings? What aspects of this subject's performance could you not make a decision about because of the lack of information? The game situation makes it difficult to catch the performance from optimal viewing angles. What other views of this performance would you be interested in seeing? Evaluation of the shooting plane and motion of the body would be improved if observations could be made from a rear view. Perform an integrated qualitative analysis of the jump shot of another subject from a different vantage point (figure 8.8).

FIGURE 8.8   Sequence images of a child shooting a junior-size basketball at an 8-foot basket. A different intervention from the Knudson et al. (1993) critical features may be needed. What should the person work on and what information leads the analyst to this decision? Time between pictures is 0.1 seconds.

Reprinted from Knudson and Morrison 1997: 138.

Subject 2

Figure 8.8 shows a 10-year-old shooting a junior basketball at an 8-foot basket. The vantage point provides an excellent perspective for most critical features, except the shooting plane. Many critical features are performed well, with weaknesses in the staggered stance and jump, the height of release, and possibly the shooting plane. Ideally the analyst would move behind the subject to check his alignment in a shooting plane with the basket. What other vantage points might be of interest?

The subject uses both the upper and lower body well and is just getting strong enough to shoot with correct jump shot form in these conditions. Note that the subject takes the ball back behind the head and coordinates the arms and legs simultaneously. The height of release is limited due to the lack of a jump, not lack of extension of the body or arm. Providing intervention for the stance and jump or the shooting plane will likely help the performer. Unfortunately, these are difficult corrections and they are related to each other.

The analyst might try this approach to intervention: "Your shot has super arm action, but let's try to get more power from your legs." The analyst might also focus on the jump by saying, "Jump first and then shoot." Providing a cue for the jump might increase the release height and ball speed enough that the shooter would not have to take the ball behind the head. This may be the best approach to intervention of this situation, since improvement in the jump may affect the weakness of taking the ball back behind the head and maintaining a shooting plane aligned with the basket. As with the previous subject, this switch from a simultaneous push to a jump with a slightly delayed upper-body shot may be difficult to develop. It may need to develop over time as this player's strength increases. An analyst coming to this conclusion could change practice by moving the performer closer to the basket. Many basketball players like to take long shots, well beyond the perimeter where they can score consistently.

Another approach to diagnosing this performance would be to prioritize the shooting plane as the most important correction. Good feedback would be, "That arm action is almost perfect. Remember to keep your shooting plane aligned with the basket." or "Try to keep the ball aligned with your dominant eye." The analyst might later explain the importance of this power line for shooting accuracy. This correction will also be difficult for the performer to change, so the analyst will need to provide motivation. Correcting the shooting plane is important because of its effect on accuracy. The problems are the difficulty of the change and the potential lack of enough strength to achieve desirable form.

Subject 3

The girl illustrated in figure 8.9 is shooting a basketball at a 7-foot basket with a technique that is transitional between a set shot and a jump shot. What would an integrated qualitative analysis of this situation suggest to help this performer?

The ball size and basket height are appropriate for this performer, but another situational factor is strongly affecting performance. This subject is attempting a shot near the limit of her strength, and it is a shot that a coach would discourage in competition because of its poor chance of success. There are weakness in the angle of release, height of release, and vertical direction of the jump, but these might be related to the distance of the shot. There appears to be good cooperation of the legs and arms, and the wrist appears to create the proper ball rotation. This performer appears to align herself with the basket, although this is a bad vantage point for this judgment.

a

b

c

d

e

f

FIGURE 8.9 Sequence images of a girl shooting a basketball at a 7-foot basket. What intervention would be appropriate based on the qualitative analysis model presented? Time between pictures is 0.1 seconds.
Reprinted from Knudson and Morrison 1997: 140.

The best intervention would be to have the player shoot several times from positions closer to the basket. If this technique persisted, the analyst should focus on the stance and vertical jump. This might help create a more effective angle of release and improve the height of release. Feedback at this stage could be "Those shots look very good. On the next few shots, concentrate on jumping straight up." The analyst would then go back to the task of observation to see if the performer effectively makes this change and if the ball's angle of release is affected. When actions are related, it is important that the analyst observe practice trials and then evaluate and diagnose those trials before intervening further.

QA Practice 8.3

Qualitatively analyze the basketball shots in the accompanying video clips. Justify your evaluation, diagnosis, and choice of intervention. These shooters are older than the shooters in the text examples.

Analyzing Overarm Throwing

Overarm throwing is an important fundamental movement pattern in many sports. This section illustrates an integrated qualitative analysis of the overarm throw in conditions with different goals. As in the previous examples, analysts will need to be sensitive to how the goal of the movement may affect the importance of critical features. Some subjects in this section will be throwing for maximum distance, while others will have varying accuracy constraints. People of all ages and abilities will be examined, so analysts need to be sensitive to physical and developmental factors that might affect throwing.

Critical Features

The high-speed overarm throw is another movement that has been extensively researched. The classic review by Atwater (1979) summarized early research on the biomechanics of overarm throwing and the related injuries. The extensive motor development research on overarm throwing is summarized in several sources (Haywood and Getchell, 2001; Roberton and Halverson, 1984; Wickstrom, 1983; Wild, 1938). Jones-Morton (1990b) proposed five critical elements for analyzing the overarm throw: (1) step with opposition, (2) open up, (3) rotate the trunk fully forward, (4) elbow leads with elbow extension, and (5) weight transfers from the back to the front foot. Kelly, Reuschlein, and Haubenstricker (1989) used five qualitative criteria for the forceful overhand throw of fourth-graders: (1) side orientation, (2) nearly complete arm extension backward in the windup, (3) weight transfer to the opposite foot, (4) marked sequential hip and shoulder rotation, and (5) follow-through beyond ball release.

We summarized this research and professional opinion on overarm throwing in a paper presenting our integrated model of qualitative analysis (Knudson and Morrison, 1996). Since forceful overarm throwing is a vital skill in many sports, this section reviews our six critical features of overarm throwing. These critical features and suggested cues are presented in table 8.5. Other major biomechanical studies have reported the effects of biomechanical feedback (Miyashita, Fukashiro, and Hirano, 1986), and an approach to qualitative analysis of baseball pitching technique has been recently published (Nicholls et al., 1999).

Overarm throwing should be analyzed relative to the goal of the throw. The conditions at release of the ball are most strongly associated with accomplishing the goal of the throw. The critical feature the analyst can easily observe in evaluating this aspect of performance is the angle of release created by the initial trajectory of the ball. Like the basketball jump shot, the outcome of the throw is largely determined by ball speed,

TABLE 8.5 Critical Features and Cues for the High-Speed Overarm Throw

Critical Feature	Cues
Torso rotation, leg drive, and opposition	Turn your side to the target; step with the opposite foot
Sequential coordination	Uncoil the body
Strong throwing position	Align arm with shoulders
Inward rotation of arm	Roll the arm and wrist at release
Relaxation	Relax your upper body
Angle of release	Throw up an incline; throw over the cutoff's head

From "An integrated qualitative analysis of overarm throwing" by D. Knudson and C. Morrison. Adapted with permission from the *Journal of Physical Education, Recreation and Dance* (August 1996): 31-36. *JOPERD* is a publication of the American Alliance for Health, Physical Education, Recreation and Dance, 1900 Association Drive, Reston, VA 22091.

spin, and, most importantly, angle of release. Biomechanical research has shown that air resistance plays a major role in the flight of most balls. In most sporting situations optimal angles of projection for throwing balls for horizontal distance are between 35 and 42 degrees above the horizontal (Dowell, 1978). A common error in young baseball players is to throw the ball with a very high trajectory. This limits the throw's effectiveness for baseball in two ways: it limits the length of the throw and increases the time it takes to cover the horizontal distance thrown.

Leg drive and opposition is the critical feature that combines the thrower's stance and step, setting up the rotations of the body to provide most of the power of the throw. The athlete creates opposition by turning the nonthrowing side of the body to the target as well as pushing off the back leg to step toward the target. Mature high-speed throwing uses a forward step greater than half the person's height (Roberton and Halverson, 1984). Research has shown that body rotation from good opposition contributes 40 to 50 percent of the ball speed, while the step contributes about 10 to 20 percent in skilled throwers (Miller, 1980). A vigorous leg drive that is channeled into body rotation is an essential technique point in high-speed throwing. Common errors are to rely too heavily (overstride) on leg action and to not transfer the energy from the stride to hip and trunk rotation.

Sequential coordination is the precise timing of accelerations of a proximal segment that transfer energy to distal segments to increase their speed. The forward acceleration of a proximal segment eccentrically loads agonists, and the later negative acceleration of the proximal segment uses joint forces or segmental interactions to speed up the distal segment. This concept of the interaction of a linked system of body segments has become known as the *kinetic link* or the *kinetic chain* (Kreighbaum and Barthels, 1985; Steindler, 1955). The sequential action of the leg drive, hip rotation, spinal rotation, arm, and forearm/hand action is required to generate high-speed throws. Figure 8.7 illustrates a side view of good overarm throwing form and sequential rotation. Roberton and Halverson (1984) have described the qualitative changes in various parts of the body in the development of sequential coordination in the overarm throw. Good form in the overarm throw is illustrated from two views in figures 8.10 and 8.11. This person is a highly skilled college baseball player.

A strong throwing position maintains alignment of the humerus at a right angle to the longitudinal axis of the spine (Plagenhoef, 1971). This position maximizes the

FIGURE 8.10   Side view of the overarm throw of a college baseball player. Note the lag of the upper arm (d) before release. Time between pictures is 0.1 seconds.
Reprinted from Knudson and Morrison 1997: 144.

speed transferred to the arm from the rotations of the hips and trunk. Atwater (1979) found this alignment (90 ± 15 degrees) to be a relatively invariant aspect of most throwing motions. In other words, there should be little difference in upper-arm position in sidearm or overarm throws, just differences in the lean of the trunk. The throwing position and trunk lean at release are observable from a rear view of the thrower (figure 8.11). The preparatory arm action in skilled overarm throwing typically involves a circular, downward backswing, with the upper arm aligned with the shoulders and the elbow maintaining a 90-degree angle.

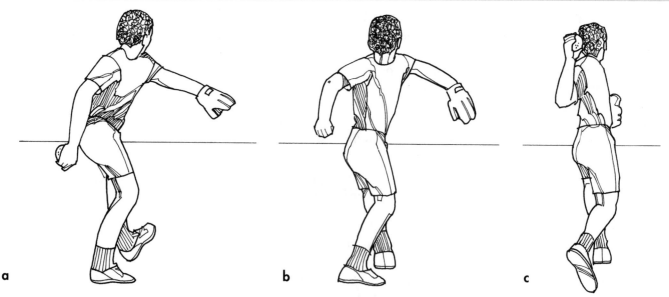

FIGURE 8.11   Rear view of the overarm throw of a college baseball player. What aspects of performance are visible in this view that are not visible in figure 8.10? Time between pictures is 0.1 seconds.
Reprinted from Knudson and Morrison 1997: 144.

d   e   f

Inward rotation of the humerus and forearm is a major propulsive and injury-protective action in the overarm throw (Atwater, 1979). The critical feature of inward rotation of the arm should be understood as the combination of humeral inward rotation, radio-ulnar pronation, and wrist flexion that provides the final propulsion of the ball. While the fingers apply important forces to create speed and spin on the ball, actual finger flexion does not occur prior to release (Hore, Watts, and Martin, 1996). This and relaxation help create the final sequentially coordinated actions of the throw. A great deal of energy is transferred up the body, and good timing of the forearm

d   e   f

pronation and wrist flexion can create that additional pop, or great ball speed, of skilled throwers. Throwing with a dead wrist does not fully utilize the energy from the more proximal segments and fails to use the final joints in the kinetic chain of the throw. Recent biomechanical studies of the kinetics of baseball pitching have increased our understanding of the stresses overarm throwing places on the body (Feltner and Dapena, 1986; Fleisig, 2001; Fleisig et al., 1995, 1996a, 1996b; Hong, Cheung, and Roberts, 2001).

Systematic Observational Strategy (SOS)

We proposed a four-phase observational strategy for the qualitative analysis of the overarm throw (Knudson and Morrison, 1996). In the initial trials, first look for timing, rhythm, signs of tension, and the trajectory of the throws. This is difficult to do from illustrations alone. This is easier in the qualitative analysis of live performances or the videotape replays on the CD-ROM. Second, observe leg drive, opposition, and hip and trunk rotation in the next few trials. Third, observe the throwing position of the arm. Last, try to look for evidence of sequential coordination in the fast actions of the arm by looking for lag in the trunk, humerus, and forearm. This kind of observational strategy, focusing on body segments and actions, is similar to the Gangstead and Beveridge (1984) observational model. Figure 8.12 illustrates the movement of a woman throwing a softball for speed and accuracy, while figure 8.13 shows the overarm throwing pattern of a child. Analyze these sequences qualitatively and prescribe intervention to improve their performances.

Compare and contrast this observational strategy with the SOSs presented earlier using live or videotaped throwing performances. Compare differences in observational strategies with different critical features, especially the stages and components discussed in the motor development literature (Roberton and Halverson, 1984; Wickstrom, 1983). What aspects of other SOSs are incorporated into the Knudson and Morrison (1996) observational strategy?

a   b   c

FIGURE 8.12 Sequence images of the overarm throw of a 20-year-old subject. What correction would help this person improve the most? Time between pictures is 0.1 second.
Reprinted from Knudson and Morrison 1997: 146.

Subject 1

The woman in figure 8.12 was an all-American college athlete, but not in a ball-throwing sport. Like many people, her throwing motor development stopped before a mature pattern had been achieved. Evaluation of performance could lead an analyst to praise the strengths of two critical features: strong throwing position and trajectory. The analyst must then diagnose the weaknesses in the remaining critical features. The major weaknesses are in her opposition and leg drive and the sequential coordination of the throw. Poor timing and coordination can be visually identified by the fact that the elbow and hand are well forward of the shoulder at release.

The best intervention for this performer may be to work on opposition and leg drive before sequential coordination. Much of the power for overarm throwing comes from a good opposition and leg drive, so the fine-tuning of sequential coordination will not be possible until the performer learns to move the legs, hips, and trunk forward powerfully as the arms move backward. The weaknesses of a relaxed performance and inward rotation of the arm are less important and should be evaluated later, when coordination has improved.

Good feedback for this performer would be to praise some aspect of her throw (arm alignment and angle of release are good) and provide cues such as "Turn your side to the target," or "Let's use that good leg drive more by first turning sideways to the target, stepping forward, and powerfully rotating your trunk into the throw." The age of the performer allows the analyst to include more information with the feedback on this critical feature.

It is not likely that good sequential coordination would develop without strong leg drive and opposition to transfer energy to the arm from the legs and trunk. Motor learning and motor development literature suggest that after good leg drive and opposition, intervention could focus on relaxation and letting the sequential coordination (lag in the arm and forearm) develop with practice. It would be a good idea to provide

d   e   f

feedback on the distance to the goal ahead and the practice required to improve throwing coordination.

Subject 2

Figure 8.13 illustrates the overarm throwing performance of a child throwing a softball for maximum distance in a competition. The goal of the performance is different from the goal in the previous example, so the analyst needs to know the desirable trajectory for throwing a ball for maximum horizontal distance. Qualitatively analyze the performance in figure 8.13 in order to help this performer throw farther.

The performer has several strong critical features of overarm throwing. He has good opposition and keeps his arm aligned with his shoulders. Improvements could be made in leg drive, sequential coordination, and the angle of release. The performer is trying so hard that he exaggerates the step, but he has limited weight transfer. It is difficult to tell from the figure, but there is limited sequential coordination (simultaneous rotation of hip and trunk) and the angle of release is a little high.

If this boy were consistently throwing the ball with this technique, the best intervention would be to correct the leg action in the throw. Good initial verbal feedback would be, "That was a strong throw, John. I'd like you to concentrate on pushing your weight from your right foot to your left." Good leg drive will provide more energy that can be channeled into body rotation and eventually to the ball. The forward thrust of the weight shift may also pull the angle of release down. This feedback could be followed up with a short cue like "step" to help him remember in subsequent practices.

Let's see why focusing on the weight shift could be the best intervention. Remember that the prioritization of corrections depends on the performer's goals and the

FIGURE 8.13 Photo sequence of the overarm throw of a boy throwing a softball for maximum distance. What correction would help this person improve the most? Time between pictures is 0.1 seconds.
Reprinted from Knudson and Morrison 1997: 146.

analyst's rationale for diagnosis. For many high-speed movements, sequential coordination is the last refinement for optimal performance. The development of sequential action will be limited until energy from the lower extremity can be channeled up the body. Correcting the angle of release will immediately improve performance because it is often an easy correction to make. But it may not be the best correction if the angle of release is related to the leg drive and subsequent loss of balance, rather than the typical child's perception that high throws go the farthest.

Analyzing Tennis Serve

Practice 8.4

Qualitatively analyze the overarm throws in the following video clips. Justify your evaluation, diagnosis, and choice of intervention. Focus on how the technique matches the apparent goal.

The qualitative analysis of the tennis serve provides an interesting contrast to the overarm throw. The overarm throw is the fundamental movement pattern associated with the tennis serve, and several authors have attempted to document the similarities between these two movements in order to examine the potential transfer of learning (Adrian and Enberg, 1971; Anderson, 1979; Miyashita et al., 1979; Rose and Heath, 1990; Wilkinson, 1996; Zebas and Johnson, 1989). Much of the tennis service action is different due to the use of a racket and rules restrictions on how the serve can be delivered. The ball must be tossed, be hit in the air without the body changing position on court, and travel over the net and land in the correct service court. Classic tennis instruction has a specific pattern of good form in the tennis serve, with small variations for different ball spins and match tactics. Note how the critical features of the tennis serve differ from overarm throwing.

You will find a wide variety of skill levels in the subjects examined. The illustrations range from beginners to a world-class tennis player.

Critical Features

Myriad tennis books, magazines, and professional articles provide opinions on the important aspects of classic form for a good tennis serve. Several models for the qualitative analysis of the tennis serve have been reported in the literature. Two physical education articles are noteworthy. Rose, Heath, and Megale (1990) proposed a model for the qualitative analysis of the tennis serve based on components similar to the motor development of the overarm throw. The integrated model for qualitative analysis of the tennis serve presented here is based on the article by Knudson, Luedtke, and Faribault (1994). They proposed six critical features of the tennis serve and cues in order of importance. The critical features and a few of the cues suggested by the article are summarized in table 8.6. There are several recent biomechanical studies that document the motion and causes of motion in skilled tennis players (Bahamonde, 2000; Chow et al., 1999; Elliott, Marshall, and Noffal, 1995).

Systematic Observational Strategy (SOS)

If these critical features are in the correct order (ultimate importance in learning and serve performance), qualitative analysis is simplified. First, the systematic observation is based on the importance of the critical features. Second, the diagnosis of performance is simplified because intervention can be provided in this order. Use the Knudson et al. (1994) qualitative analysis model for the tennis serve in the following two examples. Analyze the performance in figure 8.14, using the critical features listed in

FIGURE 8.14   Sequence images of a person performing a high-speed tennis serve. What correction would the qualitative analysis system suggest is most appropriate? How similar is this tennis serve to the overarm throw? Time between pictures is 0.2 seconds.

Reprinted from Knudson and Morrison 1997: 150.

TABLE 8.6 Critical Features and Cues for the Tennis Serve

Critical Feature	Cues
Grip	Hammer grip; loose and relaxed
Toss	Consistent placement; elevate the ball
Preparation	Trophy; coil the body; backscratch
Continuous upward motion	Uncoil; extend the wave
Follow-through	Release the wrist
Stance	Align your heels; slow and throw

Note. Critical features and cues are presented in order of importance to performance in the tennis serve. From "How to analyze the serve," by D. Knudson, D. Luedtke, and J. Faribault. Adapted with permission from *Strategies: A Journal for Sport and Physical Educators* 7(8), 19-22. Copyright 1994 by the American Alliance for Health, Physical Education, Recreation and Dance, 1900 Association Drive, Reston, VA 22091.

table 8.6. This person was a beginning tennis player in a college tennis class when the video was made.

Subject 1

The woman in figure 8.14 does not fit into the desirable range of correctness for several critical features. Her major limitations are the use of a western (frying pan) grip, a toss that is not high enough, limited upward motion in the hitting action, and an abbreviated follow-through. This situation is common for novices. They will simplify the serve to make contact with the ball and increase the chance of hitting the ball in the service court. What correction would help this performer improve the most? The

d   e   f

Knudson et al. (1994) approach suggests that the cue words *hammer grip* would be the most important feedback. The coach might say, "That serve had great timing! Check your grip. I think you need to slip your hand back to that hammer grip." Qualitative analysis of subsequent trials could help determine whether corrections were needed on the toss, upward hitting action, and follow-through.

Does the use of prioritized critical features make qualitative analysis easier? Does this qualitative analysis also have potential biases? The answer to both questions is probably yes. Diagnosis of performance is quite easy once weak critical features have been identified. The most important critical features are corrected first. This is also the potential bias of the Knudson et al. approach. Some tennis instructors would not agree with the importance placed on the grip. For decades there has been a controversy over which grip to teach beginning players: the best advanced grip (continental grip) or the easier eastern forehand grip. There is a trade-off: Will the performer have the most difficulty as a beginner getting the ball into play with the best grip, or later as an intermediate trying to improve to the next level by unlearning the eastern grip? The ideal situation would be to have research which shows that learning the continental grip is the most effective way to learn the serve. If this research has been done and the analyst has done her homework, the qualitative analysis will be biased toward the truth. Potential bias is a concern when the analyst is not sure of the priority of the critical features of the movement.

FIGURE 8.15 Sequence images of a person performing a high-speed tennis serve. What correction would the qualitative analysis system suggest is most appropriate? Time between pictures is 0.2 seconds.
Reprinted from Knudson and Morrison 1997: 150.

Subject 2

Qualitatively analyze the tennis serve of the performer shown in figure 8.15. This person was also in a college tennis class, but she had more experience than the player in figure 8.14. Will the intervention suggested by your analysis be easier or harder for the performer because of that experience?

The weaknesses of this performer are more subtle and are related to two critical features. The performer's toss has an exaggerated style that creates a toss that is too high and consequently makes the serve hitch or pause. Note the large arm rotation in preparation to toss the ball compared to the performer in figure 8.14. Experienced tennis coaches might notice that the arm action in preparation (not illustrated) is like a scissors, moving initially in opposite directions rather than the traditional down-and-up-together motion of the arms.

The second critical feature with problems is a continuous upward motion of the body. The high toss creates a pause after the weight shift. The upward action of the serve then begins without some of the energy that the lower extremities created earlier. Another possible symptom of this pause, not visible in the figure, is a slight dragging of the right toe. The sound of a dragging toe or visual inspection of the court and the performer's shoes can be clues to this limitation in performance.

d   e   f

How to provide intervention is this situation is a classic example of a major difficulty of diagnosis: the interaction of many factors that affect performance. Slowing the toss and making it lower may not directly synchronize the service action. The performer will likely go through her normal action, pause, and attempt to hit a ball that is now much lower than it should be at the contact point. Unfortunately, the other alternatives for intervention may be worse! Slowing the body preparation may not create much energy to transfer up the kinetic chain of the body or provide much eccentric muscle stretch to contribute to the hitting action. Attempting to modify stance, weight shift, or foot action affects balance, which in turn affects the other changes being made in the kinetic chain. This subject's performance would clearly improve if a slow-and-throw rhythm replaced her rush-pause-and-hit coordination. The toss, preparation, hitting action, and stance all interact to create the rhythm and service action.

The high toss and hurried racket preparation are clearly creating a hitch in the service action. Slowing down and simplifying the toss might best improve performance in the long run. Good intervention would combine a demonstration and feedback. The analyst could demonstrate the serve, focusing the player's attention on a three-count rhythm. Good feedback would include cues such as "Slow down your preparation. Remember to slow and throw." Or "Smoothly build up racket speed like

a   b   c

FIGURE 8.16   Sequence images of a person performing a high-speed tennis serve. What correction would the qualitative analysis system suggest is most appropriate? Time between pictures is 0.2 seconds.
Reprinted from Knudson and Morrison 1997: 152.

a ocean wave." Improving service rhythm will be difficult and usually results in short-term decreases in service performance.

This is another situation where the performer is mature enough to handle more advanced feedback. During a break she should be given a detailed breakdown of the strengths and weaknesses of her serve. The coach might explain that the hitting action of the serve is great, but adjusting the toss and racket preparation can improve consistency and power. The how and why of these changes and a long-term plan for improvement should be discussed. This will help motivate the player to make difficult adjustments and tolerate the initial decrease in performance.

Subject 3

Qualitatively analyze the serve shown in figure 8.16. This athlete is a professional tennis player who was an Association of Tennis Professionals (ATP) rookie of the year and has been ranked in the top 10 in the world. If you were this player's coach, what intervention would you try to sell to him? You will have to sell the change, because his results have been good and you are working for him.

This player performs all the critical features of the tennis serve well. (Few players rate among the best of a world-class field in tennis without a strong serve.) There is

d   e   f

only one aspect of his serve that could be improved: the timing of the racket preparation and toss. This athlete's toss is very high because it is not synchronized with the racket preparation. He also lifts the racket straight up, rather than the usual circular drop and lift simultaneous with the toss. It is possible that the timing of the toss/preparation and the kind of arm backswing in his serve are style factors that do not limit performance. If the player were to change his service preparation, would that substantially improve his serve? If so, how difficult will it be? Will the improved performance be worth the difficulty and initial decrease in serving ability? With a highly skilled player like this, how much input should the athlete have in this decision? Professional athletes can fire their coaches, while collegiate athletes cannot.

Let's assume that you decide that changing the subject's serve will improve his performance. You decide that a lower toss will be less affected by wind, the faster delivery will be more difficult to return, and the traditional backswing will create a larger eccentric muscular stretch prior to the upward swing. Professional tennis players compete in a year-long season. There are few long breaks during which this player could work on changing his serve, but you convince him to extend a break in tournament play. This resting phase of his periodization training cycle is extended to a month and a half. What intervention would be appropriate in practice during this break from competition? How do you motivate the athlete? How do you gauge success in practice and during the tournament play to follow?

In a one-on-one coaching situation like this, the analyst has much more time to provide intervention to improve performance than most coaches. Athletes like this one are typically more mature and knowledgeable about their sport. One approach would be, "Let's talk about some small serve changes to work on during your down cycle. You've been serving with a great first and second serve percentage, but I think with a few minor changes you could make your serve an even bigger weapon." After listening to his reply, you could propose, "The consistency and deception in your serve can be improved if we work on your toss. The power of your serve can be improved by changing your racket preparation to more of a drop and lift." Listen to the athlete's opinion on these suggestions, and together decide if and which corrections should be attempted.

As the coach, you should also lay out the long-term practice plan. Build the player's confidence that he can improve his serve and this will be the payoff. Progress can be monitored by continual qualitative analysis of the serve, radar measurements of service speed, and results and serve statistics from practice matches. It is important to show the athlete that you have a plan to monitor his progress toward the goal.

Practical Applications: Similar Skills

Have a partner perform overarm throw and tennis serves. How are the overarm throw and tennis serve similar and how are they different? Are similar critical features of the same importance in each of these skills? Do differences in the serve and throw remain consistent across different performers? Does qualitative analysis ability transfer to similar motor skills?

Perform your own mini-experiment by practicing qualitative analysis of live or videotaped tennis serve and overarm throwing performances. Both activities are difficult to analyze because of their speed. What outcome variables (ball accuracy, speed, spin) may be useful in gaining information about performance elements that are difficult to see? Do you think skill in qualitative analysis of the overarm throw will transfer to qualitative analysis of the tennis serve? Do you think skill in observation of the overarm throw helps in the qualitative analysis of the tennis serve?

Analyzing Human Gait

Most people automatically perform some qualitative analysis of gait as they passively observe others walking. We have all experienced a situation where we recognized someone we knew by the walk long before we could see the person's face. Our visual attention is drawn to specific aspects of a person's gait. Qualitative analysis of gait in physical therapy is typically done at a much deeper level. Walking, like other human movements, has important critical features. The integrated qualitative analysis system for human walking here is based on five critical features common in clinical analyses of gait. This model is simpler than the ones many therapists use. Qualitative analysis of gait in physical therapy involves greater depth of analysis into the musculoskeletal system because the therapist is knowledgeable about the patient's medical history, physical testing, and rehabilitation. In fact, the purpose of qualitative analysis of gait in physical therapy usually extends beyond observable function to what musculoskeletal limitations are affecting the patient.

Q&A Practice 8.5

Qualitatively analyze the tennis serves in the following video clips. Justify your evaluation, diagnosis, and choice of intervention. Does your diagnosis agree with the diagnosis implied by Knudson et al. (1994)?

Characteristics of Human Gait

Human gait is an example of a well-learned fundamental movement pattern that, in normal situations, is performed with a great deal of efficiency and consistency. A person's walking develops from an infant struggling to control balance against gravity to a child or adult who can walk skillfully without conscious effort. The characteristics of normal gait have been extensively documented (Whittle, 1996; Winter, 1987, 1989; Woollacott and Shumway-Cook, 1989). Gait is a classic example of the flexibility of motor control provided by the brain. In normal gait, the kinematics (angles, distances, and speeds) of the lower extremity are highly consistent. The kinetics (muscle forces and torques), however, can vary in creating the same kinematics or pattern of motion (Winter, 1984). This flexibility of neuromuscular control is an important ally of the therapist attempting to compensate for a patient's deficit, but it can be a difficult problem in the analysis and diagnosis of problems in gait.

The goals of qualitative analysis of human gait in typical clinical settings vary depending on the limitations and needs of each patient. Rehabilitation of minor injuries may require limited qualitative analysis and gait training, while more serious problems require extensive qualitative gait analysis, rehab, and gait training. In general, gait analysis has goals that vary from establishing safe gait to improving gait until it is more functional, and finally to more cosmetic gait. A cosmetically normal gait is very important to many patients. The issues that therapists usually try to evaluate are range of motion, strength, gait pattern, and the need for orthotics or assistive devices. Thus, gait qualitative analysis in physical therapy is essentially a biomechanical analysis to determine the cause of an observed gait abnormality.

Eastlack et al. (1991) identified four major observational gait analysis systems that are used in physical therapy: (1) the child prosthetic-orthotic studies observational gait analysis form (New York University), (2) the Rancho Los Amigos Hospital normal and pathological gait syllabus, (3) the functional ambulation profile, and (4) a guide to the visual examination of pathological gait (Temple University). Most of these analysis systems are organized around the biomechanical characteristics of normal gait. A good review of typical gait analysis and common gait abnormalities can be found in Lehmann (1982).

Normal gait has a high-energy stance phase (60 percent of cycle) and a lower-energy swing phase (40 percent of cycle). There is a short period (25 percent) of double support, when both feet are in contact with the ground. The key events of the stance phase are the heel strike, foot flat, midstance, and toe-off. The important events of swing are acceleration, midswing, and deceleration.

The Biomechanics of Gait

The primary biomechanical trait of human gait may be efficiency. The motor development of walking begins with the instability, wide stance, and raised arms of an infant and gradually progresses to a precisely controlled and highly efficient movement pattern. Most of the upward or side-to-side movements in walking are typically less than 2 inches, which minimizes the energy expended to move the body. One of the most well-established descriptions of normal gait is the landmark *determinants of gait* proposed by Saunders et al. (1953). These six actions of the body in normal gait minimize the motion of the body's center of gravity to make walking efficient.

Normal gait involves pelvic rotation of about 4 degrees forward and backward in the transverse plane. This pelvic motion minimizes vertical motion of the body and the amount of hip flexion/extension in walking. The second determinant of gait is about a 5-degree downward pelvic tilt in the frontal plane to keep the body from rising as it is moved over the stance leg and the other leg swings through. Normal knee flexion in midstance is 10 to 20 degrees. A small amount of ankle dorsiflexion enhances the functional length of the leg and cushioning at heel strike. Ankle plantar flexion at toe-off helps smooth out the body's vertical motion. Minimal lateral motion of the body is the final determinant that helps maintain balance over the narrow base of support in normal walking. Research is beginning to test the hypothesized kinematic benefits of these typical motions in gait (Kerrigan et al., 2001).

Readers should note that many hospitals throughout the world are beginning to rely on quantitative biomechanical analyses of gait to treat many diseases and injuries. These quantitative measures are more expensive than qualitative analyses, but quantification of biomechanical variables allows the therapists to understand and track the progress in the neuromuscular limitations of their patients. The Movement Analysis Lab of the Gillette Children's Hospital (St. Paul, Minn.) Web site has videos and CD-ROMs about the biomechanics of normal gait, pathological gait, and running (www.gillettechildrens.com/programs-services/motion-analysis/motionanalysisvideos.html). The Gait and Clinical Movement Analysis Society (www.gcmas.org/) is the professional society for biomechanics and medical professionals using quantitative biomechanical analysis to improve functional movement in clinical settings. Clinical Gait professionals have created a great Web site that offers video clips of various movement disorders and summaries of biomechanical data and treatment ideas (http://guardian.curtin.edu.au/cga/).

Critical Features of Human Gait

Based on this review of human gait literature, we propose six critical features of human gait, which are related to the three dominant biomechanical features of human gait: (1) maintenance of posture and balance, (2) support actions, and (3) control of foot recovery (Winter, 1989). Table 8.7 summarizes these critical features.

TABLE 8.7 Critical Features of Gait

Critical Feature	Cues
Minimal sway	Body over base of support
Arm opposition	Opposite arm leg
Minimal rise	Smooth recovery; smooth push-off
Cushioning	Give with the leg
Leg support	Push down and backward
Push off	Press with toes

Reprinted from Knudson and Morrison 1997: 155.

Systematic Observational Strategy (SOS)

These three areas also provide the basis for a good SOS of human gait. Most of these critical features can be evaluated from a sagittal plane view. An analyst might look at a person's overall posture and balance by visually focusing on the trunk in the first few steps. To observe the next several steps, focus on one leg in the support phase and then in the swing phase of the gait cycle. Use this observational strategy to qualitatively analyze the gait illustrated in figure 8.17. You can easily practice qualitative analysis of gait in shopping malls or other public areas where you can observe people inconspicuously. It is important that they not notice you so that they will use their natural gait (and not be alarmed that someone is watching them).

Examples of Normal Gait

The sequence in figure 8.17 illustrates half a cycle of normal walking of two young adults. Are all the critical features of gait previously discussed exhibited? Which person do you think is walking faster? Why? What critical features are difficult to evaluate and what other vantage points would be helpful for observation?

The people illustrated in figure 8.17 are in different phases of the gait cycle. The female (wearing a backpack) begins in double support with left foot toe-off and right foot strike, while the male begins in midstance on his right foot. Both walk smoothly with upright trunks, move the arms in opposition to the legs, flex the knee and hip in stance, and vigorously push off. The female is walking faster, as evidenced by the extension in the legs (compare both subjects near double support). Note that their heads become closer in successive images. A rear view is essential to evaluating the width of the base of support, lateral motion, and pelvic tilt. This sagittal plane view is an effective vantage point for evaluating step lengths, joint actions, opposition, and vertical motion of the body. How might their gait change if the backpack were very heavy, they were walking uphill, or the ground were very slippery?

A way to practice the evaluation and diagnosis of gait analysis is to create artificial gait situations. Videotape fellow students walking on the ice one winter morning. Create different foot pains by placing a small stone in your sock. Taping or bracing joints can also create an artificial injury or contracture that analysts can study by qualitatively analyzing the resulting gait. Gait can be observed or videotaped on hills, and after the performer has fatigued a muscle group with exercises. Care must be taken to ensure performer safety when setting these situations up for qualitative analysis practice.

FIGURE 8.17   Sequence images of half a walking cycle in two young adults. Are all the features of normal gait apparent? What other views would be helpful? Time between pictures is 0.1 seconds.
Reprinted from Knudson and Morrison 1997: 154.

Practice 8.6

Qualitatively analyze the walking gaits in the following video clips. Some clips represent gaits related to a specific injury or neuro-muscular condition. Justify your evaluation, diagnosis, and choice of intervention. Try to locate the body motion that seems unusual. What injury or weakness do you suspect?

Further Practice

These examples illustrate many of the important factors in qualitative analysis of human movement. Your analytical skill will develop when you make a conscious effort to improve all four tasks of qualitative analysis (preparation, observation, evaluation and diagnosis, and intervention) and practice qualitative analysis of human movement. The best practice is to analyze live performances. You may be able to observe unobtrusively at a neighborhood park, gym, or athletic field. Another good way to practice is to review videotaped performances. The videos need to be made following the recommendations in chapter 8. Most television coverage of sporting events is inadequate for practicing good qualitative analysis because you cannot change vantage points or distances, change the task, or have the performer repeat the task. You can practice qualitative analysis by watching network or cable sports coverage, but you will not have enough information to make a good integrated qualitative analysis.

Summary

Training has been shown to improve qualitative analysis ability. We presented images of several human movements to illustrate the application of the integrated model of qualitative analysis. Readers should compare their analyses of the examples presented in the text and critically examine differences. Do various qualitative analysis models lead to the same intervention?

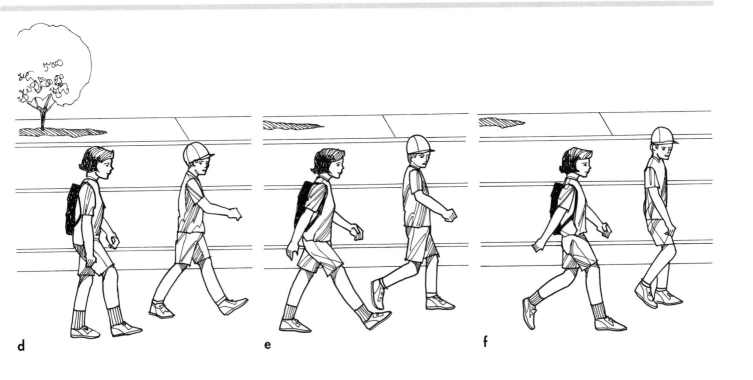

d   e   f

Discussion Questions

1. What *SOSs* are difficult to employ with the sequential images presented in this chapter?

2. Discuss the advantages of diagnosing and providing intervention based on critical features that have been prioritized according to their importance to performance.

3. Identify possible problems of diagnosing and providing intervention based on critical features that have been prioritized according to their importance.

4. What information is missing from the drawings of the movements? From the video clips? How would your evaluation and diagnosis be different if additional information were available?

Theory Into Practice Situations

© Tony Demin/International Stock

An adult at your health club is becoming very interested in weight training and has asked for your help in doing lunges. She has done lunges before but wants you to evaluate her technique and give her a lesson on the finer points. Precise body positioning and technique are essential in weight training. They ensure that the muscle groups targeted by the exercises are the muscle groups that are primarily involved in the exercises. Use the science of biomechanics to qualitatively analyze the lunge in the photograph. If she were to do several repetitions and begin to have a more forward trunk lean, what differences in muscle group involvement would you expect? (Hint: Look at the arm movement or horizontal distance from the load to the joints.) What back position (amount of lumbar arch) is associated with even or safe spinal loading?

1. Develop skill in applying integrated qualitative analysis to a variety of real-world problems.
2. Identify subdisciplines of kinesiology that provide relevant information for making decisions within qualitative analysis of human movement.

Many situations arise where a professional must integrate information from several subdisciplines of kinesiology. This chapter presents some scenarios from various kinesiology professions where an integrated qualitative analysis can be applied to help a performer. Think through each of the tasks of an integrated qualitative analysis. These situations are useful for generating discussions with other professionals. The first situation is developed as an example. Following this example you will be presented with other qualitative analysis challenges. The material is presented so these scenarios can be used as class exercises or assignments. The format will follow the comprehensive model proposed in the text: preparation, observation, evaluation and diagnosis, and intervention.

"Cleared to Play"

A sophomore coming off an anterior cruciate ligament (ACL) knee injury has asked to return to your junior college volleyball team. As head coach, you have to decide if she is ready for practice and match play because there is no athletic trainer to monitor her rehabilitation. What aspects of volleyball skills should qualitative analysis focus on? What physical tests can you give this athlete to help you make this decision? Do the athlete's personality traits have any bearing on this decision?

Preparation

In the preparation task of qualitative analysis, you should review any pre-injury information you may have on this athlete. Your research into her injury, rehab, and previous history should suggest which critical features of volleyball movements you should observe to evaluate her ability to play. Since the ACL is an important knee ligament limiting forward motion of the tibia on the femur, you should plan to observe the control of knee flexion and extension. Important volleyball movements that may stress the ACL are jumping, landing, and making vigorous changes of direction. You should also plan to focus on the player's facial expressions and body language for signs of knee pain.

Beyond observing for signs of injury, you may want to analyze how much previous ability has been recovered. If quantitative information (jump height, speed trials, agility measures) is not available, use your memory to compare the athlete's volleyball movements to those of other players. You may also plan to perform your typical qualitative analysis of selected volleyball skills to look for changes in technique.

Observation

Plan to observe carefully the athlete's control of knee flexion in landing, jumps, and changes of direction. Your observational strategy should also focus on any signs of discomfort. A good plan for observation might begin with the usual team warm-up routine so that you'll know what movements are coming and can be sure of a gradual, safe increase in movement intensity. Some volleyball movements you should plan to observe are jumps and landings in spiking and blocking. Intensity should be gradually increased. Since the ACL checks forward motion of the tibia, you might ask the athlete to hop forward and backward as far as possible on each foot six times. Landing in backward hopping creates a forward force on the lower leg that tends to stress the ACL. Major differences in distance jumped or control of the knee between the injured and uninjured legs are important points for observation. Finally, plan to monitor the athlete's affected knee for swelling after practice or physical testing.

Evaluation and Diagnosis

Your focus in evaluation is on the quality of the athlete's control of the knee during the high-energy phases of jumping, landing, and cutting movements. Evaluating the focal points of observation may be simpler than in many qualitative analyses because you are primarily interested in detecting injury-related weaknesses that would prohibit participation. The buckling or giving of the knee or unusual knee motions may merely need to be detected. Evaluating the athlete's recovery of ability relative to other athletes or evaluating her technique in the various volleyball skills is more difficult. Judging the quality of a spike is more difficult than merely detecting differences in distances or heights of jumps.

The diagnosis of the weaknesses identified in evaluation depends on your philosophy regarding the return of injured players. Since tissues that have not fully healed are more easily reinjured, some coaches might keep diagnosis simple by not allowing a player to return if she shows any signs of weakness or loss of knee control. This diagnosis of performance could also be tricky because the athlete might experience some discomfort associated with higher-intensity activity rather than overuse of tissue that is not fully healed. Here you must apply your knowledge of sports medicine and biomechanics to make sure critical features you have identified in evaluation are not related to reinjury or to limiting volleyball performance. Clearly the injury risk to the athlete is the first priority of diagnosis, with level of performance being the second priority.

Intervention

As the coach, you have many options in dealing with this athlete. If the diagnosis indicates that she is ready to return, you should provide positive feedback on her effort in rehabilitating the injury. It would also be wise to express confidence in the player's recovery and ability. Remind her that her timing and teamwork will take time to recover. Express confidence in her, but ask her to be careful and caution her that most athletes tend to rush the recovery process.

If the diagnosis indicates that the athlete should not return to the team, there are also several approaches to intervention. It is very important to be sensitive when you tell her that she needs to continue rehab before she can rejoin the team. You might say, "You've made a lot of progress, but I would like you to come back in two weeks for another tryout." Another option would be to allow limited practice with the team. You could also recommend that the athlete consider a knee brace.

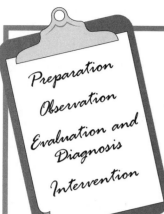

"But I Can Score!"

A high school basketball player is having great success driving to the left and scoring during a preseason practice. But he uses his right hand to execute lay-ups and is successful only because of his speed and superior jumping ability. What feedback or intervention would be appropriate? What will happen if taller and/or faster opponents guard this player or weak-side defense rotates to defend the lay-up?

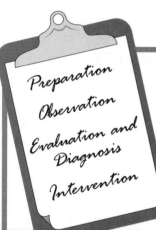

The Slump

A college softball player is struggling with her hitting. At midseason she was leading the team, but now she has been hitless in several games. What would be a good approach to the qualitative analysis of her hitting? Assume there is videotape of her hitting from earlier in the season. Should intervention focus on technique or the hitter's confidence?

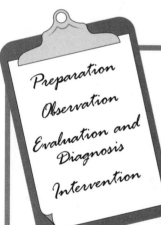

"But the Champ Does It This Way"

As a tennis coach, you notice that a promising junior tennis player is using more open-stance forehand drives during practice and matches. You think he is emulating many tennis professionals, who are using open-stance strokes rather than the traditional square stance. What intervention do you provide to this 12-year-old player?

"But I Can Lift More!"

Preparation

Observation

Evaluation and Diagnosis

Intervention

An athlete is struggling with a plateau in chest strength and asks for your help with training. During her bench press you notice the body position illustrated in figure 9.1. What intervention is appropriate for an athlete of any age with the technique illustrated? The athlete senses she can lift more with this technique, but what parts of the body does it put at risk of injury? Are there bench-press variations that would be safer? Are there alternative exercises isolating specific muscle groups that can be used together to replace the bench press? What intervention strategy will you use to motivate the use of a safer lifting technique?

FIGURE 9.1   Bench press form for a lifter. What intervention is appropriate?
Reprinted from Knudson and Morrison 1997: 160.

The Parent Distraction

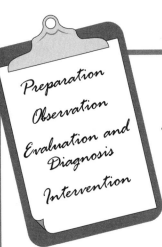

Preparation

Observation

Evaluation and Diagnosis

Intervention

An overzealous parent keeps yelling at one of your players, "Box out!" Defensive rebounding has not been a problem in this game and you have coached the team to emphasize the fast break against this opponent. How can qualitative analysis be used to identify which player the parent is yelling at and evaluate whether the players are being affected? What intervention would be appropriate?

The Final Authority

Preparation

Observation

Evaluation and Diagnosis

Intervention

You are asked to be a judge for a diving demonstration given by a local swim club. The divers will be children ages 10 to 16 who are first- and second-year students preparing for future competition. How can you increase the accuracy and consistency of your qualitative analyses of the dives? How can you avoid bias related to dive difficulty, age of the performer, and the order within the demonstration?

Preparation
Observation
Evaluation and Diagnosis
Intervention

Machine Versus Free Weights

You are asked to be part of a panel discussion on weight training at the state convention. The panel has chosen to discuss the differences between weight training with free weights and with a machine. How can you use qualitative analysis to compare free-weight arm curls with machine arm curls? What sub-disciplines of kinesiology are most relevant in analyzing each exercise?

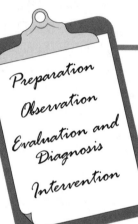

Preparation
Observation
Evaluation and Diagnosis
Intervention

Finishing Strong

You are a basketball coach whose best shooter has been shooting the lights out the entire game, but suddenly near the end of the game her shots are falling short. You may have only one or two looks at her form before you can call a time out in the final minutes of the game. What physical factors are involved and how can they be evaluated? How can you evaluate whether game pressure is affecting the athlete? What critical factors in shooting and other basketball skills should be observed? What interventions are best for different causes of this problem? Does this athlete's psychological makeup affect your intervention?

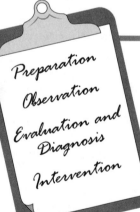

Preparation
Observation
Evaluation and Diagnosis
Intervention

Choke?

Two of the best tennis players in your junior development program have signed up for group lessons through the summer. One player excels in practice, where there are few observers and little crowd noise. This player has had difficulty in tournaments because of the crowd noise and pressure. The other player is just the opposite. He seems unmotivated in practice but thrives on pressure and has pulled off some big wins in tournaments. What can be done in practice and competition to help both performers? How can qualitative analysis be used to address the needs of each player?

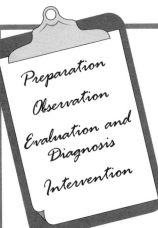

Push and Glide

You are teaching inline skating at a summer camp. One student is having difficulty with turns to the left. Your initial intervention focused on the push-off and recovery of her right leg. Like a good analyst, you immediately return to observation from intervention and find that the student is still having difficulty. Could your initial evaluation and diagnosis have been incorrect? Should you plan to evaluate the right leg again, or focus on the left leg? What aspects of leg action and balance might provide clues to the skater's problem? Could changing the task provide other clues for your evaluation?

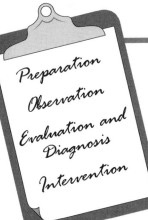

Head Over Heels, Please

One of your newer gymnastics students is having difficulty in learning the front handspring. Your observation of the first few lessons makes you think this young person is afraid of the more difficult skills. As you plan your next lesson, you set up your approach of the four tasks of qualitative analysis. What psychological cues about the gymnast's attitude do you plan to look for? What intervention will be most effective for this gymnast, motivational or technique? Could modifying the task build skills and confidence in this gymnast?

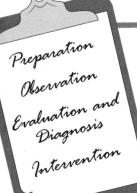

Coaching Clinic

You are a football coach worried about a player who is struggling to participate after several lower-extremity injuries in earlier years. This athlete really wants to play and is the kind of person who will ignore the pain in order to play and help the team. You plan to secretly watch this player during the school day and in physical education class to evaluate movement for signs of injury. What cues in walking gait or other locomotion might hint of an ankle or knee injury? If your initial qualitative analysis suggests that the athlete is hurt, how could you plan a more formal qualitative analysis of several movements during practice to determine if you should rest this player?

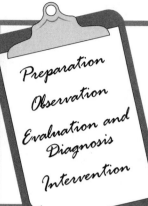

Glide

You have a class of beginning swimmers. You notice during freestyle practice that one of your swimmers plunges his hand into the water directly in front of his head. He does not roll his body onto the entry and glide before he begins to pull. What instructional cues can you use to help him get a feel for proper technique? Are there any drills you could prescribe to help him roll and glide more?

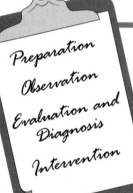

Check It Out

You are the coach of the local high school hockey team. You have a defenseman who has played on your team for three years. This player understands the game well, especially the spatial relationship of players on the ice. This understanding extends to his position in relation to an oncoming forward carrying the puck across the blue line toward the goal. He is usually in good position to force the forward to the boards close to the blue line, but he rarely completes the play successfully. By *successfully* the coach means a solid, clean check into the boards. Since this player understands correct positioning, how can you help him optimize his checking? In your preparation phase consider all the important technical information related to skating and checking. Also consider motivation and psychological factors. Plan how you will observe skating and checking technique. How will you diagnose and evaluate checking technique? What types of intervention could you use?

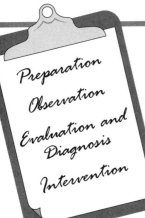

Preparation
Observation
Evaluation and Diagnosis
Intervention

Surf's Up

You are at your favorite surfing spot when you notice a young surfer trying to catch a wave. She appears to be located at the correct take-off point and gets good speed paddling to get on the wave. She also seems to be able to choose good waves. Once the wave starts moving her board, she appears to be able to make a quick and accurate transition from paddling to standing. Regardless of wave size or shape, however, she seems to fall off the board quickly, rarely gaining her balance or establishing herself in the correct standing position. How could you set yourself up to be able to observe her more closely? What will be your approach to observation? What things do you think she should know about surfing/balancing technique that would help her?

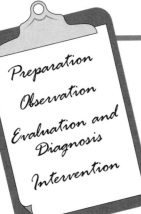

Preparation
Observation
Evaluation and Diagnosis
Intervention

Hurdle

You are a track coach with several young athletes. You have a number of good sprinters and wish to start developing some of them into hurdlers. One of your better sprinters does not seem to be as excited about the prospects of running the hurdles as some of your less-talented sprinters. Instead of approaching the hurdle with a great deal of speed, he seems to chop his steps and hesitate. This athlete seems to have all the tools of a good hurdler (height, speed, long legs, and so on). What would you do to ascertain what is limiting his ability to hurdle? How could you prepare to gather information upon which to base a decision? Could you plan an observation strategy to gather relevant information? What would you evaluate and diagnose? Could you suggest some forms of intervention based on your judgment of the problem?

Further Practice

Many readers will have assisted others in learning some motor skill. Think back to an interesting experience you have had in teaching someone to move. Translate that experience into a "theory into practice" qualitative analysis scenario. Share this scenario with your instructor or another student.

Summary

This chapter presented several real-life situations where an integrated qualitative analysis would be appropriate. Simultaneous consideration of information from several sub-disciplines of kinesiology is needed in analyzing each situation. The unique nature of each situation demands thoughtful consideration in integrating information from many subdisciplines. The qualitative analysis of the squat relies heavily on biomechanics, but information from exercise physiology and psychology is also vital in shaping the appropriate intervention. These situations are useful in stimulating discussion among professionals about the qualitative analysis of human movement.

Discussion Questions

1. What subdisciplines of kinesiology were most relevant to you in each of the scenarios presented in this chapter? Why?

2. Which scenarios were most interdisciplinary in nature? What subdisciplines of kinesiology had to be integrated?

3. What other kinds of information would you want to observe in each of the scenarios presented in this chapter?

4. Propose another "theory into practice" qualitative analysis scenario and determine if your solution is consistent with your peers' analyses.

Videotape Replay Within Qualitative Analysis

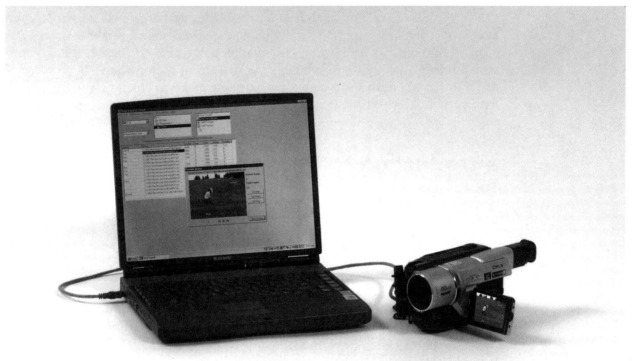

© Human Kinetics

You are a coach who has used videotape to record and qualitatively analyze an athlete. You receive information on a new video and computer system with high-tech features. Can use of this system improve your qualitative analyses? Videotape replay has often been used to extend observational power, but does this system share these advantages or does it have limitations? Which of the computer-enhanced features of the digital video clips are of real value? Which of the four tasks of qualitative analysis benefit the most from a system like this?

1. Describe the uses of videotape replay for extending observational power within qualitative analysis.
2. Explain how to use videotape to maximize qualitative analysis ability.
3. Describe spatial and temporal limitations of commercial and consumer video equipment in documenting human movement.

An important tool in extending observational power within qualitative analysis is the use of videotape replay, especially slow-motion replay. Video replay may be most useful in providing information to the analyst that is unavailable to real-time observation. Videotape can capture fast elements of the movement that are unobservable by the naked eye. This greater movement detail and unlimited capacity for replay makes video an important tool for extending the observational power of the teacher or coach within qualitative analysis. This chapter will review the factors that are important in using video to improve qualitative analysis of motor skills. These factors also apply to recent advances in computer grabbing and presentation of video clips that have been developed for qualitative analysis.

Introduction to Video Replay in Kinesiology

Many of the early studies of videotape in teaching motor skills focused on its use as visual feedback. Reviews of these early studies found that video replay used as feedback to performers is not significantly different from regular practice and teacher-augmented feedback in improving motor skills (Rothstein, 1980; Rothstein and Arnold, 1976). People seeing themselves perform on videotape replay do not appear to spontaneously perceive important aspects of their movement to improve performance. Recent studies have begun to show that video replay may have some benefits, due to the observational learning or modeling of the performer's behavior, beyond intrinsic feedback (Dowrick, 1991b; Gould and Roberts, 1982). Even though the knowledge of performance (KP) or modeling information in videotape replay is not any more useful to the performer than other inherent feedback, video replay can provide important information for the analyst to improve qualitative analysis. The section on using videotape replay for qualitative analysis will review important aspects on this research in more detail.

KEY POINT 10.1 Research has shown that videotape replay does not provide any special information to the mover beyond other forms of feedback. Videotape replay, however, can provide additional information on performance to the analyst skilled in qualitative analysis using videotape.

If used correctly, videotape replay may have benefits to the qualitative analysis of motor skills (Franks and Maile, 1991; Rothstein, 1980; Trower and Kiely, 1983). A major advantage of videotape replay is that it shows high-speed details of the movement that are not available to real-time observation. Video-recorded performances also have virtually unlimited and slow-motion replay potential to increase observational power. Computer programs can even extend and enhance these replay advantages of videotape.

Before we discuss the use of videotape in qualitative analysis, teachers and coaches should know how video imaging works and be aware of the limitations of the medium. The rest of this section describes the basics of video imaging and how these technical facts shape the analyst's use of video within qualitative analysis.

Two-Dimensional Image

A normal photographic or video image from one camera is a two-dimensional (2-D) representation of a three-dimensional (3-D) scene. This means that only objects oriented at right angles to the lens will be represented accurately, in the two dimensions of the image. These two dimensions are usually the vertical and horizontal when the camera is aligned to these important real-world directions. Anything aligned toward or away from the camera (any plane not parallel to the image) will be distorted in the image (2-D representation) taken of the real world (3-D reality). For a simple demonstration, extend your first and second fingers and hold them vertically at arms length from your eyes with your forearm pronated (looking at the back side of your hand/fingers). Note the angle formed between the fingers and how it appears to shrink when you supinate.

Suppose three TV cameras were placed next to the runway of the gymnastics vault (figure 10.1). The coach believes that the angle between the gymnast's extended arms prior to the block on the horse should be a specific angle for this athlete. The coach can get an accurate estimate of the angle between the two arms of the gymnast only when the camera is at a right angle to the motion of the arms at the instant of interest (camera B in figure 10.1). The views from cameras A and C show an arm angle that is smaller than the actual angle between the gymnast's arms. You can visualize these 2-D distortions of a 3-D event by imagining the angles viewed by cameras A and C as the shadows cast by the gymnast's arms on the back walls that are parallel to the cameras (the imagined light source). This is why an athlete can look as if he is stepping on a boundary line in one camera view, while a camera view down the boundary line shows that the athlete is inside the line.

The point to remember is that video images are 2-D representations of a 3-D reality. There are some predictable distortions of the image caused by the position and orientation of the objects in the field of view. People who use videotape for qualitative analysis should set up taping sessions to minimize these distortions and should know when these distortions may affect judgments about the performances. We will see that these distortions can also ruin many calculations that might be made with the digitizing and calculating capabilities of newer computer video systems.

> **KEY POINT 10.2** The 2-D images created by normal photography or video often provide distorted representations of the 3-D reality. For example, objects not parallel to the camera can appear smaller than they actually are.

Video Image

Video images are also limited representations of reality because they are made up of a 2-D array of dots. These dots that compose each picture are called *pixels* (short for *picture elements)*. Each picture element is given a shade on the gray scale (from black to white) for a black-and-white video picture. Color video is made up of pixels that have been given an intensity or mix of red, green, and blue light. A video picture is called a *frame* and is made up of two halves, or *fields*. One field is the odd-numbered, horizontal lines of pixels and the other field is the even-numbered, horizontal lines of pixels. This is why normal video is called *interlaced* video. The more pixels and lines of pixels in a video frame, the higher the resolution and the better the image.

Resolution

The number and size of these pixels determine the quality of the picture. Television production video equipment can have 525 (NTSC) or 625 (PAL) horizontal lines of

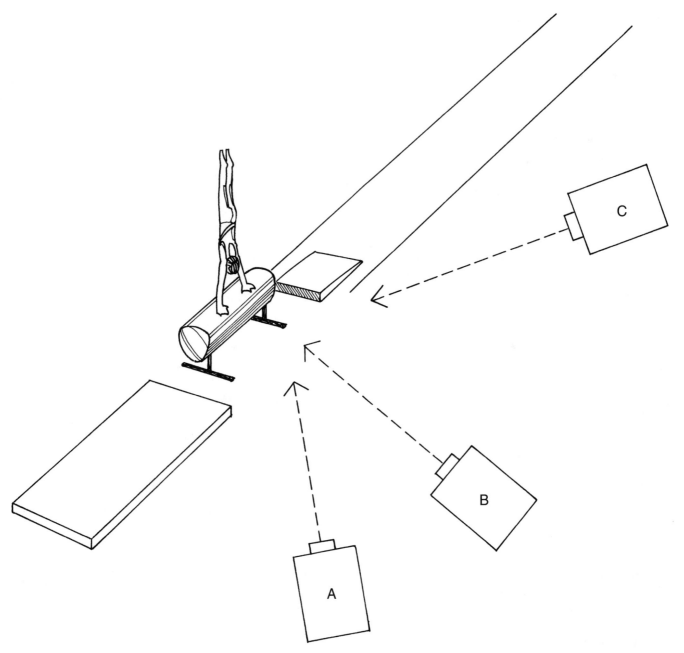

FIGURE 10.1   Schematic of three camera views of a gymnast vaulting. Only camera B provides an accurate image of the angle of the performer's arms as she blocks on the horse.
Reprinted from Knudson and Morrison 1997: 165.

pixels (Feldman, 1988). The number of pixels for a given field of view determines the resolution of the video picture and thus the image quality. Resolution in all directions is a critical issue when video is used for actual measurements (quantitative analysis), but it is still important in qualitative analyses if the images are of poor quality or the subject is small in a large field of view.

Video picture format is determined by broadcasting conventions, which vary around the world. National Television Standards Committee (NTSC) standards are used in North America and Japan. The United Kingdom, Australia, and European countries use Phase Alternation Line (PAL) video picture format, while the French and Russians use Sequential Coleur a'Memorie (SECAM) video. NTSC video has 30 frames or pictures each second; PAL and SECAM video have 25 frames per second. There is video equipment available that can switch among these international formats.

When consumer electronics are used to tape and display human movement, the resolution of the video images suffers. There is a difference between the resolution of one video component (camera) and the resolution of the whole system. For example, even a professional NTSC video signal may show up on a good TV as only 490 horizontal lines because it takes time to jump from the bottom of one frame to the top of the next. Camcorder video signals may have lower horizontal and vertical resolution than professional video. NTSC video produced by consumer camcorders, for example, generally creates images with 300 to 330 horizontal lines, with 235 to 245 pixels in each line. High-band consumer video formats (Super VHS [S-VHS] or 8 millimeter [Hi-8]) typically have 400 to 480 lines of horizontal resolution, with up to 640 pixels per line. A problem with higher resolution video is that many TVs and VCRs in the United States follow broadcast standard TV and cable formats of only 330 horizontal lines in a video frame. To take advantage of the improvements in resolution of high-band video system, one must factor in the added cost of special tapes, camcorders, and monitors.

Recently digital camcorders have become available at prices close to traditional analog cameras. Digital camcorders typically use the same TV field formatting to be compatible with analog equipment along with digital microcomputers. Note that the vertical resolution (the number of horizontal lines) is essentially fixed by the format of the video. The horizontal resolution (number of pixels in each horizontal line) varies according to how the analog video signal is sampled (digitized) or the digital video is captured. When a video ad claims 400 lines of resolution, this typically means the equipment can create 400 pixels in each horizontal line. Computer video systems can often handle larger horizontal resolutions because of differences in computer and TV displays. Added horizontal resolution depends on the video board or the digital camera that does the digitizing. Unfortunately, extra horizontal resolution will increase the size of the video files. Compression software (CODECS) is used to decrease the size of stored video files, but some reduce the quality of the images.

Some large-screen televisions are based on improved-definition television (IDTV), which creates a better-quality picture. High-definition television (HDTV) video has thousands of horizontal lines and thousands of pixels in each line. Currently some network broadcasts are being transmitted in HDTV. It will probably be a few more years before HDTV is regularly used in network and cable broadcasts because current HDTV units are very expensive.

Paused Video Image

The resolution of video, and consequently the quality of the picture, becomes worse when the VCR is put in freeze-frame or pause mode. When most consumer VCRs are put in pause mode, only one field is shown in order to prevent a flickering picture. Flicker is caused when there is motion between the two halves of a video frame (1/60 or 1/50 of a second apart), making the image seem to vibrate between the two positions on the screen. Some VCRs or frame grabbers used for computer-assisted video replay effectively give a person 60 or 50 half-pictures (fields) to look at when the frame-advance or slow-motion features are activated. Most digital camcorders in pause and frame advance show images 1/30 of a second apart. Unfortunately, most VCRs are similar and jump from the first field of a frame to the first field of the next frame when the frame advance is pushed, giving 30 lower-resolution pictures per second.

KEY POINT 10.3 The quality of a video image is strongly related to the number of picture elements (pixels) used to create that image. Many aspects of video technology affect the quality of video images that are used to extend observation within qualitative analysis.

Video pictures are physically bigger horizontally than vertically, but this is nowhere near the horizon of normal vision. Normal video has an aspect ratio (field width divided by height) of 4 to 3. This difference in field of view, combined with pixel resolution and lost resolution in freeze-frame mode, affects the quality of objects represented in these directions on most all video (analog or digital) images.

When consumer video is used for slow-motion or frame-by-frame qualitative analysis, you are most often looking at a video field, with half the vertical resolution of a normal video frame. If the video images were created with poor lighting, a small image size for the performer, a noncontrasting background, an unfavorable camera location, or some other problem, the video would probably not provide a good medium for the observation of small details. For example, if a subject's image is small and her arm rotates out of being parallel with the camera, it may be impossible to discern the position or angle of her arm.

Measurement From Video

Biomechanics research has been using video for kinematic measurements (quantitative analysis) for many years. Careful setup and procedural techniques (for example, scaling, camera alignment, shuttering, data smoothing) are needed to collect images, digitize, scale, and make accurate calculations from video data. Imagine the error in calculating elbow angle from an out-of-plane view of a movement like in QA Demonstration 5.6 (page 105).

Many biomechanical quantitative video systems are based on digital and commercial video equipment that break the video signal into each field (noninterlaced video) and may use sophisticated image processing to create subpixel resolution in measurements. Stereophotogrammetric techniques and special computer programs are needed to generate 3-D data from synchronized multiple camera images (Allard, Stokes, and Blanchi, 1995) or nonstationary (panning) camera setups. Just because a qualitative analysis software program provides some calculation features does not mean that the numbers generated will be accurate. Considerable data collection and processing expertise is required to do quantitative analysis from video. Most human movement professionals should use video for primarily qualitative analysis and not attempt measurements from video unless they are trained in these techniques or biomechanical assistance is available. Making videos for qualitative analysis is less complicated than for quantitative analysis. The following sections discuss important information in video technology and procedures for using video to enhance qualitative analysis.

Video Technology

This section will summarize the basics of video technology. The important characteristics of normal video that analysts need to be familiar with will be presented: frame rate as well as features of camcorders and VCRs.

Frame Rate

A modern analog or digital camcorder generates a video picture by using a charge-coupled device (CCD), a photosensitive array that assigns the appropriate gray scale or color to the pixels of a video frame. In the United States, the alternating current

Practical Applications: Hindsight Is 20/20

You are a first-year football coach at Metro High School and the head coach assigns you to coach the punters. Since many of the important actions of kicking are too fast to observe reliably in real time, you bring your camcorder to practice and videotape the punters trying out for the team. You record side views of the punters, maximizing the size of the punter in the field of view so that the tapes can be reviewed in freeze-frame and slow-motion replay.

As you review the tape, you can identify differences in knowledge of performance (KP) like punting technique, impact position, and ball position on the foot. Several strengths and weaknesses can be identified, and one punter is close to having the desirable punting form you expect. Unfortunately, you now realize the problem. You did not create a written or auditory record on the tape of the distance and hang time of each punt. What kind of information is the distance, hang time, and accuracy of each punt? Slow-motion video replay can extend observational power of only some of the critical features of punting. If videos are made from a position above the press box, coaches can document distance, accuracy, and hang time of the punts. In short, video replay can extend observational power in qualitative analysis, but it is not a magic bullet.

(AC) electrical power has a frequency of 60 hertz, so video standards are set up so that the phases of the current are used to scan each field of video. This gives NTSC video an effective frame rate of 30 frames per second. Normal cinematography frame rates are 24 frames per second. Compared to real-time visual observation, stop-action or slow-motion video dramatically increases the ability to see details of human movement. PAL and SECAM videos have an effective frame rate of 25 frames per second.

The sampling rates of human vision and normal video are important to understand because they help determine what aspects of human movement can be observed. For very high speed movements like pitching, tennis serving, or golf, normal video may sample at a high enough rate to consistently capture details of interest. A good example of distortions created by inadequate sampling would be the motion of the wheels of a stagecoach or wagon recorded by the typical frame rates in old westerns. When you watch these old movies, it appears that the wagon wheels are rotating backward because the frame rate is too slow to represent their actual rotation. The wheels rotate too quickly, making the spoke position of sequential frames appear behind the initial position, when in reality the spoke has rotated all the way around to a position behind the previous image.

Special high-speed video cameras are commercially available for research and other specialized tasks. Video cameras and support equipment capable of hundreds to several thousand frames per second (fps) are unnecessary for most qualitative analyses of human movement—and out of the price range of most teachers, coaches, and therapists. These high-speed video cameras would be necessary for a video analysis of the stiffness of various golf club shafts, ball rotation in baseball pitching, or the dynamics of a foot striking the ground in running.

Be aware that some consumer camcorders described as high-speed cameras are, in fact, *not* high-speed video. They are really just 30 frames per second, but with high shutter speeds (very small exposure times for each picture, for example, 1/10000 of a second). There is a marked difference in the kinematic information created between video with 30 fps and video with 200 or 1000 fps. Compare the temporal identification of impact in the illustrations in figure 10.2 that were taken from high-speed film (100 fps). Even 100 fps cannot guarantee that an image will contain impact (image b), but notice how far the racket can move (images a-c) when capturing images at 30 fps. The importance of the shutter speed will be discussed in the next section on camcorders.

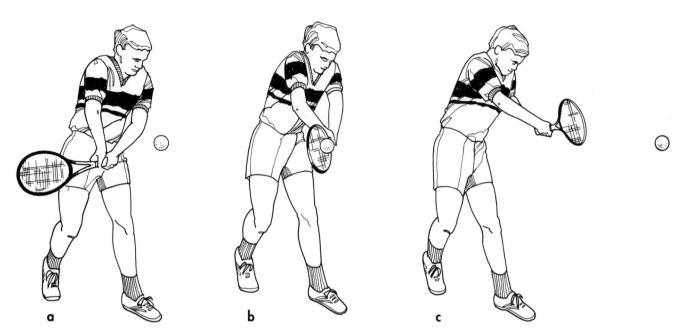

FIGURE 10.2 The difference between video sampling (30 fps) and high-speed imaging. High-speed imaging (100 fps) can usually identify impact (B), an event that lasts only 0.005 seconds. The sampling of normal video can miss high-speed events. A and B are 0.03 seconds apart.
Reprinted from Knudson and Morrison 1997: 168.

Some companies market video equipment specifically for sports instructors and coaches. Special video cameras, VCRs, editing equipment, and computer interfaces have been state-of-the-art in the imaging of football games for coaches to evaluate game plans and opponents. These game tapes have replaced the old 16-millimeter films that were used to record games and scout opponents. Many camcorders are marketed as appropriate video equipment for the analysis of sports. In fact, most camcorders have focusing, white balance, and shutter features that make them suitable for making video images for qualitative analysis. Let's look at the desirable camcorder features for qualitative analysis.

Camcorder

The camcorder is the combination of two machines that were separate in the early versions of video technology: the video camera and the recorder or machine to code the video signal on magnetic tape. Factors that help determine a camcorder's suitability include the shutter, image quality, and format.

Shutter

Perhaps the most important feature for imaging human movement for qualitative analysis is a shutter, which limits the exposure time that each field is scanned by the CCD. Capturing a field in 1/500 or 1/1000 of a second ensures that moving objects do not move much as the image is being captured. This allows the imaging of high-speed movements without blurring. The term *high-speed shutter* is a misnomer, since the shutter prevents image blurring but does not allow the camera to capture more images per second. In other words, a shutter does not make a high-speed camera, but rather the same 30 fps with crisp images of fast movements does.

The problem a shutter may create is a need for extra light when exposure times are very small. This is rarely a problem in using a camcorder outside in natural light, but

TABLE 10.1	Recommended Exposure Times for Videotaping Typical Human Movements

Activity	Exposure Time (Shutter Setting)
Walking	1/60 (off)
Sit to stand	1/60 (off)
Bowling	1/60 (off)
Basketball	1/100
Vertical jump	1/100
Jogging	1/100 to 1/200
Sprinting	1/200 to 1/500
Baseball pitching	1/500 to 1/1000
Baseball hitting	1/500 to 1/1000
Soccer kicking	1/500 to 1/1000
Tennis	1/500 to 1/1000
Golf	1/1000 or smaller

Reprinted from Knudson and Morrison 1997: 169.

indoors shuttered video may be underexposed unless extra light is used. Current camcorders have shutters that can generate exposure times as small as 1/10000 of a second. These settings are rarely necessary in capturing human movement. In fact, videotaping slower movements may not require the use of a shutter at all. Table 10.1 lists several common human movements and sports and the corresponding exposure times that may be needed to freeze the action.

It is also important to check how the camcorder operates in the stop mode. Some camcorders have a short rewind or roll-up of a couple of seconds after the tape is stopped. A good practice is to stop taping a couple of seconds after and start a couple of seconds before the action of interest.

Image Quality

Since an analyst may not have complete control over the situation being videotaped (weather, competition, logistics, and so on), the camcorder selected should have several automated features that help create good video images. These features should also be manually adjustable. Camcorders should have low-light sensitivity and autoexposure. Many camcorders have low-light sensitivity down to 1 lux. The camcorder should be able to create clear video pictures with the low levels of illumination caused by poor lighting, camera position, or the small exposure times created by a shutter. Some camcorders have a button adjustment for low-level lighting.

Other important image quality features include autofocus, autowhite balance, and a backlighting adjustment. Camcorders often automatically adjust the color sensitivity (white balance) to get uniform color in different lighting conditions. Especially important is a manual override on the autofocus feature. If the subject cannot be videotaped with the sun behind the camcorder, the backlighting adjustment is needed to prevent the light behind the subject from washing out the image.

Most camcorders use infrared beams directed at the center of the field of view to automatically focus the lens. Several conditions may not maintain a focused image, so the camcorder should have a manual override of the autofocus. An analyst may want the subject not to be in the center of the video picture to keep something else in the field of view; otherwise, other objects behind or in front of the subject may interfere with the autofocus. To focus manually, zoom in on the subject and focus, then adjust the zoom lens to the desired field of view. The camcorder should be as stable as possible to maximize image quality. A tripod is highly desirable, but some camcorders have stabilizing features to help limit motion of the field of view.

Format

One of the most important factors in choosing a camcorder used to be the format of the magnetic cassette tape. Since the 1960s large cassettes with 3/4-inch tape have been used. Two smaller 1/2-inch versions began competing for the portable/home video market: Video Home System (VHS) and a scaled-down version of professional video (Beta). Newer formats and digital video, which have now entered the video format wars, focus on two improvements: smaller size and greater resolution. Digital video and high-band formats (ED-Beta, Hi-8, and S-VHS) all have better resolution, while some formats accommodate smaller cassettes for mini-camcorders. Digital camcorders store digital video on various forms of magnetic media and have circuitry to convert the output to analog video for television playback. Digital and high-band video are not necessary for qualitative analysis, but they are desirable if the tapes and other video equipment are within your budget. In the following paragraphs the high-band format is in parentheses.

Three formats provide the smallest videocassettes: Hi-8, VHS-C, and digital. These formats have made the miniature, handheld camcorders popular. One format uses 8-millimeter tapes (Hi-8) that can store about two hours of video. This format requires that you use the recorder function to run the video signal to display or copy the images. Another format is VHS-C or (S-VHS-C), a compact version of the VHS format that can also hold up to two hours of video. These tapes have adapters so that they can be used in VCRs, which use the standard 1/2-inch magnetic tape. Digital camcorders and compact tapes typically store up to one hour of video in standard play (SP) recording. Whatever format you use, it is better to use SP recording than the expanded (LP, SLP) tape-coding speeds that degrade picture quality. Remember that not all CODECS (video compressors/decompressors) perfectly reproduce image quality, so use care in moving and saving video files.

The most popular format in the United States is VHS, whose high-band version is Super VHS (S-VHS). VHS has been more popular than Beta for years and is less expensive because of the competition with smaller camcorders. Beta's high-band version is ED-Beta (extended definition). Current VHS and Beta camcorders are larger than compact models but are not heavy or cumbersome.

Lens

Another important camcorder feature for qualitative analysis is the zoom lens. Often a camcorder cannot be placed in a desirable position because of facility or competition limitations. A zoom lens, which can accommodate a variety of distances from the subject, solves that problem. Lens focal lengths are specified in millimeters, but the range of a zoom lens is usually expressed as a ratio. Camcorders often have a zoom lens with a ratio between 12:1 and 20:1 (12:1 means that an object will appear 12 times larger in full zoom than in full wide-angle). Digital camcorders can augment this zoom capability by digitally enlarging the image, but the quality is inferior to optical. A zoom lens may allow the analyst to create video images from locations distant from the performer or from electrical power. Since electrical outlets are not always available, a long-life battery and a spare are essential.

KEY POINT 10.4 Some of the most important camcorder features related to qualitative analysis are format, shutter, low-light sensitivity, and the zoom lens.

Some camcorders provide valuable editing features. Date, titles, or time codes can be added to the image. Analysts should look up repair histories and reviews of these features in consumer publications (*Consumer Reports*, 1999) or trade magazines like *Videomaker* and *Video Review*. More on editing features will be discussed in the next section on VCRs. Good reviews of basic video technology are available (Dowrick, 1991a; Luther, 1998, 1999; McGrain, 1984).

When selecting a camcorder format for qualitative analysis, think about how and where you will be making the videos. How much time do the events take? How will the tapes be viewed? How accessible is equipment that will be needed to view, copy, or store the video? All these questions and others affect the choice of video format and camcorder features.

VCR

The VCR (videocassette recorder) is the machine that reads the videotape and generates the video signal that can be shown on various monitors, TVs, projector screens, and computers. A VCR can also code a video signal on the magnetic tape of a videocassette. Most recent models have slow-motion replay. This section discusses the important features you should evaluate when selecting a VCR for use in qualitative analysis. It does not address commercial VCRs designed for professional use.

Format

Buying a VCR can be a confusing task. Current VCRs have a bewildering array of features that may be desirable for consumers taping their favorite shows (stereo, programmability) but may not be critical for qualitative analysis. A VCR that can be used for real-time or slow-motion qualitative analysis of human movement should have several key features. The first choice to make is tape format. All tape formats are adequate for qualitative analysis. Check the most recent *Consumer Reports* review of video equipment to see what makes and models are the best and most reliable. VCRs range in price from less than $200 to thousands of dollars for commercial equipment.

Number of Heads

You need a four-head VCR to read enough videotape to obtain a clear image in freeze-frame, pause, or still mode. Look for a model that has a field advance in both directions. Some VCRs advance a whole frame, showing only the first field of each frame. Make a tape of a digital clock to take along to stores so that you can evaluate picture quality and frame advance differences. If it takes 30 frame advances to advance one second, the VCR advances two fields or a true frame advance. With many VCRs you must repeatedly press the pause or still button or use the jog-shuttle dial to advance frame by frame. Often these features are not very important to consumers, so try things out rather than rely on sales personnel.

Playback Speeds

The VCR should also have variable-speed slow motion, which can show the action at different rates of slow motion. Variable slow motion used to be a button feature, but now it is more like professional VCRs, with a jog-shuttle dial that you can turn forward or backward to change tape speeds from still to frame-by-frame, slow-motion, normal, and search. This helps you find key events in the movement and select the speed of replay.

KEY POINT 10.5 The most important VCR features for qualitative analysis are four heads, a freeze-frame function, and a jog-shuttle dial.

Time Codes

Other features in consumer VCRs relevant to qualitative analysis are title generators, time-code (address) generators, and index/search functions. An analyst may want to add titles or reminders to a video image. A particularly good or bad trial can be electronically marked by the index function so that the VCR can search for it at a later viewing. VCRs that can display or generate SMPTE time codes (hour, minute, second, frame) on the field of view are valuable for temporal analysis and finding specific frames. Picture-mixing, split-screen, or PIP (picture-in-picture) functions can be used to compare multiple video images on one screen. These high-end VCRs are modeled after expensive video editing equipment used by professionals.

Making Videos for Qualitative Analysis

Videotaping patients or athletes for qualitative analysis has been popular for several decades. There are many different objectives for capturing human movement on video. Some people videotape fast skills like a golf swing to see details in the movement not visible in live analysis. Others might record their performance over time to track improvement. Some parents tape their children's practice routines or competitions and send the tape to coaches to evaluate for possible athletic scholarships. These "daddy videos" are often of little value, however, because they may not be made from a vantage point of interest, or the conditions of the performances may not be adequate for qualitative analysis by the coaches.

Replay Options

Naturally the procedures for making a video to analyze performance qualitatively depend on the objectives of the analysis. A tape made to analyze technique in the tennis service or volley may be very different from a tape made to evaluate court movement or service return ability. Video images for qualitative analysis can be made for real-time replay and feedback to the performer or for slow-motion analysis to improve the observational power of the teacher, coach, or therapist.

Real-Time Replay

One approach to using videotape for qualitative analysis is to view or replay the recorded images at normal speed. This is real-time analysis of videotape. Creating video for real-time replay for performers or qualitative analysis by a teacher or coach requires a certain approach. The field of view needs to be several times larger than the moving subject. This gives a stable background for the subject to move against. A good rule of thumb is to have the subject between one-third and one-half of the field height.

It is important to give the observers of your real-time video a field of view that accurately represents the performance environment. Some of these tapes are made to diagnose how the performer responds to dynamic game conditions (tennis, basketball, volleyball), and analyzing the form of the performer is not the primary interest. In this situation the field size is maximized to allow observation of the whole court. Most real-time replay of video for qualitative analysis is used in this fashion by coaches or motor skill instructors to assist in the observation of performance, although sometimes it is used as feedback or intervention to improve performance.

Research on the use of real-time video replay as intervention or feedback to performers has a long history in kinesiology. Numerous studies over the past 40 years show that video replay is no more effective than traditional teacher-augmented feedback (Rothstein and Arnold, 1976). Recent studies confirm these early results but also suggest that video replay may provide useful information as intervention to improve performance. Based on her meta-analysis of videotape feedback research, Rothstein (1980) proposed that seven factors are important for using video replay for augmented feedback: (1) It should be used with verbal cues that focus the performer's attention. (2) It should be used frequently (at least five replays). Video feedback is most effective for (3) advanced beginners and (4) intermediates, not complete novices or expert players. Some research has shown that unstructured video replay can negatively affect learning in beginners (Ross et al., 1985). (5) Provide practice immediately following the video feedback. (6) Possibly zoom in on the aspect of performance you want to provide feedback about. Finally, (7) when taping, vary the camera angle and capture a field of view that is consistent with the goals and nature of the activity. For example, a close-up shot of the tennis serve would be helpful in this closed motor skill, while a view of the whole court would be helpful in analyzing how the ground stroke techniques selected relate to the environment (open motor skills).

Other recent papers have reviewed the use of videotape in the qualitative analysis or teaching of motor skills (Franks and Maile, 1991; Jambor and Weekes, 1995; Trinity and Annesi, 1996). One of the most important functions of video replay for performers has been its use for self-modeling (Dowrick, 1991b). A performer should be compared to a model of skilled performance who is similar to the performer in age, skill level, appearance, and the like. Some people exaggerate negative perceptions of themselves compared to models who are too different from them (Trower and Kiely, 1983). Most motor skills instructors who have used video have experienced the keen interest of people in watching themselves on video.

Care must be taken to monitor subject motivation and the psychological impact of anyone else who may also be watching. Some rather interesting comments and behaviors from an audience arise during video replay. The most desirable situation is one on one with the performer, eliminating extraneous effects of an audience. If other performers are watching the replay, be sure to focus group attention on good points of performance and try to limit their extraneous or negative comments.

Slow-Motion Replay

In general, video images generated for slow-motion analysis should focus on higher-speed movements that are difficult to see with the naked eye. Videos made for this kind of replay should maximize the size of the performer in the field of view. Zooming in on the subject is important for two reasons. First, the resolution of the video picture will be improved in the pause and slow-motion modes of the VCR. Second, perceptual problems with limited background information are reduced when the images are paused, slowed down, or repeated.

The ability to freeze the motion at key points in the movement and to slow down very fast movements greatly increases observational power. This is why slow-motion video analysis should not be limited to high-speed movements or sport

> **KEY POINT 10.6** Video images created for real-time qualitative analysis should have a large field of view with background features for the subject to move against. This approach is designed to simulate live qualitative analysis of human movement.

QA Demonstration 10.1

View the accompanying video clips in normal speed and determine if there is a flight phase, meaning the person is running rather than walking. Use the freeze-frame and slow-motion features of the software to see if you were correct. Was your observation improved by the slowing/stopping of the video?

KEY POINT 10.7 Video images created for slow-motion replay in qualitative analysis should zoom on the subject to maximize the performer's size in the field of view.

skills. A coach struggling to make a key diagnostic decision might use slow-motion video replay to verify certain perceptions from live analysis.

The greater observational power of videotape replay, however, comes at a cost. Slow-motion video analysis requires more time for the videotape to be positioned, played, and replayed. Time used in video analysis is often time lost in performer practice and the live qualitative analysis that could be performed.

Camera Position

Camera location should be chosen carefully to make sure that subject motion is at a right angle to the camera, or as close to a right angle as possible. Ideally the camcorder should be mounted on a tripod. Panning should generally be avoided, but limited panning may be needed in certain conditions. To avoid perspective or lens distortions, the camcorder should be as far from the subject as possible, using the zoom lens to frame the subject. Extreme examples of such distortion are a peephole in a door and a camcorder's view of a tennis court from above the fence. Objects in the foreground appear very large; objects far away appear much smaller than normal. And objects moving to and from the camera are distorted. Motion of objects in the distance is underestimated, while motion of objects near the camera is exaggerated. The farther objects of different sizes are from the camera, the smaller the differences between their sizes appear.

Limit camera motion when capturing video images for any qualitative analysis. Observers of the video you generate are attempting to detect changes in the subject's position. Changes in camera angle or camera motion will distort the actual motion of the subject. It is important to understand how camera motion affects the images created. The most accurate video representation (2-D) of reality (3-D) would be a nonmoving camera positioned on a tripod, with the subject moving parallel to the camera lens. This situation will create images of the subject moving on a 2-D background that are representative of the actual motion.

It is not always possible to set up a stationary camera to record movements. A good real-world example of how camera motion can dramatically change the perception of motion is the Indianapolis 500. A stationary camera parallel to the straightaway would capture images (very few frames!) of the cars moving past. A camera mounted looking out the side of a car in the race would see a very different view of the speeds of the cars, like what you experience on the freeway.

Now imagine you are a race fan in the stands panning your camera as cars go by. Only at one instant, when the car is moving parallel to your seat, does your video picture accurately represent the movement of the car. The car moves toward you (and in the video) slowly, gets very fast near you, and slows again after it passes you. This situation is analogous to the gymnastics example presented earlier. The motion of the car is underestimated as the car approaches. In effect, it becomes the proportional speed of the car as the car nears the camera angle of 90 degrees. The apparent length of the car is another example of this distortion. The car looks short in the distance, appears to get longer as it approaches you, and then shrinks as it moves away.

Taping Protocol

Precise control of the setting and technique of video capture are needed to generate images suitable for the qualitative analysis of interest. Although modern camcorders do well in various lighting conditions, the most desirable condition is even lighting from behind the camera. The camera location should strive for this lighting and for a contrasting background with a horizontal or vertical reference. The background should not hide the motion of the subject and should provide a directional frame of reference on which to place the subject's motion. Figure 10.3 illustrates a field of view and background that hides the motion of the person in the foreground. The protocol should provide subject identification information and some way to identify trials. Verbal cueing to the tape audio, time codes, or clocks in the field of view will help you identify key events or trials in later playback.

FIGURE 10.3 An example of a good versus bad background when videotaping.

It is crucial to make a written record of the subject, date, and notes on performance and keep it with the video. Any information about the movement or results of the movement that is not visible in the field of view should be written down. By keeping written records, the analyst does not have to play the tape to identify places to start. VCR counter numbers and indexing information can be added to the written record to help access video images quickly.

Future of Video and Computers in Qualitative Analysis

The observational power of analysts can be improved by videotape replay, especially the slow-motion replay of human movement and computer-assisted viewing. Fortunately, advances in integrating video and computer technologies and increases in computing storage and speed have made many advanced features available at lower costs. Video images contain quite a bit of data and advances in compression software have allowed efficient storage (video compression) and presentation (calculation, graphics, split screen, text) of video with off-the-shelf hardware and software. A popular feature is to compare a performer's movement with a prototype performance by split screens or overlays. These features may be motivational for a mover and help analysts evaluate the performance, however, there has been little research to see if these visuals improve learning. More expensive are commercial computer-assisted video systems designed for qualitative and quantitative analysis that can place drawings or graphics on the video to illustrate key points in the movement (see Figures 10.4 and 10.5). Advances in computer and video technology will eventually make many of these advanced video features affordable for most kinesiology professionals.

The future of video imaging will be strongly related to developments in camera and computer technology. Increases in the speed and storage capabilities of computers may make the tape storage of video obsolete. There are already cameras that interface directly with computers, enabling CCD video data to be digitized and stored directly on the computer. Technical advances in cameras to capture video and in computers to store and enhance the video images may make concerns about resolution and the speed of video less of a problem. Hardware and software are now available that sample the analog signal of video at a higher rate, allowing computers to grab or digitize higher-resolution video still images.

Video images and sound can also be stored on optical or digital videodisks (DVDs). The video images on the CD-ROM accompanying this book use this technology. Advances in erasable optical disks, video and digital data compression, and more powerful computers may make video image storage on cassette tapes obsolete.

QA Demonstration 10.2

View the video clips and determine if the golf club stays above horizontal at the end of the backswing. Did the Silicon COACH Sport drawing feature add to your ability to rate this critical feature?

In the future the line between video technology and computers will get thinner and thinner. In the past, research has focused on how separate computer technology could be used to assist in the coding and notational analysis of the movements of athletes on a team from video recordings of sport (Franks and Goodman, 1986; Franks and Nagelkerke, 1988; Patrick and Lowdon, 1987). Notational analysis is used to create counts of particular events, success rates, and other variables related to strategy and game success. Researchers and commercial vendors are looking at ways to integrate computer and video/imaging technologies. The main questions for the future are: When will good qualitative analysis video/computer support equipment be available at a cost most teachers/coaches can afford? When will the advantages of each technology be combined and readily available? Will researchers document the effectiveness of these extra features beyond traditional videotape replay for qualitative analysis?

Several companies that specialize in high-speed and research videography and biomechanics faculty have developed computerized video replay products for qualitative analysis of sport skills. Unfortunately, the names of products and vendors change rapidly. Thus, this section will list only common examples of this technology.

The German biomechanics company SIMI (Unterschleissheim, Germany, http:/www.simi.com/) has developed a lower-cost software program for manipulating and presenting grabbed video. The SIMI MoStill SE program costs about $1,500 and allows the analyst to view spilt-screen video, draw, and do simple distance and angle calculations. Figure 10.4 shows what the SIMI MoStill screen looks like.

The Silicon COACH Sport software (Siliconcoach, Dunedin, New Zealand, www.siliconcoach.com) is similar to the SIMI system. The Silicon COACH Sport program also creates customized replays and reports from PAL, NTSC, and high-speed video for the qualitative analysis of sports skills (figure 10.5). The user can display normal and split screen video clips, and use on-screen illustration and calculation capabilities to highlight various aspects of performance. The basic system runs about $450, but the professional version handles high-speed video and direct input of digital video through a fire-wire connection.

The Never Ending Athletic Trainer or NEAT system software, a commercial video system that can be used for qualitative analysis, takes grabbed video from any camcorder, stores it on a computer's hard drive, and provides custom software to replay and present the video (figure 10.6). The NEAT system (Neat Systems Inc., Annapolis, Md., www.neatsys.com) was developed in the United States and is based on typical computer hardware and 30 hertz video. The software is about $100.

Remember that many software systems that allow for instant calculations from a single video

KEY POINT 10.8 Technological advances and the integration of video and computer technology may dramatically influence the impact and use of video for the qualitative analysis of human movement.

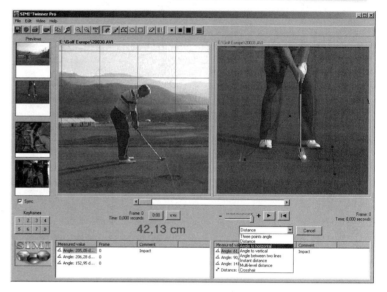

FIGURE 10.4 The MoStill SE program by SIMI provides lower-cost qualitative analysis of video with computers than traditional biomechanics research programs.
Courtesy of SIMI, Unterschleissheim, Germany.

FIGURE 10.5 The Silicon COACH Sport software program allows the capture, replay, and reporting of video clips on computer. The split-screen feature is illustrated.
Courtesy of Silicon COACH, Dunedin, New Zealand.

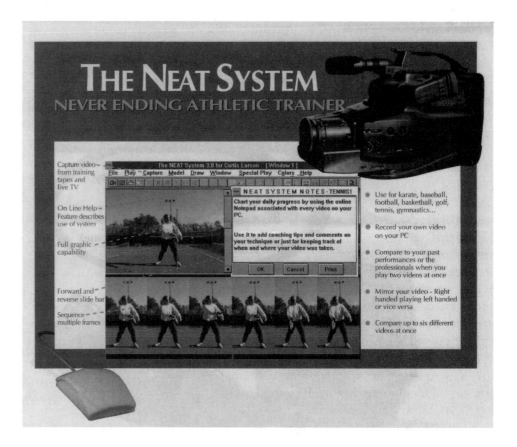

FIGURE 10.6 The NEAT video system for teaching and qualitative analysis.
Courtesy of Neat Systems Inc., Annapolis, Md.

image can result in errors. Since accurate calculations from the video require careful setup and have many technical limitations, especially in 3-D movements (Allard, Stokes, and Blanchi, 1995), special care must be taken to ensure that the angle or speed calculations are accurate. Consult the technical specifications of the software used or biomechanics experts familiar with your system.

Some biomechanists have developed their own video systems by combining inexpensive frame-grabber technology, computers, and their own custom software. These systems have the advantages of low cost and compatibility with common computer and video equipment. Some well-established systems are the Human Movement Analysis System (Hu-m-an) by Tom Duck of York University (HMA Technology, Ontario, Canada, http://www.hma-tech.com), the ATD (Analisis de la Technica Deportiva) program by Francisco Garcia and Raúl Arellano (Granada, Spain, contact: arellano@ugr.es), and the Kinematic Analysis (KA) system by Bob Schleihauf (San Francisco State University, http://kavideo.sfsu.edu). These systems are designed for quantitative biomechanical analyses, so they will have many features beyond what is needed for the qualitative analysis of movement.

Improvements in videotape technology, HDTV, and the increased integration of imaging and computers will make for an exciting future in the use of imaging for qualitative analysis. The video systems of the future designed for qualitative analysis will have many features attractive for teaching motor skills. Such systems will be portable with extended battery power. Screens will be large, flat, with hoods, and antiglare color monitors. The computer-controlled camera will be run by remote control or programmed to follow the athlete. Currently the only barriers to this technology are the cost of the equipment and the expertise of the teacher, coach, or therapist. We expect that the cost of advanced computer and video technology will come down, and that kinesiology research will help to tell us how best to use these tools together to improve the qualitative analysis of human movement.

Further Practice

This section lists some suggestions for qualitative analysis practice using videotape replay. Kinesiology professionals should develop their qualitative analysis skills through practice with videotape replay. Remember to carefully plan for the video and performance situation to get an accurate representation of performance.

- Project 1
  - ✔ Videotape a friend who wants to improve performance in a closed motor skill like in bowling, golf, or archery. Image the performance from two perspectives: to get a close-up of the technique and to capture the whole performance (KP and KR). Which perspective was most helpful in your qualitative analysis?
- Project 2
  - ✔ Videotape a friend who participates in an open environment activity or team sport. Use the video to provide several suggestions to improve performance. Use the videotape replay to illustrate the points to your friend.
- Project 3
  - ✔ Videotape a friend who is practicing a specific sport skill or technique. Use the videotape replay for qualitative analysis and feedback to your friend.
- Project 4
  - ✔ Videotape a competitive sporting contest in a public place. Qualitatively analyze the video for coaching and strategic factors. Qualitatively analyze the movements of a specific player.
- Project 5
  - ✔ Videotape yourself practicing a movement you enjoy. Qualitatively analyze your technique and write a plan for improvement. Share the video with a classmate and have her do the same for you. Then compare your plans.

Summary

Videotape is an important tool in extending observational power for qualitative analysis. Although video replay has been used as feedback for performers, the research has not shown it to be superior to teacher feedback. Slow-motion video replay, however, dramatically extends the observational ability of analysts. The ability to replay movements again and again also improves observation. Video and computer technology are changing rapidly and dramatically affect the kinesiology professional's ability to use videotape replay for qualitative and quantitative analyses. With advances in video and computer technology, many advanced video features that are currently expensive should become more readily available.

Discussion Questions

1. What views would be desirable for a qualitative analysis of a pitcher's form versus the ball flight in baseball pitching?

2. What compromises must be made in setting up the field of view for videotaping the approach to the long jump?

3. What kinds of human movements can be observed live? What kinds require normal and high-speed videotape replay?

4. A TV station would like to shoot a special on the dramatic improvement of a local pole-vaulter. What advice would you give the show's producer on how to video some of the athlete's practice vaults? How do views that exaggerate the motion for TV viewers differ from views that are good for observation of performance?

5. If video clips are to be presented on computer screen for qualitative analysis, what features are most important for the analyst? The mover?

6. Does videotape replay improve the validity of the analysis? The reliability?

Glossary

augmented feedback—Feedback that goes beyond the information normally available to a performer.

closed motor skills—A classification of motor skills that have few environmental restrictions because the performer has minimal temporal and environmental restrictions on the movement selected.

common errors—Errors that are typically observed in people learning a motor skill.

critical features—The key features of a movement that are necessary for optimal performance.

cues—Short, descriptive words or phrases used to communicate ideas about movement to learners.

deterministic model—A model linking mechanical variables with the goal of the movement, used in the Hay and Reid (1988) approach to qualitative analysis.

developmental sequence—The classification of typical phases or stages that people exhibit in the development of a movement.

diagnosis—Critical scrutiny of the strengths and weaknesses identified in evaluation to prioritize possible intervention in qualitative analysis.

dynamic visual acuity (DVA)—The accuracy of visual discrimination when there is relative movement between the observer and an object.

evaluation—The judgment of the quality of human movement to identify strengths and weaknesses of performance within qualitative analysis.

exaggeration—An intervention technique where the performer is encouraged to overcorrect or overcompensate for a persistent movement error and this feedback may bring about the small, desired change in technique.

feedback—Information about human movement.

field—Half of a video picture, composed of the even- or odd-numbered horizontal lines of a video frame (but not both).

field dependence—A way of processing information where the background information is necessary for accurate interpretation. An analyst might use this perceptual style since it relies heavily on the frame of reference.

field independence—A way of processing information without reference to any sources of information except the object or movement being observed. An observer using this perceptual style does not need background information to make sense of the movement.

filters—Processes in the brain that deal with different information to help make sense of sensory information. May deal with things like intensity, color, lines, shapes, shades, or sounds.

fixation—The focusing of the eyes on an object in the visual field.

frame—A single video picture that is composed of two halves called "fields." There are 25 or 30 frames for each second of normal video.

freeze frame—A mode of video replay that stops and holds a video image so that it can be shown on a monitor. *Freeze frame* is a misnomer because pause or still functions of a VCR usually show one field of video in freeze-frame mode.

fundamental movement pattern—A general category of human movements (for example, lift, run, jump, throw).

fusion—Putting together the two-dimensional visual information from the eyes to create the three-dimensional perception of vision.

gestalt—A way of processing visual-spatial information to get an overall impression. In a gestalt approach the whole is greater than the sum of its parts. This impression of the event uses features such as region, proximity, continuation, and closure. Gestalt is a field of study in psychology.

high-speed video—Special video technology used to create more video pictures (frames) per second than the 25 or 30 frames in normal video.

information processing—The cognitive process of organizing and making sense of sensory information, and the decision making based on that sensory information.

intervention—The fourth task of the integrated model of qualitative analysis. It involves the administration of feedback, corrections, or other change in the environment provided by the analyst to improve performance.

intrinsic feedback—Information about movement that is readily available to the performer (for example: sensory, kinesthetic, and proprioceptive information).

jog-shuttle dial—A key VCR feature that uses a dial to allow multiple-speed playback, either forward or backward.

knowledge of performance (KP)—Information about the movement of the body.

knowledge of results (KR)—Information about the outcome or results of a movement.

manual guidance—A mode of intervention within qualitative analysis where the analyst physically positions or assists the performer in making the desired movement.

mechanical guidance—A mode of intervention within qualitative analysis that uses an aid or mechanical device to help the performer make the desired movement.

moment arm—A mechanical term that describes an object's resistance to being rotated (angular acceleration).

motor program—The essential cognitive information needed to perform a movement.

observation—The second task of an integrated qualitative analysis in which sensory information is gathered about performance with a systematic observational strategy.

observational learning—The use of visual models (pictures or demonstrations) to provide information about a movement.

open motor skills—A classification of motor skills that are strongly influenced by their environment because it is unpredictable.

performance—The quality of a movement in achieving a goal, or the short-term and long-term effectiveness of a person's movement in achieving a goal.

pixel—Short for "picture element." The small dots of light that form a video image.

qualitative analysis—The systematic observation and introspective judgment of the quality of human movement for the purpose of providing the most appropriate intervention to improve performance.

reinforcement—Feedback that supports what was done so that the behavior will be repeated and eventually learned.

reliability—The consistency of a measurement or a qualitative assessment.

resolution—The number of lines of pixels that make up a video image.

sampling rate—The temporal resolution of a measurement or qualitative analysis of a continuous event. The sampling rate of normal video is 30 frames (pictures) per second.

shutter—A photo or video device that limits the exposure time of an image. This limits the chances of significant motion of the object during image capture, which would create a blurry image.

skill—An adapted fundamental movement pattern for a specific activity or goal. A baseball pitch is a skill related to overarm throwing.

smooth pursuit—The simultaneous rotation of both eyes to track a slow-moving object.

spatial ability—The ability to deal with spatial relationships and to use this information in different contexts.

static visual acuity (SVA)—The accuracy of visual discrimination in static, high-contrast conditions.

style—Aspects of movement that are personal differences, idiosyncrasies, or actions related to a specific performer.

systematic observational strategy (SOS)—A plan to gather all the relevant information about a human movement within qualitative analysis.

task modification—An intervention strategy that improves performance by changing practice to a task more appropriate for the performer.

technique—A kind of motor skill that has a specific purpose. A curveball is a technique related to the skill of baseball pitching.

validity—The extent that a measurement or a qualitative analysis assesses the true amount of some variable.

vergence—Eye movements medially and laterally to adjust for movements of objects toward and away from the observer.

zoom lens—A key feature in video camcorders that allows the field of view to be adjusted for objects at different distances.

Bibliography

Abendroth-Smith, J., and J. Kras. 1999. More BBOAT: The volleyball spike. *JOPERD* 70 (3): 56-59.

Abendroth-Smith, J., J. Kras, and B. Strand. 1996. Get aboard the BBOAT: Biomechanically based observation and analysis for teachers. *JOPERD* 67 (8): 20-23.

Abernethy, B. 1988. Visual search in sport and ergonomics: Its relationship to selective attention and performer expertise. *Human Performance* 1: 205-35.

Abernethy, B. 1989. Expert-novice differences in perception: How expert does the expert have to be? *Canadian Journal of Sport Sciences* 14: 27-30.

Abernethy, B. 1993. Searching for the minimal essential information for skilled perception and action. *Psychological Research* 55: 131-38.

Abernethy, B., and R.J. Neal. 1999. Visual characteristics of clay target shooters. *Journal of Science and Medicine in Sport* 2: 1-19.

Abernethy, B., and D.G. Russell. 1987. The relationship between expertise and visual search strategy in a racquet sport. *Human Movement Science* 6: 283-319.

Abernethy, B., J.M. Wood, and S. Parks. 1999. Can the anticipatory skills of experts be learned by novices? *Research Quarterly for Exercise and Sport* 70: 313-18.

Abernethy, B., and K. Zawi. "Pick-up of essential kinematics underpins expert perception." Unpublished Manuscript, School of Human Movement Studies, University of Queensland, Australia, n.d.

Adrian, M.J., and J.M. Cooper. 1989. *Biomechanics of human movement*. Indianapolis: Benchmark Press.

Adrian, M.J., and J.M. Cooper. 1995. *Biomechanics of human movement*. 2nd ed. Madison, Wis.: Brown & Benchmark.

Adrian, M.J., and M.L. Endberg. 1971. Sequential timing of three overhead patterns. In *Kinesiology Review*, edited by C. Widule. Washington, D.C.: AAHPER:1-9.

Adrian, M., and G. House. 1987a. Sporting miscues: Part one. *Strategies* 1 (1): 11-14.

Adrian, M., and G. House. 1987b. Sporting miscues: Part two. *Strategies* 1 (2): 13-15.

Alfano, P.L., and G.F. Michel. 1990. Restricting field of view: Perceptual and performance effects. *Perceptual and Motor Skills* 70: 35-45.

Allard, P., I. Stokes, and J. Blanchi, eds. 1995. *Three-dimensional analysis of human movement*. Champaign, Ill.: Human Kinetics.

Allison, P.C. 1985a. The development of the skill of observing during field experiences of pre-service physical education teachers. Paper presented at the meeting of the Association Internationale des Ecoles Superieures d'Education Physique, August, Garden City, N.Y.

Allison, P.C. 1985b. Observing for competence. *JOPERD* 56 (6): 50-51, 54.

Allison, P.C. 1986. Laban's movement framework as a descriptor of change in students' movement response observations. Paper presented at the national convention of the American Alliance for Health, Physical Education, Recreation and Dance, April, Cincinnati, Ohio.

Allison, P.C. 1987a. The impact of varying amounts of lesson responsibility on pre-service physical education teachers' ability to observe. Paper presented at the national convention of the American Alliance for Health, Physical Education, Recreation and Dance, April, Las Vegas, Nev.

Allison, P.C. 1987b. What and how pre-service physical education teachers observe during an early field experience. *Research Quarterly Exercise and Sport* 58: 242-49.

Allison, P.C. 1988. Strategies for observing during field experiences. *JOPERD* 59 (2): 28-30.

Allison, P.C. 1990. Classroom teachers' observations of physical education lessons. *Journal of Teaching in Physical Education* 4: 272-83.

Ammons, R.B. 1956. Effect of knowledge of performance: A survey and tentative theoretical formulation. *Journal of General Psychology* 54: 279-99.

Anderson, J.R. 1990. *Cognitive psychology and its implications*. New York: W.H. Freeman & Co.

Anderson, M.B. 1979. Comparison of muscle patterning in the overarm throw and tennis serve. *Research Quarterly* 50: 541-53.

Annett, J. 1993. The learning of motor skills: Sports science and ergonomics perspectives. *Ergonomics* 37: 5-16.

Arend, S., and J.R. Higgins. 1976. A strategy for the classification, subjective analysis and observation of human movement. *Journal of Human Movement Studies* 2: 36-52.

Armstrong, C.W. 1977a. Skill analysis and kinesthetic experience. In *Research and practice in physical education*, edited by R.E. Stadulis. Champaign, Ill.: Human Kinetics, 13-18.

Armstrong, C.W. 1977b. Effects of teaching experience, knowledge of performer competence and knowledge of performance outcome on performance error identification. *Research Quarterly* 48: 318-27.

Armstrong, C.W. 1986. Research on movement analysis: Implications for the development of pedagogical competence. In *The 1984 Olympic scientific congress proceedings VI, sports pedagogy*, edited by M. Pieron and G. Graham. Champaign, Ill.; Human Kinetics, 27-32.

Armstrong, C.W., and S.J. Hoffman. 1979. Effects of teaching experience, knowledge of performer competence, and knowledge of performance outcome on performance error identification. *Research Quarterly* 50: 318-27.

Arnell, P., and P. Bauker. 1991. The accuracy of visual gait assessment. In *Proceedings of the 11th international congress of the world confederation for physical therapy*. London: World Confederation for Physical Therapy, 431.

Arnold, P.J. 1993. Kinesiology and the professional preparation of the movement teacher. *Journal of Human Movement Studies* 25: 203-31.

Arnold, R.K. 1978. Optimizing skill learning: Moving to match the environment. *JOPERD* 49 (9): 84-86.

Arrighi, M.A. 1974. The nature of game strategy observation in field hockey with respect to selected variables. Ph.D. diss., University of North Carolina Greensboro. Abstact in *Dissertation Abstracts International* 35: 2030A.

Attinger, D., S. Luethi, and E. Stuessi. 1987. Comparison of subjective gait observation with measured gait asymmetry. In *Biomechanics: Basic and applied research*, edited by G. Bergmann et al. Boston: M. Nijhoff, 563-68.

Atwater, A.E. 1979. Biomechanics of overarm throwing movements and of throwing injuries. *Exercise and Sport Sciences Reviews* 7: 43-85.

Austin, S., and L. Miller. 1992. An empirical study of the sybervision golf videotape. *Perceptual and Motor Skills* 74: 875-81.

Bahamonde, R. 2000. Angular momentum changes during the tennis serve. *Journal of Sport Sciences* 18: 579-592.

Bahill, A.T., and T. LaRitz. 1984. Why can't batters keep their eyes on the ball? *American Scientist* 72: 249-53.

Balan, C.M., and W.E. Davis. 1993. Ecological task analysis: An approach to teaching physical education. *JOPERD* 64 (9): 54-61.

Baluyut, R., A.M. Genaidy, L.S. Davis, R.L. Sehll, and R.J. Simmons. 1995. Use of visual perception in estimating static postural stresses: Magnitudes and sources of error. *Ergonomics* 38: 1841-50.

Bampton, S. 1979. *A guide to the visual examination of pathological gait*. Philadelphia, Pa.: Temple University Rehabilitation and Research Training Center No. 8, Moss Rehabilitation Hospital.

Bard, C., and M. Fleury. 1976. Analysis of visual search activity during sport problem situations. *Journal of Human Movement Studies* 3: 214-22.

Bard, C., M. Fleury, L. Carriere, and M. Halle. 1980. Analysis of gymnastics judges' visual search. *Research Quarterly for Exercise and Sport* 51: 267-73.

Barfield, W.R. 1998. The biomechanics of kicking in soccer. *Clinics in Sports Medicine* 17: 711-28.

Barrett, K.R. 1977. We see so much but perceive so little: Why? In *Proceedings of the NAPECW/NCPEAM national conference*, edited by L.I. Gedvilas and M.E. Kneer. Chicago: University of Illinois Chicago Circle.

Barrett, K.R. 1979a. Observation of movement: An assumed teaching/coaching behavior. Unpublished manuscript, University of North Carolina Greensboro.

Barrett, K.R. 1979b. Observation of movement for teachers: A synthesis and implications. *Motor Skills: Theory into Practice* 3: 67-76.

Barrett, K.R. 1979c. Observation for teaching and coaching. *JOPER* 50 (1): 23-25.

Barrett, K.R. 1980. A system for describing and observing a spatial relationship movement task. Paper presented at the pre-convention symposium on physical education for children, Southern District of the American Alliance for Health, Physical Education and Recreation, February, Nashville, Tenn.

Barrett, K.R. 1981. Observation as a teaching behavior—research to practice. Paper presented at the national meeting of the Canadian Association for Physical Education and Health Education, June, Victoria, B.C., Canada.

Barrett, K.R. 1982. The content of observing: A model for curriculum development. Paper presented at the national convention of the American Alliance for Health, Physical Education, Recreation and Dance, April, Houston, Tex.

Barrett, K.R. 1983. A hypothetical model of observing as a teaching skill. *Journal of Teaching in Physical Education* 3: 22-31.

Barrett, K.R., P.C. Allison, and R. Bell. 1987. What pre-service physical education teachers see in an unguided field experience: A follow-up study. *Journal of Teaching in Physical Education* 7: 12-21.

Barthels, K. 1989. Applying mechanics to swimming performance analysis. *Strategies* 3 (1): 17-19.

Barthels, K., and E. Kreighbaum. 1988. A Western system of analysis and observation. Paper presented to the national convention of the American Alliance for Health, Physical Education, Recreation and Dance, April, Kansas City, Mo.

Bayless, M.A. 1980. The effect of style of teaching on ability to detect errors in performance. *Wyoming Journal for Health, Physical Education Recreation and Dance* 3: 2-4, 15.

Bayless, M.A. 1981. Effect of exposure to prototypic skill and experience in identification of performance error. *Perceptual and Motor Skills* 52: 667-70.

Behar, I., and W. Bevan. 1961. The perceived duration of auditory and visual intervals: Cross-model comparison and interaction. *American Journal of Psychology* 74: 17-26.

Behets, D. 1996. Comparison of visual information processing between preservice students and experienced physical education teachers. *Journal of Teaching in Physical Education* 16: 79-87.

Belka, D.E. 1988. What preservice physical educators observe about lessons in progressive field experiences. *Journal of Teaching in Physical Education* 7: 311-26.

Bell, F.I. 1987. The effects of two training programs on the ability of preservice physical education majors to observe the developmental steps in the overarm throw for force. Ph.D. diss., University of North Carolina Greensboro. Abstract in *Dissertation Abstracts International* 48: 1144A.

Bell, R., K.R. Barrett, and P.E. Allison. 1985. What preservice physical education teachers see in an unguided, early field experience. *Journal of Teaching in Physical Education* 4: 81-90.

Berg, K. 1975. Functional approach to undergraduate kinesiology. *JOPER* 46 (7): 43- 44.

Berger, C.G. 1999. The camcorder as a teaching tool in the weight room. *Strength and Conditioning Journal* 21 (6): 70-72.

Berger, J. 1987. *Ways of seeing.* London: British Broadcasting Corp. and Penguin Books.

Bernhardt, J., P.J. Bate, and T.A. Matyas. 1998. Accuracy of observational kinematic assessment of upper-limb movements. *Physical Therapy* 78: 259-70.

Best, J.B. 1986. *Cognitive psychology.* St. Paul: West Publishing Company.

Beveridge, S.K., and S.K. Gangstead. 1984. A comparative analysis of the effects of instruction on the analytical proficiency of physical education teachers and undergraduates. Annual convention for the American Alliance for Health, Physical Education, Recreation and Dance, Anaheim, Calif. ERIC Document Reproduction Service, ED 244-939.

Beveridge, S.K., and S.K. Gangstead. 1988. Teaching experience and training in the sports skill analysis process. *Journal of Teaching in Physical Education* 7: 103-14.

Bilodeau, I.M. 1969. Information feedback. In *Principles of skill acquisition,* edited by E.A. Bilodeau. London: Academic Press.

Bird, M., and J. Hudson. 1990. Biomechanical observation: Visually accessible variables. In *Proceedings of the VIIIth international symposium of the society of biomechanics in sports,* edited by M. Nosek, D. Sojka, P. Morrison, and P. Susan. Prague: Conex, 321-26.

Biscan, D.U., and S.J. Hoffman. 1976. Movement analysis as a generic ability of physical education teachers and students. *Research Quarterly* 47: 161-63.

Blundell, N.L. 1985. The contribution of vision to the learning and performance of sports skills: Part 1. The role of selected visual parameters. *Australian Journal of Science and Medicine in Sport* 17: 3-11.

Boehm, A.E., and R.A. Weinber. 1987. *The classroom observer: Developing observation skills in early childhood settings.* New York: Teachers College Press.

Bolt, B.R. 2000. Using computers for qualitative analysis of movement. *JOPERD* 71 (3): 15-18.

Bowers, L., and S. Klesius. 1991. Use of interactive videodisk in the analysis of skills for teaching. Paper presented at the National Convention of the American Alliance for Health, Physical Education, Recreation and Dance, April, San Francisco.

Boyce, W.F., C. Gowland, P. Rosenbaum, M. Lane, N. Plews, C. Goldsmith, D. Russell, V. Wright, S. Poter, and D. Harding. 1995. The gross motor performance measure: Validity and responsiveness of a measure of quality of movement. *Physical Therapy* 75: 603-13.

Boyer, E.L. 1990. *Scholarship reconsidered: Priorities of the professoriate.* Princeton, N.J.: The Carnegie Foundation for the Advancement of Teaching.

Braden, V. 1983. Vic Braden's startling revelations about line calls. *Tennis* (May): 37-39.

Bradley, D.R., and H.M. Petry. 1977. Organizational determinants of subjective contour: The subjective Necker cube. *American Journal of Psychology* 90(2): 253-62.

Branta, C., J. Haubenstricker, and V. Seefeldt. 1984. Age changes in motor skills during childhood and adolescence. *Exercise and Sport Sciences Reviews* 12: 467-520.

Bressan, E.S., and M.R. Weiss. 1982. A theory of instruction for developing competence, self-confidence and persistence in physical education. *Journal of Teaching in Physical Education* 2 (1): 38-47.

Brisson, T.A., and C. Alain. 1996. Should common optimal movement patterns be identified as the criterion to be achieved? *Journal of Motor Behavior* 28: 211-23.

Broadbent, D. 1958. *Perception and communication.* Oxford: Pergamon.

Broer, M.R. 1960. *Efficiency of Human Movement.* Philadelphia: Saunders.

Broker, J.P., R.J. Gregor, and R.A. Schmidt. 1989. Extrinsic feedback and the learning of cycling kinetic patterns. Abstract of XII Congress ISB. *Journal of Biomechanics* 22: 991.

Brophy, J., and T. Good. 1986. Teacher behavior and student achievement. In *Handbook of research on teaching,* edited by M. Wittrock. 3rd ed. New York: Macmillan, 328-75.

Brosvic, G.M., and S. Finizio. 1995. Inaccurate feedback and performance on the Muller-Lyer illusion. *Perceptual and Motor Skills* 80: 896-98.

Brown, E.W. 1982. Visual evaluation techniques for skill analysis. *JOPERD* 53 (1): 21-26, 29.

Brown, E.W. 1984. Kinesiological analysis of motor skills via visual evaluation techniques. In *Proceedings: Second national symposium on teaching kinesiology and biomechanics in sports,* edited by R. Shapiro and J.R. Marett. Colorado Springs, Colo.: NASPE, 95-96.

Brown, S. 1995. The effects of limited and repeated demonstrations of the development of fielding and throwing in children. Ph.D. diss., University of South Carolina, 1994. Abstract in *Dissertation Abstracts International* 55: 1868A.

Bruton, A., B. Ellis, and J. Goddard. 1999. Comparison of visual estimation and goniometry for assessment of metacarpophalangeal joint angle. *Physiotherapy* 85: 201-8.

Buckolz, E., H. Prapavesis, and J. Fairs. 1988. Advance cues and their use in predicting tennis passing shots. *Canadian Journal of Sport Sciences* 13: 20-30.

Buizza, A., and R. Schmid. 1986. Velocity characteristics of smooth pursuit eye movements to different patterns of target motion. *Experimental Brain Research* 63: 395-401.

Buizza, A., and R. Schmid. 1989. The influence of smooth pursuit dynamics on eye tracking: A mathematical approach. *Medical and Biological Engineering and Computing* 27: 617-22.

Bunn, J.W. 1955. *Scientific principles of coaching.* Englewood Cliffs, N.J.: Prentice-Hall.

Burg, A. 1966. Visual acuity as measured by static and dynamic tests: A comparative evaluation. *Journal of Applied Psychology* 50: 460-66.

Campbell, F.W., and R.H. Wurtz. 1978. Saccadic omission: Why we do not see a gray-out during a saccadic movement. *Vision Research* 18: 1297-303.

Cappozzo, A., M. Marchetti, and V. Tosi, eds. 1992. *Biolocomotion: A century of research using moving pictures.* Rome: Promograph.

Carpenter, R.H.S. 1988. *Movements of the eyes.* 2nd ed. London: Pion.

Catalano, J. 1995. The eyes have it. *Training & Conditioning* (June): 6-14.

Cavanagh, P.R. 1990. Biomechanics: A bridge builder among the sport sciences. *Medicine and Science in Sports and Exercise* 22: 546-57.

Cavanagh, P.R., and R. Kram. 1985. The efficiency of human movement: A statement of the problem. *Medicine and Science in Sports and Exercise* 17: 304-8.

Cayer, L. 1992. The skill of analysis and correction. In *Proceedings: Third national tennis seminar.* Melbourne, Australia: Tennis Australia, 1-15.

Chen, D.D. 2001. Trends in augmented feedback research and tips for the practitioner. *JOPERD* 72 (1): 32-36.

Chen, L. 1982. Topological structure in visual perception. *Science* 128 (12): 699-700.

Chow, J., L. Carlton, W. Chae, Y. Lim, and J. Shim. 1999. Pre- and post-impact ball and racquet characteristics during tennis serves performed by elite male and female players. In *Scientific proceedings of the XVIII international symposium on biomechanics in sports.* Perth, Wash.: Edith Cowan University, 45-48.

Christina, R.W., and D.M. Corcos. 1988. *Coaches guide to teaching sport skills.* Champaign, Ill.: Human Kinetics.

Chung, T.W. 1993. The effectiveness of computer-based interactive video instruction on psychomotor skill analysis competency of preservice physical education teachers in tennis teaching. Ph.D. diss., University of Northern Colorado, 1992. Abstract in *Dissertation Abstracts International* 53: 2290A.

Ciapponi, T. 1999. Skill analysis. *Strategies* 12 (5): 13-16.

Clark, J.E., C.L. Stamm, and M.F. Urquia. 1979. Developmental variability: The issue of reliability. In *Psychology of motor behavior and sport—1978,* edited by G.C. Roberts and K.M. Newell. Champaign, Ill.: Human Kinetics, 253-57.

Cloes, M., A. Deneve, and M. Pieron. 1995. Interindividual variability of teacher's feedback: Study in simulated teaching conditions. *European Physical Education Review* 1: 83-93.

Cloes, M., J. Premuzak, and M. Pieron. 1995. Effectiveness of a video training program used to improve error identification and feedback processes by physical education student teachers. *International Journal of Physical Education* 32 (3): 4-10.

Cohn, T.E., and D.D. Chaplik. 1991. Visual training in soccer. *Perceptual and Motor Skills* 72: 1238.

Coker, C.A. 1998. Observation strategies for skill analysis. *Strategies* 11 (4): 17-19.

Cole, J.L. 1981. Teacher-augmented feedback: Shortening the "fairway" between theory and instruction. *Motor Skills: Theory into Practice* 5: 81-87.

Consumer Reports. 1999. Camcorders: Time to go digital. *Consumer Reports* (October): 34-37.

Cook, D.A. 1990. Using the basic skills to organize your movement analysis. *Professional Skier* (winter): 50-52.

Cooper, J.M., and R.B. Glassow. 1963. *Kinesiology.* St. Louis: C.V. Mosby Company.

Cooper, L.K., and A.L. Rothstein. 1981. Videotape replay and the learning of skills in open and closed environments. *Research Quarterly for Exercise and Sport* 52: 191-99.

Cox, R.H. 1987. An exploratory investigation of a signal discrimination problem in tennis. *Journal of Human Movement Studies* 13: 197-210.

Cozzallio, E.R. 1986. The development of assessment instruments for screening selected gross motor skills in kindergarden children. Ph.D. diss., Florida State University, 1985. Abstract in *Dissertation Abstracts International* 47: 118A.

Craft, A.H. 1977. The teaching of skills for the observation of movement: Inquiry into a model. Ph.D. diss., University of North Carolina Greensboro. Abstract in *Dissertation Abstracts International* 38: 1975A.

Craik, R.L., and C.A. Oatis. 1995. *Gait analysis: Theory and application.* St. Louis: Mosby.

Cutting, J.E., and D.R. Proffitt. 1981. Gait perception as an example of how we may perceive events. In *Intersensory perception and sensory integration,* edited by R.D. Walk and H.L. Pick. New York: Plenium, 249-73.

Dahle, L.K., M. Mueller, A. Delitto, and J.E. Diamond. 1991. Visual assessment of foot type and relationship of foot type to lower extremity injury. *Journal of Orthopedic and Sports Physical Therapy* 14: 70-74.

Dale, E. 1984. *The educator's quotebook.* Bloomington, Ind.: Phi Delta Kappa Educational Foundation.

Daniels, D.B. 1984. Basic movements and modeling: An approach to teaching skill analysis in the undergraduate biomechanics course. In *Proceedings: Second national symposium on teaching kinesiology and biomechanics in sports,* edited by R. Shapiro and J.R. Marett. Colorado Springs, Colo.: NASPE, 243-46.

Daniels, D.B. 1987. Qualitative analysis: The coach's most important tool. In *World identification systems for gymnastic talent,* edited by B. Petiot et al. Montreal: Sport Psyche Editions, 163-72.

Darden, G., and J. Shimon. 2000. Revisit an "old" technology: Videotape feedback for motor skill learning and performance. *Strategies* 13 (4): 17-21.

Darden, G.F. 1999. Videotape feedback for student learning and performance: A learning-stages approach. *JOPERD* 70 (9): 40-45, 62.

Davids, K.W., D.R. DePalmer, and G.J.P. Savelsbergh. 1989. Skill level, peripheral vision and tennis volleying performance. *Journal of Human Movement Studies* 16: 191-202.

Davis, J. 1980. Learning to see: Training in observation of movement. *JOPER* 51 (1): 89-90.

Davis, W.E. 1984. Motor ability assessment of populations with handicapping conditions: Challenging basic assumptions. *Adapted Physical Activity Quarterly* 1: 125-40.

Davis, W.E., and A.W. Burton. 1991. Ecological task analysis: Translating movement behavior theory into practice. *Adaptive Physical Education Quarterly* 8: 154-77.

Day, M.C. 1975. Developmental trends in visual scanning. In *Advances in child development and behavior,* edited by H.W. Reese. New York: Academic Press, 154-93.

DeBruin, H., D.J. Russell, J.E. Latter, and J.T.S. Sadler. 1982. Angle-angle diagrams in monitoring and quantification of gait patterns for children with cerebral palsy. *American Journal of Physical Medicine* 61: 176-92.

Dedeyn, K. 1991. Error identification comparison between three modes of viewing a skill. In *Teaching kinesiology and biomechanics in sports,* edited by J. Wilkerson, E. Kreighbaum, and C. Tant. Ames, Iowa: NASPE Kinesiology Academy, 21-25.

DeLooze, M.P., H.M. Toussaint, J. Ensink, C. Mangnus, and A.J. Van der Beek. 1994. The validity of visual observation to assess posture in a laboratory-simulated manual material handling task. *Ergonomics* 37: 1335-43.

DePauw, K., and G. GocKarp. 1989. Systematic infusion of knowledge into the undergraduate curriculum. Paper presented at the National Association for Physical Education in Higher Education conference, January, San Antonio, Tex.

DeRenne, C., K. Ho, and A. Blitzblau. 1990. Effects of weighted implement training on throwing velocity. *Journal of Applied Sport Science Research* 4: 16-19.

DeRenne, C., K. Ho, and J. Murphy. 2001. Effects of general, special, and specific resistance training on overarm throwing velocity in baseball: A brief review. *Journal of Strength and Conditioning Research* 15: 148-56.

DeRenne, C., and T. House. 1987. The four absolutes of pitching mechanics. *Scholastic Coach* (March): 79-83.

Deutsch, J.A., and D. Deutsch. 1963. Attention: Some theoretical considerations. *Psycholocical Review* 70: 80-90.

DiCicco, G.L. 1990. The effect of tennis playing and teaching experience on ability to perform a diagnostic task. Ph.D. diss., University of Pittsburgh. Abstract in *Dissertation Abstracts International* 51: 1581A.

Donkelaar, P., and R.G. Lee. 1994. The role of vision and eye motion during reaching to intercept moving targets. *Human Movement Science* 13: 765-83.

Douwes, M., and J. Dul. 1991. Validity and reliability of estimating body angles by direct and indirect observations. In *Designing for everyone: Proceedings of the international ergonomics association,* edited by Y. Queinnec and F. Daniellou. London: Taylor & Francis, 885-87.

Dowell, L.J. 1978. Throwing for distance: Air resistance, angle of projection, and ball size and weight. *Motor Skills: Theory into Practice* 3 (1): 11-14.

Dowrick, P.W. 1991a. Equipment fundamentals. In *Practical guide to using video in the behavioral sciences,* edited by P.W. Dowrick. New York: John Wiley & Sons, 7-29.

Dowrick, P.W. 1991b. Feedback and self-confrontation. In *Practical guide to using video in the behavioral sciences,* edited by P.W. Dowrick. New York: John Wiley & Sons, 92-108.

Draper, J. 1986. Analyzing skill to improve performance. *Sports Coach* 9 (4): 33-35.

Drummond, J.L., and S.K. Gangstead. 1996. The effects of experience on analytical proficiency and observational strategy among female collegiate athletes and coaches. *Applied Research in Coaching and Athletics Annual* 11: 75-94.

Duck, T. 1986. Applied sport biomechanics for advanced coaching. *Sports Science Periodical on Research and Technology in Sport* (June): 1-6.

Dunham, P. 1986. Evaluation for excellence. *JOPERD* 57 (6): 34-36, 60.

Dunham, P. 1994. *Evaluation for physical education.* Englewood, Colo.: Morton Publishing Company.

Dunham, P., E.J. Reeve, and C.S. Morrison. 1989. *DISPE: A total instructional system for physical education.* Edina, MN: Alpha Editions.

Eastlack, M.E., J. Arvidson, L. Snyder-Mackler, J.V. Canoff, and C.L. McGarvey. 1991. Interrater reliability of videotaped observational gait analysis assessments. *Physical Therapy* 71: 465-72.

Eastman Kodak Company. 1979. *High-speed photography standard book.* No. 0-87985-165-1.

Eckrich, J.R. 1991. The effects of video observational training on video and live observational proficiency. Ph.D. diss., Purdue University, 1990. Abstract in *Dissertation Abstracts International* 52: 465A.

Eckrich, J., C.J. Widule, R.A. Shrader, and J. Maver. 1994. The effects of video observational training on video and live observational proficiency. *Journal of Teaching in Physical Education* 13: 216-27.

Elliott, B.C., R.N. Marshall, and G.J. Noffal. 1995. Contributions of upper limb segment rotations during the power serve in tennis. *Journal of Applied Biomechanics* 11: 433-42.

Emmen, H.H., L.G. Wesseling, R.J. Bootsma, H.T.A. Whiting, and P.C.W. van Wieringen. 1985. The effect of video-modelling and video-feedback on the learning of the tennis service by novices. *Journal of Sports Sciences* 3: 127-38.

Ericson, M., A. Kilbom, C. Wiktorin, and J. Winkel. 1991. Validity and reliability in the estimation of trunk, arm and neck inclination by observation. *Proceedings of the International Ergonomics Association conference.* Paris: International Ergonomics Association, 245-47.

Eriksen, C.W., and J.M. Webb. 1989. Shifting of attentional focus within and about a visual display. *Perception and Psychophysics* 45: 175-83.

Farah, M.J., K.M. Hammond, D.N. Levine, and R. Calvanio. 1988. Visual and spatial mental imagery: Dissociable systems of representation. *Cognitive Psychology* 20: 439-62.

Feldman, L. 1988. Sony VCR ED-V9000. *Video Review* (April): 66-67.

Feltner, M.E. 1989. Three-dimensional interactions in a two-segment kinetic chain. Part II: Application to the throwing arms in baseball pitching. *International Journal of Sport Biomechanics* 5: 420-50.

Feltner, M.E., and J. Dapena. 1986. Dynamics of the shoulder and elbow joints of the throwing arm during the baseball pitch. *International Journal of Sport Biomechanics* 2: 235-59.

Fife, S.E., L.A. Roxborough, R.W. Armstrong, S.R. Harris, J.L. Gregson, and D. Field. 1991. Development of a clinical measure of postural control for assessment of adaptive seating in children with neuromotor disabilities. *Physical Therapy,* 71: 981-93.

Fisher, G.H. 1981. Human information processing and a taxonomy of sporting skills. In *Vision and sport,* edited by I.M. Cockerill and W.W. MacGillivary. Cheltenham, England: Stanley Thornes.

Fisk, S.F. 1993. Seeing is believing. *Tennis* (August): 33.

Fitts, P.M. (1965). Factors in complex skill training. In *Training Research and Education,* edited by R. Glasser. New York: Wiley.

Fitts, P.M., and M.I. Posner. 1967. *Human performance.* Belmont, Calif.: Brooks/Cole.

Fleisig, G. 2001. The biomechanics of throwing. In *Proceedings of oral sessions: XIX international symposium on biomechanics in sports,* edited by J. Blackwell. San Francisco: University of San Francisco, 91-4.

Fleisig, G.S., J.R. Andrews, C.J. Dillman, and R.F. Escamilla. 1995. Kinetics of baseball pitching with implications about injury mechanisms. *American Journal of Sports Medicine* 23: 233-39.

Fleisig, G.S., S.W. Barrentine, R.F. Escamilla, and J.R. Andrews. 1996a. Biomechanics of overhand throwing with implications for injuries. *Sports Medicine* 21: 421-37.

Fleisig, G.S., R.F. Escamilla, J.R. Andrews, T. Matsuo, Y. Satterwhite, and S.W. Barrentine. 1996b. Kinematic and kinetic comparison between baseball pitching and football passing. *Journal of Applied Biomechanics* 12: 207-24.

Fleming, L.K. 1980. Identifying performance errors and teaching cues in tennis: The effectiveness of an instruction program. Master's thesis, Brigham Young University, Provo, Utah.

Foster, S.L., and J.D. Cone. 1986. Design and use of direct observation procedures. In *Handbook of behavioral assessment,* edited by A.R. Ciminero, K.S. Calhounm, and H.E. Adams. New York: Wiley, 253-324.

Franck, F. 1979. *The awakened eye.* New York: Random House.

Franks, I.M. 1993. The effect of experience on the detection and location of performance differences in a gymnastic technique. *Research Quarterly for Exercise and Sport* 64: 227-31.

Franks, I.M., and D. Goodman. 1986. A systematic approach to analyzing sports performance. *Journal of Sports Sciences* 4: 49-59.

Franks, I.M., and G. Miller. 1991. Training coaches to observe and remember. *Journal of Sports Sciences* 9: 285-97.

Franks, I.M., and L.J. Maile. 1991. The use of video in sport skill acquisition. In *Practical guide to using video in the behavioral sciences,* edited by P.W. Dowrick. New York: John Wiley & Sons, 231-43.

Franks, I.M., and P. Nagelkerke. 1988. The use of computer interactive video in sport analysis. *Ergonomics* 31: 1593-603.

Frederick, A.B. 1977. Using checklists and templates for analyzing gymnastic skills. In *Research and practice in physical education,* edited by R.E. Stadulis. Champaign, Ill.: Human Kinetics, 28-31.

Frederick, A.B., and M.U. Wilson. 1973. Web graphics and the qualitative analysis of movement. *Kinesiology III.* Washington, D.C.: AAHPER, 1-11.

French, C.A., and J.J. Plack. 1982. Effective communication: A rationale for skill instruction techniques. *Motor Skills: Theory into Practice* 6: 59-66.

Fronske, H. 2001. *Teaching cues for sports skills.* 2nd ed. Boston: Allyn & Bacon.

Fronske, H., and S.E. Dunn. 1992. Cue your students in on good swimming. *Strategies* 5 (5): 25-27.

Fronske, H., J. Abendroth-Smith, and C. Blakmore. 1995. The effect of critical cues on throwing efficiency of elementary school children. *Research Quarterly for Exercise and Sport* 66 (suppl.): A53.

Fronske, H., R. Wilson, and S.E. Dunn. 1992. Visual teaching cues for tennis instruction. *JOPERD* 63 (5): 13-14.

Gangstead, S.K. 1984. A comparison of three methodological approaches to skill specific analytical training. Annual convention of the Northern Rocky Mountain Research Association. Jackson, WY. ERIC Document Reproduction Service, ED 255-471.

Gangstead, S.K. 1987. Toward a pedagogical kinesiology: A training paradigm. Paper presented at the meeting of the International Congress of Health, Physical Education, and Recreation, June, Vancouver, B.C.

Gangstead, S.K. 1995. Development of observational and diagnostic competence: A training paradigm. *International Journal of Physical Education and Sport Science* 7: 31-41.

Gangstead, S.K., and S.K. Beveridge. 1984. The implementation and evaluation of a methodical approach to qualitative sports skill analysis instruction. *Journal of Teaching in Physical Education* 3 (winter): 60-70.

Gangstead, S.K., C. Cashel, and S.K. Beveridge. 1987. Perceptual style, visual retention and visual discrimination in qualitative sports skill analysis. Paper presented to the annual convention for the American Alliance for Health, Physical Education, Recreation and Dance, April, Kansas City, Mo.

Gassner, G.J. 1999. Using metaphors for high-performance teaching and coaching. *JOPERD* 70 (7): 33-35.

Gavriyski, V. 1969. The colours and colour vision in sport. *Journal of Sports Medicine* 4: 49-53.

Genaidy, A.M., R.J. Simmons, L. Guo, and J.A. Hidalgo. 1993. Can visual perception be used to estimate body part angles? *Ergonomics* 36: 323-29.

Gentile, A.M. 1972. A working model of skill acquisition with application to teaching. *Quest* 17: 3-23.

Gibson, E.J. 1969. *Principles of perceptual development.* New York: Appleton-Century-Crofts.

Girardin, Y., and D. Hanson. 1967. Relationship between ability to perform tumbling skills and ability to diagnose performance errors. *Research Quarterly* 38: 556-61.

Gluck, M., and L. Kerr. 1982. *Mechanics for gymnastics coaching: Tools for skill analysis.* Springfield, Ill.: Charles C. Thomas Publishers.

Godwin, S. 1975. Training powers of observation. In *Human movement behavior: Conference report,* edited by G.F. Curl. West Midlands, England: Association of Principals of Women's Colleges of Physical Education.

Goodkin, R., and L. Diller. 1973. Reliability among physical therapists in diagnosis and treatment of gait deviations in hemiplegics. *Perceptual and Motor Skills* 37: 727-34.

Gopher, D., and E. Donchin. 1986. Workload: An examination of the concept. In *Handbook of perception and human performance,* vol. 2, edited by K.R. Boff, L. Kaufman, and J.P. Thomas. New York: John Wiley & Sons.

Gould, D., and G. Roberts. 1982. Modeling and motor skill acquisition. *Quest* 33: 214-30.

Goulet, C., M. Fleury, C. Bard, M. Yerles, D. Michaud, and L. Lemire. 1988. Analyse des indices visuels preleves en reception de service au tennis. *Canadian Journal of Sport Sciences* 13: 79-87.

Gowland, C., W.F. Boyce, V. Wright, D.J. Russell, C.H. Goldsmith, and P.L. Rosenbaum. 1995. Reliability of the gross motor performance measure. *Physical Therapy* 75: 597-602.

Graham, K.C. 1988. A qualitative analysis of an effective teacher's movement task presentations during a unit of instruction. *The Physical Educator* 11: 187-95.

Graham, K.C., K. Hussey, K. Taylor, and P. Werner. 1993. A study of verbal presentations of three effective teachers. *Research Quarterly for Exercise and Sport* 64 (suppl.): 87A (abstract).

Gregg, J.R. 1987. *Vision and sports: An introduction.* Stoneham, Mass.: Butterworths Publishers.

Griffin, M.R. 1985. The utilization of product and process measures to compare the throwing, striking, and kicking proficiency of third and fifth grade students. Ph.D. diss., Florida State University, 1984. Abstract in *Dissertation Abstracts International* 45: 2797A.

Groot, C., F. Ortega, and F.S. Beltran. 1994. Thumb rule of visual angle: A new confirmation. *Perceptual and Motor Skills* 78: 232-34.

Groves, R., and D.N. Camaione. 1983. *Concepts in kinesiology.* 2nd ed. Philadelphia, PA: Saunders.

Grunwald, H.A., ed. 1986. *Artificial intelligence: Understanding computers.* Alexandria, Va.: Time-Life Books.

Hall, J. 1993. Toward outcome-based movement analysis. *Professional Skier* (spring): 10-12.

Hall, S.J. 1999. *Basic biomechanics* 3rd ed. Boston, MA: McGraw-Hill.

Halverson, L.E. 1983. Observing children's motor development in action. Paper presented at the national convention of the American Alliance for Health, Physical Education, Recreation and Dance, April, Minneapolis.

Halverson, L.E., M.A. Roberton, and C.J. Harper. 1979. Learning to observe children's motor development. Paper presented to the national convention of the American Alliance for Health, Physical Education and Recreation, April, New Orleans.

Halverson, P.D. 1988. The effects of peer tutoring on sport skill analytic ability. Ph.D. diss., Ohio State University, 1987. Abstract in *Dissertation Abstracts International* 48: 2274A.

Hamburg, J. 1995. Coaching athletes using Laban movement analysis. *JOPERD* 66 (2): 34-37.

Hamilton, G.R., and C. Reinschmidt. 1997. Optimal trajectory for the basketball free throw. *Journal of Sport Sciences* 15: 491-504.

Handford, C., K. Davids, S. Bennett, and C. Button. 1997. Skill acquisition in sports: Some applications of an evolving practice ecology. *Journal of Sports Science* 15: 621-40.

Harari, I., and D. Siedentop. 1990. Relationships among knowledge, experience and skill analysis ability. In *Integration or diversification of physical education and sport studies,* edited by D. Eldar and U. Simri. Netanyah, Israel: Emmanual Gill Publishing House, 197-204.

Harper, R.C. 1995. Effects of a videodisk instructional program on physical education majors' ability to observe the quality of performances of selected motor activities of pre-adolescents. Ph.D. diss., University of Alabama,

1994. Abstract in *Dissertation Abstracts International* 55: 3446A.

Harris, J.C. 1993. Using kinesiology: a comparison of applied veins in the subdisciplines. *Quest* 45: 389-412.

Harrison, J.M. 1973. A comparison of a videotape program and a teacher directed program of instruction in teaching the identification of archery errors. Ph.D. diss., Brigham Young University, Provo, Utah, 1973.

Harrison, J.M. 1999. *Are you a super teacher? A review of 10 years of research on teaching and learning in physical education.* Paper presented at the southwest district American Alliance for Health, Physical Education, Recreation and Dance, February, Tucson, Ariz.

Hartman, B.O., and G.E. Secrist. 1991. *Situational awareness is more than exceptional vision.* Alexandria, Va.: Aerospace Medical Association.

Hatfield, F.C. 1972. Effects of prior experience, access to information, and level of performance on individual and group performance rating. *Perceptual and Motor Skills* 35: 19-26.

Hatze, H. 1976. Biomechanical aspects of a successful motion optimization. In *Biomechanics VB,* edited by P.V. Komi. Baltimore: University Park Press, 5-12.

Haubenstricker, J.L., C.F. Branta, and V.D. Seefeldt. 1983. *Standards of performance for throwing and catching.* East Lansing, Mich.: American Society for the Psychology of Sport and Physical Activity.

Hay, J. 1983. A system for the qualitative analysis of a motor skill. In *Collected papers on sports biomechanics,* edited by G.A. Wood. Perth, Australia: University of Western Australia Press, 97-116.

Hay, J.G. 1984. The development of deterministic models for qualitative analysis. In *Proceedings: Second national symposium on teaching kinesiology and biomechanics in sports,* edited by R. Shapiro and J.R. Marett. Colorado Springs, Colo.: NASPE, 71-83.

Hay, J.G. 1993. *The biomechanics of sports techniques.* 4th ed. Englewood Cliffs, N.J.: Prentice-Hall.

Hay, J.G., and J.G. Reid. 1982. *The anatomical and mechanical bases of human motion.* Englewood Cliffs, N.J.: Prentice-Hall.

Hay, J.G., and J.G. Reid. 1988. *Anatomy, mechanics, and human motion.* 2nd ed. Englewood Cliffs, N.J.: Prentice-Hall.

Haywood, K.M. 1984. Use of image-retina and eye-head movement visual systems during coincidence-anticipation performance. *Journal of Sport Sciences* 2: 139-44.

Haywood, K.M., and N. Getchell. 2001. *Life span motor development.* 3rd ed. Champaign, Ill.: Human Kinetics.

Haywood, K.M., and K. Williams. 1995. Age, gender, and flexibility differences in tennis serving among experienced older adults. *Journal of Aging and Physical Activity* 3: 54-66.

Haywood, K.M., K. Williams, and A. Van Sant. 1991. Qualitative assessment of the backswing in older adult throwing. *Research Quarterly for Exercise and Sport* 62: 340-43.

Henderson, D. 1971. The relationship among time, distance, and intensity as determinants of motion discrimination. *Perception and Psychophysics* 10: 313-20.

Hendriks, E., J. Brandsma, Y. Heerkens, R. Oostendorp, and R. Nelson. 1997. Intraobserver and interobserver reliability of assessments of impairments and disabilities. *Physical Therapy* 77: 1097-106.

Hensley, L.D. 1983. Biomechanical analysis. *JOPERD* 54 (8): 21-23.

Hensley, L.D., J.R. Morrow, and W.B. East. 1990. Practical measurement to solve practical problems. *JOPERD* 61 (3): 42-44.

Heptulla-Chatterjee, S.H., J.J. Freyd, and M. Shiffrar. 1996. Configural processing in the perception of apparent biological motion. *Journal of Experimental Psychology: Human Perception and Performance* 22: 916-29.

Herbert, R., S. Moore, A. Moseley, K. Schurr, and A. Wales. 1993. Making inferences about muscle forces from clinical observations. *Australian Journal of Physiotherapy* 39: 195-202.

Higgins, J.R. 1977. *Human movement: An integrated approach.* St. Lous: Mosby.

Higgins, J., and S. Higgins. 1988. An Eastern system of analysis and observation. Paper presented at a national convention of the American Alliance of Health, Physical Education, Recreation and Dance, April, Kansas City, Mo.

Higgins, J.R., and R.K. Spaeth. 1972. Relationship between consistency of movement and environmental condition. *Quest* 17: 61-69.

Hoare, D. 1992. Screening for gross motor co-ordination problems in primary school children. *Sports Coach* 15 (2): 13-15.

Hoffman, S.J. 1974. Toward taking the fun out of skill analysis. *JOHPER* 45 (9): 74-76.

Hoffman, S.J. 1977a. Toward a pedagogical kinesiology. *Quest* 28: 38-48.

Hoffman, S.J. 1977b. Competency based training in skill analysis. In *Research and practice in physical education,* edited by R.E. Stadulis. Champaign, Ill.: Human Kinetics, 3-12.

Hoffman, S.J. 1977c. Observing and reporting on learner responses: The teacher as a reliable feedback agent. In *Proceedings of the NAPECW/NCPEAM national conference,* edited by L.I. Gedvilas and M.E. Kneer. Chicago: University of Illinois Chicago Circle, 153-60.

Hoffman, S.J. 1983. Clinical diagnosis as a pedagogical skill. In *Teaching in Physical Education,* edited by T.J. Templin and J.K. Olson. Champaign, Ill.: Human Kinetics, 35-45.

Hoffman, S.J. 1984. The contributions of biomechanics to clinical competence: A view from the gymnasium. In *Proceedings: Second national symposium on teaching kinesiology and biomechanics in sports,* edited by R. Shapiro and J.R. Marett. Colorado Springs, Colo.: NASPE, 67-70.

Hoffman, S.J., and C.W. Armstrong. 1975. Effects of pretraining on performance error identification. In *Movement, Actes du & symposium em apprentissage psycho-moteur et psychologie due sport.* Quebec City, Canada, 207-14.

Hoffman, S.J., and J.C. Harris, eds. 2000. *Introduction to kinesiology*. Champaign, Ill.: Human Kinetics.

Hoffman, S.J., C.H. Imwold, and J.A. Kohler. 1983. Accuracy and prediction in throwing: A taxonomic analysis of children's performance. *Research Quarterly for Exercise and Sport* 54: 33-40.

Hoffman, S.J., and J.L. Sembiante. 1975. Experience and imagery in movement analysis. In *British proceedings of sports psychology*, edited by G.J.K. Alderson and D.A. Tyldesley. Salford, England: British Society of Sports Psychology, 288-93.

Holekamp, M.J. 1987. The effect of training on physical therapy student raters evaluating videotaped motor skill performances. Ph.D. diss., University of Missouri-Columbia, 1986. Abstract in *Dissertation Abstracts International* 48: 1145A.

Hong, D., T.K. Cheung, and E.M. Roberts. 2001. A three-dimensional, six-segment chain analysis of forceful overarm throwing. *Journal of Electromyography and Kinesiology* 11: 95-112.

Hore, J., S. Watts, and J. Martin. 1996. Finger flexion does not contribute to ball speed in overarm throws. *Journal of Sport Sciences* 14: 335-42.

Hoshizaki, T.B. 1984. The application of models to understanding the biomechanical aspects of performance. In *Proceedings: Second national symposium on teaching kinesiology and biomechanics in sports*, edited by R. Shapiro and J.R. Marett. Colorado Springs, Colo.: NASPE, 85-93.

Housner, L.D., and D.C. Griffey. 1985. Teacher cognition: Differences in planning and interactive decision making between experienced and inexperienced teachers. *Research Quarterly for Exercise and Sport* 56: 45-53.

Housner, L.D., and D.C. Griffey. 1994. Wax on, wax off: Pedagogical content knowledge in motor skill acquisition. *JOPERD* 65 (2): 63-68.

Howell, M.L. 1956. Use of force-time graphs for performance analysis in facilitating motor learning. *Research Quarterly* 27: 12-22.

Hubbard, A., and C.N. Seng. 1954. Visual movements of batters. *Research Quarterly* 25: 42-57.

Hudson, J. 1985. POSSUM: Purpose/observation system for studying and understanding movement. Paper presented at the AAHPERD national convention, April, Atlanta, Ga.

Hudson, J. 1987. What goes up . . . Paper presented at the AAHPERD national convention, April, Las Vegas, Nev.

Hudson, J.L. 1990a. The value visual variables in biomechanical analysis. In *Proceedings of the 6th international symposium on biomechanics in sports*, edited by E. Kreighbaum and A. McNeill. Bozeman, Mont.: Color World Printers, 499-509.

Hudson, J.L. 1990b. Drop, stop, pop: Keys to vertical jumping. *Strategies* 3 (6): 11-14.

Hudson, J.L. 1990c. Biomechanical observation: Visually accessible variables. In *Proceedings of the VIIIth international symposium of the society of biomechanics in sports*, edited by

M. Nosek, D. Sojka, W.E. Morrison, and P. Susanka. Prague, Czech Republic: Conex, 321-26.

Hudson, J.L. 1995. Core concepts of kinesiology. *JOPERD* 66 (5): 54-55, 59-60.

Huelster, L.J. 1939. Learning to analyze performance. *Journal of Health and Physical Education* 10 (2): 84, 120-21.

Ignico, A.A. 1995. A comparison of videotape and teacher-directed instruction on knowledge, performance, and assessment of fundamental motor skills. *Journal of Educational Technology Systems* 23: 363-68.

Ignico, A.A. 1997. The effects of interactive videotape instruction on knowledge, performance, and assessment of sport skills. *The Physical Educator* 54: 58-63.

Imwold, C.H., and S.J. Hoffman. 1983. Visual recognition of a gymnastic skill by experienced and inexperienced instructors. *Research Quarterly for Exercise and Sport* 54: 149-55.

Ishigaki, H., and M. Miyao. 1993. Differences in dynamic visual acuity between athletes and nonathletes. *Perceptual and Motor Skills* 77: 835-39.

Ishigaki, H., and M. Miyao. 1994. Implications for dynamic visual acuity with changes in age and sex. *Perceptual and Motor Skills* 78: 363-69.

Ishikura, T., and K. Inomata. 1995. Effects of angle of model demonstration on learning of motor skill. *Perceptual and Motor Skills* 80: 651-58.

Jambor, E.A., and E.M. Weekes. 1995. Videotape feedback: Make it more effective. *JOPERD* 66 (2): 48-50.

James, R., and J.S. Dufek. 1993. Movement observation: What to watch . . . and why. *Strategies* 6 (2): 17-19.

Janda, D.H., and P. Loubert. 1991. A preventative program focusing on the glenohumeral joint. *Clinics in Sports Medicine* 10: 955-71.

Janelle, C.M., D.A. Barba, S.G. Frehlich, L.K. Tennant, and J.H. Cauraugh. 1997. Maximizing performance feedback effectiveness through videotape replay and a self-controlled learning environment. *Research Quarterly for Exercise and Sport* 68: 269-79.

Janelle, C.M., J. Kim, and R.N. Singer. 1995. Subject-controlled performance feedback and learning of a closed motor skill. *Perceptual and Motor Skills* 81: 627-34.

Johansson, G. 1973. Visual perception of biological motion and a model for its analysis. *Perception and Psychophysics* 14: 202-11.

Johansson, G. 1975. Visual motion perception. *Scientific American* 232 (6): 76-88.

Johnson, R. 1990. Effects of performance principle training upon skill analysis competency. Ph.D. diss., Ohio State University.

Jones, P. 1987. The overarm baseball pitch: A kinesiological analysis and related strength-conditioning programming. *NSCA Journal* 9 (1): 5-13, 78.

Jones-Morton, P. 1990a. Skills analysis series: Part I Analysis of the place kick. *Strategies* 3 (5): 10-11.

Jones-Morton, P. 1990b. Skills analysis series: Part 2 Analysis of the overarm throw. *Strategies* 3 (6): 22-23.

Jones-Morton, P. 1990c. Skills analysis series: Part 3 Analysis of running. *Strategies* 4 (1): 22-24.

Jones-Morton, P. 1990d. Skills analysis series: Part 4 The standing long jump. *Strategies* 4 (2): 26-27.

Jones-Morton, P. 1991a. Skills analysis series: Part 5 Striking. *Strategies* 4 (3): 28-29.

Jones-Morton, P. 1991b. Skills analysis series: Part 6 Catching. *Strategies* 4 (4): 23-24.

Jones, P. 1987. The overarm baseball pitch: A kinesiological analysis and related strength-conditioning programming. *NSCA Journal* 9 (1): 5-13, 78.

Juul-Kristensen, B., G. Hanson, N. Fallentin, J.H. Andersen, and C. Eckdahl. Assessment of work postures and movements using a video-based observation method and direct technical measurements. *Applied Ergonomics* 32: 517-24.

Kahneman, D. 1973. *Attention and effort.* Englewood Cliffs, N.J.: Prentice-Hall.

Kamieneski, C.D. 1980. The effectiveness of an instructional unit in the analysis and correction of basketball skills. Ph.D. diss., Brigham Young University. Abstract in *Dissertation Abstracts International* 40: 6191A.

Karn, K.S., and M.M. Hayhoe. 2000. Memory representations guide targeting eye movements in a natural task. *Visual Cognition* 7 (6): 673-703.

Kay, H. 1970. Analyzing motor skill performance. In *Mechanisms of motor skill development,* edited by K.J. Connaly. London: Academic Press, 139-59.

Keenan, A.M., and T.M. Bach. 1996. Video assessment of rearfoot movements during walking: A reliability study. *Archives of Physical Medicine and Rehabilitation* 77: 651-55.

Kelly, L.E. 1990. The effectiveness of computer managed interactive videodisk training on the development of sport skill competencies in teachers. Paper presented at the AAHPERD national convention, March, New Orleans.

Kelly, L.E., J. Dagger, and J. Walkley. 1989. The effects of an assessment-based physical education program on motion skill development in preschool children. *Education and Treatment of Children* 12 (2): 152-64.

Kelly, L.E., P. Reuschlein, and J. Haubenstricker. 1989. Qualitative analysis of overhand throwing and catching motor skills: Implications for assessing and teaching. *Journal of the International Council for Health, Physical Education and Recreation* 25: 14-18.

Kelly, L.E., P. Reuschlein, and J.L. Haubenstricker. 1990. Qualitative analysis of bouncing, kicking, and striking motor skills: Implications for assessing and teaching. *Journal of the International Council for Health, Physical Education, and Recreation* 26 (2): 28-32.

Kelly, L.E., J. Walkley, and M.R. Tarrant. 1988. Developing an interactive videodisk application. *JOPERD* 59 (4): 22-26.

Kerner, J.F., and J. Alexander. 1981. Activities of daily living: Reliability and validity of gross vs. specific ratings. *Archives of Physical Medicine and Rehabilitation* 62: 161-66.

Kernodle, M.W., and E.T. Turner. 1998. The effective use of guidance techniques in teaching racquet sports. *JOPERD* 69 (5): 49-54.

Kerrigan, D.C., P.O. Riley, J.L. Lelas, and U.D. Croce. 2001. Quantification of pelvic rotation as a determinant of gait. *Archives of Physical Medicine and Rehabilitation* 82: 217-20.

Keyserling, W.M. 1986. Postural analysis of the trunk and shoulders in simulated real time. *Ergonomics* 29: 569-83.

Kilani, H., D. Too, and M.J. Adrian. 1989. Visual perception of biomechanical characteristics of walking, jumping, and landing. In *Biomechanics in Sports V,* edited by J. Tsarouchas, J. Terauds, B.A. Gowitzke, and L.E. Holt. Athens, Greece: Hellenic Sports Research Institute, 380-92.

Kindig, L.E., and E.J. Windell. 1984. Analysis of sport skills. In *Proceedings: Second national symposium on teaching kinesiology and biomechanics in sports,* edited by R. Shapiro and J.R. Marett. Coloroado Springs, Colo.: NASPE, 231-32.

Kinesiology Academy. 1980. Guidlines and standards for undergraduate kinesiology. *JOPERD* 51 (2): 19-21.

Kinesiology Academy. 1992. Guidelines and standards for undergraduate biomechanics/kinesiology. *Kinesiology Academy Newsletter* (spring): 3-6.

Klatt, L.A. 1992. Biomechanics: Analyzing skills and performance. In *Science of coaching baseball,* edited by J. Kindall. Champaign, Ill.: Leisure Press, 49-83.

Klavora, P., P. Gaskovski, and R.D. Forsyth. 1994. Test-retest reliability of the dynavision appratus. *Perceptual and Motor Skills* 79: 448-50.

Klavora, P., P. Gaskovski, and R.D. Forsyth. 1995. Test-retest reliability of three dynavision tasks. *Perceptual and Motor Skills* 80: 607-10.

Klesius, S., and L. Bowers. 1990. The "I'm special" interactive videodisc for training teachers of handicapped children. *Florida Educational Computing Quarterly*: 2 (4): 73-76.

Kluka, D.A. 1987. Visual skill enhancement. *Strategies* 1 (1): 20-24.

Kluka, D.A. 1991. Visual skills: Considerations in learning motor skills for sport. *AAHPERD Journal* 14 (1): 41-43.

Kluka, D.A. 1994. Visual skills related to sport performance. *Research Consortium Newsletter* (winter): 3.

Kniffin, K.M. 1985. The effects of individualized videotape instruction on the ability of undergraduate physical education majors to analyze select sport skills. Ph.D. diss., Ohio State University. Abstract in *Dissertation Abstracts International* 47: 119A.

Knudson, D. 1991. The tennis topspin forehand drive: Technique changes and critical elements. *Strategies* 5 (1): 19-22.

Knudson, D. 1993. Biomechanics of the basketball jump shot: Six key teaching points. *JOPERD* 64 (2): 67-73.

Knudson, D. 1999a. Using sport science to observe and correct tennis strokes. In *Applied proceedings of the XVII international symposium on biomechanics in sports, TENNIS,* edited by B. Elliott, B. Gibson, and D. Knudson. Perth, Australia: Edith Cowan University, 7-16.

Knudson, D. 1999b. Validity and reliability of visual ratings of the vertical jump. *Perceptual and Motor Skills*: 89: 642-48.

Knudson, D. 2000. What can professionals qualitatively analyze? *JOPERD* 71 (2): 19-23.

Knudson, D. 2001. An integrated approach to the introductory biomechanics course. *The Physical Educator.*

Knudson, D., and D. Kluka. 1997. The impact of vision and vision training on sport performance. *JOPERD* 68 (4): 17-24.

Knudson, D., D. Luedtke, and J. Faribault. 1994. How to analyze the serve. *Strategies* 7 (8): 19-22.

Knudson, D., and C. Morrison. 1996. An integrated qualitative analysis of overarm throwing. *JOPERD* 67 (6): 31-36.

Knudson, D., and C. Morrison. 2000. Visual ratings of the vertical jump are weakly correlated with perceptual style. *Journal of Human Movement Studies* 39: 33-44.

Knudson, D., C. Morrison, and J. Reeve. 1991. Effect of undergraduate kinesiology courses on qualitative analysis ability. In *Teaching kinesiology and biomechanics in sports,* edited by J. Wilkerson, E. Kreighbaum, and C. Tant. Ames, Iowa: NASPE Kinesiology Academy, 17-20.

Kovar, S.K., H.M. Matthews, K.L. Ermler, and J.H. Hehrhof. 1992. Feedback: How to teach how. *Strategies* 5 (1): 21-25.

Kozak, W. 1989. Skill analysis. In *Proceedings: National coaching certification program advanced II seminar,* edited by J. Almstedt et al. Gloucester, Ontario: Canadian Amateur Hockey Association, 51-77.

Kraft, R.E., and J.A. Smith. 1993. Throwing and catching: How to do it right. *Strategies* 6 (5): 24-27, 29.

Krebs, D.E., J.E. Edelstein, and S. Fishman. 1985. Reliability of observational kinematic gait analysis. *Physical Therapy* 65: 1027-33.

Kreighbaum, E., and K.M. Barthels. 1985. *Biomechanics: A qualitative approach for studying human movement.* 2nd ed. Minneapolis: Burgess Publishing.

Kretchmar, R.T., H. Sherman, and R. Mooney. 1949. A survey of research in the teaching of sports. *Research Quarterly* 20: 238-49.

Kwak, E.C. 1994. The initial effects of various task presentation conditions on students' performance of the lacrosse throw. Ph.D. diss., University of South Carolina, 1993. Abstract in *Dissertation Abstracts International* 54: 2507A.

Lachowetz, T., J. Evon, and J. Pastiglione. 1998. The effect of an upper body strength program on intercollegiate baseball throwing velocity. *Journal of Strength and Conditioning Research* 12: 116-19.

Lafortune, M.A., and P.R. Cavanagh. 1983. Effectiveness and efficiency in bicycle riding. In *Biomechanics VIII-B,* edited by H. Matsui and K. Kobayshi. Champaign, Ill.: Human Kinetics, 928-36.

Landers, D. 1969. Effect of the numbers of categories systematically observed on individual and group performance ratings. *Perceptual and Motor Skills* 29: 731-35.

Landers, D.M. 1970. A review of research on gymnastic judging. *JOHPER* 41 (7): 85-88.

Landin, D. 1994. The role of verbal cues in skill learning. *Quest* 46: 299-313.

Landin, D.K., E. Hebert, and D.L. Cutton. 1989. Analyzing the augmented feedback patterns of professional tennis instructors. *Journal of Applied Research in Coaching and Athletics* 4: 255-71.

Langley, D. 1993. Teaching new motor patterns: Overcoming student resistance toward change. *JOPERD* 63 (1): 27-31.

Lappin, J.S., and M.A. Fuqua. 1983. Accurate visual measurement of three-dimensional moving patterns. *Science* 221: 480-82.

Larsson, L.E., M. Miller, R. Norlin, and H. Thaczuk. 1986. Changes in gait patterns after operations in children with spastic cerebral palsy. *International Orthopedics* 10: 155-62.

Latham, A., and H. Cassady. 1997. Analysis of performance: How to nurture pupils' analytical skills. *British Journal of Physical Education* (winter): 28-32.

Lee, A.M., N.C. Keh, and R.A. Magill. 1993. Instructional effects of teacher feedback in physical education. *Journal of Teaching in Physical Education* 12: 228-43.

Lee, S., and L.J. Stoner. 1985. Skill analysis through computer graphic feedback. In *Biomechanics in sports II: Proceedings of ISBS 1985,* edited by J. Terauds and J.N. Barham. Del Mar, Calif.: Research Center for Sports, 346-53.

Lehmann, J.F. 1982. Gait analysis: Diagnosis and management. In *Krusen's handbook of physical medicine and rehabilitation,* edited by F.J. Kottke, G.K. Stillwell, and J.F. Lehmann. Philadelphia: Saunders, 86-101.

Leis, H.H. 1994. The effects of two instructional conditions on sport skill specific analytic proficiency of physical education majors. Ph.D. diss., University of Southern Mississippi, 1993. Abstract in *Dissertation Abstracts International* 54 (8): 2946A.

Lenoir, M., L. Crevits, M. Goethals, J. Wildenbeest, and E. Musch. 2000. Are better eye movements an advantage in ball games? A study of prosaccadic and antisaccadic eye movements. *Perceptual and Motor Skills* 91: 546-52.

Levanon, J., and J. Dapena. 1998. Comparison of the kinematics of the full-instep and pass kicks in soccer. *Medicine and Science in Sports and Exercise* 30: 917-27.

Lindeman, B., T. Libkuman, D. King, and B. Krause. 2000. Development of an instrument to assess jump-shooting form. *Journal of Sport Behavior* 23: 335-48.

Liu, S., and A.W. Burton. 1999. Changes in basketball shooting patterns as a function of distance. *Perceptual and Motor Skills* 89: 831-45.

Locke, L. 1972. Implications for physical education. *Research Quarterly* 43: 374-86.

Locke, L.F. 1984. Research on teaching teachers: Where are we now? *Journal of Teaching Physical Education* 9 (summer): 63-85.

Lockhart, A. 1966. Communicating with the learner. *Quest* 6: 57-67.

Logan, G.A., and W.C. McKinney. 1970. *Kinesiology*. Dubuque, Iowa: William C. Brown.

Long, G.M. 1994. Exercises for training vision and dynamic visual acuity among college students. *Perceptual and Motor Skills* 78: 1049-50.

Long, G.M. and D.A. Rourke. 1989. Training effects on the resolution of moving targets: Dynamic visual acuity. *Human Factors* 31: 443-51.

Luther, A.C. 1998. *Video camera technology*. Boston: Artech House.

Luther, A.C. 1999. *Video recording technology*. Boston: Artech House.

Luttgens, K., and K.F. Wells. 1982. *Kinesiology: Scientific basis of human movement*. 7th ed. Philadelphia: Saunders.

MacLeod, B. 1991. Effects of eyerobics visual skills training on selected performance measures of female varsity soccer players. *Perceptual and Motor Skills* 72: 863-66.

Magill, R.A. 1993. Augmented feedback in skill acquisition. In *Handbook of research on sport psychology*, edited by R.N. Singer, M. Murphey, and L.K. Tennant. New York: Macmillan, 193-212.

Magill, R.A. 1994. The influence of augmented feedback on skill learning depends on characteristics of the skill and learner. *Quest* 46: 314-27.

Magill, R.A., and P.F. Parks. 1983. The psychophysics of kinethesis for positioning response: The physical stimulus-psychological response relationship. *Research Quarterly for Exercise and Sport* 54: 346-51.

Malina, R.M., and C. Bouchard. 1991. *Growth, maturation, and physical activity*. Champaign, Ill.: Human Kinetics.

Malkia, E., J. Huhtinen, and P. Luthanen. 1991. A qualitative analysis of walking in children with CP. In *The 11th international congress of the world confederation for physical therapy: Proceedings*. London: World Confederation for Physical Therapy, 1160.

Marett, J.R., J.A. Pavlacka, W.L. Siler, and R. Shapiro. 1984. Kinesiology status update: A national survey. In *Proceedings: Second national symposium on teaching kinesiology and biomechanics in sports*, edited by R. Shapiro and J.R. Marett. Colorado Springs, Colo.: NASPE, 7-15.

Marey, E.J. 1972. *Movement*. New York: Arno Press.

Marino, G.W. 1982. Qualitative biomechanical analysis of sports skills. *Coaching Science Update* 9: 20-22.

Marks, L.E. 1987. On cross-modal similarity: Auditory-visual interactions in speeded discrimination. *Journal of Experimental Psychology: Human Perception and Performance* 13: 384-94.

Martens, R., L. Burwitz, and J. Zuckerman. 1976. Modeling effects on motor performance. *Research Quarterly* 47: 277-91.

Martino, G., and L.E. Marks. 1999. Preceptual and linguistic interactions in speedec clarification: tests of the semantic coding hypothesis. *Perception* 28: 903-23.

Martino, G., and L.E. Marks. 2000. Cross-modal interaction between vision and touch: The role of synesthetic correspondence. *Perception* 29: 746-54.

Maschette, W. 1985. Correcting technique problems of a successful junior athlete. *Sports Coach* 9 (1): 14-17.

Masser, L. 1985. The effect of refinement on student achievement in a fundamental motor skill K-6. *Journal of Teaching in Physical Education* 6: 174-82.

Masser, L.S. 1993. Critical cues help first-grade students' achievement in handstands and forward rolls. *Journal of Teaching in Physical Education* 12: 301-12.

Matanin, M.J. 1993. Effects of performance principle training on correct analysis and diagnosis of motor skills. Ph.D. diss., Ohio State University. Abstract in *Dissertation Abstracts International* 54: 1724A.

Mathers, S. 1990. Training your eyes: A method of learning ski movement analysis. *Professional Skier* (winter): 30-31.

Mathias, K.E. 1991. A comparison of the effectivness of interactive video in teaching the ability to analyze two motor skills in swimming. Ed.D. diss., University of Northern Colorado. Abstract in *Dissertation Abstracts International* 51: 3676A.

Matlin, M. 1983. *Cognition*. New York: Holt, Rinehart and Winston, Inc.

McCallister, S.G., and G. Napper-Owen. 1999. Observation and analysis of skills of student teachers in physical education. *The Physical Educator* 56: 19-32.

McClenaghan, B.A., and D.L. Gallahue. 1978. *Fundamental movement: A developmental and remedial approach*. Philadelphia: Sanders.

McCormick, E.J., and M.S. Sanders. 1982. *Human factors in engineering and design*. 5th ed. New York: McGraw-Hill.

McCraw, P. 1995. The qualitative analysis of motor skills using multi-media software engineering techniques. Master's thesis, Deakin University, Melbourne, Australia.

McCullagh, P. 1986. Model status as a determinant of observational learning and performance. *Journal of Sport Psychology* 8: 319-31.

McCullagh, P. 1987. Model similarity effects on motor performance. *Journal of Sport Psychology* 9: 249-60.

McCullagh, P.M., and J.K. Caird. 1990. Correct and learning models and the use of model knowledge of results in the acquisition and retention of a motor skill. *Journal of Human Movement Studies* 18: 107-16.

McCullagh, P.M., and W.S. Little. 1990. Demonstrations and knowledge of results in motor skill acquisition. *Perceptual and Motor Skills* 71: 735-42.

McCullagh, P., J. Stiehl, and M.R. Weiss. 1990. Developmental modeling effects on the quantitative and qualitative aspects of motor performance. *Research Quarterly for Exercise and Sport* 61: 344-50.

McCullagh, P., M.R. Weiss, and D. Ross. 1989. Modeling considerations in motor skill acquisition and performance: An integrated approach. *Exercise and Sport Sciences Reviews* 17: 475-513.

McGinnis, P.M. 1999. *Biomechanics of sport and exercise.* Champaign, Ill.: Human Kinetics.

McGrain, P. 1984. Videography: An inexpensive alternative to film analysis in kinesiology and biomechanics. In *Proceedings: Second national symposium on teaching kinesiology and biomechanics in sports,* edited by R. Shapiro and J.R. Marett. Colorado Springs, Colo.: NASPE, 59-63.

McKethan, R.N., and E.T. Turner. 1999. Using multimedia programming to teach sport skills. *JOPERD* 70 (3): 22-25.

McLeod, P., J. Driver, Z. Dienes, and J. Crisp. 1991. Filtering by movement and visual search. *Journal of Experimental Psychology: Human Perception and Performance* 17 (1): 55-64.

McNaughton, L. 1986. Some drills to improve visual perception abilities in team sport players. *Sports Coach* 9 (2): 47-49.

McPherson, M.N. 1988a. Who: The physical education teacher as diagnostician. Paper presented at the national convention of the American Alliance for Health, Physical Education, Recreation and Dance, April, Kansas City, Mo.

McPherson, M.N. 1988b. The development, implementation, and evaluation of a program designed to promote competency in skill analysis. Ph.D. diss., University of Alberta, Canada.

McPherson, M.N. 1990. A systematic approach to skill analysis. *Sports Science Periodical on Research and Technology in Sport* 11 (1): 1-10.

McPherson, M.N. 1996. Qualitative and quantitative analysis in sports. *American Journal of Sports Medicine* 24: 585-88.

McPherson, M.N., and E.W. Bedingfield. 1985. Development of instructional videotape for qualitative analysis. In *Biomechanics in sports II: Proceedings of ISBS 1985,* edited by J. Terauds and J.N. Barham. Del Mar, Calif.: Research Center for Sports, 385-89.

McPherson, M.N., and J. Walsh. 1990. Application of the skill analysis approach to the nordic two skate. *Sports Coach* 13 (3): 3-7.

Mead, T.P., and J.N. Drowatzky. 1997. Interdependence of vision and audition among inexperienced and experienced tennis players. *Perceptual and Motor Skills* 85: 163-66.

Meehan, J.W., and R.H. Day, 1995. Visual accommodation as a cue for size. *Ergonomics* 38: 1239-49.

Melville, D.S. 1993. Videotaping: An assist for large classes. *Strategies* 6 (4): 26-28.

Messick, J.A. 1991. Prelongitudinal screening of hypothesized developmental sequences for the overhead tennis serve in experienced tennis players. *Research Quarterly for Exercise and Sport* 62: 249-56.

Messier, S.P., and K.J. Cirillo. 1989. Effects of a verbal and visual feedback system on running technique, perceived exertion and running economy in female novice runners. *Journal of Sports Sciences* 7: 113-26.

Metzler, M. 1989. A review of research on time in sport pedagogy. *Journal of Teaching in Physical Education* 6: 271-85.

Meyer, C.H., A.G. Lasker, and D.A. Robinson. 1985. The upper limit of human smooth pursuit velocity. *Vision Research* 25: 561-63.

Michigan Education Assessment Program. 1984. *Physical education assessment administration manual, 1984-1985.* Lansing, Mich.: Michigan Department of Education.

Mielke, D., and D. Chapman. 1987. Effectiveness of education majors in assessing children on the test of gross motor development. *Perceptual and Motor Skills* 64: 1249-50.

Mielke, D., and C. Morrison. 1985. Motor development and skill analysis: Connections to elementary physical education. *JOPERD* 56 (9): 48-51.

Miller, D.I. 1980. Body segment contributions to sport skill performance: Two contrasting approaches. *Research Quarterly for Exercise and Sport* 51: 219-33.

Miller, G., and C. Gabbard. 1988. Effects of visual aids on acquisition of selected tennis skills. *Perceptual and Motor Skills* 67: 603-06.

Miller, S., and R. Bartlett. 1993. The effects of increased shooting distance in the basketball jump shot. *Journal of Sport Sciences* 11: 285-93.

Miller, S., and R. Bartlett. 1996. The relationship between basketball shooting kinematics, distance and playing position. *Journal of Sport Sciences* 14: 243-53.

Minas, S. 1977. Memory coding for movement. *Perceptual and Motor Skills* 45: 787-90.

Miyashita, M., S. Fukashiro, and Y. Hirano. 1986. Feedback of biomechanics data. In *Biomechanics: The 1984 Olympic scientific congress proceedings,* edited by M. Adrian and H. Deutsch. Eugene, Oreg.: Microform Publications, 47-54.

Miyashita, M., T. Tsunoda, S. Sakurai, H. Nishizono, and T. Mizuno. 1979. The tennis serve as compared with overarm throwing. In *Proceedings of a national symposium on the racket sports,* edited by J. Groppel. Champaign, Ill.: University of Illinois, 125-40.

Miyazaki, S., and T. Kubota. 1984. Quantification of gait abnormalities on the basis of continuous foot-force measurement: Correlation between quantification indices and visual rating. *Medical and Biological Engineering and Computing* 22: 70-76.

Mohnsen, B., and C. Thompson. 1997. Using video technology in physical education, part II. *Strategies* 10 (6): 8-11.

Montagne, G., M. Laurent, and H. Ripoll. 1993. Visual information pick-up in ball-catching. *Human Movement Science* 12: 273-97.

Moody, D.L. 1967. Imagery differences among women of varying levels of experience, interests, and abilities in motor skills. *Research Quarterly* 43: 55-61.

Moore, J.S. 1993. The effects of an instructional strategy in naked eye analysis on elementary students' performance of the overarm throw. Ph.D. diss., University of New Mexico.

Morris, G. 1977. Dynamic visual acuity: Implications for the physical educator and coach. *Motor Skills: Theory into Practice* 2: 15-20.

Morrison, C.S. 1976. The effect of vision, motion and laterality in wrist shooting accuracy in ice hockey. Master's thesis, Springfield College, Springfield, Mass.

Morrison, C.S. 1994. Comparison of nationality, gender and type of instruction on the acquisition and retention of qualitative analysis of movement ability. In *Proceedings for the 10th commonwealth and international scientific congress: Access to active living*, edited by F.I. Bell and G.H. Van Gyn. Victoria, B.C.: University of Victoria, 169-74.

Morrison, C.S. 2000. Why don't you analyze the way I analyze? *JOPERD* 71 (1): 22-25.

Morrison, C.S., and C.M. Frederick. 1998. Relationship of initial and final scores on a qualitative analysis of movement test. *Perceptual and Motor Skills* 87: 651-55.

Morrison, C.S., S.K. Gangstead, and J. Reeve. 1990. Two approaches to qualitative analysis: Implications for future directions. Paper presented at the AAHPERD national convention, March, New Orleans, La.

Morrison, C.S., and J.M. Harrison. 1985. Movement analysis and the classroom teacher. *CAHPER Journal* 51 (5): 16-19.

Morrison, C.S., and J.M. Harrison. 1997. Integrating qualitative analysis of movement in the university physical education curriculum. *The Physical Educator* 54: 64-71.

Morrison, C.S., and E.J. Reeve. 1986. Effect of instruction units on the analysis of related and unrelated skills. *Perceptual and Motor Skills* 62: 563-66.

Morrison, C.S., and E.J. Reeve. 1988a. Effect of undergraduate major and instruction on qualitative skill analysis. *Journal of Human Movement Studies* 15: 291-97.

Morrison, C.S., and J. Reeve. 1988b. Effect of different instructional videotape units on undergraduate physical education majors' skill analysis ability. Paper presented to the Texas Association for Health, Physical Education, Recreation and Dance convention , November, San Antonio, Tex.

Morrison, C.S., and J. Reeve. 1989. Effect of different videotape instructional units on undergraduate physical education majors' qualitative analysis of skill. *Perceptual and Motor Skills* 69: 111-14.

Morrison, C.S., and J. Reeve. 1992. Perceptual style and instruction in the acquisition of qualitative analysis of movement by majors in elementary education. *Perceptual and Motor Skills* 74: 579-83.

Morrison, C.S., and J. Reeve. 1993. A framework for writing and evaluating critical performance cues in instructional materials for physical education. *The Physical Educator* 50 (3): 132-35.

Morrison, C.S., E.J. Reeve, and J.M. Harrison. 1984. The effect of two methods of teaching skill analysis and skill performance. Paper presented to the southern district American Alliance of Health, Physical Education, Recreation and Dance, February, Biloxi, Miss.

Morrison, C., E.J. Reeve, and J. Harrison. 1992. The effect of instruction on the ability to qualitatively analyze and perform movement skills. *CAHPER Journal* 58(2): 18-20.

Morrison, J.P., and B.D. Wilson. 1996. Development of a video qualitative analysis system. Paper presented at the first Australasian biomechanics conference, January, Sydney, Australia.

Morton, P. 1990. Effects of training in skill analysis on generalization across age levels. Ph.D. diss., Ohio State University, 1989. Abstract in *Dissertation Abstracts International* 50: 2424A.

Mosher, R.E., and R.W. Schutz. 1983. The development of a test of overarm throwing: An application of generalizability theory. *Canadian Journal of Applied Sport Science* 8 (1): 1-8.

Mosston, M., and S. Ashworth. 1986. *Teaching physical education*. 3rd ed. Columbus, Ohio: Merrill.

Naatanen, R. 1990. The role of attention in auditory information processing as revealed by event-related potentials and other brain measures of cognitive function. *Behavioral and Brain Sciences* 13: 201-88.

National Association for Sport and Physical Education. 1992. *NASPE/NCATE physical education guidelines: An instructional manual*. 3rd ed. Reston, Va.: American Alliance for Health, Physical Education, Recreation and Dance.

Nelson, M.A. 1991. Developmental skills and children's sports. *Physician and Sportsmedicine*, 19 (2): 67-79.

Neumaier, A. 1982. Unterschung zur funktion des blickverhaltens bei visuellen wahrnehmungsprozessen im sport. *Sportweissenschaft* 12 (1): 78-91.

Newell, K.M. 1976. Knowledge of results and motor learning. *Exercise and Sport Sciences Reviews* 4: 195-228.

Newell, K.M. 1990. Kinesiology: The label for the study of physical activity in higher education. *Quest* 42: 269-78.

Newell, K.M., L.R. Morris, and D.M. Scully. 1985. Augmented information and the acquisition of skill in physical activity. *Exercise and Sport Sciences Reviews* 13: 235-61.

Newell, K.M., J.T. Quinn, W.A. Sparrow, and C.B. Walter. 1983. Kinematic information feedback for learning a rapid arm movement. *Human Movement Science* 2: 235-69.

Newell, K.M., W.A. Sparrow, and J.T. Quinn. 1985. Kinetic information feedback for learning isometric tasks. *Journal of Human Movement Studies* 11: 113-23.

Newtson, D. 1976. The process of behavior observation. *Journal of Human Movement Studies* 2: 114-22.

Nicholls, R.L., G.S. Fleisig, B.C. Elliott, S.L. Lyman, and E.D. Osinski. 1999. Biomechanical validation of a qualitative analysis of baseball pitching. In *Scientific proceedings of the XVII international symposium on biomechanics in sports*, edited by R.H. Sanders and B.J. Gibson. Perth, WA.: Edith Cowan University, 297-300.

Nielsen, A.B., and L. Beauchamp. 1992. The effect of training in conceptual kinesiology on feedback provision patterns. *Journal of Teaching in Physical Education* 11: 126-38.

Noe, A., L. Pesoa, and E. Thompson. 2000. Beyond the grand illusion: What change blindness tells us about vision. *Visual Cognition* 7: 93-106.

Norman, R.W. 1975. Biomechanics for the community coach. *JOPERD* 46 (3) (March): 49-52.

Norman, R.W. 1977. An approach to teaching the mechanics of human motion at the undergraduate level. In *Proceedings: Kinesiology: a national conference on teaching,* edited by C.J. Dillman and R.G. Sears. Champaign, Ill.: University of Illinois, 113-23.

O'Donnell, S., S. Moise, D. Warner, and G. Secrist. 1994, *Enhancing soldier performance: A non-linear model of performance to improve selection, testing and training* (U.S. Army Research Laboratory, Report ARL-CR-193).

Ormond, T.C. 1992. The prompt/feedback package in physical education. *JOPERD* 63 (1): 64-67.

Osborne, M.M., and M.E. Gordon. 1972. An investigation into the accuracy of rating of a gross motor skill. *Research Quarterly* 43: 55-61.

Oslin, J.L., S. Stroot, and D. Siedentop. 1997. Use of component-specific instruction to promote development of the overarm throw. *Journal of Teaching in Physical Education* 16: 340-56.

O'Sullivan, M. 1988. How: The Ohio State University model. Paper presented to the national convention of the American Alliance of Health, Physical Education, Recreation and Dance, April, Kansas City, Mo.

Overdorf, V.G. 1990. Timing—in life and in sports—is everything. *JOPERD* 61 (7): 66-69.

Painter, M.A. 1990. A generalizability analysis of observational abilities in the assessment of hopping using two developmental approaches to motor skill sequencing. Ph.D. diss., Michigan State University, 1989. Abstract in *Dissertation Abstracts International* 50: 3888A.

Painter, M.A. 1994. Developmental sequences for hopping as assessment instruments: A generalizability analysis. *Research Quarterly for Exercise and Sport* 65: 1-10.

Palmer, S.E. 1992. Common region: A new principle of perceptual grouping. *Cognitive Psychology* 24: 436-47.

Palmer, S., and I. Rock. 1994. Rethinking perceptual organization: The role of uniform connectedness. *Psychomomic Bulletin and Review* 1 (1): 29-55.

Paquet, V.L., L. Punnett, and B. Buchholz. 2001. Validity of fixed-interval observations for postural assessment in construction work. *Applied Ergonomics* 32, 215-224.

Parson, M.L. 1998. Focus student attention with verbal cues. *Strategies* 11 (3): 30-33.

Partridge, D., and I.M. Franks. 1986. Analyzing and modifying coaching behaviors by means of computer aided observation. *The Physical Educator* (winter): 8-23.

Patla, A.E., and S.D. Clouse. 1988. Visual assessment of human gait: Reliability and validity. *Rehabilitation Research* (October): 87-96.

Patrick, J., and B.J. Lowdon. 1987. Computer controlled video replay of player activity in sport. *Sports Coach* 10 (3): 20-22.

Pellett, T.L., H.A. Henschel-Pellett, and J.M. Harrison. 1994. Feedback effects: Field-based findings. *JOPERD* 65 (9): 75-78.

Perry, J. 1992. *Gait analysis: Normal and pathological function.* Thorofare, N.J.: Slack.

Petrakis, E. 1986. Visual observation patterns of tennis teachers. *Research Quarterly for Exercise and Sport* 57: 254-59.

Petrakis, E. 1987. Analysis of visual search patterns of dance teachers. *Journal of Teaching in Physical Education* 6: 149-56.

Petrakis, E., and M.K. Romjue. 1990. Cognitive processing of tennis teachers/coaches during skill observation. A paper presented to the central district Association for Health, Physical Education, Recreation and Dance, Denver.

Philipp, J.A., and J.W. Wilkerson. 1990. *Teaching team sports: A coeducational approach.* Champaign, Ill.: Human Kinetics.

Phillips, S.J., and J.E. Clark. 1984. An integrative approach to teaching kinesiology: A lifespan approach. In *Proceedings: Second national symposium on teaching kinesiology and biomechanics in sports,* edited by R. Shapiro and J.R. Marett. Colorado Springs, Colo.: NASPE, 19-23.

Phillips, S.J., E.M. Roberts, and T.C. Huang. 1983. Quantification of intersegmental reactions during rapid swing motion. *Journal of Biomechanics* 16: 411-17.

Pinheiro, V. 1994. Diagnosing motor skills: A practical approach. *JOPERD* 65 (2): 49-54.

Pinheiro, V., and H.A. Simon. 1992. An operational model of motor skill diagnosis. *Journal of Teaching in Physical Education* 11: 288-302.

Pinheiro, V., and S. Cai. 1999. Preservice teachers diagnosing live motor performance. *Research Quarterly for Exercise and Sport* 70 (suppl.): A98-99 (abstract).

Pinheiro, V.E.D. 1990. Motor skill diagnosis: Diagnostic processes of expert and novice coaches. Ph.D. diss., University of Pittsburgh, 1989. Abstract in *Dissertation Abstracts International* 50 (11): 3516A.

Pinheiro, V.E.D. 2000. Qualitative analysis for the elementary grades. *JOPERD* 71 (1): 18-20, 25.

Pinheiro, V.E.D., and R.E. Marson. 1998. Teaching/training aid for the golf swing. *Strategies* 11 (4): 20-24.

Piscopo, J., and J.A. Bailey. 1981. *Kinesiology: The science of movement.* New York: Wiley.

Plagenhoef, S. 1971. *Patterns of human motion: A cinematographic analysis.* Englewood Cliffs, N.J.: Prentice-Hall.

Platt, B.B., and D.H. Warren. 1972. Auditory localization: The importance of eye movements and a textured visual environment. *Perception and Psychophysics* 12: 245-48.

Pomeroy, V. 1990. Development of an ADL oriented assessment-of-mobility scale suitable for use with elderly people with dementia. *Physiotherapy* 76: 446-48.

Portman, P.A. 1989. Parent intervention program. *Strategies* 3 (2): 13-19.

Pribram, K.H., and D. McGuiness. 1975. Arousal, activation and effort in the control of attention. *Psychological Review* 82: 116-49.

Prinzmetal, W., and L. Gettleman. 1993. Vertical-horizontal illusion: One eye is better than two. *Perception and Psychophysics* 53: 81-88.

Proctor, R.W., and A. Dutta. 1995. *Skill acquisition and human performance.* Thousand Oaks, Calif.: Sage Publications.

Putnam, C.A. 1991. A segment interaction analysis of proximal-to-distal sequential segment motion patterns. *Medicine and Science in Sports and Exercise* 23: 130-44.

Radford, K.W. 1988. Observation: A neglected teaching skill. *CAHPER Journal* 54 (6): 45-47.

Radford, K.W. 1989. Movement observation in physical education: A definitional effort. *Journal of Teaching in Physical Education* 9: 1-24.

Radford, K.W. 1991. For increased teacher effectiveness: Link observation, feedback and assessment. *CAHPER Journal* 57 (2): 4-9.

Raudensky, J. 1999. Effects of a critical element training package using self-instruction on elementary in service teachers' ability to analyze, diagnose, and provide feedback for the striking skill of batting. Ph.D. diss., Ohio State University, 1998. Abstract in *Dissertation Abstracts International* 59: 3773A.

Reeve, J., and C. Morrison. 1986. Teaching for learning: The application of systematic evaluation. *JOPERD* 57 (6): 37-39.

Regan, D. 1997. Visual factors in hitting and catching. *Journal of Sports Sciences* 15: 533-58.

Reiken, G.B. 1982. Description of women's gymnastic coaches' observations of movement. Ph.D. diss., Teachers College, Columbia University. Abstract in *Dissertation Abstracts International* 43: 397A.

Revlen, L., and M. Gabor. 1981. *Sports vision.* New York: Workman Publishing.

Reynolds, A. 1992. What is competent beginning teaching? A review of the literature. *Review of Educational Research* 2 (1): 1-35.

Riggs, L.A. 1971. Vision. In *Woodworth and Schlosberg's experimental psychology,* edited by J.W. Kling and L.A. Riggs. 3rd ed. New York: Holt, Rinehart and Winston.

Ripoll, H., and P. Fleurance. 1988. What does keeping one's eye on the ball mean? *Ergonomics* 31: 1647-54.

Roberton, M.A. 1978. Longitudinal evidence of developmental stages in the forceful overarm throw. *Journal of Human Movement Studies* 4: 153-67.

Roberton, M.A. 1983. Changing motor patterns during childhood. In *Motor development during childhood and adolescence,* edited by J.R. Thomas. Minneapolis: Burgess Publishing, 48-90.

Roberton, M.A. 1989. Future directions in motor development research: applied aspects. In *Future directions in exercise and sport science research,* edited by J. Skinner et al. Champaign, Ill.: Human Kinetics, 369-391.

Roberton, M.A., and L.E. Halverson. 1984. *Developing children: Their changing movement.* Philadelphia: Lea & Febiger.

Roberts, E.M. 1971. Cinematography in biomechanical investigation. In *Selected topics on biomechanics: Proceedings of CIC symposium on biomechanics,* edited by J.M. Cooper. Chicago, Ill.: Athletic Institute, 41-50.

Robinson, D.A. 1981. Control of eye movements. In *Handbook of physiology. Section 1: The nervous system,* vol. 2, part 2. Bethesda, Md.: American Physiological Society, 1275-320.

Robinson, S. M. 1974. Visual assessment of children's gross motor patterns by adults with backgrounds in teacher education. Ph.D. diss., University of Wisconsin, Madison.

Roemmich, J.N., and A.D. Rogol. 1995. Physiology of growth and development: Its relationship to performance in the young athlete. *Clinics in Sports Medicine* 14: 483-502.

Romance, T.J. 1985. Observing for confidence. *JOPERD* 56 (6): 47-49.

Rose, D.J., and E.M. Heath. 1990. The contribution of a fundamental motor skill to the performance and learning of a complex sport skill. *Journal of Human Movement Studies* 19: 75-84.

Rose, D.J., E.M. Heath, and D. Megale. 1990. Development of a diagnostic instrument for evaluating tennis serving performance. *Perceptual and Motor Skills* 71: 355-63.

Rose, G.K. 1983. Clinical gait assessment: A personal view. *Journal of Medical Engineering and Technology* 7: 273-79.

Ross, D., A.M. Bird, S.G. Doody, and M. Zoeller. 1985. Effects of modeling and videotape feedback with knowledge of results on motor performance. *Human Movement Science* 4: 149-57.

Rothstein, A.L. 1980. Effective use of videotape replay in learning motor skills. *JOPERD* 51 (2): 59-60.

Rothstein, A.L., and R.K. Arnold. 1976. Bridging the gap: Application of research on videotape feedback and bowling. *Motor Skills: Theory into Practice* 1: 35-62.

Runeson, S., and G. Frykholm. 1981. Visual perception of lifted weight. *Journal of Experimental Psychology: Human Perception and Performance* 7: 733-40.

Rush, D.A. 1991. Improving skill analysis for diving. Ph.D. diss., Ohio State University, 1990. Abstract in *Dissertation Abstracts International* 51: 2313A.

Sage, G.H. 1984. *Motor learning and control: A neurophysiological approach.* Dubuque, Iowa: W.C. Brown.

Saleh, M., and G. Murdoch. 1985. In defense of gait analysis. *Journal of Bone and Joint Surgery* (Br) 67: 237-41.

Sanders, R.H. 1995. Can skilled performers readily change technique? An example, conventional to wave action breaststroke. *Human Movement Science* 14: 665-79.

Sanders, R., and B. Wilson. 1989. Some biomechanical tips for better teaching and coaching: Part 1. *New Zealand Journal of Health, Physical Education and Recreation* 23 (4): 14-15.

Sanders, R., and B. Wilson. 1990a. Some biomechanical tips for better teaching and coaching: Part 2. *New Zealand Journal of Health, Physical Education and Recreation* 24 (1): 16-17.

Sanders, R., and B. Wilson. 1990b. Some biomechanical tips for better teaching and coaching: Part 3. *New Zealand Journal of Health, Physical Education and Recreation* 24 (2): 19-21.

Sanderson, D.J., and P.R. Cavanagh. 1990. Use of augmented feedback for the modification of the pedaling mechanics of cyclists. *Canadian Journal of Sport Sciences* 15: 38-42.

Sanderson, F.H., and H.T.A. Whiting. 1974. Dynamic visual acuity and performance in a catching task. *Journal of Motor Behavior* 6: 87-94.

Satern, M.N. 1986. *Apparent and actual use of observational frameworks by experienced teachers.* Paper presented at the national convention of the American Alliance for Health, Physical Education, Recreation and Dance, April, Cincinnati, Ohio. ERIC Document Reproduction Service, ED 273-588.

Satern, M.N. 1999. *Teaching undergraduate biomechanics/ kinesiology: a national survey.* Paper presented to the Biomechanics Academy at the AAHPERD National Convention, April, Boston.

Satern, M.N., M.M. Coleman, and M.H. Matsakis. 1991. The effect of observational training on the frequency of skill-related feedback given by pre-service teachers during two peer teaching experiences. *KAHPERD Journal* 60 (2): 12-16.

Saunders, J., V. Inman, and H. Eberhart. 1953. The major determinants in normal and pathological gait. *Journal of Bone and Joint Surgery* 35A: 543-58.

Schleihauf, R.E. 1983. An analysis of skill acquisition in swimming. In *Collected Papers on Sports Biomechanics,* edited by G.A. Wood. Perth, Australia: University of Western Australia Press, 117-41.

Schmidt, R.A. 1991. *Motor learning and performance: From principles to practice.* Champaign, Ill.: Human Kinetics.

Schmidt, R.A., and C.A Wrisberg. 2000. *Motor learning and performance.* 2nd ed. Champaign, Ill.: Human Kinetics.

Schneider, W., and R.W. Shiffrin. 1977. Controlled and automatic human information processing: Decision research and attention. *Psychological Review* 84: 1-66.

Scott, M.G. 1942. *Analysis of human motion.* New York: F.S. Crofts & Co.

Scully, D.M. 1986. Visual perception of technical execution and aesthetic quality in biological motion. *Human Movement Science* 5: 185-206.

Seat, J.E., and C.A. Wrisberg. 1996. The visual instruction system. *Research Quarterly for Exercise and Sport* 67: 106-08.

Secrist, G.E., and B.O. Hartman. 1993. Situated awareness: The trainability of the near-threshold information acquisition dimension. *Aviation, Space and Environmental Medicine* 64: 885-97.

Seefeldt, V.D., and J.L. Haubenstricker. 1982. Patterns, phases, or stages: An analytical model for study of developmental movement. In *The Development of Movement Control and Coordination,* edited by J.A.S. Kelso and J.E. Clark. New York: John Wiley & Sons, 309-18.

Sharpe, T. 1993. What are some guidelines on giving feedback to students in physical education? *JOPERD* 64 (9): 13.

Shea, C.H., and C. Northan. 1982. Discrimination of visual linear velocities. *Research Quarterly for Exercise and Sport* 53: 222-25.

Shea, C.H., W.L. Shebilske, and S. Worchel. 1993. *Motor learning and control.* Englewood Cliffs, N.J.: Prentice-Hall.

Sherman, A. 1980. Overview of research information regarding vision and sports. *Journal of the American Optometric Association* 51: 661-66.

Sherman, C.A., and B. Crassini. 1999. The golf swing scale: A study of the quality and outcomes of golf shots for elite and novice players. *Applied Research in Coaching and Athletics Annual* 14: 1-16.

Sherman, C.A., and B.S. Rushall. 1993 Improving swimming stroke technique: A case study. *Applied Research in Coaching and Athletics Annual* 8: 123-43.

Shields, B.C. 1995. Sucessful "Q"munication. *IDEA Today* (September): 62-63.

Shiffrar, M. 1994. When what meets where. *Current Directions in Psychological Science* 3: 96-100.

Shiffrar, M., and J.J. Freyd. 1990. Apparent motion of the human body. *Psychological Science* 1: 257-64.

Shiffrar, M., and J.J. Freyd. 1993. Timing and apparent motion path choice with human body photographs. *Psychological Science* 4: 379-84.

Shigehisa, P.M.J., T. Shigehisa, and J.R. Symons. 1973. Effects of intensity of auditory stimulation on photopic visual sensitivity in relation to personality. *Japanese Psychological Research* 15: 164-72.

Shigehisa, T., and J.R. Symons. 1973. Effect of intensity of visual stimulation on auditory sensitivity in relation to personality. *British Journal of Psychology* 64: 205-13.

Shim, J., and L.G. Carlton. 1997. Perception of kinematic characteristics in the motion of lifted weight. *Journal of Motor Behavior* 29: 131-46.

Siedentop, D. 1991. *Developing Teaching Skills in Physical Education.* 3rd ed. Mountain View, Calif.: Mayfield.

Siedentop, D., and L. Locke. 1997. Making a difference for physical education: What professors and practitioners must build together. *JOPERD* 68 (4): 25-33.

Silverman, S. 1994. Communication and motor skill learning: What we learn from research in the gymnasium. *Quest* 46: 345-55.

Simmons, R.W., and H.A. King. 1994. Expertise in the observation and subjective analysis of motor performance: A review of empirical research. *Journal of Human Movement Studies* 27: 49-74.

Simon, H.A. 1979. *Models of thought.* New Haven, Conn.: Yale University Press.

Simons, D.J., and D.T. Levin. 1997. *Change blindness: Trends in cognitive science* 1 (17): 261-67.

Simons, D.J., and D.T. Levin. 1998. Failure to detect changes to people during real-world interaction. *Psychonomic Bulletin and Review* 4 (5): 644-49.

Sinclair, G.D. 1988. Pedagogical considerations. *CAHPER Journal* 54 (3): 32-36.

Skrinar, G.S., and S.J. Hoffman. 1979. Effect of outcome information on analytic ability of golf teachers. *Perceptual and Motor Skills* 48: 703-8.

Slettum, B., C. Fox, M.A. Looney, and D.M. Jay 2001. Validity and reliability of a folk-dance performance checklist for children. *Measurement in physical education and exercise science* 5: 35-55.

Smolensky, P. 1986. Formal modeling of sub-symbolic processes: An introduction to harmony theory. In *Advances in cognitive science 1,* edited by N.E. Sharkey. Chichester, England: Ellis Horwood Limited, 204-35.

Solso, R.L. 1979. *Cognitive psychology.* New York: Harcourt Brace Jovanovich, Inc.

Spaeth, R.K. 1972. Maximizing goal attainment. *Research Quarterly* 43: 337-61.

Sparrow, W.A., and C. Sherman. 2001. Visual expertise in the perception of action. *Exercise and Sport Sciences Reviews* 29: 124-28.

Sparrow, W.A., J. Shemmell, and A.J. Shinkfield. 2001. Visual perception of action categories and the "bowl-throw" decision in cricket. *Journal of Science and Medicine in Sport* 4: 233-44.

Starek, J., and P. McCullagh. 1999. Effect of self-modeling on the performance of beginning swimmers. *Sport Psychologist* 13: 269-87.

Ste-Marie, D.M. 2000. Expertise in women's gymnastic judging: An observational approach. *Perceptual and Motor Skills* 90: 543-46.

Ste-Marie, D.M., and T.D. Lee. 1991. Prior processing effects on gymnastic judging. *Journal of Experimental Psychology: Learning, Memory and Cognition* 17: 126-36.

Ste-Marie, D.M., and S.M. Valiquette. 1996. Enduring memory-influenced biases in gymnastic judging. *Journal of Experimental Psychology: Learning, Memory, and Cognition* 22: 1498-1502.

Steinberg, G.M., S.G. Frehlich, and L.K. Tennant. 1995. Dextrality and eye position in putting performance. *Perceptual and Motor Skills* 80: 635-40.

Steindler, A. 1955. *Kinesiology of the human body under normal and pathological conditions.* Springfield, Ill.: Charles C. Thomas.

Stephenson, D.A., and A.S. Jackson. 1977. The effects of training on judges' ratings of a gymnastic event. *Research Quarterly* 48: 177-80.

Stoner, L.J. 1984. Is this performer skilled or unskilled? In *Proceedings: Second national symposium on teaching kinesiology and biomechanics in sports,* edited by R. Shapiro and J.R. Marett. Colorado Springs, Colo.: NASPE, 233-34.

Strand, B. 1988. The development of checkpoints for skill observation. *New Jersey Journal of Physical Education, Recreation, and Dance* 62 (1): 19-21.

Strohmeyer, H.S., K. Williams, and D. Schaub-George. 1991. Developmental sequences for catching a small ball: A prelongitudinal screening. *Research Quarterly for Exercise and Sport* 62: 257-266.

Stroot, S.A., and J.L. Oslin. 1993. Use of instructional statements by preservice teachers for overhand throwing performance of children. *Journal of Teaching in Physical Education* 13: 24-45.

Stuberg, W., L. Straw, and L. Deuine. 1990. Validity of visually recorded temporal-distance measures at selected walking velocities for gait analysis. *Perceptual and Motor Skills* 70: 323-33.

Suomi, R., and J. Suomi. 1997. Effectiveness of a training program with physical education students and experienced physical education teachers in scoring the test of gross motor development. *Perceptual and Motor Skills* 84: 771-78.

Swinnen, S. 1984a. Some evidence to the hemispheric asymmetry model of lateral eye movements. *Perceptual and Motor Skills* 57: 319-25.

Swinnen, S. 1984b. Some evidence to the hemispheric symmetry model of lateral eye movements. *Perceptual and Motor Skills* 58: 79-88.

Swinnen, S. 1984c. Field dependence/independence as a factor in learning complex motor skills and underlying sex differences. *International Journal of Sports Psychology* 15: 236-49.

Tant, C. 1990. A kick is a kick—or is it? *Strategies* 4 (2): 19-22.

Taylor, J.K. 1995. Developing observational abilities in preservice physical education teachers. Ph.D. diss., University of South Carolina, 1994. Abstract in *Dissertation Abstracts International* 55: 1872A.

Taylor, J. K., K.G. Hussey, P.H. Werner, J.E. Rink, and K.E. French. 1993. The effects of strategy, skill and strategy and skill instruction on skill and knowledge in ninth grade badminton. *Research Quarterly for Exercise and Sport* 64 (suppl.): 96A (abstract).

Theios, J., and P.C. Amarhein. 1989. Theoretical analysis of the cognitive processing of lexical and pictorial stimuli: Reading, naming and visual conceptual comparisons. *Psychological Review* 96 (1): 5-24.

Thorndike, E.L. 1927. The law of effect. *American Journal of Psychology* 39: 212-22.

Thornton, I.M., J. Pinto, and M. Shiffrar. 1998. The visual perception of human locomotion. *Cognitive Neuropsychology* 15: 535-52.

Tieg, D. 1983. Eyes on the PGA tour. *Golf Digest* (July): 85-89.

Tobey, C. 1992. The best kind of feedback. *Strategies* 6 (2): 19-20.

Torrey, L. 1985. *Stretching the limits: Breakthroughs in sports science that create superathletes.* New York: Dodd, Mead, & Company.

Triesman, A. 1986. Features and objects in visual processing. *Scientific American* 255 (5): 114-25.

Treisman, A.M., and G.L. Gelade. 1980. A feature integration theory of attention. *Cognitive Psychology* 12: 97-136.

Trinity, J., and J.J. Annesi. 1996. Coaching with video. *Strategies* 9 (8): 23-25.

Trower, P., and B. Kiely. 1983. Video feedback: Help or hindrance? A review and analysis. In *Using video: Psychological and social applications,* edited by P. Dowrick and S. Briggs. Chichester, England: Wiley, 181-97.

Tzetzis, G., E. Kioumourtzoglou, A.Y. Laiso, and N. Stergiou. 1999. The effect of different feedback models on acquisition and retention of technique in basketball. *Journal of Human Movement Studies* 37: 163-81.

Ulrich, B.G. 1977. A module of instruction for golf swing error detection. In *Research and practice in physical education,* edited by R.E. Stadulis. Champaign, Ill.: Human Kinetics, 19-27.

Ulrich, D.A. 1984. The reliability of classification decisions made with the objectives-based motor skill assessment instrument. *Adapted Physical Activity Quarterly* 1: 52-60.

Ulrich, D.A. 1985. *Test of gross motor development.* Austin, Tex.: PRO-ED, Inc.

Ulrich, D.A., B.D. Ulrich, and C.R. Branta. 1988. Developmental gross motor skill ratings: A generalizability analysis. *Research Quarterly for Exercise and Sport* 59: 203-09.

Valenti, S.S., and A. Costall. 1997. Visual perception of lifted weight from kinematic and static (photographic) displays. *Journal of Experimental Psychology: Human Perception and Performance* 24(1): 181-98.

Vanderbeck, E. 1979. "It isn't right but I don't know what's wrong with it": An approach to error identification. *JOPER* 50 (5): 54-56.

Vandenberg, G.S. 1971. *Mental rotations test.* Boulder, CO: Institute of Behavioral Genetics, University of Colorado.

van Wieringen, P.C.W., H.H. Emmen, R.J. Bootsma, M. Hoogesteger, and H.T.A. Whiting. 1989. The effect of video-feedback on the learning of the tennis service by intermediate players. *Journal of Sports Sciences* 7: 153-62.

Vickers, J.N. 1989. *Instructional design for teaching physical activities: A knowledge structures approach.* Champaign, Ill.: Human Kinetics.

Vincent, R.H. 1984. In or out? See if you can make this line call. *Tennis* (March): 35-37.

Walkley, J.W., and C.E. Kelley. 1989. The effectiveness of an interactive videodisk qualitative assessment training program. *Research Quarterly for Exercise and Sport* 60: 280-85.

Wang, J., and M. Griffin. 1998. Early correction of movement errors can help student performance. *JOPERD* 69 (4): 50-52.

Warren, D.H. 1970. Inter-modality interactions in spatial localization. *Cognitive Psychology* 1: 114-33.

Watkins, M.A., D.L. Riddle, R.L. Lamb, and W.J. Personius. 1991. Reliability of goniometric measurements and visual estimates of knee range of motion obtained in a clinical setting. *Physical Therapy* 71: 90-96.

Watts, R.G., and A.T. Bahill. 1990. *Keep your eye on the ball: The science and folklore of baseball.* New York: W.H. Freeman and Company.

Weiss, M.R. 1982. Developmental modeling enhancing children's motor skill acquisition. *JOPERD* 53 (9): 49-50, 67.

Welch, R.B., and D.H. Warren. 1980. Immediate perceptual response to intersensory discrepancy. *Psychological Bulletin* 88: 638-67.

Werder, J.K., and L.H. Kalakian. 1985. *Assessment in adapted physical education.* Minneapolis: Burgess Publishing.

Werner, P., and J.E. Rink. 1987. Case studies of teacher effectiveness in second grade physical education. *Journal of Teaching in Physical Education* 8: 280-97.

Whittle, M.W. 1991. *Gait analysis: An introduction.* Oxford, England: Butterworth-Heinemann.

Wickens, C.D. 1981. Processing resources in attention, dual task performance, and workload assessment. Engineering-Psychology Research Laboratory, University of Illinois. Technical Report EPL-81-3/ONR-81-3.

Wickens, C.D. 1984a. *Engineering psychology.* Columbus, Ohio: Merrill.

Wickens, C.D. 1984b. Processing resources in attention. In *Varieties of attention,* edited by R. Parasuraman and R. Davies. New York: Academic Press, 63-102.

Wickstrom, R.L. 1983. *Fundamental motor patterns.* 3rd ed. Philadelphia: Lea & Febiger.

Wiese-Bjornstal, D.M. 1993. Giving and evaluating demonstrations. *Strategies* 6 (7): 13-15.

Wild, M. 1938. The behavior pattern of throwing and some observations concerning its course of development in children. *Research Quarterly* 9: 20-24.

Wilkerson, J.D. 1985. Application of concepts: A second look. Paper presented at the AAHPERD national convention, April, Atlanta.

Wilkerson, J., K. Ludwig, and M. Butcher, eds. 1997. Fourth national symposium on teaching biomechanics. Texas Woman's University, Denton, TX.

Wilkerson, J.D., E. Kreighbaum, and C.L. Tant, eds. 1991. *Teaching kinesiology and biomechanics.* Ames, Iowa: Iowa State University.

Wilkinson, S. 1986. The effects of a visual discrimination training program on the acquisition and maintenance of physical education students' volleyball skill analytic ability. Ph.D. diss., Ohio State University. Abstract in *Dissertation Abstracts International* 47: 1650A.

Wilkinson, S. 1990. *Skill analysis: Past, present and future perspectives.* Paper presented at the AAHPERD national convention, March, New Orleans.

Wilkinson, S. 1991. The effect of an instructional videotape on the ability of physical education majors to diagnose errors in the overarm throwing pattern. In *Abstracts of research papers 1991,* edited by W. Liemohn. Reston, Va.: AAHPERD, 74.

Wilkinson, S. 1992a. Effects of training in visual discrimination after one year: Visual analysis of volleyball skills. *Perceptual and Motor Skills* 75: 19-24.

Wilkinson, S. 1992b. A training program for improving undergraduates' analytic skill in volleyball. *Journal of Teaching in Physical Education* 11: 177-94.

Wilkinson, S. 1996. Visual analysis of the overarm throw and related sport skills: Training and transfer effects. *Journal of Teaching in Physical Education* 16: 66-78.

Williams, E. 1996. Effects of a multimedia performance principle training program on correct analysis and diagnosis of throwlike movements. Ph.D. diss., Ohio State University, 1995. Abstract in *Dissertation Abstracts International* 56: 3504A.

Williams, E.U., and D. Tannehill. 1999. Effects of a multimedia performance principle training program on correct analysis and diagnosis of throwlike movements. *The Physical Educator* 56: 143-54.

Williams, J.G. 1987. Visual demonstration and movement sequencing: Effects of instructional control of the eyes. *Perceptual and Motor Skills* 65: 366.

Williams, J.G. 1989a. Motor skill instruction, visual demonstration and eye movements. *Physical Education Review* 12 (1): 49-55.

Williams, J.G. 1989b. Throwing action from full-cue and motion-only video-models of an arm movement sequence. *Perceptual and Motor Skills* 68: 259-66.

Williams, J.G. 1989c. Visual demonstration and movement production: Effects of timing variations in a models action. *Perceptual and Motor Skills* 68: 891-96.

Williams, J.G. 1992. Catching action: Visuomotor adaptations in children. *Perceptual and Motor Skills* 75: 211-19.

Williams, K. 1980. Developmental characteristics of a forward roll. *Research Quarterly for Exercise and Sport* 51: 703-13.

Williams, K., K. Haywood, and A. Van Sant. 1996. Force and accuracy throws by older adults: II. *Journal of Aging and Physical Activity* 4: 194-202.

Wilmore, J.H., and D.L. Costill. 1999. *Physiology of sport and exercise*. 2nd ed. Champaign, Ill.: Human Kinetics.

Wilson, S.J., P. Glue, D. Ball, and D. Nutt. 1993. Saccadic eye movement parameters in normal subjects. *Electroencephalography and Clinical Neurophysiology* 86: 69-74.

Wilson, V.E. 1976. Objectivity, validity, and reliability of gymnastic judging. *Research Quarterly* 47: 169-73.

Winter, D.A. 1984. Kinematic and kinetic patterns in human gait: Variability and compensating effects. *Human Movement Science* 3: 51-76.

Winter, D.A. 1987. *Biomechanics and motor control of human gait*. Waterloo, Ontario: University of Waterloo Press.

Winter, D.A. 1989. Biomechanics of normal and pathological gait: Implications for understanding human locomotor control. *Journal of Motor Behavior* 21: 337-55.

Witkin, H.A. 1954. *Personality through perception: An experimental and clinical study*. Westport, Conn.: Greenwood Press.

Witkin, H.A., P.K. Oltman, E. Raskin, and S.A. Karp. 1971. *A manual for the group embedded figures test*. Palo Alto, Calif.: Consulting Psychologists Press.

Wood, C.A., J.D. Gallagher, P.V. Martino, and M. Ross. 1992. Alternate forms of knowledge of results: Interaction of augmented feedback modality on learning. *Journal of Human Movement Studies* 22: 213-30.

Woollacott, M.H., and A. Shumway-Cook, eds. 1989. *Development of posture and gait across the life span*. Columbia, S.C.: University of South Carolina Press.

Yantis, S. 1992. Multielement visual tracking: Attention and perceptual organization. *Cognitive Psychology* 24: 295-340.

Youndas, J.W., C.L. Bogard, and V.J. Suman. 1993. Reliability of goniometric measurements and visual estimates of ankle joint active range of motion obtained in a clinical setting. *Archives of Physical Medicine and Rehabilitation* 74: 1113-18.

Youndas, J.W., J.R. Carey, and T.R. Garrett. 1991. Reliability of measurements of cervical spine range of motion: Comparison of three methods. *Physical Therapy* 71: 90-96.

Zajac, F.E., and M.E. Gordon. 1989. Determining muscle's force and action in multi-articular movement. *Exercise and Sport Sciences Reviews* 17: 187-230.

Zebas, C., and H.M. Johnson. 1989. Transfer of learning from the overhand throw to the tennis serve. *Strategies* 2 (6): 17-18, 27.

Ziegler, S.G. 1987. Effects of stimulus cueing on the acquisition of groundstrokes of beginning tennis players. *Journal of Applied Behaviour Analysis* 20: 405-11.

Zollman, D., and R.G. Fuller. 1984. Interactive videodisks: New technology for the analysis of human motion. In *Proceedings: Second national symposium on teaching kinesiology and biomechanics in sports*, edited by R. Shapiro and J.R. Marett. Colorado Springs, Colo.: NASPE, 53-56.

Index

Note: The italicized t, or f, following a page number denotes a table, or figure. The italicized ff following a page number denotes multiple figures.

About the Authors

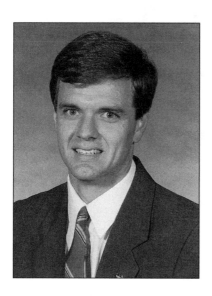

Duane V. Knudson, PhD, is an associate professor and associate chair of the department of physical education and exercise science at California State University at Chico. In addition to publishing research on qualitative analysis of human movement and its pedagogy, he has also published numerous papers on the biomechanics of sport and exercise. Dr. Knudson's presentations at national and international scientific meetings on qualitative analysis have included the International Symposium on Biomechanics and Sport. He is a fellow for the research consortium of AAHPERD and is former chairman of the biomechanics academy of NASPE. In 1994 the University of Wisconsin at Oshkosh named him Outstanding Young Alumni. His hobbies include tennis, running, and reading.

Craig S. Morrison, EdD, is a professor of and department chair for physical education at Southern Utah University. He is well published in the qualitative analysis field, authoring 10 experimental studies and five review articles in national and international journals. Additionally, Dr. Morrison has made 18 presentations on qualitative analysis at the state, regional, national, and international level. He has received three grants to produce instructional videos about qualitative analysis. The Australian Sports Commission has asked him to develop a Web-based class on qualitative analysis for its coaching certification program. In 1988 Dr. Morrison was honored by AAHPERD for a video that he helped produce on qualitative analysis. His hobbies include triathlon training, playing guitar, painting, and drawing.

*You'll find
other outstanding
biomechanics resources at*

www.HumanKinetics.com

In the U.S. call

1-800-747-4457

Australia	08 8277 1555
Canada	1-800-465-7301
Europe	+44 (0) 113 255 5665
New Zealand	0064 9 448 1207

HUMAN KINETICS
The Information Leader in Physical Activity
P.O. Box 5076 • Champaign, IL 61825-5076 USA

CD-Rom Instructions

Minimum System Requirements

This CD-ROM can be installed on a Windows®-based PC.

System compatibility:

- IBM PC compatible with Pentium® processor
- Windows® 95/98/NT 4.0
- Windows® 2000
- Windows® ME
- Pentium® processor or higher

Hardware needs:

- At least 16 MB RAM with 32 MB recommended
- 2x CD-ROM drive
- 20 MB hard drive space
- 256 colors (16-bit [65,536 colors] or higher recommended)
- At least 640 x 480 screen resolution
- Sound card
- Speakers

Installing CD-ROM for *Qualitative Analysis of Human Movement* (second edition)

1. Insert the CD-ROM for *Qualitative Analysis of Human Movement* (second edition) into the CD-ROM drive.
2. Select the Windows "Start" button.

3. Select the "Run . . ." option.
4. Type "X:\Setup.exe" in the text box. (Note: X is the letter that corresponds to your CD-ROM drive.)
5. Select the "OK" button.
6. Follow the on-screen instructions to install the software.
7. You must restart your computer to complete installation.★

★*Important notice:* If the software is installed on a Windows® 95, Windows® 98, or Windows® NT 4.0 machine, you will need to install another program before restarting your computer. Follow these instructions to install the other program located on your CD-ROM:

1. Select the Windows® Start button.
2. Type "x:Mdac_Fix.exe" in the text box. (Note: X is the letter that corresponds to your CD-ROM drive.)
3. Select the "OK" button.

Getting Started

1. Insert the CD-ROM for *Qualitative Analysis of Human Movement* (second edition) CD-ROM. (Note: the CD-ROM must be present in the drive at all times.)
2. Select the Windows "Start" button.
3. Select the "Programs" option.
4. Select the "Qualitative Analysis of Human Movement CD" program group.
5. Select the "Qualitative Analysis of Human Movement CD" icon.

Registration Procedures

1. Select the Windows "Start" button.

2. Select the "Programs" option.

3. Select the "Qualitative Analysis of Human Movement CD" program group.

4. Select the "Qualitative Analysis of Human Movement CD" icon.

5. At the next screen, enter the required information (*) to register CD-ROM for *Qualitative Analysis of Human Movement* (second edition). Press the "Register" button when you are finished.

6. Your registration code will appear onscreen. Follow the instructions to receive your unlock code. *Note: Make sure the software is running when you call customer service.* The program will prompt you to call Human Kinetics to receive your unlock code. If you purchased the program outside the U.S., a sticker will be visible on the outside of the package informing you which HK subsidiary you should contact for your unlock code.

7. If you should have any problems, call (217) 351-5076 (U.S.), e-mail support@hkusa.com, or complete the online technical support form at www.humankinetics.com/service/support/techsupport.cfm for further assistance.

8. Enter the unlock code to register CD-ROM for *Qualitative Analysis of Human Movement* (second edition) and press the "Continue" button. Once this is done, you can start using the program.

9. After CD-ROM for *Qualitative Analysis of Human Movement* (second edition) is started, Getting Started will guide you through the program.

For product information or customer support:
E-mail: support@hkusa.com
Phone: 217-351-5076
Fax: 217-351-2674
Web site: **www.humankinetics.com**